The · Book · of

Great Desserts

The · Book · of
Great Desserts

Terence Janericco

. . . .

VAN NOSTRAND REINHOLD
I(T)P A Division of International Thomson Publishing Inc.

New York • Albany • Bonn • Boston • Detroit • London • Madrid • Melbourne
Mexico City • Paris • San Francisco • Singapore • Tokyo • Toronto

Library of Congress Catalog Card Number 94-10127
ISBN 0-442-01356-6

I(T)P™ Van Nostrand Reinhold, an International Thomson Publishing Inc.
The ITP logo is a trademark under license.

Printed in the United States of America
For more information, contact:

Van Nostrand Reinhold
115 Fifth Avenue
New York, NY 10003

International Thomson Publishing GmbH
Königswinterer Strasse 418
53227 Bonn
Germany

International Thomson Publishing Europe
Berkshire House 168-173
High Holborn
London WC1V 7AA
England

International Thomson Publishing Asia
221 Henderson Road #05-10
Henderson Building
Singapore 0315

Thomas Nelson Australia
102 Dodds Street
South Melbourne, 3205
Victoria, Australia

International Thomson Publishing Japan
Hirakawacho Kyowa Building, 3F
2-2-1 Hirakawacho
Chiyoda-ku, 102 Tokyo
Japan

Nelson Canada
1120 Birchmount Road
Scarborough, Ontario
Canada M1K 5G4

International Thomson Editores
Campos Eliseos 385, Piso 7
Col. Polanco
11560 Mexico D.F. Mexico

1 2 3 4 5 6 7 8 9 10 ARC-FF 01 00 99 98 97 96 95 94

Library of Congress Cataloging in Publication Data

Janericco, Terence
    The book of great desserts / Terence Janericco.
        p.   cm.
    Includes index.
    ISBN 0-442-01356-6
    1. Desserts.   I. Title.
      TX773.J357   1994
      641.8'6–dc20

94-10127
CIP

Contents

. . . .

Introduction

Desserts—we all love them. Most of us are fairly straight forward about that and we admit to liking certain, if not all, desserts. On some occasions, at least, we succumb to a beautiful, well-prepared dessert. Oh yes, there are a few crochety souls that claim they never eat dessert and sneer that it is unnecessary, unhealthy, and fattening. Unnecessary, maybe, but so is a smile. Unhealthy? There is nothing unhealthy about fresh fruits, pure butter, the richest of cream, or the smoothest of chocolate—as long as you eat them in moderation. Too many carrots and your skin turns yellow! Fattening, possibly, but so is oat bran if you eat too much. There is room in every diet for treats—and desserts are treats—and it is the little treats that make life worth living. Desserts may also be a particularly pleasant way of maintaining a balanced diet. A macedoine of fruit provides a more interesting way of filling the fruit requirement of your diet than a plain apple. Fruits should be part of your daily diet. Served simply, they provide just a bit of sweetness. Your preparation of fruits can make them higher in calories, and it is possible to do a *lot* to them. But remember: if you eat fresh fruit desserts dresssed simply all week long, you have the freedom to indulge in a rich chocolate torte, or a raspberry macaroon mousse and walk away guilt-free and happy. Waiting for the treat always makes it taste that much better.

Fruits, whether apples, or oranges, the more exotic mangos or papayas, or the rarer carambolas or cactus pears, excite our palates. They evoke thoughts as rambling as Proust's madeleines. They remind us of the seasons, as surely as watching the flowers bloom. Berries and cherries hail late spring, into full summer. Peaches, nectarines, and plums herald summer, and the coming of fall. While the fall offerings of apples and pears tell us winter is soon to come, many of these fruits, now dried, get us through the dreary months, while reminding us of the treats to come.

Many markets sell the same fruits year round. While some fruits, such as oranges, lemons, and limes, maintain an even quality, others are unacceptable to the discerning cook. The swiftness of shipping means that we can have ripe strawberries from Chile, cactus pears from Sicily, and mangos from Thailand at almost any time of the year. These are so fresh, and so well-handled, that it is truly the next best thing to being there. But, when the offerings are California plums more suited to be polo balls than food, or the too-green pears which never ripen to perfection, disappointment is the order of the day. True, the skillful cook may be able to turn these into culinary pleasures: Poach the pears in winey syrup, bake the plums into a delicious cake, and their faults diminish. The wary shopper checks the fruit before purchasing and tries to buy only perfect, ripe fruit. He returns the less-than-perfect fruit to the shelf to send a clear message to the store.

Fruits, especially when in season, provide economical desserts, and because many fruits (apples, pears, and peaches, for example), have similar qualities, you can substitute one for another and expand your repertoire. Thus, if a desserts calls for peaches, out of season, or the selection at your market is not very good, you can substitute nectarines, apples, or pears and have a delicious, albeit different, dessert. Berries easily substitute for one another. Of course, if you have your heart set on a peach cobbler in January, you will not find the apple cobbler a suitable substitute.

Serve fruit simply. Fruits often need no more preparation than peeling, or cut several fruits to make a fruit cup or salad. Of course, with greater cooking efforts, you can create elaborate torten, charlottes, and multi-flavored mousses. Fruits are the base of most desserts, and the ability to combine them gives you the opportunity to prepare an unlimited number of delights. Chocolate and sugar also make fabulous desserts. Chocolate-flavored desserts abound in this book. At the end of the gâteau chapter, the most intensely flavored of these have a section to themselves. But do not miss the other offerings, such as the best chocolate cake ever in the Cookies, Plain Cakes and Confections chaper. In addition, the confections section has a number of easily prepared, delicious chocolate nibbles, which can provide the perfect dessert following a rich meal, or as an accompaniment to another dessert. Guests can enjoy the full dessert, or just a truffle or two, to satisfy their dessert craving, or just a bit of candied grapefruit rind for a tart-sweet lagniappe.

The majority of the recipes in this book call for fresh fruits. On rare occasion a frozen or canned fruit is acceptable, but no self-respecting cook will use canned pears or frozen melon to prepare a dessert that calls for fresh ingredients. Fresh fruit cups do not come out of a can! The result makes the few minutes of preparation worthwhile. If your recipe calls for ingredients that are not available, choose another recipe. You can often make substitutions in a recipe, but there are times that you must just let go. Too often cooks want to change a recipe to suit a dietary need. They, or someone they cook for, does not or cannot eat certain foods. They may be watching their fat and sugar intake. They may not want coffee or chocolate, for any one of a variety of reasons. Then prepare something else! Caramel custard is not the same if you omit the caramel because you do not want sugar, use egg substitutes because you are watching egg intake, and skimmed milk because you are concerned about fats. You will get a dessert, but who cares? It will be such a weak imitation of the original that it would be better to omit dessert altogether. Why not serve a macedoine of fresh fruit and a simple butter cookie or macaroon to those who can eat sugar and cream without a problem?

Chapter 1

THE BASICS

What is acidulated water? How do you make a chocolate bowl? What is the recipe for ladyfingers? The Basics always seem to be a bother. How nice it would be to just leap in—not possible. All too often, because we are successful in life and have always eaten, we assume we can cook. It is something like learning how to drive. Teenagers *know* they can drive—until they get behind the wheel. Happily, after a few weeks of driver training they can. So too, with a little training, can you produce wonderful-looking and tasting desserts. To prepare the desserts here you need to know some of the basics. What size eggs to purchase? How critical is oven temperature? What does "beating to thickened and pale" mean? How can I make a chocolate frill, or use two sauces to make a design? How do you make ladyfingers? Why? I have gathered the answers here. For new cooks it will be a great help, for well-trained cooks, a refresher course that will be of value. You decide if you want to study this now, or wait until you get started on a particular recipe.

Correct techniques make life easier. Knowing how to make a smooth chocolate glaze or to tell when eggs and sugar are thickened and pale, makes preparing desserts that much simpler and more pleasurable. We all want to make exquisite-looking and tasting desserts. And you can. But take the time to learn the basics before you sign up for the culinary Indy 500. Also, you will find here some of the professional "tricks" to make you and your desserts look good.

As a cooking teacher, I can say that the most common error made by cooks is that they do not read the recipe. They take a quick glance at the ingredients and off they go only to find themselves halfway through and in trouble. Take the few minutes needed not only to read the recipe, but also to understand the various techniques. All cooking is nothing more than a few simple steps, but you need to know the steps and the order in which to mount them. This is especially true of the cooks who choose to substitute one ingredient for another, thinking they will make the recipe easier, better, or more healthful. Often you can, but more often it leads to a truly inferior dessert or, on occasion, a complete disaster.

Some basic recipes, such as Sponge Cake, are dessert with no more than a light dusting of confectioners' sugar, or a base for a showstopper, while others, such as Praline Powder, need to be added to something. The busy cook may select a baking day to prepare these items to store for future use. To make this easier, I have indicated how and for how long to store them. None of the recipes are particularly difficult and, in most cases, are quite simple.

Equipment

Although all of the recipes can be prepared by hand, modern science has made baking much simpler with the creation of a few major pieces of equipment. If you do not have them, consider investing in them as your need arises, but remember that they are not mandatory and you can do very well with the equipement you have on hand.

ELECTRIC MIXER   Ideally you already have a good electric mixer. It does not have to be extraordinarily heavy-duty, but it should be able to hold at least 3 quarts. The stronger the motor, the more efficiently it will run, and the easier and quicker some activities will be. Speed is relative. In fact, in most instances, you can prepare the food on any speed you choose. If you run it on low, it will take longer; on high, less time. Most people choose medium as a safe rule, and it makes sense. Generally if you are whipping cream or eggs, a quick full-speed spurt at the end helps, unless it is already too well beaten.

FOOD PROCESSOR   One of the greatest machines ever built. A quality machine will give you a lifetime of service and will make many chores so much simpler. Learn to use the processor to chop, mince, puree, and mix ingredients. Generally you can forget all of the extra blades. The steel chopping blade will perform every need in this book. Remember to chop, you must use numerous on/off turns, or else you can end up with a paste. Use the processor to cream butter and sugar or to make quick cakes. Do not use it to whip cream or egg whites. Some can, but they are not as good as a mixer or doing it by hand with a wire whisk.

MICROWAVE OVEN   I came to this invention late, but have learned to use it to a maximum degree in baking. The microwave is terrific for melting chocolate and butter, softening butter and cream cheese, or bringing things to room temperature. Test your microwave, because of the different wattages, some cook more quickly than others. If you do everything on high, you will burn the chocolate and splatter the butter all over the inside of the machine. But use it on low to medium for short periods of 30 to 45 seconds, stir occasionally, and you will find a true friend.

WIRE WHISKS   No cook can perform without these. You need several sizes. Remember: A good whisk will stand in the pot without falling out. If it does, it is too large for that job. Use the largest whisk you can find to whip cream and egg whites; it makes the job much quicker and easier.

MEASURING SPOONS AND CUPS   Buy good-quality spoons and cups, with clear markings, of sturdy construction. You need two types of measuring cups: level cups and glass cups. Level measures, for measuring dry ingredients, usually have a long metal handle. Scoop into the flour, or whatever, and fill the cup to overflowing. Use a knife or metal spatula to scrape the excess off, evenly, with the top of the cup. Use glass measuring cups for liquids. They allow you to fill to the line and not worry about spilling over the top.

BAKING PANS   Select pans as you need them. Do not go out and buy a set of pans, unless you know that you will use them. Choose pans of heavy metal, I prefer tin-lined pans, but aluminum is also very good. Be sure that they are not light and flimsy, or they will warp, making for uneven cakes, or worse, might even collapse with a heavy filling. Pans come in many sizes, so select pans for the type of baking you are going to do.

Cookie Sheets. No cook can have too many cookie sheets. They are useful not only for cookies, but also to arrange hors d'oeuvres or other foods for baking, or just to have ready in the refrigerator.

Springform Pans. These also come in many sizes. A 9-inch pan will suit most recipes, although occasionally, you may want a larger or smaller pan.

Basic Ingredients and Techniques

ACIDULATED WATER   Mix 1 tablespoon of fresh or frozen lemon juice with each quart of water to keep peeled fruit from turning dark when exposed to air.

ARROWROOT   A starch used to thicken some sauces and in place of flour in some desserts. The thickening is created by absorbing liquid. Follow the recipe. If heating it, you only need to bring it to 165° F. Lengthy cooking will break down the starch and thin the glaze. Once the mixture thickens, it is important not to stir too vigorously or the mixture will break and become thin. You can substitute cornstarch, but if heating, bring to a full boil. Available in specialty stores.

BAKING POWDER   A mixture of dry acid and baking soda, baking powder comes in single- or double-acting forms. For recipes in this book, purchase double-acting baking powder in small quantities. It loses much of its potency within a year. Keep tightly covered in a dry area.

BAKING SODA   Sodium bicarbonate is used with another acid, such as molasses or chocolate, as a leavening agent. It keeps well in a cool, dry area. It tends to clump, so sift before measuring.

BUTTER   There is no substitute. You can use other fats, but since all fats are calorically equivalent, there is no real advantage. Other fats do not act in the same way to produce buttercreams, nor do they have the flavor. The recipes were tested with unsalted butter. If you substitute salted butter, omit 1 teaspoon of salt per pound.

BUTTER, CLARIFIED   Clarified butter provides clear butter oil without the milk solids present in unclarified butter. Once clarified, the butter keeps for months in the refrigerator, or indefinitely in a freezer. Since it is easier to clarify a large quantity, clarify a pound at a time to have it readily available. Once chilled, it is rock hard, so be sure to bring to room temperature before measuring.

To Clarify Butter. In a heavy saucepan, simmer the butter until the bubbling noise stops. Immediately pour through a cheesecloth-lined strainer. For extra flavor, cook the butter, watching carefully, until the solids turn the color of hazelnuts. Take care, once the water cooks off, the milk solids will fall to the bottom and can burn easily.

CANDIED OR GLACÉED FRUITS   True candied fruits are a delight to eat. They are cooked in sugar to preserve them and have a long shelf life. Unfortunately, the supermarket offerings are often insipid by comparison. Look in specialty food stores or gourmet shops for better-quality candied fruits.

CARAMEL

To Coat a Mold with Caramel. Caramel custards and flans are baked in molds lined with sugar cooked to the caramel stage. Heat the ingredients to a full rolling boil, stirring gently. When it boils, cover the pan and boil for five minutes. The steam will wash any sugar crystals from the sides of the pan. Remove the cover and wash the sides of the pan with a brush dipped into cold water. Continue to boil over high heat until the syrup turns golden brown, or to about 365° F. on a candy thermometer. If it starts to brown on one side of the pan, gently swirl the pan to caramelize the mixture evenly. Take care not to get it too dark or the caramel will taste burned. Immediately pour the caramel into the mold. Holding the mold with pot holders, tilt and turn to coat the bottom and about ¼ inch up the sides of the mold. Set aside while you prepare the filling. Because any caramel above the custard will not dissolve and can act as a hook, making unmolding difficult, if not impossible.

Safety Rules for Cooking Caramel. Caramel is not only extremely hot but also sticky. It can cause truly painful and possibly disfiguring burns. The rules here are intended to help you to work with caramel safely, not to frighten you. Do not be afraid, just use common sense to create wonderful desserts:

1.   Keep everyone out of the way, especially children.

2.   If you should spill any of the molten caramel on you, plunge the affected area under cold running water and keep it there for at least 3 minutes. *Do not try to peel off the caramel.* Let the cold water stop the burning and dissolve the caramel. Yes, the cold will be unpleasant, but a lot less so than an untended burn.

3.   If the caramel should become too dark, do not pour it down the drain until it cools. The hot melted caramel can turn the drain into a form of cannon by overheating the water in the trap and causing it to explode up into the kitchen and onto you. Let the caramel cool to room temperature. Do not worry about the pan.

To Clean a Caramel-coated Pan. No matter how badly the caramel sticks to the pan, these instructions work. Soak the pan in water until the sugar dissolves. It may take a day or two, but it *will* dissolve and the pan will be fine. Digging at undissolved sugar with can openers, spatulas, or even scrubbing equipment may destroy the pan. You can simmer the pan half-filled with water to hasten the process.

To Unmold a Caramel-lined Dessert. Chill the dessert completely. The chilling helps to firm the custard and gives the caramel a chance to dissolve and turn into a sauce. When chilled, run a knife around the outer edge of the mold. If the custard turns freely in the pan, place a serving platter on top of the mold and in one quick movement turn it upside down and lift off the mold. If the custard seems settled in one place in the mold, then dip the mold into the bowl of very hot water for about 30 seconds. Shake the pan lightly and the custard should move in place. Unmold.

A mistake many cooks make when unmolding a dessert or other food is to panic halfway through the process. They cover the mold, start to turn it over and stop in the middle. Complete the turn before you panic. If you stop in the middle, there is no question that you will create a disaster.

CHESTNUTS, FRESH AND DRIED   Purchase fresh, dried, in brine, or in syrup. For desserts, those packed in syrup are most convenient.

CHESTNUTS, CANNED   Prepared chestnuts are imported from France or Italy. Select *marrons entiers au naturel* when unsweetened chestnuts are needed and chestnuts in syrup, *marrons glacés*, or candied chestnuts, when sweetened diced chestnuts are needed. The latter are expensive, several times the cost of the *marrons entiers*. Use *puree de marrons au naturel*, sweetened with glucose, rather than *crème de marrons*, which has added sugar and is too sweet, when you need pureed chestnuts.

CHOCOLATE   Use real chocolate, not chocolate-flavored products or other imitation products. Many writers make much ado about chocolate. They insist on one brand over another as if the differences were earth-shattering. My experience is that there are many good brands, and insisting on one makes no quantifiable difference in the end result.

There are only a handful of chocolate manufacturers in the entire world. Virtually all of them produce quality chocolate, and each of them produces dozens of varieties of chocolate to suit particular purposes. For instance, chocolates that do not melt in desert heat, or a blend that perfectly suits a particular candy manufacturer. You need only go as far as your nearest supermarket or specialty store to purchase chocolate suitable for these desserts.

The recipes in this book were tested with Néstle's Peter's Superlative Coating chocolate. I use the Gibraltar for semisweet and Burgundy for bittersweet. I have prepared many of the recipes using Néstle's semisweet chocolate morsels—the same morsels used for Toll House cookies—as well as Lindt, Valrhona, Callebault, Le Notre and Ghirardelli. They are all wonderful chocolates with slightly different characteristics. But, unless you sample in a blind chocolate tasting, not different enough to require a search for a particular brand. Chocolate is similar to wine; you can select a number of fine wines that enhance your dinner, or you can sit before a legion of glasses tasting to find the nuances. Fine cooking is an art that has as much influence from the surroundings and other ingredients. If you are studying the tastes of the dessert rather than enjoying them, you are in the wrong ballpark.

I use the Peter's Coating because it is readily available to me. It has great flavor with a desirable melting point. It is sold in 10-pound blocks and the store from which I purchase it (Dairy Fresh Candies, Boston) will break those into smaller amounts. The point is to use the best chocolate you can find and enjoy the dessert rather than worry about producing an inferior result because you did not use a particular brand.

TYPES OF CHOCOLATE   Chocolate comes in many forms: unsweetened, cocoa powder, bittersweet, semisweet, milk, and white. Be sure to use the form specified in the recipe. Forget trying to make your own by mixing cocoa and oil. (One of the first rules of cookery is to be prepared.) For the most part, the required form is readily available at your local grocery store. You may have to look further afield for a rarer form like white chocolate.

Unsweetened. Wrapped in 1- or 2-ounce portions, in packages of 8 ounces or more. Keeps 6–8 months on pantry shelf. The lack of fat and sugar makes it unsuitable for eating directly.

Cocoa. Always use unsweetened and do not confuse with cocoa drink mixes. Hershey's, Droste, Van Houten, and Valrhona are all good brands. If the cocoa powder is to be mixed with water, there is no need to sift, but if it is to be folded into a meringue, batter, etc., sift to remove any lumps and to make folding easier.

Bittersweet or Semisweet. I use Peter's Burgundy for bittersweet and Gibraltar for semisweet. I have come to prefer the semisweet. I think that the desire for more and more bitter chocolate is similar to always trying to find drier white wine. It becomes too much of a good thing. It is your choice to select a bittersweet for any particular recipe.

Bittersweet chocolate is not as easily located. Unless you have a gourmet shop available, you may need to order it by mail. However, many markets sell Lindt and Tobler bittersweet bars, although the cost can be steep. Semisweet chocolate is readily available as chocolate morsels and bars in virtually every market. If it is too sweet for your taste, substitute 1–2 ounces of unsweetened for 2 ounces semisweet in each 8 ounces of semisweet. Specialty stores will carry more esoteric brands, often at great, and unnecessary, expense. Store at room temperature in a dry, airtight container for up to 2 years.

Milk. Made with the addition of milk solids and extra cocoa butter, it can go rancid more easily than bittersweet or semisweet. Store at room temperature in a dry, airtight container for no more than a year.

White. White chocolate does not have any cocoa solids and therefore is not considered "real chocolate." The better brands do have cocoa butter. I find the flavor too subtle and seldom use it. I prefer a stronger chocolate flavor. White chocolate sets much faster than dark chocolate; be prepared to work quickly. Because of the milk solids, it does not keep as long and it scorches more easily while melting. Unless you use it often, buy only as much as you need for each occasion.

MELTING CHOCOLATE   Chocolate is temperamental and must be handled with care. I prefer to melt it in a microwave oven. It is quick, efficient, and does a perfect job. Many chefs, however, prefer to use a double boiler. Because a small amount of liquid can cause chocolate to "seize" into a hard clump, it is important to keep all containers and utensils dry, and avoid any steam droplets from landing on the chocolate. If you are "making" a double boiler with a saucepan and a bowl, use a bowl with a generous lip so the steam does not fall into the chocolate. If the chocolate should "seize," stir in 1 tablespoon of vegetable oil *not* butter, as it contains water, for every 6 ounces of chocolate. This will not adversely affect most recipes. Of course there are times, when making chocolate sauce for example, when you do add liquid, but it is enough to liquefy the chocolate.

No matter how you melt the chocolate, chop it into small pieces, about the size of chocolate chips, first. Make sure that you do not heat it to more than 120° F. on a candy thermometer to prevent burning.

To Melt Chocolate in a Microwave. Since microwave ovens vary in their power, you may need to experiment to make sure you do not overheat the chocolate. Start on low power, and increase until you find the power that works best for your oven.

Place the chopped chocolate in a microwaveable bowl, microwave for 15 seconds at medium power, stir, and repeat until the chocolate is two-thirds melted. Remove from the oven and stir until the chocolate is completely melted.

To Melt Chocolate in a Double Boiler. Place the chopped chocolate in the top of a double boiler and place over hot, not boiling water, and heat, stirring occasionally, until almost fully melted. Remove the top pan from the bottom and stir until the chocolate melts. Be sure to wipe the bottom and sides of the pan before pouring out the chocolate to prevent any water from mixing with the chocolate.

TEMPERING CHOCOLATE.   When using chocolate to coat truffles, make chocolate bands, ruffles, wedges, etc., you must temper it to prevent the formation of "bloom." Bloom is the white, powdery surface that sometimes appears on chocolate in warm weather, or by overheating. The cocoa butter crystals rise to the surface and cause streaking instead of a clear dark color.

Classic Tempering Method. Use an instant-read thermometer to check temperatures. Heat the chocolate, stirring often, until the temperature is no higher than 120° F. If using a double boiler, wipe the bottom of the pan to prevent any water from dripping onto the chocolate. Pour two-thirds of the melted chocolate onto a marble slab, formica counter, or the back of a clean, dry baking sheet. Using a pastry scraper or putty knife, work the chocolate back and forth, gathering it together and spreading it out again until the chocolate begins to thicken and the temperature falls to about 80° F. Scoop into the container of the remaining melted chocolate and reheat, stirring until it reaches about 90° F. for bittersweet or semisweet chocolate, or 85° F. for milk or white chocolate. Keep chocolate fluid over hot water not more than 130° F. or place on an electric heating pad, stirring often as you use it.

Quick Tempering Methods
    Method I—Melt about two-thirds of the chocolate, remove from the heat, and stir, off the heat, until the remainder is fully melted and cooled.
    Method II—Melt about two-thirds of the chocolate, remove from the heat, and add the remaining third, finely chopped, a tablespoon at a time, until melted and cooled.
    Method III—Melt the chocolate with 1 tablespoon of vegetable oil for every 3 ounces, heating to no more than 120° F. The oil inhibits the formation of the cocoa butter crystals, but creates a softer end result.

CITRUS FRUITS AND JUICES   Use only the colored portion of the rind, called the zest. The white pith is often bitter and unappealing.

To Julienne Rind. Use a *zester,* a small five-holed tool to peel off the strips of rind. Or, with a sharp paring knife, peel off 1-inch strips. Pile the strips and, using a sharp knife, cut into the thinnest possible shreds.

To Grate Rind. With a four-sided box or similar grater, proceed as follows: Take the lemon in hand, take a deep breath and exhale slowly—RELAX. Gently rub the lemon across the smallest, or next-to-smallest-holes in the grater *in a circular motion*, rolling the lemon as you grate. You will remove the colored rind without the pith and not grate your knuckles.

Citrus Juice. For the freshest flavor, use fresh oranges or lemons. To acidulate water feel free to use frozen lemon juice. Avoid bottled juice, it has a chemical flavor.

COCONUT   None of the recipes call for freshly grated coconut. Take advantage of the various forms found ready-to-use on the market shelf. Select grated, shredded, or flaked according to personal preference. Consider the use: Flakes are too large for the Coconut Thistle Confection, but can look pretty once toasted and sprinkled on top of a Lime Mousse.

CORNSTARCH   A starch thickener that must reach a full boil to thicken completely. Do not cook too long or it will break down. Use to thicken sauces, glazes, and pastry creams. It is also used in some cakes, to lighten without adding gluten. When using with hot liquid, it must be mixed with a cold liquid first.

CREAM   Most of the recipes in this book using cream require heavy cream. It has a butterfat content of 36 to 40 percent. Avoid half-and-half, which is half light cream and half milk, light cream with only 20 percent fat, or so-called whipping cream; their fat contents are too low to whip properly.

To Whip Cream. In a cold bowl, with cold beaters, whip the cream on medium speed until it starts to thicken. Add the sugar and flavoring and increase the speed to medium high. Beat until stiff enough for the particular use. To fold into other ingredients the cream should form soft peaks, when it will mound and hold the shape. To pipe, beat the cream until it is stiff enough to stand on its own. Be careful not to overwhip the cream or it will start to break down and turn into butter. If you have not overbeaten it too much, you can often redeem it by mixing in a little unwhipped cream.

To Flavor Cream for Whipping. Generally, each cup of cream requires 1 teaspoon of vanilla, or as much as 1 tablespoon of a liqueur such as Cognac, kirsch, etc. Whip the cream to form soft peaks, add the flavoring, and sweeten to taste. Whip to the desired consistency.

Chocolate Whipped Cream
  • *With cocoa*
Add 1 tablespoon of cocoa to each cup of cream, stir, and let stand 10 minutes. Whip to form soft peaks, sweeten to taste. For a more intensely flavored cream, add 2 tablespoons of cocoa.
  • *With semisweet chocolate*
Add 3 tablespoons of melted semisweet chocolate to the cream and whip to the desired consistency. Use immediately if piping, or it may set. If the cream does set, heat over low heat until melted, chill until cold, and whip again.

Mocha Whipped Cream. In a bowl, mix 4 teaspoons of instant espresso powder, 1 tablespoon of boiling water, and vanilla, to taste. Cool, stirring, for 1 minute. Add 1⅓ cups of heavy cream and beat until soft peaks form. Add ½ cup of sugar and beat to the desired consistency. Yields 2½ cups.

CREAM OF TARTAR   Otherwise called tartaric acid. Add 1 teaspoon for each cup of egg whites to prevent overbeating. When boiling, add ⅛ teaspoon to each ½ cup of sugar to inhibit crystallization. You can beat egg whites and dissolve sugar without it, but the risk of a problem is much greater.

EGGS   Eggs are vital to many desserts. Treat eggs correctly for each use and they will reward you with great success, otherwise, you could have a dismal failure. There is some limited concern about using uncooked eggs. Many classic recipes have used uncooked recipes for centuries. If this is of concern, I can only recommend that you select some other recipe.
   Recommendations for working successfully with eggs:
  • Always use fresh eggs.
  • Never buy cracked eggs and if you find one return it to the market.
  • Keep refrigerated until ready to use.
  • In most instances, you will want eggs to be at room temperature. They whip to greater volume and incorporate into other ingredients more easily.
   The recipes were tested using large eggs. If you use medium-size, you should add an additional egg for every 5 large eggs. Extra large eggs will give greater volume, but were not found to affect any recipe critically.

Cracking Eggs. Crack eggs on the countertop with a sharp, distinct rap, rather than the edge of the bowl. You will be less likely to get bits of shell into the bowl.

Separating Eggs. There are several methods for separating eggs:
  • Crack the shell, separate the two ends of the shell, and roll the yolk back and forth between the shell sections, letting the white drop into a container.
  • Crack the egg, drop the whole egg into one hand, and let the white fall between the fingers. You can easily feel and separate the chalaza (the white chord that holds the yolk in suspension in the shell).
  • Use an egg separator, a metal or plastic gadget with a center area to hold the yolk and holes along the sides, to allow the yolk to run off into the bowl.

Beating Whole Eggs. The manner in which you beat the eggs, the ratio of sugar to eggs, and the temperature of the eggs all affect the final result of beating eggs.
  Until thickened and pale in color. Beat whole eggs or egg yolks with or without sugar until they are light in color and somewhat thickened.
  To form a ribbon. With further beating they will become thick enough to form a "ribbon." This means that a portion of the mixture, dropped from a spoon or beater, will form a slowly dissolving ribbon of batter on top of the batter in the bowl.
  To the consistency of mayonnaise. With further beating, they will look pale in color, triple in volume, and have the consistency of mayonnaise. These are used for mousses, sponge cakes, etc. I recommend using an electric mixer because it takes a great deal of time and effort. If you must beat them by hand, warm the eggs and sugar to help them mount more rapidly.
  When using an electric mixer, many bakers find that separating eggs and whites is unnecessary, even in those recipes suggesting it, because with a little rearranging of the process, they can whip the whole eggs, and possibly extra whites or yolks, and the sugar to this consistency. The remaining ingredients are carefully folded into the beaten eggs.
  To heat eggs for beating. In the mixing bowl, stir the eggs and sugar, place over a pan of hot, not boiling water, and heat until hot to the touch, about 110° F. Stir often until they are hot. If tap water is hot enough, you can place the bowl directly in a sink of hot water. In a bowl, beat the egg yolks and sugar until the sugar is partially dissolved. The eggs should be considerably paler in color and form a slowly dissolving ribbon when dropped from the beater.

To whip egg whites. In a mixer, or copper bowl with a wire whisk, beat the egg whites until foamy and start to hold a shape. Add cream of tartar, if using, and sugar, if required, and beat until they hold firm peaks. Since beaten egg whites, except for meringues, are always folded into something else, take care not to overbeat. They should hold soft peaks to allow for easy folding.

For meringue. To make meringue, beat the eggs with the sugar and cream of tartar until they hold stiff, unwavering peaks. Because the quantity of sugar is so great, the mixture becomes quite heavy. I recommend using an electric mixer.

FLOUR   The recipes were tested using all-purpose flour, unless stated otherwise. Any of the major brands will suit. Measure by scooping up the flour and scraping off the excess. Do not shake or tap the measure to level it.

Cake Flour. Use cake flour when specified. I have not found a noticeable difference making sponge cakes and pound cakes from cake flour or all-purpose flour. Bread flour and high-gluten flours are not recommended for cake making.

FOOD COLOR   A few recipes in this book require food color. Omit the color if you prefer. Use the liquid vegetable food colorings available in grocery stores, with caution. The color tends to intensify when exposed to the air and a pale pink can become rather shocking.

GELATIN   Gelatin always means unflavored gelatin. Gelatin mixtures with sugar and flavoring added have less gelatin per tablespoon and will not set properly. Gelatin is most commonly sold in small ¼-ounce packets containing slightly less than 1 tablespoon, which is enough to set 2 cups of liquid.

To Dissolve Gelatin. In a small saucepan, sometimes a bowl, soften the gelatin in cold water or other liquid for at least 5 minutes. Dissolve over low heat, stirring, or by adding to a hot liquid and stirring. Check the back of a metal spoon. If you can see granules of gelatin on it, it is not fully dissolved. The gelatin continues to thicken over a 24-hour period, so using too much can make a dessert leathery. Freezing does not affect its thickening power.

GINGER   Fresh gingerroot is occasionally used to flavor desserts. Peel and grate or shred, according to recipe instructions. Preserved ginger is packed in syrup. Drain the ginger and mince. Use the syrup as a flavoring for whipped cream or as a sauce on fresh fruits.

Crystalized or Candied Ginger. Crystallized, or candied, ginger is sold sliced or minced and is available in some supermarkets and most gourmet shops. In most recipes you can substitute preserved ginger for crystallized ginger.
    Dried ground ginger is available in the spice section of the supermarket. Use it to flavor cakes, cookies, or whipped cream.
    Ginger marmalade or preserves is available in most supermarkets.

HERBS   Use fresh herbs, unless the recipe specifies dried. "Mint" means peppermint. Beware of the dozen different varieties found in the local nursery: Pineapple mint and some other exotics could work, but may give a completely different flavor than intended. Although, for a change of pace, a sprig of lemon mint or apple mint can add variety.

LIQUEURS   Quality liquers enhance many desserts. You need not buy the most expensive brands, but remember the rule of use for any alcohol in cooking: If you will not drink it, do not use it. In other words, leftover, off-taste wine is not suitable. However, there are some liqueurs that many of us would never choose to drink, but which do wonders for other ingredients. Specifically eau de vie, such as kirsch or mirabelle.
    Strictly speaking, a liqueur is fruit syrup with alcohol, such as raspberry cordial, although we also include flavored brandies, such as Grand Marnier. Some of the more common flavors used in desserts are amaretto, or almond, triple sec and Cointreau or orange, cassis or currant, and anisette or licorice.
    Eau de vie, on the other hand, are distillates of the fruit and are always clear in color. The more common flavors are: kirsch (cherry), mirabelle (plum), framboise (raspberry) and Poire or Poire William (pear) for many of the recipes. Advokaat and kümmel are flavored with caraway.
    Brandies, rums, and whiskies are also used in desserts. I prefer to use Cognac, but any well-flavored brandy will do. In most instances, I prefer a dark rum for a richer flavor. Any good brand of whiskey will do, but be sure to select bourbon for bourbon, etc.

MASCARPONE   Mascarpone is an Italian cream cheese that is the consistency of clotted cream. It has a rich, luscious flavor that enhances many desserts in addition to being the base for many others. Available in specialty markets and gourmet shops.

MILK   The recipes have all been tested wth whole milk. Lower-fat versions provide for somewhat insipid desserts. If you are watching your fat, select another recipe instead of trying to pass off a skimmed milk, custard sauce, etc.

Remember this a book of *great desserts*, not how to cut fat from your diet. There are many great desserts, based on fruits, that will leave you satisfied and happy. Skimmed milk custard sauce will leave you wishing for more.

NUTS   Many desserts require nuts in one form or another. If you rarely prepare desserts it is probably wisest to buy what you need as you need it. If you prepare desserts more often, then consider buying in larger quantities. My preference is to shop at a store that specializes in bulk sales of nuts such as candy shops, Middle Eastern stores, etc.

Be careful of purchasing nuts from markets with small turnover; the nuts may be rancid. If you have a question, open the package on the spot to smell and taste them. Nuts keep for months in a cool dry area. If your environment is hot or humid, or both, it is best to store the nuts in the freezer.

Blanching and Peeling Nuts.

Almonds—Blanch in boiling water for about 30 seconds, drain, and pinch each nut out of its skin.
Hazelnuts—Bake in a 350° F. oven for about 20 minutes or until golden and the skins start to split. Turn the nuts onto a coarse towel, wrap, and let stand for about 20 minutes. Rub and roll the nuts in the towel to scrape and chip off the husks. Pick the nuts out of the husks. I use a spaetzle maker/chestnut roaster, a sieve-like instrument with holes just slightly smaller than the nuts. The husks fall through and the nuts stay in the roaster. One student bought hardware cloth (a wire mesh) and shaped it into a box. The holes of colanders are usually too small to be of much help.
Walnuts, Pecans, etc.—Blanch in boiling water and rub in a towel. Dry in a 350° F. oven for 10 minutes to recrisp.

Roasting or Toasting Nuts. Roasting nuts enhances the flavor and also makes them crisper. Place the nuts in a single layer on a baking sheet and bake at 350° F. for about 10 minutes. Check periodically to make sure the nuts on the edge of the sheet are not browning too quickly. Stir as needed.

Toast small nuts, such as pine nuts, in a dry skillet over medium heat, tossing and stirring constantly until evenly golden.

Almonds. Sold blanched or unblanched, whole, sliced, slivered, chopped, or ground (meal). I recommend that you maintain a supply of blanched almonds and purchase unblanched, sliced, or slivered as needed. Use the food processor to chop or grind them.

Sugar-toasted Almonds or Other Nuts. In a small skillet, bring 1 cup of chopped almonds, 2 tablespoons of water, 2 tablespoons of sugar, and 1 teaspoon of almond extract to a boil. Cook, stirring for 2 to 3 minutes, or until the almonds are dry and light brown. Remove from the heat and stir until cool. With other nuts, omit the almond extract.

Hazelnuts. Sold skinned or unskinned. Purchase skinned hazelnuts to save time and effort, since hazelnuts are almost always skinned before using.

Pecans. Buy shelled pecans and maintain a supply that you will use within a month. They tend to go rancid more quickly than other nuts.

Walnuts. Buy shelled and maintain a supply that you will use within a few months.

Unusual nuts. Buy as needed unless you know that you will be using a particular nut. Stocking quantities of Brazil or macadamia nuts could lead to spoilage and waste.

POTATO FLOUR/STARCH   A starch used to add lightness, without adding gluten, to some tortes. Available in most grocery stores.

RAISINS   If directed, plump by soaking in a liquid for 15 minutes before using.

SALT   Some of the recipes call for a small amount of salt. I advise that you use it since the salt enhances the sweet flavor without making it too sweet. Omitting the salt often results in a flat-tasting product. The amount used is so small that it will not affect any diet.

SUGAR   The recipes were tested using cane sugar. If using another sugar, you may need to skim the scum when boiling it for caramel or spun sugar. If the package does not say "cane," it will come from another source, such as beets.

    Use granulated sugar unless a recipe stipulates a particular sugar such as light brown, confectioners', or superfine. Measure granulated sugar by scooping the measuring cup into the sugar.

To measure brown sugar: light or dark, pack into a cup until it holds its shape when removed from the cup.

Measure confectioners' sugar by following directions for granulated sugar. Sift it when indicated, otherwise you need not.

THERMOMETERS   Thermometers are invaluable for many aspects of dessert making. They provide the precise temperature for custard sauce (180° F.), the correct temperature for sugar cookery, and how hot the deep fat is for fritters.

Instant-read thermometers are the easiest to use and, because of their metal construction, last longer than the more fragile glass tube thermometers of the past. Be sure to select a thermometer to suit your particular needs. Some are calibrated for low temperatures for yeast breads, while others go higher for roasts and boiling water, while a third type goes as high as 550° F., to cover all needs.

VANILLA BEAN   Some recipes call for vanilla bean. It must be fresh and not dried out to have flavor. If wrapped in cellophane, you should be able to smell it. If in a jar, uncap and make sure that it has flavor. To use, split the bean lengthwise and scrape out the seeds. Let the seeds and beans steep in the liquid as the recipe directs. You can reuse a bean once. Rinse it off, dry until needed. Then store used beans in containers of sugar to make vanilla sugar to sprinkle over pastries.

VANILLA EXTRACT   The recipes indicate an equivalent for vanilla extract. The supermarket brands are suitable as long as they are real vanilla and not an imitation. Take care not to add too much, or the alcohol can add a bitter taste to the dessert.

CRYSTALLIZED VIOLETS   These are real violets dipped in sugar. They have a delicate violet color and almost no flavor. They are available from gourmet shops. They are a conceit that many contemporary chefs replace with fresh, edible flowers.

WATER BATH   A water bath (or *bain-marie*) is more a technique than a piece of equipment. It allows food to bake more gently: The water protects the food from overcooking, and from browning on the bottom and sides. Essential for certain baked custards, water baths also protect other foods, such as cheesecakes and some chocolate tortes. Fortunately it is easy to create.

To Prepare a Water Bath. Put the custard, or other food, in its mold, into a roasting or layer cake pan that is at least 1 inch larger on all sides. Fill the larger pan with enough water to come at least 1 inch, if not halfway up the sides of the mold. The water should be almost boiling when added to the pan, to aid in the cooking, but during baking, the water must *not* boil. If it boils, the custard could develop holes, become watery and split apart when unmolded, or, in the worst case, curdle. The degree of damage depends on how long and how vigorous the boiling. If you find the water simmering or boiling when you check it during baking, immediately add some ice cubes to the water to stop the boiling, and lower the oven temperature. (Not all ovens are accurate, and the oven temperature could be higher or lower by 50° F. or more. This is one good reason not to accept the time stated in a recipe without testing for doneness first.) If the water boiled only briefly, the custard may still come out perfectly. Unless it has curdled, continue with the recipe; it will taste good even if it should split when unmolded.

Basic Recipes

EGG-LEAVENED CAKES   Some of the finest cakes use only eggs for leavening. Sponge cakes and génoise are the two best-known. These classics from European pastry shops are easily prepared and infinitely useful. Keep several in the freezer for emergencies. Making them by hand requires work, but an electric mixer, either hand-held or on a stand, makes it easy and relatively quick.

To gain the maximum height, warm the eggs or egg whites in a bowl, over hot water, until hot to the touch, about 120° F., before beating.

To prepare the pan, butter the bottom, but not the sides, of the baking pans (the batter needs to cling to the sides as it cools). Many chefs prefer to flour the pan, or to line it with parchment, and butter the parchment.

Use any size pan to create the shape dessert you want. With a little experience, you will see that the only difference is the baking time. Jelly rolls take about 12 minutes, layers take about 20 to 25 minutes, and a decorative tube pan can take about 55 minutes. To test for doneness, tap the top; it should spring back when baked. Cool in the pan and then unmold. Serve dusted with confectioners' sugar for a quick, simple dessert.

BISCUIT DE SAVOIE (Sponge Cake)

6 eggs, separated	1 tablespoon lemon juice
Pinch of salt	1 teaspoon vanilla
1 cup sugar	1 cup sifted flour
1 teaspoon grated lemon rind	

1. Preheat the oven to 350° F. Lightly butter the bottoms but not the sides and dust with flour one of the following pan alternatives:
9- or 10-inch tube pan
2 (9-inch) layer pans
3 (7-inch) round cake pans
11 × 17-inch jelly roll pan
2 (10-inch) pans
2 (9 × 5-inch) loaf pans

2. Beat the whites with the salt until they form soft peaks. It's helpful to use an electric mixer to get greater volume. Beat in the sugar gradually, 1 tablespoon at a time, until stiff peaks form.

3. In another bowl, stir the egg yolks with a fork and add the lemon rind, lemon juice, and vanilla.

4. Fold one-fourth of the egg whites into the yolks to lighten. Sprinkle the flour on top. With a rubber spatula, your hand, or the mixer on low speed, fold in the remaining whites. Do not overmix.

5. Pour into the prepared pans and bake for 10 to 40 minutes (depending on the pan size). To test for doneness, touch the cake with your finger; it should spring back. The cake will also start to pull away from the sides of the pan.

6. Cool in the pan for 10 minutes. Run a spatula around the edge and unmold. Cool.

Alternate Method

Electric mixers make this method much easier. Put the whole eggs and sugar into a bowl. Bring to room temperature, or warm, by placing over a pan of hot, not boiling, water and heat, stirring often, until hot to the touch. Beat on high speed until tripled in bulk and the consistency of mayonnaise. Fold in the flavoring and flour.

Variations

- *Chocolate*. Omit the lemon rind and juice and substitute ½ cup of un-sweetened cocoa for ½ cup of the flour.
- *Nutted*. Fold ½ cup of finely ground toasted nuts in with the flour.
- *Nougat/Praline*. Add ⅔ cup of Praline Powder (see page 30) to the cake with the flour.

TO ROLL A SPONGE CAKE   Cut two 20-inch sheets of waxed paper and place on a counter, overlapping, so they are wider than the sponge roll. Sprinkle the paper with confectioners' sugar and unmold the cake on top. Roll the warm cake, tightly, and keep wrapped in a damp towel for 20 minutes.

GÉNOISE (Butter-flavored Sponge Cake)

6 large eggs	**½ cup Clarified Butter, melted,**
1 cup sugar	**page 4, see Note**
1 cup sifted flour	**1 teaspoon vanilla**

1.   Preheat oven to 350° F. Lightly butter and flour one of the following pan alternatives:
2 (8- or 9-inch) cake pans
3 (7-inch) round cake pans
1 (11 × 17-inch) jelly roll pan
2 (10-inch) layer pans

2.   In a large bowl, mix the eggs and sugar over hot, not boiling, water, stirring often until hot to the touch. Do not cook.

3.   In an electric mixer, beat the egg mixture until it is light and fluffy and the consistency of mayonnaise.

4.   Sprinkle the flour over the eggs, a little at a time, and fold into the eggs. Fold in the melted butter and vanilla. Be careful not to overmix.

5.   Pour into the prepared pan. Bake for 10 to 40 minutes (depending on pan size), or until the cakes pull away from the sides of the pan and are golden and springy when touched lightly.

6.   Cool for 10 minutes and unmold onto a cooling rack. Keeps 1 day covered at room temperature or up to 3 months in the freezer.

NOTE: Cool the melted butter until it is still fluid, but not hot. If it is too hot, it will fall to the bottom of the bowl. If it is not hot enough, it will harden into clumps.

Alternate Method

This cake can also be made by separating the eggs and folding all the ingredients together, as directed for Sponge Cake, (see page 19).

Variations

- *Chocolate*. Substitute ½ cup of cocoa for ½ cup of the flour.
- *Lemon* or *Orange*. Add 1 teaspoon of orange or lemon rind and 2 tablespoons of juice to the butter.
- *Nougat/Praline*. Substitute ⅔ cup of nougat or Praline Powder (page 30) for ½ cup of the flour.
- *Nutted*. Add ½ cup of finely ground toasted walnuts or other nuts with the flour.

LADYFINGERS

6 eggs	**1 teaspoon grated lemon rind**
¾ cup sugar	**1½ cups sifted flour**
1 teaspoon vanilla	**Confectioners' sugar**

1. Preheat the oven to 350° F. Line a baking sheet with parchment paper, or butter and flour the pan.

2. Fit a large pastry bag with a #8 plain tip.

3. Using an electric mixer, beat the eggs and sugar to the consistency of mayonnaise.

4. Fold in the vanilla, lemon rind, and flour. Using the pastry bag, pipe strips of batter, 3 inches long and 2 inches apart, along the baking sheet. Place the confectioner's sugar in a sieve and sift generously over the ladyfingers.

5. Bake 12 to 15 minutes or until pale brown. Cool on the baking sheets and remove from the paper, if used.

Yields about 50 ladyfingers

These become stale quickly. To serve as a cookie, serve on the same day or freeze. Prepare them ahead and store in an airtight container, at room temperature, to use in charlottes. Can be frozen.

Alternate Method

If an electric mixer is not available, separate the eggs and beat the yolks with the sugar until thickened and pale. Beat the egg whites until stiff but not dry peaks form. Fold the whites into the yolks with the vanilla, grated lemon rind, and flour.

BASIC NUT CAKE

This recipe allow you to prepare nut layers in almost any flavor. Select your favorite nut to suit your particular needs.

6 eggs	**1½ cups ground nuts**
1 cup sugar	**¾ cup flour**
1½ teaspoons vanilla	**⅓ cup butter, melted and**
Pinch of salt	**cooled**

1.   Preheat the oven to 350° F. Butter 2 (9-inch) round cake pans or 1 (11 × 19-inch) jelly roll pan. Line the pan with parchment paper and butter the paper.

2.   In the bowl of an electric mixer, stir the eggs and the sugar to combine. Place the bowl over hot, not boiling, water and heat until warm, about 100° F.

3.   Add the vanilla and salt. Beat to the consistency of mayonnaise.

4.   Stir the nuts to aerate them and fold into the batter with the flour. Fold in the butter, turn into the pan, and smooth the top.

5.   Bake for 15 to 17 minutes for the jelly roll pan or up to 25 minutes for the round pan or until the tops feel springy. Loosen the edges and invert the cake onto a rack and peel off the paper. Turn right side up and cool.

NOTE: Substitute half brown sugar to enhance the nut flavor.

Variation

• *Chocolate Nut*. Substitute 3 tablespoons cocoa for 3 tablespoons of flour.

Suggested Uses

• Split 9-inch layers and fill with buttercream, mousse, whipped cream, or top with fruits.
• Roll the sheet cake and fill with buttercream, mousse, whipped cream, plain or with fruits folded in, or chocolate-flavored whipped cream.

Meringues

Meringue may be divided into two basic types: soft and hard. Soft meringue is baked on top of desserts such as lemon meringue pie until it colors lightly. The recipe for this is with the particular dessert. Hard meringue are dried out in a low oven to create crisp layers. Use hard meringue as the base of cakes or to make shells or cups to hold fruit, or other fillings.

Hard meringue can be prepared by three methods: common, sometimes called French; Swiss; and Italian. The methods use the same ratio of 2 parts of sugar to 1 part egg white by weight. For the ease of home cooks, the recipes are written in cup measures. Prepare common meringue by beating egg whites at room temperature with the sugar until very stiff. Prepare Swiss meringue by beating the egg whites and sugar while heating over hot water to produce greater stability and volume. Prepare Italian meringue by beating a hot sugar syrup (prepared by cooking half the weight of water as sugar to 240° F.) into the egg whites.

Meringues are tricky. They are dried out in the oven rather than baked. The egg whites and sugar must hold stiff, unwavering peaks to dry properly. Also, humidity affects them, so prepare to bake longer on a humid day. If your oven has a pilot light, leave the meringue in the unlighted oven until dry and ready to use. In electric ovens, it helps to prop the door open with a potholder or wooden spoon after the first hour. Ideally these do not take on any color. Store meringues in an airtight container. Pipe extra meringue into arabesques, stars, curlicues, etc., to use to garnish other desserts, or pipe into individual cases.

With electric mixers, all of these meringues are reasonably easy to prepare so select the method you like best to make any of the following recipes.

PÂTE À MERINGUE (Plain Meringue)

4 egg whites
1 cup sugar
1 teaspoon vanilla

1.   Preheat the oven to 225° F. Line baking sheets with parchment, or butter and flour. Fit a pastry bag with a pastry tip suited to the meringue shape you are preparing (see page 24).

2.   Warm the egg whites to room temperature before beating to allow for greater volume. (You may follow directions for Swiss or Italian meringue, above.)

3. Using an electric mixer, beat the egg whites until they form soft peaks. Beat in ½ cup of sugar, a tablespoon at a time, until the meringue is thick, glossy and holds stiff peaks. Add the vanilla and fold in the remaining sugar.

4. Pipe meringue onto the baking sheet (see Meringue Shapes, below). Bake for about 1 hour, or until dry and crisp.

Yields 2 (9-inch) layers or approximately 12 shells or cups

Can be stored in an airtight container at room temperature for up to 3 months.

MERINGUE SHAPES

- *Cakes and Individual Rounds*. With a large pastry bag fitted with a #5 or larger plain tip, pipe the meringue in spirals to the desired shape and size. If there are any spaces between spirals, smooth with a spatula.
- *Shells*. With a pastry bag fitted with a #8 star tip, press out large 2- to 3-inch-long shell shapes and sprinkle with sugar. Bake 30 minutes. While they are still warm, hold them shell-side down and press in the underside to make a hole. Place back in the oven and bake 30 minutes longer, or until dried.
- *Nests or Cups*. With a pastry bag fitted with a #4 star tip, pipe a 3-inch spiral of meringue. Pipe a ring on the outside edge of the spiral. Sprinkle with sugar and bake for about 40 minutes. Fill with whipped cream, pastry cream, berries, ice cream, mousses, etc.

COCOA MERINGUE

3½ tablespoons cocoa   12 tablespoons sugar
  1 cup confectioners' sugar
  4 egg whites

1. Preheat the oven to 250° F. or as recipe directs. Line a baking sheet with parchment, or butter and flour the baking sheet.

2. In a bowl, mix the cocoa and confectioners' sugar.

3. Using an electric mixer, beat the egg whites until they start to form soft peaks. Add 3 tablespoons of the sugar and beat until stiff. Fold in the remaining sugar and the cocoa mixture.

4. Pipe the meringue on the baking sheet. Bake for 1 hour, or until dry. Check color and lower heat, if necessary.

Yields 4 cups

NOTE: For the Concorde (see page 437), pipe 3 (10 × 5-inch) oval disks on one baking sheet and, on a separate sheet, pipe strips as long as the sheets. The strips will bake in about 50 minutes.

SUCCÈS (Nutted Meringues)

Succès, dacquoise, and Japonaise are all names for meringue made with ground nuts, making them less sweet than regular meringue. They often have richer fillings such as buttercream and ganache.

1 cup ground, toasted, hazelnuts, see Note	¾ cup sugar
1½ tablespoons cornstarch, see Note	6 egg whites

1.   Preheat the oven to 325° F. Line a baking sheet with parchment or foil. Fit a pastry bag with a #8 plain tip.

2.   In a processor, pulse the nuts, cornstarch, and ½ cup of sugar until well mixed.

3.   Using an electric mixer, beat the egg whites until they form soft peaks. Continue beating, adding the remaining sugar, a tablespoon at a time, until stiff peaks form. Fold in the nut mixture.

4.   Fill the pastry bag. Pipe 2 (9- or 10-inch) or 3 (7-inch) circles on the baking sheet. Bake for 1 hour, turn off the oven, and let dry in the oven for another hour.

Yields 2 (9-inch) or 3 (7-inch) layers

Can be prepared ahead and kept in an airtight container.

NOTE: The cornstarch helps to absorb the oil from the nuts. Be extra careful not to grind the nuts to a paste. Walnuts have too much oil to make crisp layers.

Variations

• Substitute almonds for the hazelnuts.
• Substitute ½ cup of almonds for ½ cup of hazelnuts.

ALMOND MACAROONS

Almond macaroons are used as part of many other desserts as well as being served as a cookie.

1 cup almonds, finely ground	½ teaspoon almond extract
1 cup sugar	½ teaspoon vanilla
2–3 egg whites	Blanched almonds, optional

1.   Preheat the oven to 400° F. Line baking sheets with parchment or foil. Fit a pastry bag with a #5 plain or star tip.

2.   In a bowl, mix the almonds with ⅔ cup of sugar and gradually add the egg whites until the mixture is the consistency of mashed potatoes. With a wooden spoon, beat hard for 3 minutes. Beat in the almond and vanilla extracts.

3.   Pipe 1½-inch rounds onto the baking sheets about 1 inch apart. Sprinkle with the remaining sugar and press an almond into each cookie, if desired.

4.   Bake 15 minutes, or until the tops are crackled and lightly browned. Cool.

Yields about 24 cookies

Can be prepared ahead and stored in an airtight container, or frozen.

CRÈME PÂTISSIÈRE (Pastry Cream)

2 cups milk	¾ cup sugar
1 (3-in) piece vanilla bean	⅓ cup flour
4–6 egg yolks	Pinch of salt

1.   In a saucepan, scald the milk with the vanilla bean. Turn off the heat, cover, and let stand 10 minutes.

2.   In another saucepan, beat the egg yolks, sugar, flour, and salt until they are thickened and pale. Add the scalded milk, stirring constantly.

3.   Cook, stirring, over medium heat, until the mixture reaches a boil. Cook for 2 to 3 minutes, stirring constantly.

4.   Strain into a bowl. Cool, stirring often, to prevent a skin from forming, or dot the surface with butter, or cover tightly with plastic wrap. Refrigerate until cold.

Yields about 3½ cups

Can be prepared 2 days ahead.

Variations

- *Crème au Chocolat*. Add 2 ounces of melted unsweetened chocolate to the milk.
- *Crème au Moka*. Flavor *crème au chocolat* with 3½ tablespoons of triple-strength coffee.
- *Crème au Café*. Flavor pastry cream with ¼ cup of triple-strength coffee or 2 tablespoons of instant coffee dissolved in ¼ cup of hot water. For texture as well as flavor, fold in 1 tablespoon of very finely ground espresso coffee beans.
- *Liqueur-flavored*. Add 1–2 tablespoons, or to taste, of rum, kirsch, or other liqueur.

MINCEMEAT

- 1½ pounds raisins, chopped
- 1 pound black currants, chopped
- ¾ pound suet, chopped
- ½ pound cooked beef, chopped
- ½ pound cooked beef tongue, chopped
- 2 cups brown sugar
- 2 cups diced apple
- 2 cups Cognac or rum
- ½ cup chopped candied citron
- ½ cup chopped candied cherries
- ½ cup chopped candied pineapple
- ½ cup dry sherry
- ¼ cup chopped candied lemon peel
- ¼ cup chopped candied orange peel
- ¼ cup lemon juice
- Grated rind of 1 orange
- Grated rind of 1 lemon
- 1 teaspoon nutmeg
- 1 teaspoon cinnamon
- ½ teaspoon ground cloves
- ½ teaspoon allspice
- ½ teaspoon salt

In a large, nonreactive container, combine the raisins, currants, suet, beef, tongue, brown sugar, apple, Cognac, citron, cherries, pineapple, sherry, candied lemon peel, candied orange peel, lemon juice, grated orange rind, grated lemon rind, nutmeg, cinnamon, cloves, allspice, and salt. Mix well. Keep covered for at least 3 weeks before using. The mincemeat will keep for months in tightly sealed jars in a cold place. If necessary, add more Cognac and sherry to keep the mixture somewhat fluid.

Yields about 3½ quarts

Can be prepared several months before using.

APPLE PUREE

More familiarly known as applesauce.

Peel, core, and slice or chop the apples. Place in a saucepan, cover and simmer for 15 minutes. Stir and add sugar to taste. If the apples are very watery, remove the cover and cook, stirring often, until thickened.

LEMON CURD

4 egg yolks	**¼ cup butter, softened**
⅔ cup sugar	**Pinch of salt**
¼ cup lemon juice	

1.   In a nonreactive saucepan, beat the egg yolks and sugar until thickened and pale. Place over low heat and beat in the lemon juice, butter, and salt. Cook, stirring, until thick enough to coat the back of a spoon. It must not boil or it will curdle.

2.   Immediately strain into a bowl and cool, stirring, or cover with plastic wrap. Refrigerate until cold.

Yields 3½ cups

Can be refrigerated in covered containers for up to 2 weeks.

NOTE: The hot lemon curd will be thin. It will continue to thicken as it cools.

NESSELRODE MIX

1½ cups diced candied fruit, page 39	**¼ cup dark rum, Cognac, or kirsch**
12 chestnuts in syrup, chopped	

In a bowl, mix the fruit, chestnuts, and liqueur. Macerate for at least 1 hour.

Yields about 2 cups

Can be stored for as long as 6 months in a sealed jar.

PEAR-ALMOND PUREE

Use this versatile puree in place of applesauce, as a tart filling, as a base for fresh raspberries or strawberries, as a sauce for ice cream or gingerbread.

4 pounds pears, peeled, cored, and sliced	**ground, optional**
	⅓ cup sugar
3 tablespoons water	**2 tablespoons pear liqueur**
2 ounces toasted almonds,	**1 tablespoon lemon juice**

In a saucepan, cook the pears in the water, stirring occasionally about 25 minutes or until soft. Drain the pears. In a processor, puree the pears and add the almonds, sugar, pear liqueur, and lemon juice.

Yields about 1 quart

Can be prepared 3 days before serving, or frozen.

RASPBERRY PUREE

In a processor, puree the raspberries and strain through a fine sieve to remove the seeds. Sweeten to taste.

Can be stored in a refrigerator for 2 to 3 days.

Variations

• Other fruits such as strawberries and peaches adapt well to this technique.
• Substitute frozen, unsweetened raspberries for fresh. If using sweetened, frozen raspberries, drain syrup and puree the fruit.

DESSERT SYRUP

1 cup sugar
1 cup water
2–3 tablespoons liqueur

1. In a saucepan, simmer the sugar and water for 5 minutes. Add the liqueur and cool to lukewarm.

2. Brush over cake layers to keep them moist.

Yields about 1½ cups

Can be stored in a covered container at room temperature for a week or longer.

PRALINE POWDER

Praline is usually made from almonds, sometimes walnuts, and Duja is made from an equal mix of almonds and hazelnuts.

1 cup sugar   **½ teaspoon vanilla**
¼ cup cold water
1 cup blanched almonds

1. In a saucepan, cook the sugar and water until the sugar dissolves. Add the nuts and cook over moderate heat until the sugar is well caramelized. Add the vanilla.

2. Pour onto the baking sheet, spread evenly, and cool until the praline hardens. Break up and put into a blender or processor and process to a fine powder. Sift through a sieve, reprocessing any large chunks.

Yields about 1¼ cups

Can be stored in a tightly covered container in the freezer for up to 6 months.

Variations

• Substitute hazelnuts, walnuts, Brazil nuts, or macadamia nuts for the almonds.
• Substitute ½ cup of hazelnuts for ½ cup of almonds.

Buttercream Frostings

There are many versions of buttercream frostings, made with all egg yolks, all egg whites, or a mixture of the two. Whichever recipe you choose, it must be made with butter. Attempting to substitute an imitation butter will produce an unpleasing result, if not a total disaster.

CLASSIC BUTTERCREAM

⅔ **cup sugar**
  Pinch of cream of tartar
⅓ **cup water**
5 **egg yolks**
1 **cup butter, softened**
  Flavoring, see below

1.   In a heavy saucepan, boil the sugar, cream of tartar, and water until the mixture reaches 238° F.

2.   In a electric mixer, beat the egg yolks until fluffy. With the machine running, beat the syrup into the egg yolks in a thin, steady stream. Continue beating until the mixture cools, and becomes thickened and pale.

3.   When cooled to lukewarm, beat in the butter in small amounts. Beat in the flavoring.

Yields about 2 cups

Can be prepared several days ahead and stored in the refrigerator or frozen. Let come to room temperature before using.

Variations

- *Chocolate*. Add 1 ounce of cooled melted unsweetened chocolate.
- *Coffee*. Add 1 tablespoon of extra-strong coffee.
- *Mocha*. Add 1 ounce of cooled melted unsweetened chocolate and 1 tablespoon of extra-strong coffee.
- *Liqueur*. Add 1 tablespoon of liqueur, or to taste.
- *Praline*. Add 2 tablespoons of Praline Powder, (see page 30).
- *Lemon*. Add 2 tablespoons of grated lemon rind and 1 teaspoon of lemon juice.
- *Orange*. Add 1 tablespoon of grated orange rind and 1 tablespoon of orange juice.
- *Almond*. Add 1 teaspoon of almond extract.

NEOCLASSIC BUTTERCREAM

This is an adaption of a buttercream created by Rose Levy Bernbaum. It is easier than the method used above.

6 egg yolks	**Flavoring, double amount**
¾ cup sugar	**for Classic Buttercream,**
½ cup corn syrup	**page 31**
2 cups butter, softened	

1.   Lightly oil a 1-cup glass or metal measuring cup.

2.   In a electric mixer, beat the egg yolks until light in color.

3.   In a small saucepan, heat the sugar and the corn syrup, stirring constantly, until the sugar dissolves. Bring to a rolling boil and immediately pour into the measuring cup.

4.   Hold the measuring cup at the side of the mixing bowl. With the machine running, let the syrup flow down the side of the bowl, beating constantly. Continue to beat until cool. Beat in the butter, bit by bit, and flavor to taste.

Yields about 4 cups

Can be prepared ahead and kept in the refrigerator, or frozen. Let come to room temperature before using.

QUICK BUTTERCREAM

4 egg yolks	**1¼ cups butter, softened**
¼ cup sugar	**Flavoring, see Classic**
1 teaspoon vanilla	**Buttercream, page 31**

In a processor, beat the egg yolks, sugar and vanilla for 2 minutes. Add the butter, bit by bit, until fully incorporated, and flavor to taste.

Yields about 2 cups

Can be prepared ahead and kept in the refrigerator or frozen. Let come to room temperature before using.

EGG WHITE BUTTERCREAM

1 cup egg whites
1 pound confectioners' sugar
2 cups butter, at room
  temperature

Flavoring, double amount for
Classic Buttercream, page 31

1. In a large bowl, mix the egg whites and sugar over hot, not boiling water, until they reach 90° F.

2. In a electric mixer, beat the egg white mixture until stiff and cool. Add the butter, a little at a time, until the butter is well incorporated and smooth. It may look a bit separated in the beginning. Keep beating. Beat in the flavoring and refrigerate until ready to use.

Yields about 4 cups

Can be prepared the day before and kept in the refrigerator or frozen. Let come to room temperature before using.

CARAMEL BUTTERCREAM

2 cups butter, softened
10 egg yolks
1 cup sugar

⅓ cup plus 2 tablespoons
water

1. In a bowl, cream the butter until light and fluffy. Set aside.

2. In an electric mixer, beat the egg yolks until light in color.

3. In a saucepan, dissolve the sugar in ⅓ cup of water, over low heat. Bring to a boil and cook to the golden brown caramel stage (see page 5). Remove from heat and cool 1 minute. Add the remaining water to the caramel and stir to combine.

4. With the machine running, slowly pour the hot caramel down the side of the bowl into the yolks and beat until cool. Beat in the creamed butter and refrigerate until thick, about 30 minutes.

Yields about 4 cups

Can be prepared the day before and kept in the refrigerator, or frozen. Let come to room temperature before using.

ROYAL ICING

3 egg whites	**sugar**
½ teaspoon cream of tartar	
1 pound sifted confectioners'	

In a mixer, beat the egg whites and cream of tartar until foamy. Beat in the sugar, ½ cup at a time, until smooth. Continue beating until stiff peaks form.

Yields 3½ cups

Store at room temperature in an airtight container.

NOTE: Use to decorate petit fours. It becomes hard after a few hours exposed to the air.

Ganache

In recent years ganache, a combination of melted bittersweet or semisweet chocolate and heavy cream, has become one of the most popular of cake and dessert toppings. Ganache can vary from equal quantities of chocolate and cream, by weight, to twice the weight of cream to the weight of chocolate. For light, airy filling that almost dissolves in the mouth, prepare the ganache with 8 ounces of chocolate and 2 cups (1 pound) of heavy cream to yield 4 cups. For a denser, more fudge-like filling, use 1 pound of chocolate with 2 cups of heavy cream. Once the ganache is prepared, cool to room temperature, and pour over the cakes to use as a glaze, or put into an electric mixer and beat until light and whipped. The heavier the chocolate, the heavier and more fudge-like the ganache. In many instances, butter is added for greater richness.

   Ganache, once whipped, especially with a high chocolate content, must be used immediately, or it will become too stiff to spread. Should that occur, melt over hot water until fluid, refrigerate until cold, and whip again.

GANACHE FOR SUCCÈS LAYERS

24 ounces semisweet chocolate, chopped	**2¼ cups heavy cream**
8 ounces butter	

1. In a bowl, combine the chocolate and the butter.

2. In a saucepan, bring the cream to a full boil and pour over the chocolate and butter. Let stand for 3 minutes, stir until smooth and refrigerate until cold.

Yields about 4 cups, or enough to fill and frost 2 (9-inch) or 3 (7-inch) succès layers

Can be prepared the day before.

GANACHE WHIPPED TOPPING

If you overbeat it, or it becomes too stiff, you can melt, cool, and rewhip.

8 ounces semisweet chocolate, chopped
2 cups heavy cream

1. Place the chocolate in a large bowl.

2. In a saucepan, bring the cream to a full boil and pour over the chocolate. Stir until smooth, and refrigerate until cold.

3. In an electric mixer, beat until soft peaks form. Do not overbeat, or it will become grainy.

4. Use immediately. It will continue to stiffen after you stop beating.

Yields 4 cups

Keeps at room temperature for a day, or can be frozen.

CHOCOLATE GLAZE

Pour over cakes for a thin, shiny coating to seal in freshness.

8 ounces semisweet chocolate, chopped
1 cup heavy cream

1 tablespoon Cognac or other liqueur, optional

1. In a double boiler, over hot, but not boiling, water, or in a microwave, melt the chocolate in the cream. Stir until smooth. If necessary, heat another 30 seconds. Stir in the Cognac. Strain into a clean bowl.

2. Cool until tepid and pour over the center of the cake, tilting and turning the cake, or use a thin metal spatula to spread to the edges and around the sides. For a thicker coating, refrigerate the cake for 20 minutes and pour on a second coating. Refrigerate until set.

Yields enough for 1 (9-inch) cake layer

NOTE: Save any leftover glaze for another use or thin and serve as a chocolate sauce.

CHOCOLATE DIP (for cookies, etc.)

    4 ounces semisweet   **shortening**
      chocolate
    2 teaspoons vegetable

1. In a double boiler, over hot, not boiling water, or in a microwave, melt the chocolate and shortening.

2. Cool to 90° F. and dip the cookies halfway into the chocolate. Dry on a wire rack.

Yields about ½ cup

Prepare and use immediately.

CONFECTIONERS' SUGAR GLAZE

    1 cup confectioners' sugar
1–2 tablespoons liqueur or
      water

1. Mix ingredients until they form the consistency of heavy cream. You can use kirsch, Cognac, or Madeira as liqueurs, or water for a more neutral glaze.

2. Use as directed.

NOTE: For a stiffer glaze, add additional sugar.

APRICOT OR CURRANT GLAZE

    1 cup apricot preserves or   **liqueur**
      currant jam, strained
    4 tablespoons water or

In a small saucepan, boil the preserves and water for 1 minute. Use to glaze fruit tarts and cakes.

Yields about 1 cup

Can be prepared in large quantity and stored in an airtight container.

CARAMEL GLAZE

2 cups sugar
⅔ cup water
1 teaspoon cream of tartar or

lemon juice

1. In a saucepan, simmer the sugar, water, and cream of tartar or lemon juice, stirring gently, until the sugar dissolves, brushing down the sides of the pan with cold water.

2. Cover and boil for 5 minutes.

3. Remove the cover and boil without stirring until it starts to turn golden. Swirl the pan to mix the color evenly. When it reaches the desired color, remove from the heat and place the saucepan in a pan of hot water to stop the cooking.

Yields about 1¼ cups

Use while warm.

SPUN SUGAR

Literally throw the syrup from the ends of the fork by swinging your arm in a long arc. Ideally, stand on a stool to give your arm room to swing to make the thinnest possible threads.

4 cups sugar
2 cups water
Pinch of cream of tartar

1 teaspoon light corn syrup
Food coloring, optional

1. Oil broom handles and place on the backs of 2 chairs, back-to-back, 2 to 4 feet apart. Place newspapers on the floor.

2. In a heavy saucepan, heat the sugar and water to 270° F., brushing the sides of the pan with cold water to remove any sugar crystals.

3. Add the cream of tartar and corn syrup and heat to 310° F.

4. Remove from the heat and set the saucepan in a pan of cold water to stop cooking. Then, place in a pan of warm water.

5. Stand on one chair, with a fork dipped in sugar syrup, and swing the syrup over the broom handles to create the spun sugar. Gather threads and wrap around the edge of the dessert.

Yields 2 cups syrup—enough spun sugar for a large dessert

NOTE: Must be served immediately.

CANDIED ORANGE RIND I

Use these to garnish desserts.

  2 oranges
  1 cup water
  ½ cup sugar

1. With a zester, remove tiny strips of rind from the oranges, or use a vegetable peeler to remove the colored rind only and cut into the thinnest possible strips, small circles, or other shapes.

2. Blanch the rind in boiling water for 5 minutes, drain, refresh under cold water, and drain again.

3. In a saucepan, simmer 1 cup water and the sugar for 5 minutes. Add the peel and cook, turning often, for about 10 minutes, or until the peel is translucent.

4. Cool in the syrup.

Yields about ½ cup

Can be stored in syrup for months.

Variation

• Substitute lemon or lime rinds.

CANDIED ORANGE RIND II

Use this as a confection.

4 thick-skinned oranges
2 cups water
1½ cups sugar
   Coarse sugar, optional

1. Cut the ends from the oranges and cut the oranges into quarters. With a spoon or your fingers, pry the rind from the flesh. Save the flesh for another use.

2. Cut the rind into ½-inch-wide strips. Place in a saucepan with enough cold water to cover. Simmer 10 minutes. Drain.

3. In a saucepan, bring the 2 cups of water and the sugar to boil, stirring until the sugar dissolves. Add the orange rind and simmer, uncovered, for 2 hours. Cover and let stand at room temperature for 12 hours.

4. Store in the syrup until ready to use.

Yields about 75 strips

Can be stored in syrup for up to 6 months.

NOTE: For a confection, drain well, roll in coarse sugar, and let dry on racks. Or, use as candied rind in recipes.

Variation

• Substitute lemon rinds.

CRÈME FRAÎCHE

Use this in lieu of heavy cream for a richer dessert.

1 cup heavy cream, see Note
1 tablespoon buttermilk

1. In a saucepan, warm the cream to 90° F.

2. Remove from the heat and whisk in the buttermilk. Let stand for 24 hours, or until thickened to the consistency of sour cream.

Yields 1 cup

Keeps up to 3 weeks, refrigerated.

NOTE: This will not work with ultra-pasteurized cream.

VANILLA POACHED FRUITS

6 pears, peaches, apples, apricots, or pineapples	2 teaspoons lemon juice
1 cup sugar	1 cup water
Pinch of salt	1 (2-in) piece vanilla bean, split

1.   Peel, core, and cut the fruit as directed in the recipe.

2.   In a saucepan, simmer the sugar, salt, lemon juice, water, and vanilla for 3 minutes.

3.   Add the fruit and simmer gently until tender, turning often. Cool in the syrup.

Yields 6 servings

Can be prepared the day before serving.

NOTE: You can double or triple the syrup according to needs. With the quantity listed it may be necessary to poach in batches. Pears have a tendency to darken on the inside if prepared ahead. Since you cannot see the condition until you cut into the fruit, it is best to prepare them no more than a day ahead.

COOKING TIMES FOR POACHED FRUIT   The time required to poach fruit depends on the fruit. Some, such as strawberries, poach in a minute or less, while others may take much longer. There are two major types of pears when ripe, the hard Seckle, and Bosc varieties and the soft Bartlett, Anjou, and comice varieties. The harder pears take longer to poach and will still be quite firm when cooked. The softer pears become quite soft during cooking depending on ripeness. It is impossible to specify cooking times because some pears will cook in as little as 10 minutes while others will require as much as 35 minutes. If the pears are ripe and soft, start checking with a small sharp knife or skewer after 10 minutes. If they are hard-type pears, poach or bake at least 20 minutes before testing.

Chocolate Garnishes

CHOCOLATE RUFFLES

The chocolate frill takes some practice. A few broken pieces are not a problem.

METHOD I   Melt and temper about 8 ounces of semisweet chocolate, (see page 8). On the back of a baking sheet, spread a very thin layer of chocolate over the whole surface. Let stand at room temperature for about 20 minutes. (The room must be no more than 70° F., 65° F. is even better.) Or, refrigerate for 10 minutes. With the aid of a pastry scraper, scrape off a 2-inch-wide band of the chocolate. It should form pleats. If it breaks, it is too cold and if it does not form pleats, it is still too warm. Let it stand at room temperature for about 5 minutes and try again. Hold your thumb against one end of the base of the chocolate to get the frill to form a fan.

Arrange the pleated pieces over the top of the cake, starting at the outside edge and working in concentric circles toward the center. The top of the cake should look like a ruffled blouse. (See illustration.) Can be prepared the day before serving.

METHOD II   If the method described above is too difficult, try this simpler method.

Place sheets of waxed paper on the back of baking sheets. Melt and temper about 8 ounces semisweet chocolate, (see page 8). Thinly spread the melted chocolate on the waxed paper. Cool at room temperature, or in the refrigerator, until firm enough to handle, but not hard. Cut the sheets into 2- to 3-inch strips. Dip your hands into ice water, if they are warm, and peel the paper off a ribbon of chocolate and quickly shape it into a ruffle and place on the top of the cake. Remember, the frills do not have to be perfect. If they are not as appealing as you would like, sift some confectioners' sugar over the top.

CHOCOLATE CAKE BANDS

Place sheets of waxed paper on the back of baking sheets. Melt and temper about 8 ounces of semisweet chocolate, (see page 8). Thinly spread the melted chocolate on the waxed paper. Cool at room temperature, or in the refrigerator, until firm enough to handle, but still supple. Once firm enough to handle, cut the sheets into strips as wide as the cake is tall. Wrap around the cake and refrigerate until set. Peel off the paper. The strips can overlap, if necessary. Use a little icing as glue, if needed.

CHOCOLATE WEDGES

Line the bottom of a cake pan the same diameter as the cake with a circle of waxed paper. Melt and temper about 3 ounces of semisweet chocolate (see page 8). Pour the chocolate into the pan and tilt to coat evenly. Refrigerate until set. Run a knife around the edge of the pan and unmold the chocolate onto a board. Peel off the paper. Run a knife under hot water and wipe dry. Cut the disk into wedges.

CARAQUE, OR CHOCOLATE SHAVINGS

Melt and temper 3 ounces of chocolate (see page 8). Spread the chocolate on a marble slab or the back of a baking sheet. Cool until almost set. Hold a long, thin sharp knife almost at a right angle and shave off long chocolate scrolls or flakes using a slight sideways sawing motion.

Can be prepared a week or two before using. Store in an airtight container in a cool place, not in the refrigerator.

Chocolate can also be carefully shaved from a block. This will create a fluffy garnish for the top of desserts. Hold the chocolate firmly and draw a vegetable peeler along the block in a downward motion. Make sure you do this over a pan so that the shavings do not scatter.

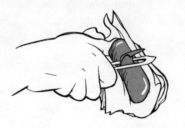

Chocolate Ornaments

CIRCLES, TRIANGLES, SQUARES, OR OTHER SHAPES

Melt and temper 3 ounces of semisweet chocolate (see page 8). Spread the chocolate on the back of a baking sheet or marble slab and cool until set. Run a sharp knife or a metal cookie cutter under hot water and dry completely, or, using a cookie cutter, cut out the desired shapes. You can remelt the trimmings to make more or to use in a dessert.

CHOCOLATE FENCES

Instead of surrounding a cake with a band of chocolate, you may wish to prepare a chocolate fence. Melt and temper 3 ounces of semisweet chocolate (see page 8). Spread a sheet of waxed paper on a counter or the back of a baking sheet. Put the warm chocolate into a pastry bag fitted with a #2 plain tip or use a paper cone and snip the opening as large as needed. Mark the paper in strips as wide as the cake is tall and long enough to surround it..

   Using the pastry bag, pipe the chocolate in a series of interlocking scrolls and swirls over the marked area. Or, pipe a decorative strip along the top of the marked area and another along the bottom of the marked area. Make Xs between the two strips connecting the top and bottom strips. Cool until flexible but firm. Carefully lift the waxed paper strip and wrap around the cake. Carefully peel off the waxed paper, pressing the chocolate into the icing to secure.

CHOCOLATE PALM TREES

Melt and temper 3 ounces of semisweet chocolate (see page 8). Spread a sheet of waxed paper on a counter or the back of a baking sheet. Put the warm chocolate into a pastry bag fitted with a #2 plain tip or use a paper cone and snip an opening as large as needed.

   Hold the pastry tip close to the waxed paper. Moving the tip back and forth, make a ½-inch-wide base and work to the top of the trunk making it about ¼ inch wide. Using the same back-and-forth movement, move the tip in a half-circle toward one side of the trunk and again to the opposite side. Make two more palm fronds above the first two. Refrigerate until set. Store at room temperature. Use these to decorate individual ice creams or assemble around the top of a cake.

CHOCOLATE BUTTERFLIES

On a sheet of paper, make an outline of a butterfly as large as you wish. Make these small for individual servings, or, for a more impressive look, one very large butterfly for the top of a cake. Place the drawing under a sheet of waxed paper.

Melt and temper 3 ounces of semisweet chocolate (see page 8). Spread a sheet of waxed paper on a counter or the back of a baking sheet, with the drawing underneath. Put the warm chocolate into a pastry bag fitted with a #2 plain tip, or use a paper cone and snip an opening as small or as large as needed.

Hold the tip ½ inch above the paper and follow the outside edges of the drawing. Draw each wing section separately. Pipe scrolls of chocolate filling in the center of each wing to look like lace. Pipe a separate, long, thick center section to make the body of the butterfly. Refrigerate until set. Once firm, place the body of the butterfly on a baking sheet. Pipe some melted chocolate along part of the body and carefully place a wing section against the body at an angle. Use crumpled waxed paper as a support for the wing. Repeat with the remaining wings. If necessary, pipe more chocolate over the wings where they attach to the body. Refrigerate until set and store at room temperature.

CHOCOLATE LEAVES

One of the easiest decorations to put on a cake is chocolate leaves. Select clean dry leaves with good veining on the underside. Rose, hibiscus, cabbage, and maple leaves all suit perfectly.

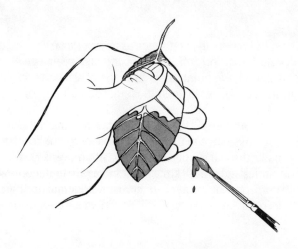

Melt and temper about 4 ounces of semisweet chocolate (see page 8). With a pastry brush or small artist's brush, brush the chocolate on the *underside* of each leaf and place on a baking sheet. Refrigerate about 10 minutes or until set. Carefully peel the leaf from the chocolate.

Store the chocolate leaves in an airtight container until needed. Keeps a week or longer. Place a cluster of leaves on the center of the cake or off to one side.

CHOCOLATE VERMICELLI

One of the best-known chocolate decorations, especially atop mounds of ice cream. Also known as jimmies, sprinkles, and shots.

SAUCE DECORATIONS FOR PLATES

Many dessert cooks would not think of serving a dessert on a plain plate. They feel a need to decorate the plate as lavishly, and sometimes even more lavishly, than the dessert. Dinner-size plates make these decorations impressive. On smaller plates they look cramped.

Plate Decoration I. Place a piece of foil-covered cardboard in the center of the plate. Pour one sauce on one side and another sauce on the opposite side. Remove the cardboard.

Plate Decoration II. Twist the cardboard into a "S" shape and follow previous directions.

Plate Decoration III. Pour one sauce in the center of the plate and tilt to fill the well. Put the second sauce in a squeeze bottle with a small tip and place drops around the outer edge. Use a small knife point to draw the drops into commas.

Plate Decoration IV. Prepare the first sauce as above. Place the dessert in the center and drizzle 3 or more fine lines of the second sauce around the dessert. With a sharp knife point, draw from the center out every 2 inches, and then from the center in between those lines.

Plate Decoration V. Pour the first sauce on the plate and place the dessert off-center. With the second sauce in the squeeze bottle, draw a line through the first sauce and make the leaf shapes off the line. At the top of the line, make 3 or 4 concentric circles and draw a knife point in them to create a flower. Dust the plates with confectioners' sugar and garnish with small arrangements of berries or other fruits.

Chapter 2

FRUIT PREPARATION AND PRESENTATION

Serve fruits alone, as a snack, a simple meal, or dessert. Serve them hot, cold, raw, poached, or baked. Sprinkle with sugar, top with cream, lace with liqueurs, or use a combination of these suggestions. Serve with a sauce, or two. Turn them into the most elaborate and elegant of mousses, charlottes, or soufflés. Just select the best fruits at the height of perfection and handle them properly.

Proper Handling

When the fruit arrives from the market, remove it from the packaging, and, if you did not hand-select it at the store, inspect it. Set aside any bruised fruits for immediate use, and discard any that are damaged or rotted. Spread berries on paper toweling, and discard any stalks, leaves, or twigs, as well as any underripe or overripe berries.

Do not wash fruit until just before serving. If you wash it long before you use it, the water can cause the fruit to deteriorate. Return picked-over berries or grapes to the original container or a colander so air can pass around them. When ready to wash them, rinse them quickly under cold running water, drain well, and dry on paper toweling. Porous berries such as strawberries absorb water if left to soak. In the past, it was not uncommon for recipes to suggest you rinse the berries in wine — Champagne specifically — to clean them. The idea is only a little precious. The wine gives the berries added flavor and, once the grit settles to the bottom, it becomes a refreshing drink for the cook. Be sure to dry the berries and keep them cool until ready to serve.

For the best flavor, let the fruit come to just below room temperature before serving. Fruits served directly from the refrigerator have less flavor. If the fruit has just arrived and seems a little warm, try the Italian method: Place the fruit (not porous fruitlike strawberries) in a bowl half-filled with cool water. The evaporation will cool the fruit to the right temperature. Try this with a bunch of grapes.

Preparing Individual Fruits

Most fruits are quickly and easily prepared, but some require special attention. The techniques needed for this chapter and throughout the book follow. The following are elements to keep in mind:

WASHING   My basic belief is, If it isn't dirty, don't wash it. Running an apple or bunch of grapes under cold water gets the fruit wet, but not much else. If you think the fruit is chemically coated, you may feel better if you wash it first. However, many fruits suffer from too much water, specifically berries. If you must wash them, rinse them quickly under cold water in a colander and shake to drain. Immediately roll them onto paper toweling to dry. If left wet, they will quickly rot.

BLANCHING   You must blanch certain fruits, such as peaches and nectarines, to peel them. Bring a pot of water to a full boil and add the fruit. Cook 20 seconds and immediately plunge the fruit into cold water. When cool enough to handle, use a paring knife to peel off the skin. If the fruit is ripe, it will peel easily. If not, you will have difficulty. If the fruit is slightly overripe, blanching longer will help, but be careful not to cook the fruit.

APPLES   If serving apple slices to children or wary adults, slice the apple horizontally to expose the seed casings. They form a star. For most recipes, peel apples with a vegetable peeler. Core apples whole by inserting an apple corer through the center. To halve or slice, cut from the stem to blossom end and use a sharp knife or melon baller to remove the core. To slice, cut into quarters, remove the core, and slice.

APRICOTS   Peel, if directed, by blanching (see above). To pit, cut around the apricot at the dimple and twist the halves to separate and pry out the pit.

AVOCADOS   Avocados appear in a few fruit desserts. With a sharp knife, cut into the flesh, encircling the pit from top to bottom. Twist the two halves and pull apart. Pry out the pit with a sharp knife and scoop out the flesh with a spoon. Use the pulp right away, or to prevent browning, put into an airtight container and refrigerate for as short a time as possible, not more than a few hours.

BANANAS   Cut off the ends and peel the skin in sections. Use immediately, or brush with lemon juice if it is necessary to hold longer than a few minutes, but not more than an hour. Under refrigeration, the skins turn an unappealing brown, discouraging eating out of hand, but the fruit may still be white and firm.

BLACKBERRIES   Pick over berries discarding any leaves, twigs, or molds berries. Wash just before using and dry on toweling. Use within a day or two.

BLUEBERRIES   See Blackberries.

CACTUS PEARS   See Prickly Pears.

CARAMBOLA OR STARFRUIT   This citrus-flavored fruit makes a flavorful accompaniment to fruit cups. Slice to expose the star shape.

CHERRIES   Serve raw with or without a cherry pitter. Be sure to pit before using in recipes. Cherry pitters are available at gourmet shops. Some cooks suggest pushing the pit out of the cherry with a chopstick.

CHESTNUTS

To Peel Raw Chestnuts. With a sharp knife, cut an X on one side of each chestnut. Put into boiling water and simmer for 20 minutes. Drain and cool. Peel the shell and rub off the brown skin. This is tedious work.

To Rehydrate Dried Chestnuts. Soak the chestnuts in water to cover for 12 hours and drain. Or, in a saucepan with water to cover, simmer the chestnuts until tender, about 20 minutes.

COCONUTS   With an ice pick or screwdriver, pierce the "eyes," the dark spots on top of the coconut. Drain out the watery liquid and discard. Place the coconut on its side and gently rap around the center with a hammer or heavy cleaver, while turning the coconut until it splits. When split, break into sections and, using an old table knife, pry the meat from the shell. Use a vegetable peeler to pare the bark-like skin from the meat. Grate the coconut on a four-sided grater using the largest holes, or shred in a processor, using the shredding blade.

To Toast Coconut. Preheat oven to 350° F. Spread coconut evenly on a baking sheet and bake 5 minutes. Stir the coconut and bake 5 minutes longer.

DATES   They are sold fresh or dried, pitted or unpitted. If dried and unpitted, cut a slit along one side of the date, open the flesh, and remove the pit. Occasionally found fresh. Serve like grapes. Warn your guests about pits.

FIGS   Cut off the blossom end and peel the skin in sections toward the stem end, if desired. I do not usually peel figs. Cut the hard stem from dried figs.

GRAPES   Store grapes in their original container or a colander to allow for air circulation. Pull from the stems and use whole or halved. If you want, use a small sharp knife to peel the skin from the stem end in sections.
    To seed grapes, cut in half and pry out the seeds. Or, to seed whole grapes, open a paper clip, leaving the smaller bend in place; insert this bend into the stem end of the grape and "worry out" the seeds. Best to buy seedless grapes.

GRAPEFRUIT   See Lemons.

KIWIS OR CHINESE GOOSEBERRIES   Cut off the ends and peel the skin with a vegetable peeler before slicing horizontally.

LEMONS   Wash lemons well before preparing the rind in any of the forms listed below.

To Julienne. Use a vegetable peeler to remove the zest, the yellow outermost layer. (The white is called the pith.) Stack a bundle of strips and cut into the finest possible shreds with a large knife. Or, use a special tool called a *zester*. A zester has four or five small holes. Pull it down the fruit from stem to blossom end, removing the outer layer of skin in long, thin strips (julienne).

To Make Lemon Strips. Remove larger strips with a *stripper*. This tool has a single large hole and removes ¼-inch-wide strips. Use the same way as a zester.

To Remove the Whole Rind. Cut off both ends and cut a slit down one side of the lemon, cutting through the pith but not the flesh. Ease a teaspoon between the flesh and the pith and pry the rind from the lemon. Cut the rind into thin strips. You may cut off the pith.

To Grate Lemon Rind. Use the finest side of a four-sided grater and gently grate the lemon in a rotary motion, removing just the color (zest) of the lemon and none of the white pith. Relax and grate in a gentle circular motion while rotating the lemon to remove the zest and not grate your knuckles.

For larger quantities—more than half a cup—use a vegetable peeler or stripper to remove the zest from the lemon and mince in a processor. The blade must be sharp; processor blades do dull! Plan to replace it as needed.

Lemon Cups. Cut a slice from the top or side of each lemon, about one-third the height of the lemon. With a spoon, or grapefruit knife, remove the flesh from inside the shell. You can make a more elaborate shell by cutting the lemon to create a handle, or cutting notches into the upper edge. If necessary, make a thin slice on the side opposite the opening, so the shell will stand upright. For added decoration, use a stripper to create designs in the skin of the shell.

Use these cups to Serve fresh fruit, mousse, or sherbet.

LIMES   See Lemons.

MANGOES   To serve raw, cut around the seed at the widest side of the mango. Use a spoon to slip under the meat and over the seed. Remove the mango halves. With a knife, cut a crosshatch into the flesh, but not the skin, of the fruit. Press the skin toward the flesh to make a mound with the cubes of mango standing up. To serve in fruit cups, etc., peel with a sharp knife or vegetable peeler, and cut slices lengthwise into the pit of the mango; then cut underneath the flesh and over the seed to remove.

MELONS   Use melons as containers for other foods, cut into wedges, scooped into balls, or decorated as a centerpiece. Except for watermelon, cut melons in half, discard the seeds, and cut the melon into serving pieces. Serve individual halves of small melons.

Melon Wedges. Cut the melon in half lengthwise and cut each half into wedges. Cut underneath the fruit to separate it from the rind. Cut fruit into ½-inch-wide sections. To arrange attractively, poke alternating sections ½ inch toward the center.

For a more elaborate presentation, cut into the sides of the wedge with a melon baller without removing the ball. This gives it a sculptural quality. Fill

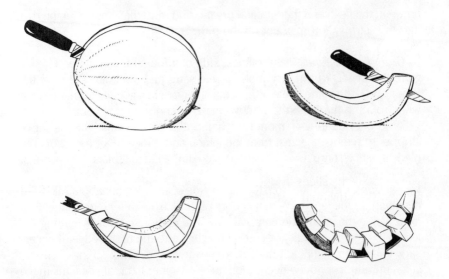

the center of the wedge with more melon balls or other fruits. You also can cut out the balls from the sides and replace with balls cut from a different-colored melon.

Melon Balls. Press a melon baller firmly into the melon and twist to remove the ball. (Watch out for the juices that spurt from the small hole.) Snap your wrist over a bowl to remove the ball.

Melon Flowers. With a thin sharp knife or a vegetable peeler cut thin slices from the sides of a peeled melon wedge. Wrap one or more slices around a

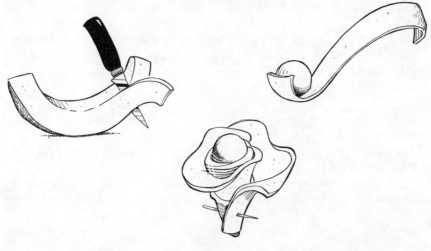

melon ball, preferably of a contrasting color, and secure with a wooden skewer. Soak the slices in salted water for 10 minutes to make them more pliable. Use individual flowers to garnish dessert plates, or make a nosegay of flowers to decorate a fruit or meat platter.

Melon Containers. Use halves of small melons to hold individual portions of other fruits. For large melons, cut off the top third of one side. Scoop out the flesh with a melon baller or cut out with a knife and dice it. Use the knife or scoop to make the inside as neat as possible. Scallop, serrate, or "cannel" the edges of the melon and/or use a lemon stripper to cut a design into the skin of the melon. Decorate the container with skewers of other fruits. Skewer orange slices and strawberries and place around the upper edge of the melon. Or, with a small sharp knife or a wooden skewer, make holes and insert flower stems into the edges of the melon.

Let your imagination soar. Carve the melon vertically or horizontally, create a handle, or carve to create a swan. Cut a thin slice off the bottom to steady the melon. To serve a large melon vertically, place the base in a wok ring and decorate the ring with fruits, flowers, and leaves.

NECTARINES

To Peel. Bring a pot of water to a full rolling boil, add the nectarines and blanch about 20 seconds. Transfer to a bowl of cold water to stop the cooking. Then, with a sharp knife and your thumb, pull the skin away. Rub the fruit with lemon juice to prevent the fruit from darkening. This fruit is often served with the skin attached.

To Pit. With a sharp knife, cut into the nectarine at the dimple to the pit and encircle the fruit. Twist the two halves and pull apart, exposing the pit. Pry the pit from the fruit. To prevent the flesh from darkening, put into acidulated water or a bowl of sliced citrus fruits.

ORANGES

To Peel. Slice off both ends of the oranges and place a cut end on a board. With a sharp knife, cut down the side of the orange to remove a section of the rind, including the pith, exposing the fruit. Continue around the orange. Slice horizontally.

To Segment. Peel the orange as above. With a sharp knife, cut along one side of a membrane, repeat on the other side of the same membrane, and cut along the side of the next membrane to remove the segment. Continue to cut around the orange to remove all the segments.

PAPAYAS   With a sharp knife or vegetable peeler, pare the rind from the fruit. Cut in half and remove the seeds. Cut the papaya into slices, either lengthwise or crosswise.

PEACHES   See Nectarines.

PEARS   With a vegetable peeler or sharp knife, peel around the globular base and then peel from the center of the pear to the stem end. This method of peeling enhances the pear shape.

To Hollow Pears. Use an apple corer inserted part or all the way into the bottom of the pear to remove the core and leave the stem, or to remove the stem completely. If necessary to accommodate a filling, use a melon baller inserted from the bottom to enlarge the inner cavity.

To Core Pears. Cut the pears in half and remove the core with a melon baller or pear corer (a pear-shaped metal strip attached to a wooden handle). If using a pear corer, use the large end to remove the core and seeds and the narrow neck to remove the stem. A melon baller makes a good substitute for a pear corer.

PINEAPPLES

Pineapple Wedges. Cut the pineapple in half from top to bottom, cutting through the frond. Cut each half into halves or thirds, from top to bottom, cutting through the frond. Cut the hard core from each wedge and undercut the meat in the shell. Cut the meat into ½-inch slices and push alternating slices ½ inch toward the center of each wedge.

To Peel. Cut off the frond and base. Stand the pineapple on end and, with a heavy knife, cut off the sides, cutting deeply enough to remove the eyes.

To Peel in a Spiral. For a more decorative presentation, leave or remove the frond as you wish. Cut off the base. With the tip of a small sharp knife, cut diagonally underneath a spiral of eyes from top to bottom. Turn the pineapple upside down and cut again under the opposite side of the same strip of eyes to remove a diagonal strip. Repeat around the pineapple.

Pineapple Slices. Slice a peeled pineapple horizontally. Use an apple corer or a small sharp knife to remove the center core. For smaller slices, cut the pineapple into halves or quarters and remove the core before slicing.

Pineapple Container. Cut off the frond about ½ inch from the top and set aside to use as a lid for the container. With a sharp, long, thin knife, cut straight down into the pineapple about ½ inch from the outside edge, cut a circle around the pineapple to create a center core. Remove the knife. Insert the knife into the base of the pineapple, about 1 inch from the bottom and

twist it in place to cut toward one side. Remove the knife, turn the blade in the opposite direction, reinsert in the same hole, and cut in the opposite direction. With a kitchen fork, remove the "plug" of pineapple in the center. It may be necessary to go over the original cuts to make sure that you have cut it completely. Use a small pat of softened butter to seal the hole at the base of pineapple to prevent juices from escaping.

PLUMS Do not peel. See Nectarines for pitting.

PRICKLY PEARS Cut off both ends of the fruit and cut a slit in the skin from end to end. Put a fork into the slit and with the back of a knife wedged between the flesh and the skin, pull the skin away from the fruit. Slice the fruit horizontally.

PRUNES Prunes are dried plums. Steep in a liquid such as tea, fortified wine, or a liqueur. Pit if required.

QUINCES See Apples.

RASPBERRIES The recipes are written for fresh or frozen unsweetened raspberries. Sweetened frozen raspberries will work out, but adjust the sweetening to taste.

RHUBARB Rhubarb leaves are poisonous but the stalks are edible. Be sure to cut off any leaf attached to the stalks. Slice stalks as directed in the recipe.

STARFRUIT See Carambola.

STRAWBERRIES See Blackberries. Do not let sit in water or the fruit will become soggy.

To Hull. With a small sharp knife, cut a circle under the hull and pull off the green top. The white core will pull out as well. Discard the flavorless core and hull.

TANGERINES Peel the skin from the tangerine with your fingers and remove the network of bitter membrane. Separate into segments.

Special Fruit Presentations

FROSTED FRUITS   Use these to garnish main courses as well as desserts. They add a wintery quality to holiday dishes and cheese boards. Customarily done with grapes, the method works very well with citrus fruits and berries.

Beat 1 to 2 egg whites until frothy, but not stiff. Dip the fruit into the egg white and roll in a dish of granulated sugar. Place the fruit on a wire rack and dry for several hours. Store in a cool room overnight, if needed. Do not store in the refrigerator, the moisture causes the sugar to dissolve.

BREAD CORNUCOPIA

Use the cornucopia to present fresh fruits and assorted cookies in a decorative way.

1 package active dry yeast	2¼ tablespoons salt
2 cups lukewarm water	7–8 cups flour
1 tablespoon sugar	1 egg

Hand Method

1.   In a bowl, dissolve the yeast in the water with the sugar. Let stand for 3 minutes. It should show signs of movement and growth.

2.   Stir in 2 tablespoons of salt and 3 cups of flour and beat well. Add additional flour, 1 cup at a time, until the dough looks shaggy. Turn onto a lightly floured board and knead until smooth and elastic, adding enough additional flour to make a medium-firm dough.

3.   Place in a bowl, dust with flour, and cover with a warm damp towel, wrung out well. Let rise until doubled, about 1 hour. Punch down. Proceed with the directions for shaping the cornucopia.

Food Processor Method

1.   Insert a dough blade into the processor (this is a shortened, plastic blade in many models) and mix the yeast, water, and sugar with on/off turns. Let sit until it starts to show movement and growth.

2.   Add the salt and 3 cups of flour and process for 1 minute. Add 3 more cups of flour and process until it comes together. Turn onto a lightly floured board and knead until smooth and elastic, adding additional flour to make a medium-firm dough. Let rise about 1 hour or until doubled.

3.   Proceed with the directions for shaping the cornucopia.

Preparing the Foil Form. Unroll several yards of aluminum foil and crush and shape it roughly into a cone. Keep wrapping lengths of foil around the cone until it is the size you want. Concentrate on keeping the cone shape. When large enough, curl the point toward one side until it resembles a cornucopia. You can also make a cone from chicken wire and wrap it in a sheet of foil. To make it easier to remove the foil, wrap the foil lengthwise along the cone and press to smooth the edges. Lightly oil the foil.

Wrapping the Form with Dough

4.   After the dough rises, punch it down and place on a lightly floured board. Roll into a large rectangle or square about ¼ inch thick. Cut the dough into long strips about 2 inches wide. Brush one side of each strip with cold water.

5.   With the wet side out, starting at the tip, wrap the dough around the form, overlapping each piece generously. Press the end of each new strip onto the end of the preceding strip and continue until you reach the opening of the cornucopia. Do not let the ends of the pastry drape over the opening or you will have trouble removing the foil.

6.   Use several strips of dough to make a twisted or braided rope and set around the opening. If the dough sags, use wooden skewers to hold in place until after baking. (To remove without damaging the cornucopia, twist the skewers in place *before* withdrawing them.) If the dough seems too soft to hold a shape, work in more flour. Remember, no one is going to eat it.

7.   Place on a lightly oiled baking sheet, opening down, if the oven is tall enough, or on its bottom. Use sheets of crumpled foil to support it if needed. Let it rise for about 20 minutes, or until it begins to look puffy.

Baking the Cornucopia

8.   Preheat the oven to 400° F.

9.   In a small bowl, beat 1 egg with the remaining salt. Brush over the cornucopia, let rest for 10 minutes, and repeat.

10.   Bake the cornucopia for 30 to 50 minutes, or until the dough sets and is golden brown. Gently pull some of the foil from the center and check the interior. If the dough is not cooked, bake until it is no longer soggy-looking. The interior does not have to brown. Remove from the oven and cool.

11.   Gently remove the foil with a twisting motion to remove as much as you can. If it sticks in the tip of the cornucopia, cut off the foil and pack any remaining foil into the tip.

NOTE: For a more elaborate cornucopia, you can run strips of dough lengthwise along the cone and weave strips of dough among them for a basket-like effect.

Fruit and Cheese Platters

Fruit and cheese are natural partners that complement each other beautifully. Serve them as an accompaniment to cocktails or as dessert. Classic pairings include Cheddar and apples, Roquefort and pears, and Brie and grapes, but most cheeses complement most fruits, so do not worry too much about what is the best pairing. Serve them attractively. The bread cornucopia mentioned above is perfect for a large party, but for a few people, a more modest presentation is in order.

Plan to use fruits that you can eat easily out of hand, unless plates, forks, and knives are available. Serve the cheese on pottery, porcelain, marble, or in leaf-lined baskets. Arrange the fruit and the cheese together or separately. Accompany the fruit and cheese with unshelled nuts, a nutcracker, and crackers or breads, if desired.

Serve most cheeses with a knife on the side and let guests serve themselves. For a large group, cut firm cheeses like Gruyère, Cheddar, Muenster, etc., into cubes for easy eating.

To Serve Stilton. To Serve Stilton properly, wrap it in a white linen napkin. Cut off the upper crust in the kitchen. Place the napkin-wrapped Stilton on a silver tray and, with a sharp knife, cut it into wedges about ½-inch thick around the top. When the first layer is consumed, cut into the next layer. At this point, it will look like a staircase. This allows you to eat as much as you wish at one sitting. To store, put the upper crust on top, wrap in a port-soaked cloth, and keep in a cool dark place until the next occasion. For a large party, serve with a Stilton scoop.

Chapter 3

FRUIT DESSERTS: MACÉDOINES, CUPS, AND COMPOTES

An apple picked from the tree or a grape plucked from the vine is among the simplest of desserts. You may enhance these arcane pleasures with a sweetener, a dollop of cream, or a sauce prepared from another fruit. You can cook them in syrup, butter, or a little cream and go on to greater effort with bases of cakes or puddings, and embellish all with great swirls of meringue and glazes of chocolate or halos of caramel. But sometimes, nothing is as good as a fruit, simply prepared. An apple out-of-hand tastes good, and an apple charlotte may perfectly suit an occasion, but in midwinter, a baked apple with fresh cream satisfies best. A bowl of fresh strawberries needs no accompaniment until mid-season, when they seem all too ordinary. Renew their sparkle with a different sauce or mix them with other fruits.

We think of simple fruit desserts as a way of keeping the family quiet. No uprisings if we toss them a bowl of berries, or bake an apple, or poach a pear. Yet these very desserts may make perfect company desserts, just because they are so simple. After a large meal, a poached peach or pear served with a simple cookie might be far more appealing than an elaborate gâteau. And, for the cook who feels pushed to get dinner, they provide a delicious sweet with a minimum of fuss. Often they are better if prepared the day before; others bake while you are eating.

This chapter features particular fruits, or fruit combinations. Other chapters feature fruits as part of the recipe—for instance, a souffle or pudding with fruit as the flavoring. If you have a particular fruit on hand and want ideas, check the index for suggestions.

In Chapter 15, you will find many sauces that enhance fruits. Raspberry Sauce, for instance, seems to improve almost any other fruit, as well as complement ice cream, puddings, and cakes. When inspiration is low, look there for ideas to help you turn a simple bowl of melon balls into something extraordinary. Serve Custard Sauce (*Crème Anglaise*) to make a perfectly poached pear into a company treat. Or, flavor the sauce with a liqueur or garnish with another fruit puree to give the poached pear star quality. The Basic Recipes in Chapter 1 have directions on poaching fruits as well as many other ideas to inspire you. Give it a quick look when imagination lags.

PURÉE DE POMMES AU CITRON
(Apple Sauce with Lemon and Orange)

2 pounds McIntosh apples, peeled, quartered, and cored	½ cup water
	Sugar to taste
	1 unpeeled orange, thinly
Juice of ½ lemon	sliced, for garnish

1. In a saucepan, cook the apples, lemon juice, and water, covered, over low heat, until the apples soften.

2. Beat with a wire whisk and add sugar to taste.

3. Chill and garnish with orange slices.

Yields 3 cups

Can be prepared several days before serving.

CARAMELIZED APPLE SLICES

For more texture, cook the apples uncovered, with the salt, sugar, and cinnamon over high heat just until tender-crisp.

6 Cortland apples, peeled, cored, and sliced	3 tablespoons brown sugar
	½ teaspoon cinnamon
3 tablespoons butter	Heavy cream, whipped and
Pinch of salt	sweetened, to taste, optional

1. In a skillet, cook the apples in the butter, covered, over low heat, for 10 minutes, or until they begin to soften.

2. Sprinkle with the salt, sugar, and cinnamon and cook over high heat until evenly glazed.

3. Serve warm with whipped cream, if desired.

Yields 6 servings

Can be prepared 1 day ahead and reheated.

BRANDIED APPLES

Serve plain, with heavy or whipped cream, as an ice cream topping, or over pancakes or waffles.

½ **cup butter**	**peeled, cored, and thinly**
¾ **cup dark brown sugar**	**sliced**
2 **tablespoons lemon juice**	1 **teaspoon dark rum**
2 **tablespoons orange juice**	2 **teaspoons Cognac**
3 **Golden Delicious apples,**	

1. In a skillet, melt the butter. Add the sugar and cook until the sugar dissolves.

2. Stir in the lemon and orange juices, apples, rum, and Cognac.

3. Simmer until the apples are tender, about 5 minutes. Serve warm.

Yields 4 to 6 servings

Can be prepared 1 day ahead and reheated.

Baked Apples

BASIC BAKED APPLES

Every apple-growing region has its favorite baked apple. Here is a basic recipe with a list of variations. Peel a strip of skin around the middle, or a quarter to halfway down the apple to avoid bursting. Leave the skin on the lower half to help maintain the shape.

6 Cortland apples, cored	¼ teaspoon cinnamon
through the center	¼ teaspoon nutmeg
2 tablespoons sugar	⅛ teaspoon ground cloves
2 tablespoons butter	

1. Preheat the oven to 350° F.

2. Peel a strip of skin around the middle of each apple. Place the apples upright in a baking pan just large enough to hold them. Put 1 teaspoon of sugar and the butter into the center of each apple. Season each opening with the cinnamon, nutmeg, and cloves. Add ¼ inch of water to the pan.

3. Bake for 40 minutes, or until tender. With a small, sharp knife, pierce the apple to test for tenderness. Serve warm, at room temperature, or cold.

Yields 6 servings

Can be prepared 1 day ahead and reheated.

Variations

- Add 1 teaspoon of raisins or currants to each apple.
- Substitute honey, maple syrup, or molasses for the sugar.
- Add apple cider or white wine to the pan instead of water.
- Substitute honey for the sugar and 3 teaspoons of minced mint for the cinnamon, nutmeg, and cloves.
- *Baked Apples with Brazil Nuts and Ginger.* Omit the sugar, cinnamon, nutmeg, and cloves. In a bowl, mix 1 cup of chopped Brazil nuts, ½ cup of chopped dates, ⅓ cup of chopped candied ginger and fill the centers of each apple. In a saucepan, simmer 1 cup of light corn syrup, and 1 teaspoon of ground ginger for 5 minutes and brush over the apples. Bake 40 minutes. Preheat the broiler and glaze, basting apples often with the remaining syrup.

BAKED APPLES ON TOAST WITH RED WINE

6 thin (¼ inch) slices French	6 apples, cored
bread	1 cup red wine
5 tablespoons butter	6 tablespoons sugar

1. Preheat the oven to 350° F. Butter both sides of the bread and arrange in a baking pan.

2. Peel a strip of skin around the middle of each apple and place on the bread slices. Fill the centers with the remaining butter. Pour the wine over the apples and sprinkle with the sugar.

3. Bake for 35 minutes, basting often, or until the apples are tender and the wine reduces to a glaze. With a small, sharp knife, pierce the apple to test for tenderness. Serve warm.

Yields 6 servings

Best if served shortly after baking.

FRANSK APPELKAKA
(Baked Apple Halves with Almond Topping, French-style)

This is a Swedish version of a French dessert.

2 **cups cold water**	1 **cup butter, softened**
¼ **lemon**	3 **eggs, separated**
2 **teaspoons lemon juice**	½ **cup ground blanched**
½ **cup plus ⅔ cups sugar**	**almonds**
4 **large tart apples, peeled,**	2 **teaspoons lemon juice**
halved, and cored	**Pinch of salt**

1. Preheat the oven to 350° F.

2. In a saucepan, simmer the water, lemon quarter, squeezed, and the apples with ½ cup of sugar, for 6 to 8 minutes, or until the apples are tender. Drain the apples on a cake rack.

3. Butter a baking dish just large enough to hold the apples in one layer. Place the apples in the dish, cut side down.

4. In a processor, cream the butter with the remaining sugar. Add the egg yolks, almonds, and remaining lemon juice.

5. In a separate bowl, beat the egg whites with the salt until stiff, but not dry. Fold into the egg yolk mixture and spread over the apples. Bake for 20 minutes or until golden brown. Serve warm.

Yields 4 to 8 servings

Can be prepared several hours ahead and served at room temperature.

POMMES AU FOUR FRANGIPANE
(Baked Apples with Almond Cream)

6 apples	1 egg
Lemon juice	½ cup light cream
¾ cup blanched almonds	½ teaspoon almond extract
1 tablespoon flour	2–3 tablespoons Calvados, or to
1 cup confectioners' sugar	taste
½ cup butter, softened	2 cups heavy cream, optional

1.   Preheat the oven to 350° F.

2.   Peel the top inch of each apple. Remove the stem and core, leaving the bottom intact. Enlarge the opening to about 1 inch. Rub the cut surface with lemon juice. Arrange apples in a gratin with ¼ inch of water and cover with foil. Bake for 15 minutes.

3.   Meanwhile, in a processor, grind the almonds with the flour and set aside.

4.   In the processor, cream the sugar and butter. Add the almond mixture, egg, light cream, almond extract, and Calvados, to taste.

5.   Fill the apples with the mixture and bake, uncovered, until tender, about 20 minutes longer. Serve with cream, if desired.

Yields 6 servings

Can be prepared 1 day ahead and reheated.

APPLE HEDGEHOG

Do not let the unflattering name deter you. This is a party dessert that will bring raves when you present it.

12 Cortland apples, peeled and cored	Grated rind of 1 lemon
1 cup plus 2 tablespoons sugar	3 egg whites
	Confectioners' sugar
1¼ cups water	½ cup sliced almonds

1.   Leave 6 apples whole and chop the remaining apples.

2. In a saucepan, bring 1 cup of sugar, the water, and lemon rind to a boil. Add the whole apples and poach until just tender. Drain, reserving the syrup. Add the chopped apples to the reserved syrup and cook to a thick puree.

3. Preheat the oven to 375° F. On a heatproof serving platter, arrange the whole apples in a pyramid and spread evenly with the apple puree.

4. In a bowl, beat the egg whites with the remaining sugar until stiff, but not dry. Using a pastry bag fitted with a #5 star tip or a metal spatula, pipe or spread the meringue over the apple mound. Sprinkle the mound with confectioners' sugar and stud the mound with the almond slices.

5. Bake about 12 minutes, or until the meringue is light golden. Serve warm.

Yields 6 servings

Except for the meringue, this can be prepared for baking several hours ahead. Make and spread the meringue shortly before baking and serving.

POMMES BOURGEOISES
(Apples in Custard with Mixed Fruit)

6 Vanilla Poached Apples, halved and cored, page 40	**½ cup toasted slivered almonds or Almond Macaroon crumbs, page 26**
¾ cup mixed glacéed fruits	**Sugar, to taste**
2 cups Pastry Cream, page 26	

1. Preheat the oven to 450° F. Place the apples on a heatproof serving dish, cut side up, and fill the cavities with the glacéed fruits. Coat the apples with the pastry cream and sprinkle with the almonds and sugar.

2. Bake for 5 to 7 minutes, or until glazed. Serve hot or at room temperature.

Yields 6 servings

Can be prepared for glazing the day before serving. Bring to room temperature before glazing.

Variation

• *Rice Pudding with Apples.* Make, or use leftover, rice pudding. Spread about ½ cup of pudding on the bottom of a heatproof serving dish. Top with the poached apples. Omit the glacéed fruits. Roll the apples in 1 cup of Pastry Cream. Sprinkle with ½ cup of toasted almonds and sugar to taste. Brown under a hot broiler and serve.

COMPOTE DE PRUNEAUX ET POMMES
(Prune and Apple Compote)

24 prunes	6 apples, peeled, cored
2 cups tawny port	through the center
2 cups red wine	1 tablespoon butter
10 tablespoons sugar	½ cup heavy cream
2 tablespoons vanilla	

1.   Soak the prunes in the port for 24 hours.

2.   Simmer the prunes in the port with the wine, 9 tablespoons of sugar, and the vanilla over low heat, until reduced by two-thirds. Chill the prunes in the liquid.

3.   In a skillet, saute the apples in the butter until tender. Add the remaining sugar and cook until the sugar caramelizes.

4.   Arrange the apples in a serving dish, fill the centers with the cream, and surround with the prunes and their liquid.

Yields 6 servings

Can be prepared several hours ahead. Reheat the apples just before serving.

ABRICOTS FINES BOUCHES
(Apricots with Kirsch Butter Sauce)

12 Vanilla Poached Apricots,	1 tablespoon sugar
page 40, see Note	6 tablespoons butter, softened
2 egg yolks	½ cup sliced almonds, toasted
2 tablespoons kirsch	

1.   Arrange the apricots on a serving dish, cut side up, and chill.

2. In a saucepan, using a wire whisk, beat the egg yolks, kirsch, and sugar over low heat, until the mixture starts to thicken. Beat in the butter, a tablespoon at a time, and cook until the sauce is thick and creamy.

3. Pour the warm sauce over the apricots and sprinkle with the almonds.

Yields 6 servings

Can be prepared several hours ahead and refrigerated until ready to serve.

NOTE: Canned apricots will suit, if fresh apricots are not available.

ABRICOTS AUX COGNAC
(Apricots with Cognac)

Serve these richly flavored fruits with heavy cream, whipped cream, or ice cream.

  1 pound dried apricots
  ⅓ cup sugar
  Cognac

In a covered container, combine the apricots, sugar, and enough Cognac to cover. Let macerate for at least 24 hours, and up to two weeks.

Yields 6 servings

ABRICOTS HÉLÈNE
(Apricots in Custard with Ladyfingers)

  ¼ pound stale Ladyfingers,   **12 Vanilla Poached Apricots,**
  page •••   **page 40, see Note**
  1½ cups milk, heated   **24 cherries**
  ¼ cup sugar   **Apricot Sauce, page 547**
  4 eggs

1. Preheat the oven to 350° F. Butter a 2-quart soufflé dish.

2. In a bowl, soak the ladyfingers in the milk for 10 minutes. Force through a sieve and beat in the sugar and the eggs. Pour into the prepared dish and bake for 40 minutes, or until set.

3.   Unmold and surround with the apricot halves, cut side up. Fill the center of each apricot with a cherry and serve the sauce on the side. Serve warm or cold.

Yields 6 servings

Can be prepared 1 day ahead.

NOTE: Canned apricots will suit.

APRICOT COMPOTE

½ **pound dried apricots**	3 **whole cloves**
½ **cup sugar**	⅓ **cup chopped crystallized**
2 **cups water**	**ginger**
¼ **cup currants**	2 **tablespoons pine nuts or**
¼ **cup golden raisins**	**almonds**
2 **cups Sauterne**	

1.   In a saucepan, simmer the apricots, sugar, and water for 20 minutes, or until the apricots are soft. With a slotted spoon, remove the fruit and set aside.

2.   Reduce the liquid to 1 cup. Pour over the apricots and add the currants, raisins, Sauterne, and cloves. Chill for 12 to 36 hours.

3.   Discard the cloves. Sprinkle with the ginger and pine nuts.

Yields 6 servings

Can be prepared 1 day ahead.

NOTE: Serve with Custard Sauce (see page 545), heavy cream, whipped cream, sour cream, or yogurt.

AVOCADO CHARTREUSE DESSERT

This strange-sounding dessert is delightful. A student who rejected it initially, later carried the ingredients in his car to prepare at a moment's notice.

3 **large ripe avocados**	**Chartreuse**
1 **cup sugar**	½ **cup heavy cream**
4 **tablespoons lime juice**	6 **thin lemon slices, for**
2 **tablespoons green**	**garnish**

1. Cut the avocados in half, discard the pits, and scoop out the flesh with a spoon without damaging the skins.

2. In a processor, puree the pulp with the sugar, lime juice, and Chartreuse. Fill the avocado shells with the puree.

3. In a bowl, whip the cream until stiff peaks form. Using a pastry bag fitted with a #4 open star tip, pipe the whipped cream onto the avocado mixture. Garnish each serving with a lemon slice and serve cold.

Yields 6 servings

Do not prepare more than 4 hours ahead or the avocado mixture may turn brown.

BANANAS AND GRAPES IN CARAMEL SYRUP

    6 tablespoons water
    ¾ cup sugar
    ¼ teaspoon ground ginger
    Grated rind and juice of 1
    lime
    3 tablespoons rum
    4 bananas, sliced
    1½ cups seedless grapes

1. In a small saucepan, heat 2 tablespoons of water and the sugar over low heat until the sugar dissolves. Raise the heat to high and cook without stirring, until the mixture turns golden. Remove from the heat, add the remaining water and stir until the mixture is smooth. Be careful of splattering (see page 5).

2. Stir in the ginger, lime juice, and rum. Chill.

3. Place the bananas and grapes in a serving dish. Just before serving, sprinkle with the syrup and the grated lime rind.

Yields 6 servings

Prepare the sauce several days ahead, but do not prepare the fruit until just before serving.

BANANES FLAMBÉES
(Liqueur-flavored Bananas)

6 bananas, halved lengthwise

2 tablespoons Clarified
   Butter, page •••

2 tablespoons sugar, or to

taste

¼ cup rum, kirsch, or orange
   liqueur

1.   In a large skillet, sauté the bananas in the butter until they start to turn golden. Sprinkle with the sugar and cook until the sugar starts to caramelize.

2.   Add the liqueur and ignite. Serve flaming or just after the flames die. Serve hot or warm.

Yields 6 servings

Prepare just before serving.

Variations

• *Bananes Flambées Maltaise.* Add the grated rind of one orange and the juice of 2 oranges. Cook until the juices are syrupy and then stir in orange liqueur.
• *Bananes Flambées au Rhum.* Use brown sugar and ½ cup of dark rum.

BANANAS FOSTER

This classic dessert, created at New Orleans' Brennan's Restaurant over 50 years ago, is still a must.

6 bananas, halved lengthwise
   and crosswise
   Lemon juice

¼ cup butter

1 cup brown sugar

¼ teaspoon cinnamon

¼ cup banana liqueur

¼ cup dark rum

   Vanilla ice cream, optional

1.   Dip the bananas in the lemon juice.

2. In a large skillet, melt the butter and the sugar. Sauté the banana for 3 minutes. Sprinkle with the cinnamon and the banana liqueur. Add the rum and carefully ignite. Spoon the juices over the bananas until the flames die. Serve with ice cream, if desired.

Yields 6 servings

Prepare just before serving.

BANANAS IN ORANGE-CARAMEL CREAM

¼ cup butter	6 bananas
3 tablespoons brown sugar	2 tablespoons banana liqueur
1 tablespoon grated orange rind	2 tablespoons orange liqueur
	2 tablespoons Cognac
½ cup orange juice	¼ cup golden raisins
3 tablespoons lemon juice	1 cup heavy cream
Pinch of nutmeg	

1. In a large skillet, heat the butter and the sugar until melted. Stir in the orange rind, orange juice, lemon juice, and nutmeg. Cook the bananas in the mixture until heated, about 3 minutes. Remove the bananas to a serving platter.

2. Over high heat, cook the juices until syrupy. Add the banana and orange liqueurs and Cognac and reduce by half. Add the raisins and cream and reduce by one-third. Pour over the bananas. Serve warm.

Yields 6 servings

Can be prepared ahead and reheated.

NERUPPU VAZHAI
(Bananas with Coconut and Cardamom)

This delicacy originated in India.

6 bananas	½ cup slivered blanched almonds
¼ cup orange juice	
½ cup brown sugar	1 teaspoon ground cardamom
1 cup grated coconut	¼ cup melted butter

1.   Preheat the oven to 400° F. Butter a baking dish just large enough to hold the bananas in one layer. Arrange the bananas in the dish.

2.   Pour the orange juice over the bananas and sprinkle with the sugar, coconut, almonds, cardamom, and butter.

3.   Bake for 25 minutes, or until the bananas are tender. Serve warm.

Yields 6 servings

Can be prepared several hours ahead and reheated.

BANANAS BRAZILIAN-STYLE

Bananas baked with orange juice and coconut.

6 bananas, halved lengthwise	**Pinch salt**
½ cup orange juice	**2 tablespoons butter**
1 tablespoon lemon juice	**1 cup grated coconut**
¼ cup brown sugar	

1.   Preheat the oven to 400° F. Butter a baking dish just large enough to hold the bananas in one layer. Arrange the bananas in the dish.

2.   In a bowl, mix the orange juice, lemon juice, sugar, and salt. Mix well. Pour over the bananas and dot with the butter.

3.   Bake for 10 to 15 minutes, or until tender. Remove from the oven and sprinkle with the coconut.

Yields 6 servings

Can be prepared ahead and reheated.

BANANES MERINGUÉES
(Bananas Topped with Meringue)

3–6 ripe bananas, halved
   lengthwise
  2 tablespoons orange liqueur
  2 tablespoons Clarified
   Butter, page 4

1 egg yolk, lightly beaten
1 tablespoon flour
2 egg whites
6 tablespoons sugar

1. Preheat the oven to 300° F. If the bananas are long, cut in half crosswise; place in a baking dish. Sprinkle with the orange liqueur and macerate for 1 hour. Drain, reserving the liqueur.

2. In a skillet, sauté the bananas in the butter until golden, in batches, if necessary. Arrange the bananas in one layer in the baking dish. Add the reserved liqueur to the skillet, carefully ignite, and pour over the bananas.

3. In a bowl, mix the egg yolk and flour. In another bowl, beat the egg whites and the sugar until stiff. Fold into the egg yolk mixture and spread with a spatula over the bananas.

4. Bake until crisp and golden, about 30 to 40 minutes. Serve warm.

Yields 6 servings

Can be prepared up to 2 hours ahead.
For a prettier presentation, pipe the meringue through a pastry bag fitted with a #5 open star tip.

ORANGE-GLAZED BAKED BANANAS

  6 bananas, halved lengthwise
¾ cup orange juice
¼ cup orange liqueur
  3 tablespoons butter
⅓ cup chopped walnuts

⅓ cup brown sugar
Vanilla ice cream, sour
  cream, or whipped cream,
  for garnish

1. Preheat the oven to 450° F.

2. In a baking dish, arrange the bananas in a single layer. Sprinkle with the orange juice and liqueur and dot with butter. Bake for 10 minutes, basting twice.

3. Sprinkle with the nuts and sugar and bake until the sugar melts and the nuts glaze, about 5 minutes longer. Serve warm with ice cream, sour cream, or whipped cream, if desired.

Yields 6 servings

Can be prepared ahead and reheated.

Variation

· Add 1 tablespoon of minced ginger with the orange juice.

GINGERED BLUEBERRY COMPOTE

1 pint blueberries	2 tablespoons minced
1 cup orange juice	preserved ginger
1 tablespoon lemon juice	Mint leaves, for garnish
¼ cup confectioners' sugar	

1. Pick over the berries and place in a bowl. In another bowl, mix the orange juice, lemon juice, sugar, and ginger.

2. Pour over the berries and let macerate for 1 hour. Serve cold, garnished with mint leaves, if desired.

Yields 6 servings

Can be prepared the day before serving.

CERISES AU COGNAC
(Cherries in Cognac)

3 pounds of cherries, pitted, if desired	¼ pound sugar
	3 tablespoons water
Cognac	

1. In a wide-mouth canning jar, pack the cherries firmly and cover with the Cognac. Cover jar tightly and store in a cool place for 6 weeks.

2. In a small saucepan, dissolve the sugar in the water. Add the juices from the macerated cherries. Bring to a boil and pour over the cherries in the jar.

3. Cover tightly and store until ready to use. Serve hot or cold with ice cream or on cake.

Yields 3 pints

Can be prepared up to 6 months ahead.

NOTE: Use these as an ice cream topping, to flavor baked goods, or as part of a fruit macédoine.

CHERRY COMPOTE

1½ **pounds cherries, pitted**	**orange**
1 **tablespoon sugar**	1 **tablespoon cornstarch or**
Pinch of cinnamon	**arrowroot**
½ **cup red wine**	2 **tablespoons water**
3 **tablespoons currant jelly**	**Ice cream, optional**
Grated rind and juice of 1	

1. In a saucepan, heat the cherries, sugar, and cinnamon, covered, for 5 to 10 minutes, or until the juices flow. Turn into a bowl.

2. Add the wine to the pan and reduce by half. Stir in the jelly, orange rind, and juice, and heat until the jelly melts. Strain the juices from the cherries into the wine mixture.

3. In a bowl, mix the arrowroot and water. Add to the wine mixture and bring to a boil, stirring. Pour over the cherries and let cool.

4. Serve cold, plain, or with ice cream.

Yields 6 servings

CERISES MONTMORENCY
(Cherries with Orange, Macaroons, and Cream)

1 **recipe Cherry Compote, see**	1½ **cups heavy cream**
above	12 **Almond Macaroons, page 26**
4 **sugar cubes**	2 **tablespoons kirsch**
1 **orange**	

1.   Prepare the cherry compote and let cool.

2.   Rub the sugar cubes over the rind of the orange until well soaked with the orange oil. Crush the cubes in a bowl with the juice from the orange.

3.   In another bowl, whip the cream until stiff peaks form and fold in the orange juice mixture.

4.   In a large flat serving bowl, arrange the macaroons in a layer. Spoon the cherries and a little of their juice over the macaroons. Sprinkle with the kirsch and spread the whipped cream over the fruit. Chill until ready to serve.

Yields 6 servings

Can be prepared the day before serving.

NOTE: For color, grate some orange rind over the whipped cream.

CERISES AUX LIQUEURS
(Cherries with Liqueurs)

2½ quarts cherries, pitted   **Crème Fraîche, page 39,**
 ⅔ cup cassis syrup, see Note   **optional**
 ⅓ cup framboise

1.   In a bowl, sprinkle the cherries with the cassis and framboise.

2.   Let stand in the refrigerator for 4 hours or longer. Serve with crème fraîche, if desired.

Yields 8 servings

Can be prepared several days ahead.

NOTE: Cassis syrup is available in gourmet shops.

CHERRIES IN CREAM

2 pounds cherries, pitted   **1 teaspoon cinnamon**
3 tablespoons kirsch   **Grated semisweet chocolate,**
1 cup sour cream   **for garnish**
2 tablespoons sugar

1.   In a bowl, toss the cherries with the kirsch and chill until serving time.

2. In a separate bowl, mix the sour cream, sugar, and cinnamon and chill. When ready to serve, pour the sour cream mixture over the fruit and sprinkle with the chocolate, if desired.

Yields 6 servings

Can be prepared up to 2 days before serving.

CHERRIES JUBILEE

An old-fashioned restaurant treat that is worth reviving.

1½ **pounds cherries, pitted**	**Pinch of salt**
1 **cup sugar**	1 **tablespoon cornstarch**
2 **cups plus 2 tablespoons**	½ **cup Cognac**
water	6 **scoops vanilla ice cream**

1. In a saucepan, simmer the cherries, sugar, 2 cups of water, and the salt for 5 minutes. Remove from the heat and cool.

2. Drain the cherries, reserving 1 cup of the juice in the saucepan.

3. In a small bowl, mix the remaining water with the cornstarch, and stir into the reserved juice. Bring to a simmer and add the cherries.

4. When ready to serve, reheat the cherries in the syrup. In a separate saucepan, heat the Cognac. Ignite the Cognac and pour over the warm cherries. While still flaming, ladle over the scoops of ice cream.

Yields 6 servings

Prepare the cherry mixture several hours ahead.

FICHI ALLA GRITTI
(Figs in Kirsch and Cream)

18 **fresh ripe figs, peeled if**	½ **cup heavy cream**
desired	
2 **tablespoons kirsch**	

1. In a large flat serving dish, arrange the figs.

2. In a small bowl, mix the kirsch and cream and spoon over the figs.

3.   Let stand for 1 to 2 hours at room temperature before serving.

Yields 6 servings

Can be prepared the day before serving.

FIGS WITH RASPBERRY CREAM

1 cup heavy cream	thawed and drained
¼ cup sugar	12 fresh figs, peeled
1 (10-ounce) package frozen	1 cup fresh raspberries, for
unsweetened raspberries,	garnish

1.   Beat the cream until soft peaks form and mix in the sugar. It should be just firm enough to hold a shape, not stiff.

2.   Force the thawed raspberries through a sieve and discard the seeds. Fold the raspberry puree into the whipped cream.

3.   Cut three-quarters of the way through each fig from the pointed end to create quarters or sixths. Spread the figs to resemble flowers. Spoon the raspberry cream onto the plates, top with the figs, and garnish with the fresh raspberries, if desired.

Yields 6 servings

Can be prepared up to 2 hours before serving.

FIGS IN CRÈME DE CACAO

1 cup sour cream	desired
2 tablespoons crème de cacao	½ teaspoon cocoa
12 fresh figs, peeled, if	

In a bowl, mix the sour cream and the crème de cacao. Dip each fig into the mixture to coat completely and arrange on a serving platter. Sprinkle with the cocoa. Chill.

Yields 6 servings

Can be prepared up to 4 hours ahead.

FIGS IN ORANGE LIQUEUR

12 fresh figs, peeled, if desired, and quartered	1 cup heavy cream
1 tablespoon Cognac	⅓ cup orange liqueur

1. Arrange the figs in a serving bowl. Sprinkle with the Cognac and macerate for 30 minutes, or up to 24 hours.

2. In another bowl, mix the cream, orange liqueur, and any unabsorbed Cognac. Beat with a wire whisk until it just starts to hold a shape. Spoon over the figs.

Yields 6 servings

FIGS WITH PORT AND HONEY SABAYON SAUCE

12 fresh figs, peeled, if desired	3 tablespoons honey
¾ cup port	1½ teaspoons vanilla
6 egg yolks	¾ teaspoon lemon juice

1. Cut each fig ½ inch down from the pointed end, and macerate in the port for 4 to 24 hours.

2. When ready to prepare, drain the port into a measuring cup and add enough additional port to make ½ cup. Arrange the figs on a serving platter.

3. In a saucepan, mix the port, egg yolks, honey, vanilla, and lemon juice. Place over medium heat and cook, beating constantly with a hand-held mixer, until the mixture is the consistency of mayonnaise and tripled in volume.

4. Spoon the warm sauce over the figs.

Yields 6 servings

Can be prepared several hours ahead.

FIGS, DATES, AND WALNUTS
IN SHERRIED WHIPPED CREAM

1½ pounds fresh figs, stemmed   1 cup chopped walnuts
   and halved lengthwise   2 cups heavy cream
¼ pound pitted dates   ½ cup confectioners' sugar
¼ cup cream sherry

1.   In a bowl, macerate the figs, dates, and 2 tablespoons of sherry for 30 minutes. Fold in the walnuts. Arrange the fruit in individual bowls, or 1 large serving dish.

2.   In a bowl, whip the cream and the sugar until stiff. Fold in the remaining sherry. Spoon the whipped cream over the fruit.

Yields 6 servings

Can be prepared 24 hours before serving.

FIGUES AU THYM
(Figs in Thyme)

1 pound dried figs, stems   ½ teaspoon dried thyme
   removed   3 tablespoons honey
2 cups red wine

1.   In a saucepan, simmer the figs, wine, thyme, and honey for 30 minutes, or until the figs are tender. Remove the figs to a bowl and strain the syrup into a saucepan.

2.   Reduce the syrup by one-third. Pour over the figs and serve hot or cold.

Yields 6 servings

Can be prepared 2 days ahead.

HOT OR COLD GINGERED FIGS

1 pound dried figs, stems   6 slices gingerroot
   removed   Sugar
3 tablespoons lemon juice   4 lemon slices
1 tablespoon thinly sliced   Cream, optional
   lemon rind

1. In a saucepan, cover the figs with water and add 2 tablespoons of lemon juice, the lemon rind, and the gingerroot. Simmer until the figs are tender, about 30 minutes. Drain the liquid into a measuring cup and discard the lemon rind and the gingerroot. Arrange the figs in a serving dish.

2. Measure the reserved liquid and place in a saucepan. Add half as much sugar. Simmer until syrupy, about 20 minutes. Add the remaining lemon juice and the lemon slices.

3. Pour over the figs and serve warm, at room temperature, or cold with cream, if desired.

Yields 6 servings

Can be prepared 2 days before serving.

POACHED FIGS WITH CHARTREUSE-FLAVORED CHEESE

½ **pound cream cheese**	**Chartreuse**
½ **pound farmer cheese**	2 **Pinches of cardamom**
½ **cup sour cream**	1½ **cups water**
¾ **cup plus tablespoons sugar**	12 **dried figs, stems removed**
2 **tablespoons green**	2 **(1-in) strips lemon rind**

1. In a bowl, mix the cream cheese, farmer cheese, sour cream, sugar, 1½ tablespoons of Chartreuse, and cardamom, until smooth.

2. Line a colander with a double layer of cheesecloth, wrung out in cold water. Add the cheese mixture and fold the edges of the cheesecloth over the top. Put a saucer on top and place a 1-pound weight on the saucer. Set the colander in a cake pan and refrigerate overnight or up to 3 days. (The longer it drains, the drier the cheese becomes.)

3. In a saucepan, dissolve the remaining sugar in the water over low heat. Add the figs, lemon peel, and cardamom and simmer until the figs are tender. Chill the figs in the syrup.

4. Unmold the cheese onto a serving platter and surround with drained figs. Add the remaining Chartreuse to the syrup and spoon over the cheese.

Yields 6 servings

Prepare at least 1 day before serving.

SEEDLESS GRAPES IN SOUR CREAM

1½ cups sour cream
¾ cup light brown sugar
6 cups seedless grapes

1.   In a bowl, mix the sour cream and ½ cup of sugar. Fold in the grapes and arrange in a serving dish.

2.   Sprinkle with the remaining sugar.

Yields 6 servings

Can be prepared the day before.

GRAPES IN BRANDY

¾ cup honey
6 tablespoons Cognac
1 tablespoon lemon juice

1 pound seedless grapes
1 cup sour cream

1.   In a bowl, mix the honey, Cognac, and lemon juice. Fold in the grapes and chill for at least 2 hours.

2.   Serve with the sour cream on the side.

Yields 4 to 6 servings

Can be prepared the day before.

RED AND GREEN GRAPES WITH MINT-RICOTTA SAUCE

1¼ cups ricotta cheese
¼ cup confectioners' sugar
2 teaspoons lemon juice
2 tablespoons minced mint

¾ pound red seedless grapes
¾ pound green seedless grapes
Mint sprigs, for garnish

1.   In a processor, puree the ricotta, sugar, and lemon juice. Add the mint with on/off turns.

2.   Separate the grapes from the stems and put into a bowl. Fold in the sauce and chill for 30 minutes before serving.

Yields 6 servings

Can be prepared the day before serving.

NOTE: For a smoother mixture, force the ricotta through a sieve before mixing with the sugar, lemon juice, and mint.

Alternate Method

Cut the grapes into clusters and arrange in a bowl or on a platter. Serve each person a small bowl of chilled sauce garnished with mint and let them dip the grapes.

CANTALOUPE IN CABERNET SAUVIGNON

½ cups cabernet sauvignon	8 large mint leaves
¼ cup sugar, or to taste	1 cantaloupe
1 (1-in) piece vanilla bean, split	4 small mint sprigs, for garnish

1. In a saucepan, boil the wine, sugar, vanilla bean, and large mint leaves until reduced to 1 cup, about 15 to 20 minutes. Remove sauce from heat and chill completely.

2. Cut melon into balls or 1-inch dice. Divide the melon among serving bowls. Strain sauce around the fruit, and garnish with the mint sprigs, if desired.

Yields 4 to 6 servings

Prepare the sauce several days in advance.

MELON WITH ORANGE AND RUM

1 large cantaloupe	3 tablespoons rum
¼ cup honey	
½ cup orange juice	

1. Cut the melon into balls or 1-inch dice. In a bowl, mix the honey, orange juice, and rum.

2. Fold in the melon and keep covered until ready to serve.

Yields 4 to 6 servings

Prepare no more than 3 hours before serving.

MELON-ORANGE-BLUEBERRY CUP

3 quarts honeydew melon
balls
¾ cup orange juice
¼ cup orange liqueur
2 tablespoons sugar

2 teaspoons grated orange
rind
1 pint blueberries
Mint sprigs, for garnish

1.   In a serving bowl, mix the melon balls, orange juice, orange liqueur, sugar, and orange rind.

2.   Refrigerate for up to 6 hours.

3.   Just before serving, add the blueberries, and garnish with mint sprigs.

Yields 8 servings

Prepare no more than 6 hours ahead.

MINTED CANTALOUPE AND BLUEBERRIES

Substitute any other melon of your choice.

1 cup sugar
½ cup water
1 tablespoon minced mint
2 cups cantaloupe or other
melon balls
1 cup blueberries
Mint sprigs, for garnish

1.   In a saucepan, boil the sugar, water, and minced mint for 3 minutes. Let the syrup stand until cool, and strain. Chill.

2.   Just before serving, mix the melon and blueberries in a serving bowl and spoon the syrup over the top. Garnish with the mint sprigs, if desired.

Yields 4 to 6 servings

Prepare the sauce several days ahead.

MELON WITH PERNOD AND MINT

3 cups water
1 cup plus 2 tablespoons
sugar
1 cup mint leaves

¼ cup Pernod
3 cantaloupes or honeydews,
cut into balls or wedges
Mint sprigs, for garnish

1.   In a saucepan, boil the water and sugar over medium heat, stirring, for 5 minutes. Add the mint leaves and let stand 1 hour. Strain into a bowl and add the Pernod.

2.   Arrange the melon in one or two layers in a flat dish. Pour the syrup over it and macerate 3 hours, turning occasionally.

3.   Drain the melon. Serve garnished with mint sprigs, if desired.

Yields 6 servings

The syrup can be prepared as much as a week ahead. The drained syrup may be reused.

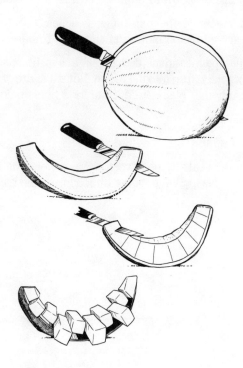

MELON DE SCHEHERAZADE (Fruit-filled Melon)

This is a beautiful dessert. If all of the fruits listed here are not available, use about 4 cups of any combination that is available.

1 large Persian melon	18 strawberries, hulled
Salt	3½ tablespoons sugar
2 pineapple slices, cored and diced	2 cups Champagne
	½ cup crème de menthe
2 peaches, peeled, pitted, and sliced	¼ cup maraschino liqueur
	¼ cup kirsch
1 banana, sliced	1 tablespoon butter, softened,
18 raspberries	optional, see Note

1. Cut off the top third of the melon. With a melon baller, scoop balls from the top and bottom sections and reserve. With a knife, cut the interior as smoothly as possible without breaking through the shell. Salt the inside lightly and turn upside down to drain for at least 20 minutes.

2. In a bowl, macerate the pineapple, peaches, banana, raspberries, strawberries, reserved melon balls, and sugar for 1 hour.

3. Pour the Champagne, crème de menthe, maraschino, and kirsch over the fruit and mix gently. Turn into the melon. Butter the rim of the melon and press the top firmly into place. Refrigerate for 2 hours before serving.

Yields 6 to 8 servings

Can be prepared up to 6 hours before serving.

NOTE: The butter seals in the flavors. If you prefer, omit the butter and wrap the melon in plastic wrap. Serve directly from the melon.

NECTARINES AND COGNAC

6 nectarines, peeled, pitted,
and quartered
¾ cup sugar
1 cup water
5 tablespoons Cognac

1½ teaspoons vanilla
1 cup sour cream
1 tablespoon confectioners'
sugar

1. In a saucepan, simmer the nectarines, sugar, and water for 1 minute. Remove from the heat and add 3 tablespoons of Cognac and the vanilla. Refrigerate for 24 hours.

2. Just before serving, drain and arrange the fruit in a serving dish. In a small bowl, mix the sour cream, confectioners' sugar, and the remaining Cognac. Spoon over the nectarines and serve.

Yields 6 servings

Prepare the nectarines and the sauce the day before, but assemble just before serving.

NECTARINES FLAMBÉ

While vanilla ice cream is the standard, ginger, black raspberry, or butter pecan ice cream can also be used to create greater excitement.

1 cup sugar
1½ cups water
6 nectarines, peeled, halved,

and pitted
¼ cup orange liqueur
Vanilla ice cream, optional

1. In a saucepan, simmer the sugar and water for 10 minutes. Add the nectarines and simmer until tender, about 5 minutes. Remove the nectarines and set aside until ready to serve. Reserve ½ cup of the syrup.

2. In the blazer of a chafing dish or a large skillet, bring the nectarines and ½ cup of the reserved syrup to a simmer. Add the orange liqueur and ignite.

3. Serve over ice cream, if desired.

Yields 6 servings

Prepare the fruit the day before.

NECTARINES AND PLUMS WITH PARMESAN

2 nectarines, pitted and   ¼ cup red wine
   sliced   4 teaspoons sugar
2 plums, pitted and sliced   ¼ pound Parmesan

1.   Macerate the fruits in the wine and sugar for 30 minutes. Arrange fruit slices on individual plates.

2.   Shave the Parmesan in broad slices over the top.

Yields 4 servings

Do not prepare more than an hour before serving.

NECTARINES POACHED IN PORT

1–2 oranges   3 whole cloves
 1 lemon   1 (1-in) piece cinnamon stick
2½ cups sugar   ¼ teaspoon nutmeg
1½ cups water   6 nectarines, peeled
 ¾ cup port

1.   With a knife, remove 2 (1-inch-wide) strips of rind from 1 of the oranges and squeeze ½ cup of orange juice from the oranges. Remove 1 (1-inch-wide) strip of rind and squeeze 3 tablespoons of lemon juice from the lemon.

2.   In a saucepan, bring the sugar and water to a simmer and cook until the sugar dissolves. Add the orange and lemon juices, strips of rind, port, cloves, cinnamon stick, and nutmeg. Return to a boil.

3.   Add the nectarines and just enough additional water to cover, if needed. Poach for 5 minutes. Cool in the poaching liquid for 1 hour.

4.   Drain the nectarines and place in a separate container. Reduce the cooking liquid by one-third and pour over the nectarines. Let cool.

Yields 6 servings

Can be prepared the day before serving.

ORANGES WITH NUTMEG

Blood oranges make this dessert extra-special.

6 blood oranges, if available
¼ cup Cointreau
 Grated nutmeg

1. Grate the rind from the oranges and then peel completely. Slice the oranges discarding any seeds.

2. Sprinkle with the grated rind, Cointreau, and nutmeg.

Yields 6 servings

Prepare shortly before serving.

SPICY ORANGES WITH CINNAMON AND CLOVES

8 large oranges, peeled and
 thinly sliced, with juices
 reserved
¼ teaspoon cinnamon
½ teaspoon ground cloves
¼ cup sugar
16 amaretti cookies, crushed,
 see Note
½ cup orange liqueur

1. Put the oranges in a glass bowl and toss with the cinnamon, cloves, and sugar. Refrigerate until cold.

2. Just before serving, sprinkle with amaretti crumbs, reserved orange juice, and liqueur.

Yields 8 servings

Prepare the oranges the day before.

NOTE: Amaretti cookies, made from apricot kernels, are available in gourmet shops and better supermarkets.

ORANGE SLICES IN CASSIS

6 navel oranges
⅔ cup orange juice
3 tablespoons cassis
2 teaspoons lemon juice

1. With a zester or knife, julienne the rind of 2 oranges and place in a saucepan with cold water to cover. Bring to a boil and drain. Set aside.

2. Peel all the oranges, removing all the pith. Cut the oranges into segments and place in a bowl with the orange juice, cassis, lemon juice, and cooled orange rind.

3. Chill, covered, for 2 hours before serving.

Yields 6 servings

Can be prepared the day before, if desired.

ORANGES WITH GINGER AND WHITE WINE

6 navel oranges	½ cup orange juice
5 ounces preserved ginger in	1 tablespoon lemon juice
syrup	¾ tablespoon sugar
⅔ cup dry white wine	¼ cup diced crystallized ginger

1. With a zester or knife, julienne the rind of two oranges. Wrap and refrigerate.

2. Peel all the oranges removing all the pith. Cut into thin slices. Arrange in a serving bowl.

3. In a processor, with on/off turns, mince the preserved ginger in the wine, orange juice, lemon juice, and sugar. Pour over the orange slices, cover, and chill for up to 24 hours.

4. Sprinkle with the reserved rind and crystallized ginger just before serving.

Yields 6 servings

Prepare the day before serving.

ORANGES IN RED WINE

1 cup water	2 whole cloves
1 cup dry red wine	2 slices lemon
¾ cup sugar	6 large oranges
1 cinnamon stick	

1. In a saucepan, simmer the water, wine, sugar, cinnamon stick, cloves, and lemon slices for 5 minutes.

2. With a zester or knife, julienne the rind of three oranges and set aside.

3. Peel all the oranges, removing all the pith. Cut the oranges into segments and place in a bowl. Pour the hot wine syrup over the oranges and sprinkle with the orange rind. Chill.

Yields 6 servings

Can be prepared 2 days ahead.

ARANCI CARAMELATI (Caramelized Oranges)

6 navel oranges	**1½ cups sugar**
1 cup plus 5 tablespoons	**3 tablespoons Cognac**
water	**½ cup diced candied fruit**

1. With a zester or a knife, julienne the rind of 2 of the oranges. Blanch the julienne in boiling water for 5 minutes. Drain, refresh under cold water, and drain again.

2. Peel all the oranges, removing all the white pith, and set aside.

3. In a saucepan, simmer 1 cup of water and ½ cup of sugar for 10 minutes. Add the julienned rind and simmer 10 minutes longer. Strain, reserving the syrup and rind.

4. In another saucepan, boil the remaining sugar and the remaining water until a deep golden caramel color. Stir in ½ cup of the reserved syrup. Remove from the heat and stir in the Cognac.

5. Arrange the oranges, whole or sliced, in a shallow dish and pour the caramel mixture over the top. Sprinkle the reserved julienned rind and the candied fruit and spoon the remaining reserved syrup over the top. Chill.

Yields 6 servings

Prepare the syrup and caramel mixture the day before, but assemble no more than 2 hours before serving.

NOTE: Carefully read the safety instructions for handling caramel in Chapter 1.

Variation

• Omit the Cognac and candied fruit if desired.

ORANGES GLACÉES AU GRAND MARNIER
(Glazed Oranges with Grand Marnier)

6 navel oranges
2 tablespoons honey
¼ cup orange juice

¼ cup Grand Marnier

1.   Peel the rind from the oranges and candy the rind, following the instructions for Candied Orange Rind (page 38). Julienne the candied rind and add the honey to the candying syrup.

2.   Peel the pith from the oranges and cut the fruit into slices. Arrange the slices in a shallow serving dish.

3.   Add the orange juice and the Grand Marnier to the candied rind and syrup. Spoon over the oranges. Chill.

Yields 6 servings

Can be prepared 2 to 3 days ahead.

ORANGE SLICES IN ROSEMARY SYRUP

Flavoring fruits with herbs is an ancient culinary tradition.

½ cup sugar
2 tablespoons minced
   rosemary
1 cup water

6 navel oranges, peeled and
sliced
Rosemary sprigs, for
garnish, optional

1.   In a saucepan, simmer the sugar, minced rosemary, and water for 5 minutes. Remove from the heat and let cool.

2.   Arrange the orange slices in a serving dish and spoon the syrup over the top. Refrigerate for 2 to 3 hours.

3.   Garnish with rosemary sprigs just before serving, if desired.

Yields 6 servings

Can be prepared a day ahead.

ORANGES AND CHESTNUTS IN VANILLA SAUCE

Chestnuts in syrup are also available in gourmet shops.

2 cups water
¾ cup sugar
1 (1-in) piece vanilla bean
1 pound chestnuts, peeled

and skinned, page 6, see
Note
3 large oranges, peeled and
thinly sliced

1. In a saucepan, boil the water, sugar, and vanilla bean for 5 minutes. Add the chestnuts and simmer 30 minutes, or until soft.

2. Cool. Discard the vanilla bean. Add the oranges and mix gently shortly before serving.

Yields 6 servings

The chestnuts can be prepared several days ahead.

NOTE: Use these chestnuts in other recipes that call for candied chestnuts in syrup.

MARINATED CITRUS FRUITS WITH CHEESE-FLAVORED ZABAGLIONE

3 oranges, peeled and sliced
1 lemon, peeled and sliced
1 lime, peeled and sliced
½ cup plus 3 tablespoons
Marsala
½ cup plus 1 tablespoon
sugar

6 egg yolks
1 tablespoon vanilla
1 tablespoon grated Parmesan
1 tablespoon finely chopped
Gorgonzola

1. Remove the center core and any seeds from the fruits and arrange the slices alternately in an ovenproof serving dish. Sprinkle with 3 tablespoons of Marsala and 1 tablespoon of sugar. Cover and macerate, refrigerated, for several hours.

2. Preheat the broiler. Drain the marinade into a large bowl. Stir in the egg yolks and the remaining sugar and whisk until pale and creamy. Set the bowl over a pan of simmering water and slowly add the remaining Marsala and the vanilla. With a hand-held mixer, beat until the mixture forms soft mounds. Remove from the heat and blend in the cheeses. Spoon over the fruits and broil until just browned.

Yields 6 servings

Can be prepared for broiling 2 hours before serving.

BAKED PAPAYAS

3 papayas, peeled, halved, and seeded	**2 teaspoons vanilla**
2 tablespoons butter	**¼ cup brown sugar**
	Heavy cream, optional

1. Preheat the oven to 350° F.

2. In a baking dish, arrange the papayas, cut side down. Add ½ inch of water and dot with the butter. Sprinkle with the vanilla and sugar. Bake until tender, about 25 minutes.

3. Serve hot or cold and pass a pitcher of cream, if desired.

Yields 6 servings

Can be prepared several hours ahead and reheated.

OVOS MOLES DE PAPAIA, MOZAMBIQUE
(Papaya and Egg Yolk Pudding)

The large number of egg yolks reveals the Portuguese influence on this dessert from Mozambique.

1 papaya, peeled, seeded, and chopped	**2 cups sugar**
¼ cup lime juice	**1 cinnamon stick**
¼ cup water	**4 whole cloves**
	5 egg yolks

1. In a blender, puree the papaya, lime juice, and water. Rub the puree through a fine sieve into a saucepan.

2. Add the sugar, cinnamon stick, and cloves and cook, stirring, until the syrup reaches 230° F. Remove from the heat and discard the cinnamon stick and cloves.

3. In a deep bowl, beat the egg yolks for 1 minute, or until slightly thickened. Beating constantly, pour the hot syrup into the yolks in a thin, steady stream. Continue to beat until smooth, thick, and bright deep yellow. Turn into dessert dishes. Chill.

Yields 4 to 6 servings

Can be prepared the day before serving.

PEACHES IN WINE

6 peaches, peeled, pitted, and
sliced

Red or white wine, to cover

Sugar, to taste

In a serving bowl, mix the peaches, wine, and sugar, to taste. Macerate for up to 12 hours.

Yields 6 servings

Serve within 12 hours.

PEACHES WITH HONEY-LIME SAUCE

6 peaches, peeled, pitted, and
sliced

2 tablespoons honey

2 tablespoons lime juice

1 teaspoon grated lime rind

Dash of mace

In a serving bowl, mix the peaches, honey, lime juice, lime rind, and mace. Macerate for at least 2 hours.

Yields 6 servings

Can be prepared up to 6 hours before serving.

PÊCHES À LA FERMIÈRE
(Peaches Farmer-style)

6 peaches, peeled, pitted, and
sliced

2 tablespoons sugar

⅓ cup peach brandy

8 ounces cream cheese, or

mascarpone cheese,
softened

½ cup confectioners' sugar

1 cup heavy cream

2 cups blueberries

1. In a bowl, mix the peaches with the sugar and brandy. Refrigerate, covered, for 3 hours.

2. In a bowl, mix the cream cheese and confectioners' sugar. In another bowl, beat the heavy cream until it forms soft peaks and fold into the cheese mixture.

3. Just before serving, drain the peaches and arrange in a bowl. Fold the blueberries into the cream mixture and spoon over the peaches.

Yields 6 servings

Can be prepared up to 6 hours before serving.

NOTE: If the cheese is too stiff to fold easily, add some of the macerating liquid. Instead of folding the berries into the cheese, arrange on top.

PÊCHES AU SABAYON MOUSSELLINE
(Peaches with Fluffy Sabayon Sauce)

6 peaches, peeled, halved,	**page 544**
and pitted	**Pinch of cinnamon**
Juice of 1 lemon	**Pinch of nutmeg**
½ cup peach brandy	**½ cup heavy cream**
2 tablespoons sugar	**Toasted almond slices, for**
2 cups cold Sabayon Sauce,	**garnish**

1.   In a bowl, toss the peaches with the lemon juice, brandy, and sugar. Refrigerate, covered, for 4 hours.

2.   Season the sabayon sauce with cinnamon and nutmeg. Beat the cream until it forms soft peaks and fold into the sabayon sauce. Pour over the peaches and garnish with the toasted almonds, if desired.

Yields 6 servings

Can be prepared up to 6 hours before serving.

PESCHE RIPIENE FREDDO
(Cold Stuffed Peaches)

6 peaches, peeled, halved,	**½ teaspoon vanilla**
and pitted	**12 amaretti cookies, crushed**
2 tablespoons lemon juice	**1 cup heavy cream, whipped**
2 cups dry white wine	**1 egg yolk, lightly beaten**
¾ cup sugar	

1.   Scoop part of the pulp out of each peach half and reserve. Brush the peach halves with lemon juice.

2.   In a saucepan, bring the wine, sugar, and vanilla to a boil. Add the peach halves and poach for 2 minutes. Remove from the heat and cool the peaches in the syrup. Remove the peaches and set aside. Simmer the syrup until thickened.

3. Measure 2 tablespoons of amaretti crumbs and reserve. In a processor, puree the reserved pulp. Fold into the whipped cream with the remaining amaretti crumbs and the egg yolk. Fill the peach halves with the cream mixture and arrange on a serving dish. Refrigerate.

4. Just before serving sprinkle with the syrup and reserved amaretti crumbs.

Yields 6 servings

Prepare the ingredients the day before, but do not assemble until shortly before serving.

Variation

• Substitute nectarines for the peaches.

PESCHE RIPIENE CALDO
(Hot Stuffed Peaches)

6 peaches, halved and pitted	3 egg yolks
6 amaretti cookies	½ cup light rum
2 tablespoons sugar	12 whole almonds, blanched

1. Preheat the oven to 350° F. Butter a baking dish and set aside.

2. With a melon baller, scoop out a little of the pulp from each peach and reserve it and the outer shell.

3. Place the amaretti in a processor and crush coarsely. Add the sugar, peach pulp, and egg yolks and process 30 seconds. Fill the peach cavities with the mixture.

4. Place the peaches in the prepared baking dish and bake until tender, about 30 minutes, basting with a little rum every 5 minutes.

5. Decorate each peach half with an almond. Serve warm or at room temperature.

Yields 6 servings

Can be prepared the day before and reheated.

GLAZED BAKED PEACHES

6 peaches, peeled, pitted, and sliced	**1–2 tablespoons sugar**
2 tablespoons butter	**½ cup Cognac**

1. Preheat the oven to 350° F. Butter a baking dish.

2. Arrange the peach slices in the dish. Dot with butter and sprinkle with sugar. Bake for 30 minutes.

3. Pour the Cognac over the peaches and ignite.

Yields 6 servings

Prepare ahead and reheat. Add the Cognac and ignite just before serving.

Variation

• *Glazed Baked Peaches II.* In a processor, cream ¼ cup of softened butter, 1 cup of sugar, ½ cup of orange liqueur, and ¼ cup of lemon juice. Pour over the peaches in the baking pan and sprinkle with ¼ cup of slivered almonds. Bake until soft, basting with the juices.

NUT-STUFFED PEACHES, PEARS, OR NECTARINES

½ cup raspberry jam	**12 (3-in) Génoise circles, page 20**
¾ cup finely chopped pecans	
6 Vanilla Poached Peaches, Pears, or Nectarines, page 40	**1 cup heavy cream, whipped and sweetened, to taste for garnish**

1. In a bowl, mix the jam and pecans. Cut the poached fruit in half and remove each pit or core. Fill the hollows with the jam, to resemble the pit.

2. Place génoise circles on serving plates. Arrange the halves on the cake circles, jam side up. Using a pastry bag fitted with a #4 open star tip, pipe a whipped cream garnish.

Yields 12 servings

Can be prepared up to 4 hours before serving.

NOTE: If using pears, cut the cake in a pear shape.

Try substituting Vanilla Poached Pears or Nectarines for the Vanilla Poached Peaches.

POIRES AU COINTREAU
(Pears in Cointreau)

6 pears peeled, cored, and sliced	¼ cup Cointreau
1 tablespoon sugar	1 teaspoon lemon juice
1 cup orange juice	Julienned rind of 1 orange

1. In a bowl, mix the pears, sugar, orange juice, Cointreau, and lemon juice. Macerate in the refrigerator for at least 1 hour.

2. Sprinkle with rind just before serving.

Yields 6 servings

Can be prepared up to 6 hours before serving.

PERE RIPIENE ALLA GORGONZOLA FREDDO
(Cold Gorgonzola-stuffed Pears)

6 pears, peeled, halved, and cored	softened
1½ tablespoons lemon juice	3 tablespoons ground walnuts, pistachios, or pine nuts
3 ounces Gorgonzola cheese	
3 tablespoons butter,	

1. Scoop a scant tablespoon of pulp from each pear. Brush the pear inside and out with the lemon juice.

2. In a bowl, cream the Gorgonzola and butter until soft and fluffy. Fill the cavities of the pears with the cheese and press the halves together. Roll the pears in the nuts. Chill for 2 hours before serving.

Yields 6 servings

Can be prepared up to 6 hours before serving.

Variation

• For a simpler version, fill the pear cavities with mashed Gorgonzola, omit the nuts, and serve immediately.

Poached Pears

There are dozens and dozens of desserts based on poached pears. The flavoring for the poaching liquid may be red or white wine, herbs, spices, or vanilla. The flavors of vanilla and pears combine beautifully and marry well with other ingredients such as cream, custard, chocolate, and fruit purees. There are numerous suggestions here, but I hope that you will use these ideas as inspiration to create a special dessert. See page 40 for the basic recipe for poaching fruit.

POIRES AU VIN ROUGE
(Pears in Red Wine)

There are literally dozens, if not hundreds, of recipes for pears poached in wine. Here is a basic recipe with many alternatives.

1 lemon	Strawberry or Raspberry
Rind of 1 orange, julienned	Puree, page 29, or 2
2 cups strong red wine	tablespoons raspberry or
1 cup sugar	currant preserves
6 pears, peeled, see Note	Juice of 1 lemon
2 tablespoons fresh	

1.   With a zester or knife, remove the rind from the lemon, and cut into julienne. Squeeze the lemon and reserve the juice.

2.   In a large saucepan, simmer the rinds, wine, and sugar for 5 minutes. Add the pears and simmer, covered, until tender, basting often, and turning so they color evenly. Remove the pears to a serving dish.

3.   Add the puree or preserves to the wine and simmer for 15 minutes. Stir in the reserved lemon juice and pour over the pears.

Yields 6 servings

Can be prepared the day before.

NOTE: Usually the pears are whole and uncored, but you may core the pears from the bottom, or halve and remove the core, or core and slice.

Variations

• *Angevine.* Omit the orange and lemon rinds and add 1 cinnamon stick to the poaching liquid. When cooled, add 1 tablespoon of pear brandy.

- *Au Porto.* Substitute 1 cup of port and 2 cups of water for the wine. Omit the lemon juice.
- *Poires à la Bordelaise (Pears Bordeaux-style).* Omit the lemon and the orange rinds and add 2 tablespoons of rum or Cognac to the cooled syrup.
- *Pere al Vino (Pears with Red Wine).* Replace the wine with 4 cups of Chianti and 1 cup of tawny port. Omit the lemon, orange rinds, and the raspberry puree or preserves.
- *Poires Bourguignon (Pears Burgundy-style).* Omit the lemon and orange rinds and lemon juice and add 2 tablespoons of kirsh or orange liqueur.
- *Poires en Sabayon (Pears with Wine-flavored Sabayon).* Reduce the poaching liquid to 1½ cups and use to prepare a Sabayon Sauce (see page 544).
- *Poached Pears with Wine and Basil.* Omit the orange rind. Reduce the liquid until syrupy. Swirl in ½ teaspoon of butter and 20 minced basil leaves. Macerate for 1 hour. Strain the syrup and discard the basil leaves and, lemon rind. Omit the puree or preserves.
- *Poached Pears à la Vigneronne (Pears Wine Growers–style).* Substitute white wine for the red, add 1 cinnamon stick, and 1 (1-inch) piece of vanilla bean to the poaching liquid. Omit the raspberry puree. When the pears are cool, drain the syrup, and simmer with ¼ cup of orange marmalade and ¼ cup of apricot preserves until syrupy. Pour over the pears. Discard the cinnamon stick and vanilla bean before serving.
- *Pere al Mirtilli (Pears with Blueberries).* Omit the orange rind and the raspberry puree. In a processor, puree 2 cups of blueberries. Reduce the cooking liquid to ¾ cup, stir into the blueberries, and serve with the pears.

POIRES PRALINÉES AU PORTO BLANC
(Poached Pears in White Port Sabayon with Praline)

6 pears, peeled, halved, and cored	**¼ cup sugar**
	¼ teaspoon vanilla
3 cups white port	**¾ cup heavy cream, whipped**
6 egg yolks	**⅓ cup Praline Powder, page 30**

1. In saucepan, poach the pears in the port until tender. Cool in the liquid.

2. Drain the pears, reserving the liquid. In a saucepan, beat the egg yolks, sugar, and vanilla until thickened and pale. Add 1 cup of the reserved liquid.

Cook over medium heat, beating, until the mixture is thick and frothy. Remove from the heat and cool. Fold in the whipped cream.

3.   Preheat the broiler. In an ovenproof serving dish, arrange the pears, cut side down, and spread the sauce over them. Sprinkle with the praline powder.

4.   Broil until golden. Watch carefully; it can burn quickly. Refrigerate until cold.

Yields 6 servings

Can be prepared the day before serving.

POMMES ET POIRES FLAMBÉ
(Apples and Pears Flambé)

2 pounds apples, peeled, cored, and chopped	**from the bottom**
1½ cups sugar	**3 cups red wine**
½ cup chopped walnuts	**¼ teaspoon cinnamon or 1 cinnamon stick**
6 pears, peeled, and cored	**¼ cup rum**

1.   In a saucepan, cook the apples with ½ cup of sugar, covered, until very soft.

2.   In a processor, puree the apple mixture and stir in the walnuts. Arrange the applesauce on a heatproof serving platter.

3.   In another saucepan, simmer the pears in the wine, the remaining sugar, and the cinnamon until the pears are tender. Arrange the pears on the applesauce.

4.   Reduce the poaching liquid to a syrup. Add the rum and ignite and pour, flaming, over the pears. Serve hot or at room temperature.

Yields 6 servings

Can be prepared the day before, but allow to come to room temperature before serving.

POACHED PEARS AND PLUMS IN WINE

Rind of 1 orange, julienned	**1 cinnamon stick**
2 tablespoons orange liqueur	**1 (2-in) strip lemon rind**
6 pears, peeled	**3 whole cloves**
2 tablespoons lemon juice	**12 plums**
3 cups dry red wine	**½ cup currant jelly**
1½ cups sugar	

1.   Blanch the orange rind in boiling water for 5 minutes and drain. Place the rind in a bowl, add the orange liqueur, and set aside. Place the peeled pears in a bowl of water acidulated with 1 tablespoon of lemon juice.

2.   In a saucepan, simmer the wine, sugar, cinnamon, lemon rind, and cloves for 2 minutes. Poach the pears, 2 or 3 at a time, covered, until tender. Remove the pears to a bowl and repeat with the remaining pears.

3.   Add the plums to the liquid and poach for about 10 minutes. Put into the bowl with the pears.

4.   Reduce the poaching liquid until it thickens and lightly coats the back of a spoon. Add the jelly and the remaining lemon juice. Strain the sauce over the pears and plums. Sprinkle with the julienned rind.

Yield 6 servings

Can be prepared the day before serving.

PEARS IN CIDER

6 pears, peeled	**1 vanilla bean, split**
½ lemon	**1 cinnamon stick**
2½ cups apple cider	**1½ cups heavy cream**
½ cup sugar	**1½ tablespoons Cognac**
1 (1-in) strip of lemon rind	

1.   Trim the bottoms of the pears so they stand straight. Rub the pears with the lemon half.

2.   In a saucepan, simmer the cider, sugar, lemon rind, vanilla bean, and cinnamon stick for 5 minutes. Poach the pears until tender. Discard the lemon rind, vanilla bean, and cinnamon stick. Transfer the pears to a serving dish. Reduce the cooking liquid to a syrup and pour over the pears.

3.   In a bowl, whip the cream until stiff peaks form, blend in the Cognac, and put into a serving bowl. Pass the whipped cream separately. Serve warm or cold.

Yields 6 servings

Can be prepared 1 day ahead.

POIRES AU SIROP
(Pears in Pepper and Honey Syrup)

The fire of the pepper accents the fruit flavor.

4⅓ cups water   2 whole cloves
1¾ cups sugar   ¾ teaspoon black peppercorns
⅔ cup honey   6 pears, peeled
3 bay leaves

1.   In a saucepan, simmer the water, sugar, honey, bay leaves, cloves, and peppercorns for 2 minutes.

2.   Poach the pears until tender. Cool in the syrup.

3.   Strain the syrup and discard the bay leaves, cloves, and peppercorns.

Yields 6 servings

Can be prepared 2 days before serving.

GINGERED PEARS

2 cups water   2 tablespoons chopped
2 cups sugar   gingerroot
1 cinnamon stick   6 pears, peeled, cored, and
2 (1-in) strips lemon rind   sliced
1 teaspoon whole cloves

1.   In a saucepan, simmer the water, sugar, cinnamon stick, lemon rind, cloves, and gingerroot for 2 minutes.

2.   Poach the pears until tender. Cool in the syrup.

3.   Strain the syrup and discard the cinnamon stick, lemon rind, cloves, and gingerroot.

Yields 6 servings

Can be prepared the day before serving.

POACHED PEARS IN CARAMEL SYRUP

6 pears, peeled	⅓ cup coffee liqueur
Juice of 1 lemon	Heavy Cream whipped and
3 cups water	sweetened, optional
2 cups sugar	

1. Cover the pears in water acidulated with the lemon juice.

2. In a saucepan, simmer the water and 1 cup of sugar for 2 minutes. Poach the pears until tender. Drain the pears, reserving the syrup. Place the pears on a platter.

3. In a saucepan, heat 1 cup of reserved syrup with 1 cup of sugar until the sugar dissolves. Raise the heat to high and boil, without stirring, until it starts to turn golden brown.

4. Remove from the heat. Wearing an oven mitt or wrapping your hand in a towel, stir in the remaining syrup. Bring to a boil and add the coffee liqueur. Pour the sauce over the pears and chill.

5. Pass the whipped cream separately, if desired.

Yields 6 servings

Can be prepared 2 days ahead.

POACHED PEARS WITH CHESTNUTS

2 cups water	12 whole plus ½ cup chopped
2 tablespoons lemon juice	chestnuts in syrup, see Note
¾ cup sugar	2 cups Custard Sauce, page
1 (1-in) piece cinnamon stick	545
6 pears, peeled, halved, and	¼ cup syrup from the chestnuts
cored	

1. In a saucepan, simmer the water, lemon juice, sugar, and cinnamon stick for 3 minutes. Poach the pears until tender. Cool the pears in the syrup, drain, and chill. Discard the syrup or save for another use.

2. Arrange the pears, cut side up, on a serving plate and fill each cavity with a whole chestnut. In a bowl, mix the Custard Sauce and chopped chestnuts with the chestnut syrup. Mix well and pour over the pears.

Yields 6 servings

Can be prepared for assembly the day before serving.

NOTE: Gourmet shops and better supermarkets sell chestnuts in syrup. If you wish to prepare them, prepare the chestnuts as suggested in Oranges and Chestnuts in Vanilla Syrup (page 95).

POIRES ROSEMOND (Pears Rosamond)

Pears in custard with pineapple.

3 cups water	**⅓ cup plus 1 tablespoon rum**
1½ cups sugar	**3 egg yolks**
6 pears, peeled and cored	**Grated rind of 1 lime**
from the bottom	**⅓ cup dry white wine**
⅓ cup minced pineapple	

1.   In a saucepan, bring the water and 1 cup of sugar to a simmer. Poach the pears until tender. Drain the pears and cool.

2.   In a bowl, macerate the pineapple in the rum for at least 10 minutes.

3.   In a saucepan, beat the egg yolks and remaining sugar until thickened and pale. Beat in the lime rind. Place the pan over low heat, add the wine, and beat constantly until the mixture becomes light and fluffy and the consistency of mayonnaise. Remove from the heat.

4.   Stuff the cooled pears with the pineapple and arrange on a serving plate. Coat the pears with the warm sauce.

Yields 6 servings

The pears and pineapple can be prepared the day before, but prepare the sauce within an hour of serving.

POACHED PEARS MARY GARDEN

At the turn of the century, one of the great honors a chef could give to a star, such as the opera singer Mary Garden, was to name a dish after her.

6 Vanilla Poached Pears, page 000, cooled	1½ teaspoons cornstarch
¼ cup candied cherries, soaked in hot water to cover, until softened	1 tablespoon water
	1 tablespoon kirsch
	1 cup heavy cream, whipped and sweetened
¾ cup raspberry jam	

1. Cool the pears in the poaching syrup and drain well.

2. In a saucepan, melt the jam. In a bowl, mix the cornstarch and water and stir into the jam and cook until thickened. Strain and stir in the kirsch.

3. Drain the cherries and dry on paper toweling. Stir into the raspberry mixture.

4. Spoon the sauce onto serving plates and top with an upright pear. Using a pastry bag fitted with a #5 star tip, pipe the cream over the pears.

Yields 6 servings

Assemble just before serving.

POIRES SUSANNE
(Susanna's Pears)

I created this dessert for Susanna Gourley using many of her favorite flavors.

6 Vanilla Poached Pears, page 40	1 tablespoon kirsch
4 ounces cream cheese	Sugar, to taste
¼ cup ground walnuts	Grated semisweet chocolate, for garnish

1. Chill the pears and core by cutting into the bottom of each pear, leaving the stem intact. Cut a slice off the bottom so the pears will stand upright.

2. In a small bowl, cream the cheese until light and fluffy and fold in the walnuts, kirsch, and sugar to taste. Using a pastry bag fitted with a plain round tip, stuff the pears from the bottom and stand upright on serving plates.

3.   Spoon the poaching syrup around the pears and sprinkle the grated chocolate over the pears.

Yields 6 servings

Can be prepared the day before serving.

POIRES VEFOUR
(Poached Pears Grand Vefour)

This dessert was created at the Grand Vefour, one of Paris' oldest restaurants, often considered one of its finest.

2 cups Pastry Cream, page 26
  Grand Marnier, to taste
12 Almond Macaroons, page 26
6 cold Vanilla Poached Pears,
  page 40, halved and cored

1 cup heavy cream, whipped,
  sweetened, and flavored with
  Grand Marnier, to taste
  Crystallized violets, for
  garnish, see Note

1.   In a bowl, mix the pastry cream and Grand Marnier to taste, and spread a thin layer on a serving platter.

2.   Pour some Grand Marnier into a small bowl and dip the macaroons into the liqueur. Arrange them on top of the pastry cream.

3.   Spoon the remaining pastry cream over the macaroons and arrange the pears on top.

4.   Using a pastry bag fitted with a #5 open star tip, pipe the whipped cream around the pears. Garnish each with a crystallized violet.

Yields 6 servings

Can be prepared several hours before serving.

NOTE: The violets give much-needed color.

Variations
• Shape the macaroons in a pear shape or substitute slices of sponge cake.
• Garnish with raspberries, blackberries, or blueberries instead of the violets.

POIRES À LA CARDINALE
(Pears with Raspberry Sauce)

6 cold Vanilla Poached Pears, page 40, halved and cored	Sugar, to taste
1 cup raspberries, sieved	⅓ cup chopped toasted almonds
2 teaspoons lemon juice	

1. Arrange the pear halves on plates.

2. In a bowl, mix the sieved raspberry puree with the lemon juice and sugar to taste. Pour the sauce over the pears and sprinkle with the almonds.

Yields 6 servings

Poach the pears and prepare the sauce the day before.

NOTE: For a different presentation, pour the sauce onto serving plates, cut the pear halves into thin slices horizontally or vertically and fan onto the sauce.

POIRES ARMENONVILLE
(Pears Armenonville-style)

10-ounce package frozen unsweetened raspberries, sieved	6 cold Vanilla Poached Pears, page 40
¼ cup port	½ cup sour cream
	½ cup heavy cream, whipped

1. In a bowl, mix the raspberry puree and port. Add the pears, turning to coat. Refrigerate for several hours, basting often with the raspberry sauce. Arrange the pears on serving plates with the sauce.

2. In a bowl, fold the sour cream into the heavy cream and spoon over the pears.

Yields 6 servings

Arrange just before serving.

ALMOND-FILLED PEARS WITH RASPBERRY SAUCE

Rose water is available in gourmet shops.

6 cold Vanilla Poached Pears, page 40, cored from the bottom, stems intact
1 cup blanched almonds, toasted
¼ cup sugar

2 tablespoons rose water
¼ teaspoon almond extract
20 ounces frozen raspberries, thawed and drained
Framboise or kirsch, to taste

1.   Drain the pears, reserving the poaching liquid.

2.   In a processor, grind the almonds, sugar, rose water, and almond extract until the mixture forms a paste. Stuff the pears with the almond mixture and stand upright in a serving dish.

3.   In a processor, puree the raspberries with ¾ cup of reserved poaching liquid and strain to remove the seeds. Add more poaching liquid to thin, if needed, and flavor with the framboise or kirsch, to taste.

4.   Chill until serving time. Spoon the sauce over the pears and serve.

Yields 6 servings

Can be prepared the day before.

POIRES FIORETTA (Pears Little Flower)

This lovely presentation has several steps which, fortunately, you can do ahead.

¼ cup semolina flour
½ cup sugar
½ teaspoon salt
2 cups milk
1 (2-in) piece vanilla bean
1 tablespoon gelatin
¼ cup cold water

1 cup heavy cream, whipped
6 Red-Wine Poached Pears, page 102
¼ cup red currant jelly
10 (1-in) circles Candied Orange Rind, page 38
¼ cup grated pistachio nuts

1.   Lightly oil an 8-inch ring mold.

2.   In a saucepan, simmer the semolina, sugar, salt, milk, and vanilla bean, stirring constantly, for 5 to 10 minutes, or until it thickens.

3.   In a bowl, soften the gelatin in the cold water. Stir the gelatin into the hot semolina until it dissolves. Discard the vanilla bean.

4.   Turn the mixture into a bowl and place the bowl in a pan of ice water. Cool, stirring often. When cool to the touch, remove from the pan of water and fold in the whipped cream. Turn into the mold. Chill until set, about 2 hours.

5.   Remove the pears from the poaching liquid and cook the syrup until it reaches 230° F. Stir in the jelly. Set aside.

6.   Unmold the semolina onto a serving platter. Drain the pears, dip four of them into the syrup, and place in the center of the mold. Cut the remaining pears in half, core, and arrange them around the side of the mold. Garnish the top of the mold with circles of candied orange rind and sprinkle with the pistachios.

Yields 6 servings

Can be assembled up to 3 hours before serving.

POACHED PEARS AND APPLES

4 cups Sauterne	3 pears, peeled, cored, and
1½ cups sugar	quartered
1 large piece lemon rind	2 Red Delicious apples,
1 cinnamon stick	peeled, cored, and sliced
1 (3-in) piece vanilla bean	½ cup apricot jam
3 whole cloves	

1.   In a saucepan, simmer the wine, sugar, lemon rind, cinnamon stick, vanilla bean, and cloves for 20 minutes. Add the pears and apples and poach until just tender.

2.   With a slotted spoon, transfer the pears and apples to a serving bowl. Add the apricot jam to the syrup and simmer for 3 minutes. Strain the sauce over the fruit and chill.

Yields 6 servings

Can be prepared the day before serving.

GOURMANDISE DOMFRONTAISE
(Fresh Pears Baked with Pear Brandy and Cream)

4 Anjou pears, peeled, halved, and cored	3 eggs
1 tablespoon Poire William	Pinch of salt
¼ cup plus 1 tablespoon sugar	Pinch of cinnamon
	½ cup heavy cream
	1 tablespoon flour

1.   Preheat the oven to 350° F. Cut each pear half into four sections. Arrange in the bottom of a large casserole dish. Sprinkle with the liqueur and 1 tablespoon of sugar. Bake for 15 minutes.

2.   Meanwhile, in a bowl, beat the remaining sugar, eggs, and the salt until thickened and pale. Stir in the cinnamon, heavy cream, and flour. Pour over the pears and bake 35 to 40 minutes, or until lightly browned.

Yields 6 servings

Can be prepared ahead and reheated.

PERE IN FORNO AL RUM (Pears Baked with Rum)

6 pears, peeled, halved, and cored	¼ cup water
Juice of 1 lemon	6 whole cloves
2 tablespoons brown sugar	1 pint vanilla ice cream or ½ cup heavy cream, whipped and sweetened, optional
¼ cup rum	

1.   Preheat the oven to 250° F.

2.   Place the pears, cut side down, in a baking dish with a tight-fitting lid. Squeeze the lemon juice over the top and sprinkle with the sugar. Pour the rum and water over the pears and scatter the cloves around, but not on, the fruit.

3.   Bake the pears for 1½ to 2 hours, basting occasionally. Discard the cloves and serve with the ice cream or whipped cream, if desired.

Yields 6 servings

Can be prepared ahead and reheated.

BAKED PEARS WITH CHEDDAR CHEESE

6 pears, peeled, halved, and
cored
¾ cup dry white wine
6 tablespoons sugar

1 teaspoon cinnamon
½ cup butter
¼ pound shredded Cheddar
cheese

1.   Preheat the oven to 375° F. In a shallow baking dish, arrange the pears.

2.   In a saucepan, simmer the wine, sugar, cinnamon, and butter for 5 minutes. Pour over the pears and bake for 25 minutes, or until tender, basting often. Add more wine, if needed.

3.   Sprinkle the pears with the cheese and serve.

Yields 6 servings

Can be prepared the day before and reheated.

BAKED PEARS WITH CHÈVRE

3 pears, peeled, halved, and
cored
Juice of 1 lemon
3 tablespoons port
3 tablespoons amaretto
¼ cup sugar
½ teaspoon cinnamon
½ teaspoon mace

¼ teaspoon ground cloves
1 teaspoon grated orange or
lemon rind
½ pound chèvre cheese, such
as Montrachet
1 cup amaretti cookie crumbs
Strawberries, for garnish

1.   Preheat oven to 350° F. Butter a baking dish large enough to hold pears in a single layer and arrange the pears in the dish. Brush with the lemon juice and sprinkle with the port and amaretto liqueur.

2.   In a bowl, mix the sugar, cinnamon, mace, and cloves and sprinkle over the pears. Cover and bake for 15 minutes, basting often. Remove the cover and bake until tender. Arrange the pears on a serving plate and set aside.

3.   Increase oven to 375° F. In a saucepan, reduce the poaching liquid with the grated orange rind by half, and strain into a bowl.

4.   Slice the cheese into 12 rounds, brush lightly with the poaching liquid, and roll in the amaretti crumbs. Place on a baking sheet and bake until heated, about 3 minutes.

5.   Garnish the pears with strawberries and the baked cheeses.

Yields 6 servings

Can be prepared ahead. Bake the cheese just before serving.

ALMOND BAKED PEARS

3 egg yolks	6 pears, peeled and cored
½ cup plus 2 tablespoons	from the bottom
confectioners' sugar	1½ cups dry white wine
½ teaspoon almond extract	6 tablespoons amaretto
2 cups slivered toasted,	½ cup heavy cream
almonds, chopped	

1.   Preheat the oven to 375° F.

2.   In a bowl, beat the egg yolks and ½ cup of sugar until thickened and pale. Stir in ¼ teaspoon of almond extract and all but 2 tablespoons of almonds. Stuff the pears with the mixture and stand upright in a baking dish.

3.   Add the wine and the amaretto to the dish. Cover and bake the pears, basting often, until tender.

4.   Transfer the pears to a serving dish and reduce the cooking liquid to 6 tablespoons. Spoon over the pears.

5.   In a bowl, whip the cream and fold in the remaining sugar and almond extract. Spoon over the pears and sprinkle with the reserved almonds.

Yields 6 servings

Can be prepared the day before and reheated. Add the cream just before serving.

PERE RIPIENE ALLE MILANESE
(Stuffed Pears Milan-style)

6 pears, halved and cored	ground
¾ cup confectioners' sugar	¼ teaspoon almond extract
4 marschino cherries, minced	½ cup sherry
½ cup toasted almonds,	

1.   Preheat the oven to 375° F. Arrange the pears in a single layer in a baking dish, cut side up.

2. In a bowl, mix the sugar, cherries, almonds, and almond extract. Fill the pears with the mixture and drizzle on the sherry.

3. Bake for 15 minutes, or until the pears are tender.

Yields 6 servings

Can be prepared the day before.

PEARS STUFFED WITH AMARETTI

6 pears, peeled and cored from the bottom	softened
12 amaretti cookies	6 tablespoons sugar
3 egg yolks	1½ cups white wine
1½ tablespoons butter,	Custard Sauce, page 545, optional

1. Preheat the oven to 375° F.

2. With a melon baller, scoop out some of the inside pear flesh to make a larger opening.

3. In a processor, grind the amaretti to a powder. Add the flesh from the pears, the egg yolks, butter, and 3 tablespoons of sugar and blend. Stuff each pear with the mixture and arrange upright in a baking pan.

4. Bake for 40 minutes, or until the pears are tender. Remove the pears to a plate.

5. Place the baking dish over direct heat and pour the wine and remaining sugar into the baking dish. Simmer, deglazing the pan, until reduced to a thin syrup. Spoon the syrup over the pears. Serve warm or cold with custard sauce.

Yields 6 servings

Can be prepared 2 days before serving.

BAKED PEARS WITH BRANDY

3 tablespoons dried currants	2 teaspoons grated lemon rind
⅓ cup brandy	
6 tablespoons butter, softened	6 pears, peeled and cored from the bottom
⅓ cup light brown sugar	

1. Preheat the oven to 375° F.

2. In a bowl, macerate the currants in the brandy for 15 minutes. Drain the currants, reserving the brandy.

3. In a bowl, cream the butter and sugar until light and fluffy. Fold in the currants and lemon rind and stuff the pears with the mixture.

4. In a baking dish just large enough to hold them, arrange the pears upright. Pour on the reserved brandy and bake, about 25 minutes, basting often, until tender. Cool to room temperature.

Yields 6 servings

Can be prepared the day before.

CARDAMOM-FLAVORED PEARS

6 pears, peeled, cored, and sliced	**1 cup heavy cream, whipped and flavored with 2 tablespoons orange liqueur, optional**
¼ cup sugar	
½ cup orange liqueur	
1 teaspoon ground cardamom	

1. Preheat the oven to 375° F.

2. Arrange the pears in a shallow baking dish and sprinkle with the sugar, liqueur, and cardamom. Bake until tender. Refrigerate until cold.

3. Serve topped with the cream, if desired.

Yields 6 servings

Can be prepared the day before serving.

HONEY BAKED PEARS

6 pears, peeled, halved, and cored	**½ cup honey**
3 tablespoons lemon juice	**¾ teaspoon cinnamon**
	2 tablespoons butter

1. Preheat the oven to 350° F.

2. Arrange the pears in a baking dish and sprinkle with the lemon juice, honey, and cinnamon. Dot with the butter.

3. Bake, basting often, until tender, about 20 minutes. Serve hot or cold.

Yields 6 servings

Can be prepared 2 days before serving.

ORANGE MUSCAT PEARS

6 pears, peeled and cored from the bottom	**Julienned rind of 1 orange**
1 bottle sweet muscat wine, such as Muscat de Beaumes de Venise	**1 tablespoon honey**
	Pear or orange sherbet or vanilla ice cream, optional
1 cup orange juice	

1. Preheat the oven to 350° F.

2. In a 2-quart soufflé dish, arrange pears upright. Pour the wine and orange juice into the dish.

3. Bake 1 hour, basting occasionally, or until very tender. Stand the pears upright on a serving platter.

4. Pour the juices into a saucepan, add the rind and honey and simmer, until reduced to ⅓ cup and caramel-colored. Pour over the pears. Serve warm or at room temperature with sherbet or ice cream, if desired.

Yields 6 servings

Can be prepared the day before serving.

PEARS WITH MERINGUE AND CHOCOLATE SAUCE

12 ounces apricot jam	**½ cup mixed candied fruit**
1 cup sugar	**1 tablespoon rum**
½ cup water	**2 egg whites**
6 pears, peeled and cored from the bottom	**6 ounces semisweet chocolate, grated**

1. Preheat the oven to 425° F.

2. In a saucepan, simmer the jam, ½ cup of sugar, and water for 3 minutes. Poach the pears in batches, turning and basting often, until tender.

3. In a small bowl, mix the candied fruit with the rum. Remove the pears from the poaching liquid and, when cool enough to handle, fill the centers with the candied fruit. Arrange the pears in a large baking dish, at least 3 inches apart.

4. In a bowl, beat the egg whites until stiff peaks form and carefully fold in 7 tablespoons of sugar. Using a pastry bag fitted with a #4 open star tip, pipe a rosette of meringue onto each pear. Sprinkle the meringue with the remaining sugar. Bake until the meringue browns, about 8 minutes.

5. Meanwhile, stir the grated chocolate into the poaching liquid in the saucepan and heat, stirring until melted. Pour some sauce onto each serving dish and place a cooked pear in the center.

Yields 6 servings

Can be prepared about 6 hours before serving.

BAKED PEARS WITH MAPLE NUT SAUCE

You can substitute walnuts or Brazil nuts for the pecans.

6 pears, peeled, halved, and cored	**½ cup dark brown sugar**
½ cup water	**2 tablespoons butter, melted**
½ cup maple syrup	**¼ cup chopped pecans**

1. Preheat the oven to 350° F.

2. Place the pear halves, cut side up, in a small, deep casserole dish. Add the water, maple syrup, sugar, and butter. Cover and bake until the pears are tender. Sprinkle with the nuts and serve.

Yields 6 servings

Can be prepared the day before and reheated.

POIRES CUITES À LA SAVOYARDE
(Baked Pears Savoyarde)

6 pears, peeled, cored, and quartered	**2 tablespoons water**
¾ cup sugar	**6 tablespoons butter**
	½ cup heavy cream

1. Preheat the oven to 400° F.

2. Arrange the pears in a baking dish. Sprinkle with the sugar and water. Dot with the butter.

3. Bake for about 40 minutes or until the sugar caramelizes. Pour on the cream and serve hot.

Yields 6 servings

Can be prepared up to 2 hours before serving.

POIRES BRAISÉE À LA BRESSANE
(Braised Pears Bress-Style)

This recipe from a region in France, adjacent to Savoy, is a more elaborate version of the previous recipe.

6 pears, peeled, cored, and halved	**2 cups heavy cream**
¼ cup sugar	**3 tablespoons Cognac**
3 tablespoons butter	**2 tablespoons honey**
	½ teaspoon vanilla

1. Preheat the oven to 400° F.

2. Arrange the pears, cut side down, in a baking dish. Sprinkle with the sugar and dot with the butter. Bake for 35 to 40 minutes, or until tender.

3. Lower the heat to 350° F. and pour 1 cup of cream over the pears. Bake until the sauce thickens and turns caramel-colored, about 10 minutes, basting several times.

4. In a bowl, whip the remaining cream and fold in the Cognac, honey, and vanilla.

5. Serve the pears at room temperature and pass the whipped cream.

Yields 6 servings

The pears can be baked the day before and reheated.

VERMOUTH-GLAZED PEARS

6 pears, peeled, with stems left attached, cored from the bottom	½ cup amaretti cookies, crushed
Juice and grated rind of 1 lemon	¼ cup chopped toasted almonds
⅔ cup apricot preserves	3 tablespoons dark rum
⅓ cup vermouth	1 pint vanilla ice cream, softened

1. Preheat the oven to 350° F. Arrange the pears in a baking dish, no more than 1 inch apart. Squeeze the lemon juice over the pears.

2. In a saucepan, simmer the apricot preserves, vermouth, and grated lemon rind for 1 minute and pour over the pears.

3. Sprinkle the pears with the amaretti crumbs and nuts. Bake, basting often, until the pears are tender, about 30 minutes.

4. In a bowl, beat the rum into the softened ice cream. Keep well chilled until ready to serve.

5. Transfer the pears to serving plates and pass the ice cream separately. Serve warm.

Yields 6 servings

The pears can be made the day before and reheated.

SAUTÉED PEARS WITH RASPBERRY SAUCE

6 pears, peeled, cored, and sliced	½ cup raspberry preserves, strained
Juice of ½ lemon	¼ cup sliced almonds, toasted
4 tablespoons butter	½ cup heavy cream, whipped and sweetened
¼ cup orange liqueur	

1. In a bowl, toss the pear slices in the lemon juice.

2. In a large skillet, over high heat, sauté the pears in the butter until tender. Transfer the pears to a platter or serving dishes.

3. Add the orange liqueur and the raspberry preserves to the skillet and cook, stirring, over high heat, until slightly thickened. Pour over the pear slices and sprinkle with the nuts.

4. Pass the whipped cream on the side.

Yields 6 servings

Can be prepared ahead and reheated.

PINEAPPLE WITH GINGERED YOGURT SAUCE

2 cups plain yogurt

1 tablespoon sugar, or to
taste

1 teaspoon minced

crystallized ginger

1 pineapple, cut into rings or
dice

1. In a bowl, mix the yogurt, sugar, and ginger.

2. Arrange the pineapple on serving plates and coat with the sauce or pass separately.

Yields 6 servings

Can be prepared the day before serving.

ANANAS ROMANOFF
(Pineapple with Rum Cream)

1 large pineapple, cut into
1-in wedges

½ cup confectioners' sugar

3 tablespoons rum

3 tablespoons Cointreau

1½ cups heavy cream

3 tablespoons kirsch

Grated rind of 1 orange

1. In a bowl, toss the pineapple with ¼ cup of sugar, and sprinkle with the rum and Cointreau. Refrigerate for up to 24 hours.

2. One hour before serving, whip the cream with the remaining sugar and the kirsch. Spoon the whipped cream over the pineapple and mix to coat. Turn into a serving bowl and sprinkle with the grated orange rind.

Yields 6 servings

Can be prepared up to 24 hours before serving.

PINEAPPLE IN PERNOD

1 pineapple, cut into cubes
2–4 tablespoons Pernod, see
Note
Sugar, to taste

In a bowl, mix the pineapple and Pernod. Sprinkle with sugar, to taste.

Yields 6 servings

Can be prepared the day before serving.

NOTE: Any anise-flavored liqueur will do in place of Pernod.

PINEAPPLE IN RUM CUSTARD

1 large pineapple
1½ cups Custard Sauce, page
545, flavored with rum

1.   Cut the pineapple in half through the fronds and then cut each half into thirds. With a sharp knife, cut the flesh from each section and remove the core.

2.   Cut each section into small slices and rearrange them in the pineapple shells. Serve with the sauce on the side.

Yields 6 servings

The pineapple and sauce can be prepared the day before serving.

ANANAS À L'ORANGE
(Pineapple in Orange Syrup)

1 orange	**1 pineapple, peeled, cored,**
2 cups sugar	**and cut into ½-in slices**
2 cups water	**¼ cup orange liqueur**

1.   Julienne the orange rind and set aside. Peel off the white pith and discard. Slice the orange.

2.   In a saucepan, simmer the sugar and water for 1 minute. Add the orange rind, orange slices, and pineapple and poach for 5 to 10 minutes, or until the pineapple is tender.

3. With a slotted spoon, remove the fruit to a bowl. Simmer the sauce until slightly thickened. Remove from the heat and stir in the orange liqueur. Pour over the fruit. Serve warm or cold.

Yields 6 servings

Can be prepared the day before serving.

ANANAS AU RHUM (Pineapple with Rum)

This is a particularly delicious method to use with most fruits. Change the liquor to suit your taste.

6 tablespoons Clarified Butter, page 4	Sugar, to taste
1 pineapple, peeled, cored, and cut into ½-in slices	2 tablespoons butter
	¼ cup rum

1. In a large skillet, heat the clarified butter and sauté the pineapple slices until golden on both sides. Sprinkle with the sugar and add the 2 table-spoons of butter.

2. Cook, shaking the pan, until the sugar starts to caramelize. Add the rum and ignite. Serve immediately.

Yields 6 servings

PINEAPPLE FLAMBÉ

¼ cup sugar	1½ cups currant jelly
½ cup sherry	½ cup Cognac
½ cup water	Vanilla ice cream
1 pineapple, peeled, cored, and thinly sliced	Almond Macaroon crumbs, page 26, for garnish

1. In a saucepan, simmer the sugar, sherry and water for 3 minutes. Poach the pineapple for 5 minutes. Drain the pineapple.

2. In a skillet, melt the jelly and add the pineapple slices. Cook, basting the pineapple with the jelly, for 5 minutes longer.

3. Add the Cognac to the pan, and ignite. Spoon the flaming Cognac over the pineapple. Serve the hot fruit over ice cream and sprinkle with the macaroon crumbs, if desired.

Yields 6 servings

Can be prepared ahead and reheated just before serving.

ANANAS BRULÉES (Broiled Pineapple)

¼ **cup butter**	¼ **teaspoon almond extract**
1¼ **cups dark brown sugar**	2 **pineapples, quartered**
½ **cup dark rum**	**lengthwise, with fronds**
½ **teaspoon lemon juice**	**intact**

1. In a saucepan, cook the butter, 1 cup of sugar, rum, lemon juice, and almond extract, stirring, for 10 minutes.

2. Cut the flesh free from the skin of each pineapple section. Cut into 1-inch slices. (See Chapter 2.)

3. Preheat the broiler. Wrap the fronds with foil and place the pineapple quarters on a baking sheet. Spoon the sauce over each pineapple section. Sprinkle with the remaining sugar and broil until the mixture begins to bubble. Remove the foil and serve.

Yields 8 servings

Can be prepared for broiling several hours ahead.

NOTE: Watch carefully when broiling; the sugar burns quickly.

PIÑA NATILLAS (Baked Pineapple)

1 **pineapple, cut as a**	¼ **cup butter**
container, page 55	2 **cups cold Vanilla Custard**
¼ **cup sugar**	**Sauce, page 545**
2–3 **tablespoons rum**	

1. Preheat the oven to 350° F.

2. Cut the flesh of the pineapple into bite-sized pieces and place in a bowl. Mix in the sugar and rum. Fill the pineapple shell with the mixture and dot with the butter. Place on a baking sheet and bake for 20 minutes.

3. Serve immediately with cold sauce on the side.

Yields 6 servings

Can be prepared for baking the day before serving.

ANANASSO AL CIOCCOLATO
(Glazed Pineapple with Chocolate Sauce)

1 pineapple	¾ cups heavy cream, whipped
2 cups confectioners' sugar	2 tablespoons slivered
½ cup dark rum	almonds
3 tablespoons kirsch	2 cups Salsa al Cioccolato,
3 tablespoons orange liqueur	page 541
1 pint vanilla ice cream	

1. Peel and core the pineapple and cut into 6 slices.

2. In a skillet, cook the pineapple slices, over moderate heat, with the sugar, rum, and kirsch until the juices start to turn golden. Transfer the pineapple slices to dessert bowls. Pour ½ tablespoon of orange liqueur over each slice and top with ice cream and whipped cream. Sprinkle with the almonds and serve with the sauce.

Yields 6 servings

Can be prepared the day before serving.

ANANAS CRÈME CHANTILLY
(Pineapple with Cream)

1 pineapple, peeled, cored,	1 teaspoon kirsch
and cut into slices,	Sugar, to taste
reserving the juice	Crystallized violets, for
1 cup heavy cream	garnish
1 vanilla bean, split	

1. Arrange the pineapple slices on a platter.

2. Pour the reserved juice into a bowl with the cream. Scrape the vanilla seeds into the cream and add the kirsch. Beat until stiff peaks form, adding sugar, to taste.

3. Using a pastry bag fitted with a #5 open star tip, pipe the whipped cream onto the pineapple slices or dollop with a spoon, and garnish with the violets.

Yields 6 servings

The pineapple and cream can be prepared the day before, but assemble just before serving.

ANANAS SURPRISE
(Stuffed Pineapple)

1 pineapple, cut into a container, page 55	6 ounces candied cherries
1 grapefruit, cut into sections	½ cup maraschino liqueur or kirsch
2 oranges, cut into sections	½ cup sugar
2 apples, peeled and diced	

1. Cut the pineapple pieces left over from creating the pineapple container into ¾-inch cubes.

2. In a bowl, mix the grapefruit, oranges, apples, pineapple cubes, cherries, maraschino liqueur, and sugar. Macerate for at least 10 minutes.

3. Fill the pineapple shell, replace the top, and chill until ready to serve.

Yields 6 servings

Can be prepared the day before serving.

Variation

• Substitute 2 apricots, pitted and diced; 4 cherries, pitted and halved; 1 peach, peeled, pitted, and diced; and 4 strawberries, sliced, in place of the citrus and apple.

APPLE, PINEAPPLE, AND PAPAYA MÉLANGE

3 small pineapples, halved
1 papaya, peeled and diced
1 apple, thinly sliced

1. Cut the flesh from each pineapple half, leaving a ½-inch-thick shell. Cut the pineapple flesh into bite-sized pieces and mix with the papaya and the apple.

2. Refill the pineapple shells with the fruit.

Yields 6 servings

Chill for up to 6 hours before serving.

ANANAS ET FRAISES CRÉOLE
(Pineapple Creole-style)

1 large pineapple
3 tablespoons plus 1
teaspoon kirsch
2 tablespoons sugar
1 pint strawberries, hulled

Sugar, to taste
½ cup heavy cream, whipped,
sweetened and flavored with
kirsch, page 11

1. Cut the pineapple into quarters or sixths, lengthwise, through the frond. Remove the pulp and cut into thin slices. Put the slices into a bowl and sprinkle with 3 tablespoons of kirsch and the 2 tablespoons of sugar. Mix gently. Chill the slices and the shells, covered, until serving time.

2. Arrange the pineapple shells on a platter and set the slices back into the shells.

3. In a processor, puree the strawberries. Strain the puree and sweeten with sugar, to taste. Coat the pineapple slices with the strawberry puree.

4. Using a pastry bag fitted with a #5A star tip, pipe rosettes of whipped cream down the center of each serving.

Yields 4 to 6 servings

The fruit can be prepared the day before serving.

CHISTERA AUX FRUITS
(Pineapple Baskets)

2 pineapples, cut into thirds
lengthwise
3 bananas, quartered
lengthwise and halved
½ cup maraschino liqueur

½ cup apricot brandy
¾ cup white rum
10 tablespoons sugar
1 quart vanilla ice cream

1. Cut the pulp from the pineapple, leaving ¼-inch-thick shells. Cut the pulp into wedges.

2. In a skillet, warm the pineapple, bananas, maraschino, apricot brandy, ½ cup of rum, and the sugar. Spoon the hot fruit into the shells and top with the ice cream.

3. In a saucepan, warm the remaining rum and ignite. Pour, flaming, over the ice cream and fruits.

Yields 6 servings

Best prepared just before serving.

PLUMS ORIENTAL-STYLE

12 plums, halved and pitted	**¼ cup honey**
24 walnut or pecan halves	**Brown sugar, for garnish**
1 cup plain yogurt	

1. Place the plums, cut side up, on a serving platter or individual plates. Put a walnut in the center of each half.

2. In a bowl, mix the yogurt and honey and spoon over the plums. Chill until ready to serve.

3. Just before serving, sprinkle with brown sugar.

Yields 6 servings

Can be prepared several hours before serving.

POACHED PLUMS IN PORT

2 pounds plums, pitted	**orange rind**
2 cups tawny port	**1 cinnamon stick**
⅔ cup sugar	**6 whole cloves**
2 tablespoons julienned	**1 cup heavy cream, whipped**

1. In a saucepan, simmer the plums, port, sugar, orange rind, cinnamon stick, and cloves until tender, about 10 minutes. Discard the cinnamon and cloves. Refrigerate.

2. Pass the whipped cream separately.

Yields 6 servings

Can be prepared the day before serving.

PRUNES SUEDOISE
(Plums Swedish-style)

1½ pounds plums, halved and pitted	1 tablespoon gelatin
½ cup sugar	12 blanched almonds
2 cups cold water	Custard Sauce, page 545, or heavy cream

1. In a saucepan, poach the plums in the sugar and 1½ cups of water until tender. Drain, reserving the syrup. Set 12 of the best-looking plum halves aside.

2. In a processor, puree the remaining fruit with 1 cup of reserved poaching syrup.

3. In a small saucepan, sprinkle gelatin over ½ cup of cold poaching liquid; let soften. Stir into the plum puree. Heat until the gelatin dissolves.

4. Place a blanched almond into each reserved plum half and place, cut side down, in a 1-quart mold. Add the puree and chill at least 4 hours, or until set.

5. Unmold and serve with custard sauce or cream, if desired.

Yields 6 servings

Can be prepared the day before serving.

CROUTES AU PRUNES (Plum Toasts)

This is one of the easiest and most delicious desserts. It is suitable for family and the most particular of guests.

6 (½-in) slices bread	6 tablespoons brown sugar
¾ cup butter	
12–18 plums, halved and pitted	

1. Preheat the oven to 350° F. Butter the bread on both sides and arrange in a baking dish. Crowd 4 to 5 plum halves on each slice and dot with remaining butter.

2. Sprinkle with the sugar and press down gently. Cover lightly with foil and bake until the bread slices are golden and crispy and the plums are coated with a sugary syrup, about 30 minutes. If necessary, bake 10 minutes without the foil.

Yields 6 servings

Can be prepared for baking several hours ahead.

Variation

• Substitute peaches, apricots, nectarines, pears, or apples for the plums.

PURPLE PLUM COMPOTE WITH CARAMEL CRACKLE

1¼ cups sugar	1 (1-in) slice lemon
3¼ cups water	½ cup ruby port
1 vanilla bean, split	Crème Fraîche, page 39, or
12 purple plums	sour cream
1 (2-in) slice orange	

1.   Lightly oil a 9-inch pie pan. In a small saucepan, boil ½ cup of sugar and ¼ cup of water until it caramelizes. Pour onto the pie pan and, holding the pan with pot holders, tilt to spread in an even layer. Set aside to cool. (See page 5.)

2.   In another saucepan, simmer the remaining water and sugar and the vanilla bean for 5 minutes, or until the syrup thickens slightly. Add the plums, orange and lemon slices, and the port, and poach until the plums are tender, about 5 minutes. Refrigerate in the syrup. Remove and discard the vanilla bean and the orange and lemon slices.

3.   Arrange the plums and syrup in dessert bowls. With the handle of a heavy knife, tap the caramel and break into small pieces. Sprinkle the caramel pieces over each serving. Pass the crème fraîche separately.

Yields 6 servings

Can be prepared the day before serving.

BAKED QUINCE

6 quinces, peeled	½ cup butter, softened
Lemon juice	1¼ cups heavy cream
1½ cups sugar	

1.   Preheat the oven to 375° F. Cut the quince and remove cores from the tops, about three-quarters of the way to the bottom. Sprinkle with lemon juice and stand in a buttered baking dish.

2.   In a bowl, beat ⅔ cup of sugar, the butter, and 3 tablespoons of cream. Fill the quinces with the mixture.

3.   Bake 30 minutes. Add ⅓ cup of sugar and 1 tablespoon of cream to the baking pan. Bake until tender, about 30 minutes longer. Sprinkle with the remaining sugar and pass the remaining cream. Serve warm.

Yields 6 servings

Can be prepared ahead and reheated.

QUINCE COMPOTE

6 quinces, peeled, cored, and sliced	1 cinnamon stick
3 cups water	2 whole cloves
2 cups sugar	1 tablespoon lemon juice

In a saucepan, simmer the quinces with the water, sugar, cinnamon stick, cloves, and lemon juice until tender, about 1 hour. Cool and discard cinnamon stick and cloves.

Yields 6 servings

Can be prepared up to 2 days before serving.

RASPBERRIES IN SHERRY CREAM

2 eggs, separated	½ teaspoon almond extract
2 tablespoons sugar	Pinch of salt
1 cup heavy cream, scalded	1 quart raspberries, chilled
2 tablespoons dry sherry	

1.   In a saucepan, beat the egg yolks and sugar until thickened and pale. Slowly pour in the hot cream, beating constantly.

2.   Heat, beating constantly until the mixture is smooth and thickened. Remove from the heat.

3. Stir in the sherry, almond extract, and salt. Beat the egg whites until stiff, but not dry, and fold into the hot sauce. Serve the warm sauce over the raspberries.

Yields 6 servings

Prepare just before serving.

RASPBERRIES HAMILTON

In the backwoods of Maine, Bill Hamilton created this marvelous dessert when he found a bramble of wild raspberries.

1½ quarts raspberries	**Heavy cream, sour cream,**
¼ cup honey	**plain yogurt, or cream,**
1 tablespoon lemon juice	**whipped**

1. In a saucepan, mix 2 cups of raspberries, the honey, and lemon juice, and bring to a boil, stirring constantly.

2. Arrange the remaining raspberries in dessert glasses and spoon the hot sauce over them. Pass the cream or yogurt separately.

Yields 6 servings

NOTE: You can substitute strawberries, blueberries, or blackberries, but raspberries are best.

RASPBERRY BRULÉE WITH BASIL

1 quart raspberries	**3 cups cold Sabayon Sauce,**
½ cup lightly packed basil	**page 544, flavored with 2**
leaves	**tablespoons of framboise**
¾ cup heavy cream	**6 tablespoons sugar**

1. Preheat the broiler.

2. In a processor, puree 1½ cups of the raspberries with the basil. Press through a sieve, discarding the seeds.

3. In a bowl, beat the cream until soft peaks form. Fold into the sabayon sauce with the raspberry and basil puree.

4. Divide the remaining raspberries and the sauce among six ramekins, custard cups, or put all in a gratin pan.

5. Spoon the sauce over the raspberries and sprinkle with the sugar. Broil until just lightly browned, taking care not to burn the sugar. Serve at once.

Yields 6 servings

Can be prepared for broiling 2 hours before serving.

STEWED RHUBARB

6 cups sliced rhubarb
Juice of 1 orange
¾ cup sugar

1. In a saucepan, cook the rhubarb, orange juice, and sugar over low heat, stirring occasionally for 15 minutes, or until tender.

2. Serve warm or cold.

Yields 6 servings

Can be prepared several days before serving.

Variation

• Omit orange juice. Refrigerate until cold and fold in 1 cup of sliced strawberries, raspberries, or blueberries.

FRAGOLE AL LIMONE (Strawberries with Lemon)

1½ quarts strawberries, hulled
½–1 cup confectioners' sugar
Juice of 2 lemons

1. In a large bowl, crush ½ cup of strawberries and stir in the sugar and lemon juice, to taste.

2. Fold in the remaining strawberries. Refrigerate until ready to serve.

Yields 6 servings

Can be prepared up to 6 hours before serving.

FRAISES AUX LIQUEURS
(Strawberries in Liqueurs)

1 quart strawberries, hulled and sliced	2 tablespoons Cognac
½ cup confectioners' sugar	10 × 15-in Sponge Cake, page 19
1 tablespoon Cointreau	Cream, whipped and
1 tablespoon kirsch	sweetened, for garnish

1. In a bowl, mix the strawberries with the sugar. Pour on the Cointreau, kirsch, and Cognac, and mix gently. Chill for 3 to 4 hours.

2. Cut six 3-inch circles from the sponge cake and place on serving plates. Spoon the strawberries over each circle of sponge cake and garnish with whipped cream.

Yields 6 servings

Can be prepared up to 6 hours before serving.

Variation

• Substitute any favorite berry, or use sliced peaches, nectarines, or cactus pears.

FRAISES AU RHUM
(Strawberries with Rum Custard)

2 cups cold Custard Sauce, page 545	1 pint strawberries, hulled
¼ cup light brown sugar	1 pint vanilla ice cream, softened
2 tablespoons rum	

1. Mix the custard sauce with the brown sugar and the rum.

2. Arrange the strawberries in a bowl and cover with scoops of softened ice cream. Pour sauce over all.

Yields 6 servings.

The custard sauce can be prepared the day before serving.

FRAISES CORDON BLEU I
(Strawberries Cordon Bleu I)

6 sugar cubes

1 large orange

¼ cup Cognac

1½ pints strawberries, hulled

1. Rub the sugar cubes over the orange rind until saturated with oil from the orange.

2. In a bowl, crush the sugar cubes, add the juice from the orange, and the Cognac. Stir until the sugar dissolves. Pour over the strawberries and chill for 2 to 3 hours before serving.

Yields 6 servings

Can be prepared up to 8 hours before serving.

FRAISES CORDON BLEU II
(Strawberries Cordon Bleu II)

1½ pints strawberries, hulled
and sliced

¾ cup Almond Macaroon
crumbs, page 26

Grated rind and juice of 1
orange

2 tablespoons sugar

1 cup heavy cream

1. In a serving bowl, layer the berries and macaroon crumbs. Moisten with half the orange juice.

2. In another bowl, mix the remaining orange juice, orange rind, and sugar. Stir until the sugar dissolves.

3. Whip the cream until stiff peaks form and fold into the orange syrup. Spoon onto the berries. Chill 1 hour before serving.

Yields 6 servings

Can be prepared up to 6 hours before serving.

FRAISES À LA CARDINALE
(Strawberries with Cardinal Sauce)

1½ pints strawberries, hulled
1½ cups Cardinal Sauce, page 554

6 tablespoons chopped toasted almonds

1. Arrange the strawberries in a bowl.

2. Spoon the sauce over the strawberries and sprinkle with almonds.

Yields 6 servings

Can be prepared up to 6 hours before serving.

STRAWBERRIES WITH COINTREAU AND PISTACHIOS

1½ pints strawberries, hulled
⅓ cup Cointreau
Sugar, to taste

¼ cup chopped pistachios

1. In a serving bowl, macerate the strawberries, Cointreau, and sugar, to taste. Chill until ready to serve.

2. Sprinkle with the pistachios just before serving.

Yields 6 servings

Can be prepared up to 2 hours before serving.

FRAISES MARINÉES AUX CALVADOS
(Strawberries Marinated in Calvados)

1 quart small strawberries, hulled
2 tablespoons Calvados

¼ cup sugar
1 cup heavy cream
Cinnamon

1. In a bowl, macerate the strawberries in the Calvados for 1 hour.

2. Add the sugar and mix gently.

3. Whip the cream to stiff peaks and spread in the center of each plate. Sprinkle the edges of the cream with cinnamon and place the strawberries in the center.

Yields 6 servings

Assemble just before serving.

STRAWBERRIES WITH GRAND MARNIER SAUCE

This is one of the best fruit-and-sauce combinations. Be sure to try it.

1 quart strawberries, hulled
2 cups Grand Marnier Sauce,
 page 545

1. Halve the strawberries and refrigerate until cold.

2. Arrange the berries in serving dishes and coat with the sauce.

Yields 6 servings

The sauce can be prepared the day before serving.

STRAWBERRIES ROMANOFF I

1 quart strawberries, hulled	**1 cup vanilla ice cream,**
6 tablespoons Cointreau	**softened**
2 tablespoons sugar	**1 teaspoon lemon juice**
½ cup heavy cream	

1. In a bowl, macerate the berries with the Cointreau and sugar for 1 hour.

2. In a bowl, whip the cream until stiff peaks form.

3. In another bowl, with a whisk, whip the ice cream until smooth. Fold in the lemon juice, whipped cream, strawberries, and their juices. Transfer to a serving bowl or dessert dishes.

Yields 6 servings

Assemble just before serving.

STRAWBERRIES ROMANOFF II

Grated rind and juice of 1 orange	**1 cup heavy cream**
2 tablespoons sugar	**2 pints strawberries, hulled and halved**

1. In a bowl, mix the orange rind, juice, and sugar, until the sugar dissolves.

2. Whip the cream until it forms soft peaks and fold in the orange mixture. Fold in the strawberries and spoon into a serving bowl or dessert dishes. Chill for 30 minutes.

Yields 6 servings

Can be prepared 2 hours before serving.

STRAWBERRIES IN RASPBERRY CREAM

1½ pints strawberries, hulled	**1 cup raspberries**
Juice of ½ orange	**¼ cup confectioners' sugar**
1 tablespoon kirsch	**1½ cups heavy cream**
Sugar, to taste	

1. In a bowl, mix the strawberries, orange juice, kirsch, and sugar, to taste. Cover and chill.

2. In a processor, puree the raspberries and strain through a sieve, discarding the seeds. Stir in the confectioners' sugar and set aside.

3. In a bowl, beat the cream until it holds soft peaks and fold in the raspberry puree. Spoon over the strawberries.

Yields 6 servings

Strawberries and raspberry puree can be prepared the day before. Do not assemble until shortly before serving.

FRAGOLE AL ACETO
(Strawberries with Vinegar)

1½ pints strawberries, hulled	**Confectioners' sugar**
1 cup red or white wine	
2 tablespoons white vinegar	

1. In a bowl, swirl the strawberries and the wine, and let stand for 5 minutes.

2. Drain the berries. Discard the wine and any grit.

3. Return the strawberries to the bowl and sprinkle with the vinegar and sugar. Mix gently.

Yields 6 servings

Can be prepared up to 6 hours before serving.

PICKLED STRAWBERRIES

2 pints strawberries, hulled	**2 teaspoons balsamic vinegar**
2 tablespoons sugar	**1 bottle, dry, sparkling wine**
Pinch of cinnamon	

1. In a bowl, mix the strawberries, sugar, and cinnamon. Macerate for 30 minutes, stirring 2 or 3 times.

2. Sprinkle with the vinegar and mix. Refrigerate until ready to serve.

3. Distribute the strawberries in goblets and pour the wine over the berries.

Yields 6 servings

Can be prepared up to 6 hours before serving. Add the wine just before serving.

STRAWBERRIES FLAMBÉ

2 tablespoons butter	**2 tablespoons orange liqueur**
2 tablespoons sugar	
2 pints strawberries, hulled	

1. In a skillet, cook the butter and sugar until the sugar dissolves and thickens slightly. Add the strawberries and heat.

2. Add the liqueur, and ignite. Serve.

Yields 6 servings

Serve plain, or with crepes, ice cream, or whipped cream, if desired.

TANGERINES IN KIRSCH

6 tangerines, peeled and	Confectioners' sugar, to
separated into segments	taste
2 tablespoons kirsch	

1.   Arrange the tangerines in serving dishes and sprinkle with the kirsch and sugar, to taste.

2.   Macerate for at least 2 hours before serving.

Yields 6 servings

Can be prepared the day before serving.

SHERRIED WATERMELON

4 cups cubed watermelon,	1 cup dry sherry
seeded	Mint leaves, for garnish
¼ cup sugar	

1.   In a bowl, mix the watermelon with the sugar and sherry and macerate for 2 hours.

2.   Serve garnished with mint leaves.

Yields 6 servings

Can be prepared 24 hours before serving.

WINED WATERMELON

To add a little zest to your Fourth of July melon.

1 whole watermelon
1 bottle red wine

1.   Cut a plug from one end of the watermelon. Stand the melon on end and slowly pour in the bottle of wine. Replace the plug, sealing the opening with softened butter, if desired.

2.   Chill the melon for 24 hours, shaking once or twice.

Yields 10 to 20 servings

NOTE: Set the melon in a wok ring to stabilize it while adding the wine or even to serve it.

MACEDOINE DI FRUITS I
(Macedoine of Fruit I)

1½ cups seedless grapes	1½ cups fresh berries
1½ cups seedless orange sections	⅓ cup confectioners' sugar
	3 tablespoons Cognac
3 cups peaches or plums, pitted and sliced	3 tablespoons kirsch
	3 tablespoons orange liqueur

1. In a bowl, mix the grapes, orange sections, peaches, berries, and sugar. Refrigerate for at least 2 hours.

2. Just before serving, pour on the Cognac, kirsch, and orange liqueur.

Yields 12 servings

Can be prepared up to 24 hours before serving.

MACEDOINE DI FRUITS II
(Macedoine of Fruit II)

1 pineapple, peeled and diced	1 teaspoon minced gingerroot
½ pound peaches, peeled, pitted, and diced	1 teaspoon grated lemon rind
	¼ cup port
1 pint strawberries, halved	Sugar, to taste

In a bowl, mix the pineapple, peaches, strawberries, gingerroot, lemon rind, and port. Add sugar to taste.

Yields 12 servings

Can be made up to 24 hours in advance.

MACEDOINE DI FRUITS III
(Macedoine of Fruit III)

2 grapefruits, cut into
sections

3 oranges, cut into sections

1 small melon, cut into balls

2 pears, peeled, cored, and
sliced

½ pound plums, halved and
pitted

2 bananas, sliced

¼ pound cherries, pitted

3 peaches, peeled, pitted, and
sliced

¼ pound seedless grapes

Juice of 1 lemon

Kirsch or Cointreau

Candied Orange, Lemon,
and Lime Rinds in syrup,
page 39, reserving the
syrup

1. In a bowl, arrange the fruit in layers with grapefruit sections on the bottom and the grapes on the top. Sprinkle with the lemon juice and the kirsch. Refrigerate until serving time.

2. Just before serving, pour on ½ to 1 cup of the syrup from cooking the rinds and sprinkle with the rinds.

Yields 12 or more servings

Prepare the fruits up to 6 hours before serving, but do not add the syrup until minutes before serving; it will thin out the juices.

MACEDONIA DI FRUTTA IV
(Macedoine of Fruit IV)

2 quarts strawberries, hulled

1 pound cherries, pitted

1 pound seedless grapes,
halved

2 bananas, sliced

4 peaches, peeled, pitted, and

sliced

½ cup kirsch, or to taste

2 tablespoons confectioners'
sugar, or to taste

6 tablespoons lemon juice

1. In a bowl, mix the strawberries, cherries, grapes, bananas, and peaches. Stir in the kirsch, sugar, and lemon juice.

2. Refrigerate until ready to serve. Add more kirsch or sugar, if desired.

Yields 12 or more servings

Can be prepared up to 6 hours before serving.

Variation

• Add 1½ cups orange juice and the grated rind of 1 lemon.

MELANGE DE FRUITS
(Mixture of Fruit)

2 cups strawberries, hulled and halved, or pears or apples, sliced and cored	sugar
	2 tablespoons Grand Marnier
1 orange, cut into sections	1 tablespoon kirsch
2 tablespoons orange juice	1 tablespoon Cognac
3 tablespoons confectioners'	1 tablespoon framboise

1. In a bowl, mix the strawberries, orange sections, orange juice, and sugar. Refrigerate for at least 1 hour.

2. Just before serving, mix in the orange liqueur, kirsch, Cognac, and framboise.

Yields 6 servings

Can be prepared up to 6 hours before serving.

NOTE: Pears, peaches, grapes, oranges, cherries, strawberries, and raspberries would all work well.

MIVEH MAKHLOUT
(Persian Fruit Melange)

1 honeydew melon, cut into balls	almonds
	¼ cup chopped pistachios
1 cantaloupe, cut into balls	1 cup seedless grapes
1 pint strawberries, hulled and halved	2 tablespoons rose water
	1½ cups orange juice
2 tablespoons slivered	½ cup kirsch

In a bowl, mix the melon balls, strawberries, almonds, pistachios, grapes, rose water, orange juice, and kirsch. Macerate for up to 6 hours before serving.

Yields 6 to 8 servings

Can be prepared up to 6 hours before serving.

FRUITS AU VIN ROUGE
(Fruit in Red Wine)

1¼ cups dry red wine
½ cup water
3 tablespoons sugar
1 vanilla bean, split
   lengthwise
6 cups assorted fresh fruits,
in season (pears, peaches,
grapes, oranges, cherries,
strawberries, raspberries,
etc.)
6 mint leaves, for garnish

1. In a saucepan, simmer the wine until reduced by half. Add the water, sugar, and vanilla bean. Simmer 2 minutes longer. Refrigerate until cold.

2. Prepare the fruits and put into a bowl. Add the wine and refrigerate for at least 1 hour.

3. Discard the vanilla bean and garnish with the mint leaves.

Yields 6 servings

Can be prepared the day before serving.

TERRINE OF FRUITS

This is an excellent dessert for large crowds. You can prepare it easily and ahead of time. The slices are colorful and, of course, it tastes wonderful.

5 teaspoons gelatin
1½ cups milk
1 vanilla bean, split
   lengthwise
1 cup plus 2 tablespoons
   sugar
4 egg yolks
1 cup heavy cream
2 cups peeled and cubed
   peaches
½ pint raspberries
¾ cup strawberries, hulled and
   halved, if large
¾ cup blackberries
2 cups Raspberry Sauce, page
   552

1. Line a 9 × 5-inch loaf pan with plastic wrap and oil lightly. In a small bowl, sprinkle the gelatin over ½ cup of milk and let soften.

2.   In a heavy saucepan, heat the remaining milk, the vanilla bean, and 1 cup of sugar, stirring until the sugar dissolves and the milk is scalded. Set aside.

3.   In a bowl, whisk the egg yolks with the remaining sugar until thickened and pale. Whisk in the hot milk and mix well. Return the yolk mixture into the saucepan and cook, stirring over medium heat, until thick enough to coat the back of a spoon, about 180° F. DO NOT BOIL. Strain into a clean bowl and stir in the softened gelatin. Refrigerate until it is cold, and it barely starts to mound when dropped from a spoon.

4.   In a bowl, whip the cream until soft peaks form and fold into the custard. Gently fold in the fruit and pour into the prepared pan. Bang once or twice on the counter to remove any air holes. Chill until set, at least 4 hours.

5.   Unmold onto a chilled platter. Cut into ¾-inch-thick slices and serve with the raspberry sauce.

Yields 10 to 12 servings

Can be prepared the day before serving.

FRUITES FRAIS À LA GELÉE D'AMANDE (Fresh Fruit with Almond Jelly)

This is a French version of a Chinese standard. For an Asian effect, serve with arbutus, lychee, and loquats (see Note).

1½ teaspoons gelatin	3 cups assorted fruits
1 tablespoon cold water	(berries, cherries, grapes,
½ cup milk	oranges, pears, apples,
½ teaspoon almond extract	etc.)

1.   In a bowl, soften the gelatin in the water.

2.   In a saucepan, bring the milk to a simmer and pour over the gelatin, stirring until it dissolves. Stir in the almond extract and pour into a 7-inch cake pan. Chill until set, at least 3 hours.

3.   Arrange the fruits on a serving platter or on individual plates. Cut the almond mixture into diagonals, squares, rectangles, or other shapes, and place on the platter.

Yields 6 servings

The almond mixture can be prepared the day before. Prepare the fruit no more than 2 hours before serving.

NOTE: Canned arbutus, lychee, and loquats are available in Asian markets.

BROILED FRUIT WITH PASTRY CREAM BRÛLÉ

4 cups assorted fruits
    (blueberries, strawberries,
    pears, cherries, grapes,
    oranges, etc.)
2 tablespoons superfine

sugar
2 tablespoons framboise,
    kirsch, or orange liqueur
1 cup Pastry Cream, page 26
¼ cup dark brown sugar

1. Preheat the broiler.

2. Prepare the fruits and mix in a bowl with the sugar and liqueur. Spoon into individual ramekins or a 1-quart, shallow, ovenproof serving dish and coat with the pastry cream.

3. Sprinkle with the sugar. Broil until the sugar melts and browns.

Yields 6 servings

Can be prepared for broiling 2 hours before serving.

GRATIN DE FRUITS
(Broiled Fruits with Sabayon Sauce)

This is a more sophisticated version of the previous recipe.

3 peaches or pears, peeled,
    pitted or cored, and sliced
2 tablespoons lemon juice
2 oranges, peeled and
    sectioned

1 pint strawberries
½ cup brown sugar
1½ cups Sabayon Sauce, page
    544

1. Preheat the broiler.

2. In a bowl, mix the peaches with the lemon juice. Drain. Add the oranges and strawberries, and refrigerate until ready to serve.

3. When ready to serve, arrange the fruit in ramekins or a 1-quart shallow ovenproof serving dish and top with the sauce. Broil until golden.

Yields 6 servings

Assemble just before serving.

WARM FRUIT COMPOTE

The perfect winter dessert, and a far better choice than woody strawberries, rock-hard pears, and other out-of-season fruit.

2 **apples, peeled, cored, and sliced**	½ **teaspoon ground cloves**
12 **ounces pitted prunes**	2 **pears, peeled, cored, and sliced**
6 **dried figs, quartered**	2 **oranges, peeled and sectioned**
6 **ounces dried apricots**	1 **cup seedless grapes**
½ **cup water**	**Heavy cream, plain yogurt,**
⅓ **cup apple juice**	**or sour cream**
Juice of 1 lemon	
2–3 **cinnamon sticks**	

1. In a saucepan, simmer the apples, prunes, figs, apricots, water, apple juice, lemon juice, cinnamon sticks, and cloves, for 5 minutes.

2. Add the pears and cook until the fruit is tender. Just before serving, stir in the orange sections and grapes. Discard the cinnamon sticks. Pass the cream or yogurt, if desired.

Yields 6 or more servings

Can be prepared the day before and reheated.

Variation

• Substitute 4 sliced, dried, pear halves, for the fresh pears, and simmer with the other dried fruit.

Chapter 4

CREAMS, FOOLS, SNOWS, AND WHIPS

Every couple of decades these old-fashioned desserts, forgotten or unknown by many cooks, reappear to be rediscovered and praised for their simplicity and goodness. Most often they need only a fruit puree and a whipped egg white or some cream to finish the dessert.

Once cooks carefully distinguished among these various desserts. Today many cooks confuse the names, because the dish reminds them of a snow or a cream, even if it might truly be a whip or a fool. Do not worry about the name, just enjoy them all.

You can prepare some of them ahead, while you must serve others immediately to maintain their airiness. Gelatin or freezing helps to keep some others stable. The creative cook will quickly see how to create a signature dessert using what is in season. Do not hesitate to exchange one fruit for another, or one liqueur for another.

Creams

Usually fruit is not folded in, but surrounds the unmolded cream. The foundation of the cream may be whipped cream and cheese or egg whites. Although gelatin firms some creams, others need to be drained to make them firm enough to hold a shape. Use special baskets of wicker or porcelain to mold these desserts or drain them in a colander. Porcelain or pottery pudding molds suit hot desserts, but their thick walls make unmolding cold desserts difficult.

To Prepare a Basket to Drain Creams. Cut two sheets of very fine cheesecloth, large enough to line the bottom and sides of the basket or a colander. Wring out the cheesecloth in cold water and line the basket. Fill the basket with the cream and set over a bowl or baking pan. Lift the edges of the cheesecloth over the cream and drain for at least 6 hours and up to 36 hours. The longer the cream drains, the drier and firmer it will become. To serve, unmold the cream onto a serving platter and remove the cheesecloth. Some chefs pour a coating of heavy cream over the top before garnishing with seasonal fruits. You decide if you want that further enrichment.

Fools

Fools, from the French *fouler* meaning "to crush," are among the simplest of desserts to prepare. Puree a fresh fruit or simmer any fruit in a little water until tender. Strain the fruit, sweeten to taste, and chill completely. Some recipes suggest adding cornstarch to the cooked fruit just before it finishes cooking to make a thicker puree. You prepare the fruit several days before serving. For each cup of fruit, add 2 cups of whipped cream, folding them together so the fruit creates a marbled effect. Serve individually in parfait glasses, wine glasses, or, for a party, in a large glass bowl.

Snows

Snows are the same as whips, except that dissolved gelatin, folded into the mixture, provides greater stability. Fruit juices, especially citrus juices, flavor snows. Plan to use a pretty bowl as the mold and serve in scoops, or prepare individual servings in your prettiest glasses or individual bowls.

Whips

The difference between fools and whips is that whipped cream holds the fruit together in fools and stiffly beaten egg whites hold the fruit in a whip. Because the egg whites are more delicate, plan to serve the whips within a few hours or they may lose their fluffiness. Prune whip, which gets baked, is the exception to the rule. You may bake other whips for greater stability, but you lose a certain freshness. Serve them in parfait glasses or wine glasses. The mixture does not bear up to scooping once assembled, so do not serve from a large bowl.

CRÈME LOUISA

1 tablespoon gelatin	½ teaspoon almond extract
2 tablespoons cold water	2 tablespoons Cognac or
1 cup heavy cream	Cointreau
½ cup milk	3 cups crushed and sweet-
½ cup sugar	ened berries, peaches,
Pinch of salt	apricots, etc., for garnish
1 cup sour cream	

1. In a small bowl, soften the gelatin in the water.

2. In a saucepan, beat the cream, milk, sugar, and salt over low heat until the sugar dissolves. Stir the gelatin into the hot cream mixture until it dissolves.

3. Remove from the heat, let cool 5 minutes, and whisk in the sour cream until smooth. Stir in the almond extract and the Cognac. Pour into six ½-cup bowls and chill about 4 hours, or until set.

4. Unmold and garnish with the fruit of your choice.

Yields 6 servings

Can be prepared the day before serving.

COEUR À LA CRÈME (Cream Heart)

If you do not have the special heart-shaped dessert mold, drain the cheese in a colander or a sieve and unmold onto a platter. You may pat it into a heart shape.

1 pound cottage cheese	2 cups heavy cream
1 pound cream cheese,	3–4 cups strawberries,
softened	raspberries, or other fresh
Pinch of salt	fruit, for garnish

1. Line a 6-cup *Coeur à la Créme* mold, six 1-cup molds, or a colander with cheesecloth.

2. Force the cottage cheese through a sieve or a food mill into a bowl. Beat in the cream cheese and the salt until smooth. Beat in the heavy cream until smooth. Turn into the mold and drain overnight in the refrigerator.

3.   When ready to serve, unmold onto a serving platter. Surround with fruit.

Yields 6 to 8 servings

Can be prepared up to 36 hours before unmolding and serving.

Variations

• Substitute chèvre or Roquefort for part or all the cottage cheese.
• For a sweeter cheese, add sugar to taste when adding the salt.
• Flavor unsweetened leftover cheese with 1 to 2 tablespoons minced herbs and perhaps a clove of minced garlic. Serve as an hors d'oeuvre.

ANGELA PIA (Angel Cream)

3 eggs, separated	¼ cup cold water
½ cup sugar	1 cup heavy cream, whipped
2 tablespoons Cognac	1 teaspoon vanilla
2 tablespoons rum	Seasonal fruits, or fruit
1 tablespoon gelatin	sauces, for garnish

1.   In a bowl, beat the egg yolks and the sugar until thickened and pale in color. Beat in the Cognac and the rum.

2.   In a small saucepan, soften the gelatin in the water. Heat over low heat, stirring until the gelatin dissolves. Stir into the egg yolk mixture.

3.   In a clean bowl, beat the egg whites until stiff. Fold into the yolk mixture with the whipped cream and the vanilla. Pour into sherbet glasses and chill about 2 hours, or until set.

4.   Serve with fruits or fruit sauces of your choice.

Yields 6 servings

Can be prepared the day before serving.

CREMETS D'ANGERS
(Molded Cream)

1½ cups heavy cream
3 egg whites
3–4 cups fresh berries

1. Line a sieve or heart-shaped *Coeur à la Crème* mold with cheesecloth.

2. In a bowl, beat 1 cup of cream until stiff. In another bowl, beat the egg whites until almost stiff and fold into the cream. Pour into the mold and drain overnight in the refrigerator.

3. When ready to serve, unmold onto a serving platter. Pour on the remaining cream. Garnish with the berries.

Yields 6 servings

Can be prepared the day before serving.

FONDANT DE NOIX AU CHOCOLAT
(Walnut Fondant with Chocolate Sauce)

4 egg yolks	1 cup plus 2 tablespoons
1½ cups confectioners' sugar	butter, softened
2½ teaspoons cornstarch	3 cups finely chopped walnuts
2½ teaspoons flour	Walnut halves, for garnish
5 tablespoons kirsch	Chocolate Sauce, page 540
1½ cups heavy cream	

1. Line the bottom of a 1-quart charlotte mold with parchment. In a bowl, beat the egg yolks and ¼ cup of sugar until they are thickened and pale. Beat in the cornstarch and the flour. Blend in the kirsch.

2. In a saucepan, bring the cream to a boil. Stir into the yolk mixture. Return to the saucepan and cook, stirring constantly, until it just comes to a boil and thickens. Refrigerate, covered, until slightly thickened.

3.   Using an electric mixer, cream the butter and the remaining sugar until smooth.

4.   Beat in the cooled cream mixture and fold in the walnuts. Pour into the mold and refrigerate about 4 hours, or until fully set.

5.   Unmold and garnish with walnut halves. Serve with sauce.

Yields 8 servings

Can be prepared up to 2 days before serving.

COUNTRY CHEESE WITH BERRIES

1 quart sour cream	**1 cup sugar**
6 egg yolks	**3–4 1-in strips of lemon rind**
8 ounces cream cheese,	**1 pint raspberries, or other**
softened	**berries**

1.   Place a strainer over a bowl and line with cheesecloth.

2.   In a saucepan, heat the sour cream until hot, but not boiling.

3.   In a bowl, beat the egg yolks with 1 cup of hot sour cream. Beat in the cream cheese and the sugar. Stir in the remaining hot sour cream and the lemon rind. Return to the saucepan and cook, over low heat, stirring, until thickened. Do not boil. Remove from the heat. Place the saucepan in a larger pan of hot water for 15 minutes. Discard the lemon peel.

4.   Pour the cheese mixture into the strainer and drain at room temperature for 2 hours. Cover the cheese with the ends of the cloth and drain for 24 hours in the refrigerator. Turn onto a serving platter. Serve garnished with the berries.

Yields 6 servings

Can be prepared 2 days before serving.

POMMES À LA NEIGE (Apple Snow)

6 apples, Cortland or Rome Beauties	¼ cup sugar
2 teaspoons gelatin	Grated rind and juice of 1 lemon
1½ tablespoons water	3 egg whites

1. Preheat the oven to 350°F. With a sharp knife, peel a strip of skin around each apple one-third of the way from the top to help prevent the skin from bursting. Place the apples upright in a baking pan just large enough to hold them. Add ¼ inch of water to the pan. Bake for 30 minutes, or until tender. Cool.

2. In a saucepan, soften the gelatin in the water. Heat over low heat, stirring until the gelatin dissolves.

3. When the apples are cool, slice off the caps and scoop out the centers, without damaging the shells. Reserve the shells and the scooped-out pulp but discard the cores.

4. In a processor, puree the apple pulp with 2 tablespoons of sugar, the lemon rind, juice, and dissolved gelatin. Scrape into a bowl.

5. In a clean bowl, beat the egg whites until stiff with the remaining sugar. Fold into the apple mixture. Spoon the snow into the reserved apple skins and replace the caps. Refrigerate for 1 hour, or until fully set.

Yields 6 servings

Can be prepared the day before serving.

NOTE: If you do not want to use the baked apple skins, spoon the snow into glasses and serve garnished with a dollop of whipped cream.

APPLE WHIP

1 cup Apple Puree, page 28	4 egg whites
1½ tablespoons sugar, or to taste	1½ cups Custard Sauce, page 545

1. In a bowl, mix the puree and sugar.

2.   In another bowl, using an electric mixer, beat the egg whites until stiff and fold into the puree. Pour into a serving dish and chill until fully set. Serve the sauce on the side.

Yields 6 servings

Do not prepare more than 6 hours before serving.

APPLE AND PRALINE CREAM

2 **pounds McIntosh apples,** **peeled, cored, and sliced**	⅓ **cup minced crystallized** **ginger**
½ **cup honey**	1 **tablespoon gelatin**
Grated rind and juice of 1 **lemon**	¼ **cup water**
2 **tablespoons butter**	¼ **cup light rum**
1 **teaspoon vanilla**	1½ **cups heavy cream**
1 **cup Praline Powder made** **with walnuts, page 30**	⅓ **cup sugar**

1.   In a large skillet, cook the apples, honey, lemon rind, lemon juice, butter, and vanilla about 15 minutes, or until the apples are soft and the liquids evaporate. Transfer to a bowl and with a wire whisk beat to a puree. Stir in ½ cup of praline powder and the ginger.

2.   In a small saucepan, soften the gelatin in the water. Dissolve over low heat. Stir into the apples and blend in the rum. Let cool until almost set, about 30 minutes, stirring occasionally. It must not set completely.

3.   Whip the cream until it forms soft peaks. Beat in the sugar until almost stiff. Fold into the apple mixture and pour into a serving bowl.

4.   Chill about 4 hours, or until set.

5.   Sprinkle with the remaining praline powder just before serving.

Yields 6 to 8 servings

Can be prepared 1 day before serving.

CRÈME AUX ABRICOTS (Apricot Cream)

12 ounces dried apricots	**1 cup heavy cream, whipped,**
1 tablespoon gelatin	**sweetened, and flavored**
¼ cup cold water	**with vanilla, to taste**
½ cup blanched almonds	**Fresh or stewed apricots, for**
1 tablespoon milk	**garnish**

1. Lightly oil a 3-cup mold and refrigerate.

2. In a saucepan, simmer the apricots, in water to cover, 30 minutes or until tender.

3. In a processor, puree the apricots. Soften the gelatin in the water. Add to the hot puree with on/off turns. Transfer to a bowl and refrigerate. While the mixture chills, stir occasionally, until the mixture is about to set.

4. In the processor, grind the almonds and milk to a paste and stir into the apricot mixture. Fold in the whipped cream and scrape into the mold.

5. Refrigerate about 3 hours, or until set. Unmold onto a serving platter and garnish with fresh or stewed apricots.

Yields 6 servings

Can be prepared the day before serving.

NOTE: Serve with Raspberry Sauce or Chocolate Sauce (see pages 552 and 540).

BANANA WHIP WITH ORANGE SABAYON SAUCE

4 ripe bananas	**3 egg whites**
¼ cup sugar	**Pinch of salt**
½ cup orange juice	**Orange Sabayon Sauce,**
¼ cup light rum	**page 544**

1. In a processor, puree the bananas with the sugar, orange juice, and rum. Taste and add more sugar if desired.

2. In a bowl, beat the egg whites with the salt until almost stiff. Fold into the banana mixture and chill for several hours until fully set. Spoon into individual dessert dishes. Spoon the sauce over each portion.

Yields 6 servings

Can be prepared up to 6 hours before serving.

BLUEBERRY FOOL

4 cups blueberries	1½ tablespoons crème de
2 large strips lemon rind	cassis or 3 tablespoons
¾ cup sugar	orange liqueur
	2 cups heavy cream

1.   In a 2-quart saucepan, simmer the blueberries, lemon rind, and sugar for about 15 minutes, or until thick, stirring occasionally. Discard the lemon rind and puree the blueberries in a food mill or processor. The mixture should be quite thick. Refrigerate until cold. Stir in the crème de cassis.

2.   Meanwhile, in another saucepan, reduce the cream to 1 cup. Refrigerate until cold.

3.   Beat the chilled cream until it forms soft peaks. Partially fold it into the blueberry mixture to create a marbled effect. Spoon into a serving dish and chill until fully set.

Yields 6 servings

Can be prepared up to 12 hours before serving.

CHESTNUT FOOL

2 cups sweetened chestnut	1 cup heavy cream
puree, see Note	1 teaspoon vanilla
2 tablespoons maraschino	
liqueur	

1.   In a bowl, beat the chestnut puree with the maraschino liqueur until smooth.

2.   In another bowl, whip the cream with the vanilla until almost stiff and partially fold into the chestnut puree to create a marbled effect. Spoon into serving glasses and chill until fully set.

Yields 6 servings

Can be prepared up to 12 hours before serving.

NOTE: Gourmet shops and better supermarkets sell canned sweetened chestnut puree.

FOOL DE FIGUES (Fig Fool with Walnuts)

2 ounces toasted walnuts,
chopped
1–2 tablespoons anisette, to
taste

1½ cups heavy cream, whipped
2 pounds fresh figs
6 walnut halves, for garnish

1. In a bowl, fold the chopped nuts and anisette into the whipped cream.

2. Halve the figs and scoop out the pulp. Mash the pulp with a fork and partially fold into the whipped cream mixture to create a marbled effect. Spoon into dessert glasses and chill for 2 to 4 hours, or until fully set. Garnish each serving with a walnut half.

Yields 6 servings

Can be prepared up to 12 hours before serving.

GINGER SYLLABUB

½ cup ginger marmalade
3 tablespoons Advokaat
liqueur, see Note

1½ cups heavy cream
Strips of preserved ginger in
syrup, drained, for garnish

1. In a processor, puree the marmalade and liqueur.

2. In a bowl, beat the cream until it forms stiff peaks and fold in the marmalade mixture. Spoon into dessert glasses and chill. Just before serving, garnish with slivers of preserved ginger.

Yields 6 servings

Can be prepared up to 12 hours before serving.

NOTE: Advokaat liqueur can be purchased in liquor stores.

GOOSEBERRY FOOL

1 **pint gooseberries**	3 **egg yolks**
Sugar, to taste	1 **teaspoon cornstarch**
2 **teaspoons orange flower**	1 **cup milk, scalded**
water, see Note	1¼ **cups heavy cream**

1.   In a saucepan, simmer the gooseberries with water to cover for 15 minutes. Strain, discarding the seeds and reserving the fruit and the juice. Measure the pulp and add enough juice to make 2½ cups. Add sugar, to taste, and the orange flower water. Refrigerate until slightly thickened.

2.   In a saucepan, beat the egg yolks with the cornstarch until smooth, and stir in the milk. Over medium heat, cook, stirring, until thickened and then simmer 1 minute. Remove from the heat and stir in the gooseberry puree. Refrigerate until slightly thickened.

3.   Whip the cream until it holds soft peaks and partially fold it into the cold gooseberry mixture to create a marbled effect. Spoon into a serving bowl or dessert glasses.

Yields 6 servings

Can be prepared the day before serving.

NOTE: Gourmet shops, Middle Eastern markets, drugstores, and better supermarkets sell orange flower water.

Variation

• Substitute blackberries, raspberries, tamarinds, or plums for the gooseberries.

HONEY ALMOND CREAM

8 **ounces amaretti cookies**	2 **tablespoons almond liqueur**
1 **cup honey**	2 **cups heavy cream**
6 **tablespoons Scotch**	

1.   In a processor, pulverize the cookies.

2. In a bowl, mix the honey, Scotch, and almond liqueur. In another bowl, whip the cream until it forms soft peaks. Fold one-third of the whipped cream into the honey mixture to lighten it. Then fold in the remaining whipped cream and the amaretti crumbs. Spoon into a serving bowl or dessert glasses.

Yields 6 servings

Can be prepared the day before serving.

Variation

• For a frozen soufflé, collar a 1-quart dish or six ¾-cup soufflé dishes (see page 239) and fill with the honey almond cream. Freeze for at least 4 hours. Pulverize 2 more ounces amaretti cookies (approximately). After you remove the collar, press the crumbs against the edge above the soufflé dish so it looks "baked."

KIWI FOOL

14 kiwi, peeled	**⅓ cup sugar**
4 teaspoons cornstarch	**2 cups heavy cream**
2 tablespoons water	

1. In a processor, coarsely puree 12 of the kiwi.

2. In a cup, combine the cornstarch and the water. In a saucepan, mix 1 cup of puree, the sugar, and the cornstarch mixture. Over medium heat, cook, stirring, until thickened and clear. Pour into a bowl and cool slightly. Beat in the remaining puree and refrigerate until slightly thickened.

3. In a saucepan, reduce the cream to 1 cup. Refrigerate until cold.

4. Beat the cold cream until it forms soft peaks and partially fold it into the cold puree to create a marbled effect. Spoon into a serving bowl or dessert glasses. Garnish with the remaining kiwi, sliced or cut into wedges.

Yields 6 servings

Can be prepared the day before serving.

LEMON SNOW

2 tablespoons gelatin	½ teaspoon grated lemon rind
2 cups water	6 egg whites
1⅓ cups sugar	Candied violets, for garnish
⅔ cup lemon juice	

1.   In a large saucepan, soften the gelatin in the water. Stir in the sugar. Heat over low heat, stirring, until the gelatin dissolves. Stir in the lemon juice and rind. Refrigerate until the mixture is syrupy, about 1 hour.

2.   Beat the egg whites until stiff and fold into the lemon mixture. Spoon into a serving bowl or dessert glasses. Garnish with candied violets.

Yields 6 servings

Can be prepared up to 12 hours before serving.

Variation

For a subtler flavor, fold in 1 cup of heavy cream, whipped and sweetened to taste, after the egg whites.

COLD LEMON POSSET

This posset is a more elaborate version of lemon snow.

2½ cups heavy cream	½ cup plus 2 tablespoons sugar
1½ teaspoons grated lemon rind	3 egg whites
¼ cup dry white wine	Candied violets, for garnish
¼ cup lemon juice	Mint sprigs, for garnish

1.   In a bowl, whip the cream with the lemon rind until they form soft peaks. Gradually beat in the wine, lemon juice, and ½ cup of sugar until stiff.

2.   In a clean bowl, beat the egg whites until they form soft peaks. Add the remaining sugar and beat until stiff. Fold into the whipped cream mixture and pour into a serving bowl or dessert glasses. Garnish with the violets and mint.

Yields 6 servings

Can be prepared up to 6 hours before serving.

LEMON CREAM

The base of this cream is similar to lemon meringue pie filling and, with the cream folded in, makes a delicious pie filling. Plan to use it in meringues or as a spread for sponge cake, to top with berries.

4 egg yolks
½ cup sugar
3 tablespoons lemon juice

2 tablespoons grated lemon rind
1 cup heavy cream, whipped
Berries, for garnish

1. In a saucepan, beat the egg yolks and the sugar until thickened and pale in color. Beat in the lemon juice and rind. Cook over low heat, stirring constantly, for about 10 minutes, or until thickened about 180°F.

2. Refrigerate until slightly thickened and fold in the whipped cream. Spoon into a serving bowl or dessert glasses and garnish with the berries.

Yields 6 servings

Can be prepared up to 12 hours before serving.

ORANGE CHANTILLY

6 oranges
1 cup heavy cream
6 tablespoons sugar
2 tablespoons maraschino liqueur

5 tablespoons chopped walnuts

1. Cut off the top third of the oranges and scoop out the flesh, saving the juice, the pulp, and the shells. Cut the pulp free of seeds and membranes and dice.

2. In a bowl, whip the cream until stiff, and fold in the sugar, maraschino liqueur, walnuts, orange pulp, and juice. Fill the orange shells and chill until fully set.

Yields 6 servings

Can be prepared the day before serving.

NOTE: These oranges freeze well. Serve them directly from the freezer, arranged on green leaves.

CRÈME AUX PÊCHES (Peach Cream)

1 cup chopped fresh peaches
½ cup confectioners' sugar
1 tablespoon dark rum
1 tablespoon gelatin
¼ cup cold water

1 cup heavy cream
2 egg whites
Peach slices, for garnish
¼ cup lemon juice

1. Oil a 1½-quart mold.

2. In a bowl, marinate the chopped peaches, sugar, and rum for 10 minutes. In a saucepan, soften the gelatin in the water. Heat over low heat, stirring until the gelatin dissolves. Stir into the peaches.

3. In a bowl, beat the cream until it forms soft peaks. In another bowl, using clean beaters, beat the egg whites until they form soft peaks. Fold the whipped cream and egg whites into the peaches. Pour into the mold and chill for at least 2 hours, or until fully set.

4. Unmold and garnish with peach slices, dipped in lemon juice, just before serving.

Yields 6 servings

Can be prepared the day before serving.

PEAR SNOW

1 cup heavy cream
3 cups Pear Puree, page 29
3 egg whites
  Pinch of salt

¼ cup sugar
¼ teaspoon almond extract
Brown sugar, for garnish

1. In a bowl, beat the cream until stiff and fold in the pear puree.

2. In another bowl, beat the egg whites and the salt until they form soft peaks. Beat in the sugar and the almond extract until almost stiff. Fold into the pear mixture and spoon into a serving bowl or dessert dishes and refrigerate for at least 2 hours, or until fully set. Just before serving, sprinkle with brown sugar.

Yields 6 servings

Can be prepared up to 6 hours before serving.

PINEAPPLE FOOL

2 cups minced fresh
pineapple
1 cup heavy cream
2 tablespoons confectioners'
sugar

1 teaspoon vanilla
Pineapple wedges, for
garnish

1.   In a colander, drain the minced pineapple for 20 minutes.

2.   In a bowl, whip the cream until it forms soft peaks, add the sugar and vanilla, and beat until stiff. Cover the cream with plastic wrap and chill until fully set.

3.   Just before serving, fold the drained pineapple into the cream and spoon into a serving bowl or dessert glasses. Garnish with pineapple wedges.

Yields 6 servings

Can be prepared up to 6 hours before serving.

PRUNE WHIP

⅓ pound pitted prunes
½ cup sugar
5 egg whites

½ teaspoon lemon juice
Custard Sauce, page 545

1.   Preheat the oven to 350°F. Butter an 8 × 11-inch baking dish.

2.   In a saucepan, simmer the prunes, with water to cover, until soft. Puree in a processor. Add the sugar and return to the saucepan. Simmer until thickened. Cool.

3.   In a clean bowl, beat the egg whites until stiff, but not dry, and fold into the cooled prune mixture with the lemon juice. Pour into the prepared dish and bake for 20 minutes, or until it tests done. Chill until cold.

4.   Serve with the custard sauce.

Yields 6 servings

Can be prepared the day before serving.

PRUNE FOOL WITH PORT

½ pound pitted prunes
⅔ cup sugar
   Rind of 1 lemon, cut into
   strips
1 cup port wine

1 cup heavy cream
3 tablespoons confectioners'
   sugar
   Slivered blanched almonds,
   for garnish

.1.   In a saucepan, simmer the prunes, sugar, and lemon rind, with water to cover, until tender. Drain and return the prunes and the lemon rind to the pan. Add the port and simmer 20 minutes. Discard the rind.

2.   In a processor, puree the prunes and add more sugar, if desired.

3.   In a bowl, whip the cream until it forms soft peaks. Fold half of it into the prunes. Spoon the prune mixture into a serving bowl or dessert dishes. Fold the confectioners' sugar into the remaining whipped cream and pipe through a pastry bag fitted with a #5 open star tip, or dollop with a spoon. Garnish with the almonds.

Yields 6 servings

Can be prepared up to 12 hours before serving.

RASPBERRY WHIP

1¼ cups raspberries
1 cup confectioners' sugar
3 egg whites

Vanilla Custard Sauce, page
545

1.   In a processor, puree the raspberries with the sugar. Strain to remove the seeds.

2.   In a bowl, beat the egg whites until stiff and fold into the raspberry puree. Spoon into a serving bowl or dessert dishes and chill until fully set. Serve the custard sauce on the side.

Yields 6 servings

Can be prepared 6 hours before serving.

RASPBERRY COEUR À LA CRÈME
(Cream Cheese Heart with Raspberries)

20 ounces frozen unsweetened raspberries, thawed	8 ounces cream cheese, softened
4 tablespoons raspberry liqueur, see Note	½ cup confectioners' sugar
	1½ cups heavy cream

1.   Line a 2-cup *Coeur à la Crème* mold, or a small colander or sieve, with cheesecloth.

2.   Drain the juice from 10 ounces of raspberries, reserving the juice and the berries. In a processor, puree the remaining raspberries with the reserved juice, strain into a bowl, and discard the seeds. Stir in 2 tablespoons of raspberry liqueur. Refrigerate the sauce until ready to serve.

3.   In a processor, cream the cream cheese and sugar until light and fluffy. Scrape into a bowl. In a bowl, whip the cream until stiff. Fold into the cream cheese mixture with the reserved drained raspberries and the remaining raspberry liqueur.

4.   Fill the mold, cover the cheese with the ends of the cheesecloth, and drain overnight in the refrigerator. Unmold the cheese onto a serving platter and pass the raspberry sauce separately.

Yields 8 servings

Can be prepared up to 2 days before serving.

NOTE: Raspberry liqueur, unlike framboise, an eau de vie, is red and has a sweet taste. You can substitute framboise.

RASPBERRY PARFAIT

1 pint fresh raspberries, or 10 ounces frozen unsweetened raspberries, thawed	2 egg whites
	½ cup sugar
	1½ cups heavy cream

1.   In a processor, puree the raspberries and strain through a fine sieve. Discard the seeds. Put the puree into an ice cube tray, cover with foil, and freeze overnight.

2. About 1 hour before serving, in a bowl, beat the egg whites until they hold soft peaks. Add the sugar and beat until stiff. In another bowl, whip the cream to form soft peaks.

3. Place the raspberry puree into a bowl and whisk to break down the ice crystals. Fold the cream and egg whites together and fold into the semi-frozen raspberry puree. Spoon into parfait glasses. Keep in the coldest part of the refrigerator until ready to serve.

Yields 6 servings

Assemble no more than 2 hours before serving.

RHUBARB FOOL

1½ pounds rhubarb, cut into	**½–¾ cup sugar**
1-in pieces	**2 cups heavy cream**

1. In a saucepan, simmer the rhubarb and ½ cup sugar, stirring often, about 20 minutes, or until the rhubarb is very soft. Add more sugar, if desired. Chill.

2. In a bowl, whip the cream until it forms soft peaks and partially fold into the rhubarb to create a marbled effect. Turn into a serving bowl or dessert dishes and chill until fully set.

Yields 6 servings

Can be prepared up to 6 hours before serving.

Variations

- Add 1 cup of sliced strawberries during the last 5 minutes of cooking. Mix and cook the fruits until chunky.
- Add 2½ tablespoons of minced crystallized ginger.

STRAWBERRY RHUBARB CREAM

2 cups sliced rhubarb	**1½ cups plain yogurt**
1 pint strawberries	**½ cup heavy cream, whipped**
⅓ cup crème de cassis or	**6 whole strawberries, for**
framboise	**garnish**
4 tablespoons strawberry	
preserves	

1. In a saucepan, simmer the rhubarb, strawberries, crème de cassis, and preserves about 20 minutes, or until thickened. Refrigerate until cold.

2. Fold in the yogurt and the whipped cream. Spoon into a serving bowl or dessert glasses and garnish with whole strawberries.

Yields 6 servings

Can be prepared up to 6 hours before serving.

Variations

• Substitute sour cream for the yogurt.
• Omit yogurt and use 2 cups heavy cream, whipped.

FRAISES EUGÉNIE (Strawberry Cream)

1 pint strawberries	1 tablespoon gelatin
2 tablespoons kirsch or	¼ cup cold water
framboise	1½ cups heavy cream
5 tablespoons sugar	Raspberry Sauce, page 552

1. Lightly oil a 2-quart soufflé dish and refrigerate.

2. Set aside a few strawberries for garnish and slice the remainder. Macerate the sliced berries in 1 tablespoon of kirsch and 2 tablespoons of sugar.

3. In a saucepan, soften the gelatin in the water. Heat over low heat, stirring until dissolved.

4. In a bowl, whip the cream until it forms soft peaks. Add the remaining sugar and kirsch and beat until stiff. Fold the gelatin into the whipped cream with the sliced strawberries and spoon into the prepared mold.

5. Chill about 4 hours, or until fully set. Unmold onto a serving platter and garnish with the reserved whole strawberries. Pass the raspberry sauce.

Yields 6 servings

Can be prepared the day before serving.

MANSIKKALUMI (Finnish Strawberry Snow)

1 pint strawberries	Pinch of salt
½ cup sugar	¾ cup heavy cream, whipped
4 egg whites	18 strawberries, for garnish

1.   In a processor, puree the berries and stir in the sugar.

2.   In a bowl, beat the egg whites and the salt until they hold stiff peaks and fold in the strawberry puree and whipped cream. Spoon into a serving bowl or dessert glasses and garnish with strawberries.

Yields 6 servings

Can be prepared up to 6 hours before serving.

WIENER GÖTTERSPEISE (Viennese Food for the Gods)

Oh! Truly, this is a heavenly dessert.

1 cup crushed Almond Macaroon, page 26	2 tablespoons sugar
	1 cup heavy cream, whipped
¼ cup rum	1 quart strawberries
1 egg yolk	Confectioners' sugar

1.   Rinse a 3-cup mold in cold water.

2.   In a bowl, mix the macaroon crumbs with 2 tablespoons of rum, the egg yolk and sugar. Fold into the whipped cream and turn into the mold. Smooth the top and freeze for at least 2 hours.

3.   Unmold the dessert onto a serving platter. Dip the strawberries in the remaining rum, roll in confectioners' sugar, and arrange around the mold.

Yields 6 servings

Can be prepared several days ahead.

NOTE: If the dessert freezes for more than 2 hours, temper in the refrigerator for 2 to 3 hours before serving.

Italian Cream Desserts

There are many Italian desserts that are similar to French and English creams. The principal difference is that they require mascarpone, a super-rich cream cheese that is slightly thicker than sour cream but nowhere near as thick as cream cheese. I have found that substituting cream cheese is suitable, although different. These desserts are sometimes made with ricotta cheese, which makes a drier-tasting dessert. Considering the calories and money saved, it is an acceptable substitute. Do try at least one of the recipes with mascarpone to taste the silky, luxurious quality of the real thing. If you use cream cheese, bring to room temperature, and even then, depending on the brand, you may wish to thin it with a little heavy cream. If you are using ricotta, use freshly made Italian ricotta from a cheese shop instead of the commercial product, if possible. If that is not available, drain the commercial product in a cheesecloth-lined colander or sieve for at least an hour to remove the excess moisture.

CREMA DI MASCARPONE (Mascarpone Cream)

The ground espresso beans provide texture and flavor.

4 eggs, separated	Pinch of salt
¾ cup sugar	1 tablespoon espresso coffee
15 ounces mascarpone or	beans, finely ground, for
ricotta	garnish
1 ounce dark rum	

1. In a bowl, beat the egg yolks and the sugar until thickened and pale. Beat in the mascarpone and rum until blended.

2. In a separate bowl, beat the egg whites with the salt until stiff. Fold the egg whites into the mascarpone mixture, spoon into dessert dishes, and chill until fully set. Just before serving, sprinkle with the ground coffee.

Yields 6 servings

Can be prepared the day before serving.

LA COPA ORESTE
(Amaretti and Mascarpone Dessert)

24 amaretti cookies

¼ cup rum

¼ cup anisette

4 eggs

½ cup sugar

1 pound mascarpone

1 ounce semisweet chocolate,
shaved or grated, for garnish

1.   Put 3 cookies in each dessert bowl.

2.   In a bowl, mix the rum and anisette and drizzle over the cookies.

3.   In another bowl, beat the eggs and sugar until thickened and pale. Beat in the mascarpone until smooth and creamy. Spoon into the bowls, cover, and chill about 2 hours, or until fully set. Sprinkle chocolate shavings over each dessert.

Yields 8 servings

Can be prepared the day before serving.

TIRAMI SÙ I (Mascarpone Dessert I)

This is the simpler version of this easily prepared Italian favorite.

5 egg yolks

¼ cup sugar

1¼ cups mascarpone

1 cup heavy cream, whipped

12–18 Ladyfingers, page 21

¾ cup espresso

¼ cup cocoa powder, for
garnish

1.   In a bowl, beat the egg yolks and the sugar until thickened and pale. Beat in the mascarpone. Fold in the whipped cream.

2.   Dip the ladyfingers in the espresso and arrange in the bottom of a shallow 9 × 5 × 2-inch serving dish. Pour the cheese mixture over and smooth the top. Dust the top with cocoa and chill for at least 3 hours, or until fully set.

Yields 6 to 8 servings

Can be prepared the day before serving.

NOTE: There is no substitute for mascarpone. Some chefs make a second layer of the ladyfingers and mascarpone.

TIRAMI SÙ II (Mascarpone Dessert II)

This is a more elaborate version of the previous dessert.

¼ cup rum	2 eggs, separated
½ cup strong black coffee	5 tablespoons confectioners'
2 tablespoons Cognac	sugar
16–20 Ladyfingers, page 21	3–4 ounces semisweet chocolate,
1 pound mascarpone	grated, for garnish

1. In a small bowl, mix 2 tablespoons of rum, the coffee, and Cognac. Dip the ladyfingers and arrange in a shallow 6-cup serving dish.

2. In another bowl, beat the mascarpone, egg yolks, and sugar with the remaining rum.

3. Beat the egg whites until stiff, but not dry, and fold into the mascarpone mixture. Spread over the ladyfingers and sprinkle with the chocolate. Chill overnight.

Yields 8 servings

Should be prepared the day before serving.

TORTA MASCARPONE (Mascarpone Torte)

In this dessert *torta* means a dessert layered in a dish or goblet. Parfait glasses would be perfect.

1 cup mascarpone	1 cup heavy cream, whipped
½ cup confectioners' sugar	2 egg whites
⅓ cup dry Marsala	20 amaretti cookies
1 teaspoon vanilla	Strawberries or raspberries,
3 ounces semisweet	for garnish
chocolate, grated	

1. In a bowl, beat the mascarpone, sugar, Marsala, and vanilla until smooth. Fold in the chocolate and whipped cream.

2. In a clean bowl, beat the egg whites until stiff and fold into the mascarpone mixture.

3. In a processor, pulverize the amaretti with on/off turns.

4. In 6 dessert dishes or goblets, spoon one-third of the mascarpone mixture and sprinkle with one-third of the amaretti. Repeat the layers two more times ending with the amaretti layer. Chill at least 4 hours, or until fully set. Just before serving, garnish with the berries.

Yields 6 servings

Can be prepared the day before serving.

TORTA AL MASCARPONE
(Mascarpone Cheesecake Torte)

3 **eggs, separated**	40 **Biscottini di Rona or vanilla**
9 **tablespoons sugar**	**cookies**
1 **pound mascarpone**	½ **cup chopped Sugar-Toasted**
¾ **cup cold, strong, black**	**Almonds, page 16, for**
coffee	**garnish**
2 **tablespoons rum**	

1. In a bowl, beat the egg yolks with 4½ tablespoons of sugar until thickened and pale. Beat in the mascarpone.

2. In another bowl, beat the egg whites until they start to hold a shape. Add the remaining sugar, and beat until they form soft peaks. Fold into the egg yolk mixture.

3. In a small bowl, mix the coffee and rum. In a 1-quart crystal bowl, place a layer of cookies dipped into the coffee mixture. Spread with a layer of the cheese mixture. Continue making layers, ending with the cheese mixture.

4. Sprinkle with the almonds and chill at least 4 hours, or until fully set, before serving.

Yields 6 servings

Can be prepared up to 2 days ahead.

NOTE: Biscottini di Rona can be found in Italian grocery stores.

CHOCOLATE AND PRALINE MASCARPONE WITH VANILLA CUSTARD

6 ounces semisweet
 chocolate
1 cup mascarpone
1¼ cups heavy cream, whipped
¼ cup Praline Powder made
 with hazelnuts or pecans,
 page 30

1½ cups Vanilla Custard Sauce,
 page 552
6 strawberries, for garnish

1. Melt the chocolate and cool to room temperature.

2. In a large bowl, fold the mascarpone into the chocolate. Fold in the whipped cream.

3. Spoon into 6 dessert dishes or goblets and sprinkle with the praline powder. Spoon custard sauce over the top. Chill 1 hour, or until fully set. Just before serving, top each dessert with a strawberry.

Yields 6 servings

Can be prepared the day before serving.

SEMIFREDDO DI CIOCCOLATA
(Chilled Chocolate Swirl)

4 ounces semisweet
 chocolate, melted
1 tablespoon butter
1 cup mascarpone

¾ cup sugar
1 teaspoon almond extract
1 tablespoon orange liqueur
1 cup heavy cream, whipped

1. Stir the butter into the melted chocolate and cool to room temperature.

2. In a bowl, beat the mascarpone, sugar, almond extract, and orange liqueur until smooth. Fold in the whipped cream and pour into a serving bowl.

3. In a thin stream, pour the cooled chocolate in circles over the mascarpone mixture. With a knife blade, swirl the chocolate to create a marbled effect. Cover and chill for 6 hours.

Yields 8 servings

Can be prepared the day before serving.

Variation

• Substitute 1 cup ricotta for the mascarpone. Drain the ricotta in a sieve lined with cheesecloth, suspended over a bowl, for 1 hour before using in the recipe.

SEMIFREDDO DI FRUTTA MISTA
(Berries in Ricotta Cream)

Use one or a combination of berries, whatever are in season.

1 tablespoon gelatin	**½ teaspoon vanilla**
¼ cup cold water	**3 cups assorted berries**
1 cup ricotta	**1 cup heavy cream, whipped**
½ cup sugar	**Mint sprigs, for garnish**

1.   In a small saucepan, soften the gelatin in the water. Dissolve, stirring, over low heat.

2.   In a processor, puree the gelatin, ricotta, sugar, vanilla, and 2½ cups of berries until smooth. Pour into a bowl and fold in the whipped cream and remaining berries.

3.   Spoon into a serving bowl or dessert dishes. Chill until fully set. Garnish with mint before serving.

Yields 6 servings

Can be prepared the day before serving.

SEMIFREDDO AL CAFFÉ
(Chilled Coffee Cream)

6 egg yolks	**1 teaspoon vanilla**
1 cup sugar	**1 tablespoon anisette**
¼ cup cornstarch	**1½ cups heavy cream, whipped**
1 cup espresso	**24 candied coffee beans, for**
1 cup milk	**garnish**
1 ounce semisweet chocolate,	
grated	

1. In a saucepan, beat the egg yolks and sugar until thickened and pale. Beat in the cornstarch, espresso, and milk. Cook over low heat, stirring, until it boils and thickens. Remove from the heat and stir in the chocolate, vanilla, and anise. Pour into a bowl, cover with plastic wrap, and refrigerate until set.

2. Reserve ¾ cup of whipped cream for garnishing. Fold the remaining whipped cream into the coffee mixture.

3. Spoon into a serving bowl, dessert dishes, or goblets. Using a pastry bag fitted with a #4 open star tip, pipe rosettes of the reserved whipped cream or dollop with a spoon. Decorate each with coffee beans, if desired.

Yields 6 servings

Can be prepared the day before serving.

NOTE: Candied coffee beans are available in gourmet shops. Substitute grated chocolate or finely ground espresso coffee beans for the candied coffee beans.

SEMIFREDDO ALLA NOCCIOLE
(Chilled Hazelnut Cream)

Serve alone or accompanied with a butter cookie and a small bunch of green grapes.

2½ cups heavy cream	⅔ cup sugar
2 tablespoons hazelnut or amaretto liqueur	⅔ cup Praline Powder made with hazelnuts, page 30
8 egg yolks	

1. In a bowl, beat the cream until it begins to thicken. Add the liqueur and beat until stiff peaks form.

2. In another bowl, beat the egg yolks with the sugar until thickened and pale. Fold into the whipped cream with ⅓ cup of the praline powder. Spoon into glasses. Chill until fully set.

3. Sprinkle with the remaining praline powder before serving.

Yields 6 servings

Can be prepared the day before serving.

Chapter 5

CUSTARDS, CRÈME BRÛLÉES, AND BAVARIAN CREAMS

These subtle, light, delicious desserts are sometimes called "nursery desserts." In years past, good mothers *knew* that spicy, highly flavored foods excited children. (Well, European and American mothers, anyway; Mexicans, Indians, and the other four-fifths of the world did not necessarily agree.) Therefore, to keep the children calm, parents fed them bland foods. These desserts were easily eaten, readily digested, and minimally flavored. Adult versions were laced with liqueurs and much more emphatic flavors while retaining the original textures. Adults could indulge in the comforts of the nursery and not appear infantile. Whatever the age, when properly made, these desserts are a treat.

These desserts are an ideal example of how a few ingredients used with thought and skill can generate many different tastes and textures. The desserts consist of eggs, sugar, cream, and flavoring extract, often with the addition of fruit puree and/or a liqueur. Some require the addition of gelatin or a ring of ladyfingers, but the essence of most is the eggs and cream. Although rich, their lightness makes them a delicious offering after a full dinner.

Custards

There are two major types of custard: baked and unbaked or stirred. For baked caramel custards, such as a *crème caramel renversée*, flan, or caramel-coated custard, prepare the caramel mixture and pour into the mold. Prepare the custard ingredients and strain into the mold over the caramel. (It is important to strain the custard to remove the "chalaza" and any undissolved bits of sugar.) Set the baking dish in a *bain-marie* or water bath (see below) and bake until the mixture is almost set. Chill the custard for several hours, unmold onto a serving platter, and serve in slices. Similar recipes instruct you to bake the custards in individual molds and serve them directly from the molds, but you could unmold and slice them, like the filling of a custard pie.

For unbaked or stirred custards, cook the ingredients in a saucepan (many prefer a double boiler), until the custard thickens slightly, 180°F. on a thermometer. Once cooled, the result will be the consistency of a thick sauce. For some preparations—*crème brûlée*, for example—the cooked custard will be almost thick enough to hold a shape in a spoon. Stir the custard as it cools to prevent a skin from forming on the surface.

Stirred custard is often the base for Bavarian creams, charlottes, and some cold soufflés. It also serves as the base for desserts such as *Oeufs à la Neige*, a pool of custard sauce topped with pillows of poached meringue.

Baked Custards

BAIN-MARIE OR WATER BATH   A *bain-marie*, or water bath, allows food to bake more gently. The water protects the food from overcooking and from browning on the bottom and sides. Essential for certain baked custards, water baths also protect other foods such as *pâtés* and puddings.

To prepare a water bath, put the custard, or other food, in its mold into a pan that is at least 1 inch larger on all sides. A baking pan or layer cake pan does nicely. Fill the larger pan with enough hot water to come at least 1 inch, if not halfway, up the sides of the mold. The water should be almost boiling when added to the pan to aid in the cooking, but during baking the water must not boil. If it boils, the custard could develop holes, or become watery and split apart when unmolded, or, in the worst case, curdle into an unsightly mass of curds and whey. The degree of damage depends on how long and how vigorous the boiling. If you find the water simmering or boiling when you check it during cooking, immediately add some ice cubes to the water to stop the boiling and lower the oven temperature. (Not all ovens are accurate and though the dial may indicate one temperature the oven temperature could be higher or lower by 50°F. or more. This is one good reason not to accept the time stated in a recipe without testing for doneness first.) If the water boiled only briefly, the custard may still come out perfectly. Unless it curdled, continue with the recipe; it will taste good even if it does split when unmolded.

TO TEST BAKED CUSTARDS FOR DONENESS To test a custard for doneness, insert a thin-bladed knife halfway between the edge of the custard and the center. It should come out clean. The center of the custard will be slightly undercooked at this point, but it will finish cooking as the custard cools. If you bake the custard until the knife comes clean when inserted in the center, the retained heat can overcook the custard. Remove the custard from the water bath as soon as it is baked; cool on a rack and refrigerate until cold.

Stirred Custards

TO COOK UNBAKED OR STIRRED CUSTARDS Some other custards require a less firm texture than baked custards. Prepare them by cooking the ingredients on top of the stove until the mixture is thick enough to coat the back of a spoon. Some cooks prefer to use a double boiler. My experience is that there is no difference between the two methods. What *is* necessary is that the heat be no more than moderate and that the water in a double boiler never be more than barely simmering. I prefer to use direct heat because I feel I have more control.

Cook the ingredients, stirring in a figure eight pattern, scraping the bottom and sides of the pan, to keep the custard moving and to distribute the heat evenly throughout the custard. A kitchen thermometer should read 180°F. I prefer to remove it from the heat at 175°F. and let the retained heat finish the cooking. If a thermometer is not available, test for doneness by checking if the custard coats a spoon. Dip a spoon into the custard, turn it over, and run your finger down the back of the spoon. If a clear track remains and does not fill immediately, the custard is cooked. Constant motion will help keep the custard from curdling. To avoid "cooking" the eggs with the hot liquid, add the scalded milk gradually.

Once cooked, immediately strain the custard through a fine sieve, into a clean, dry bowl. If left in the pot, the retained heat could curdle the custard. There is no remedy for curdled custard, except to start again. (If it is not too curdled, put it in a processor for about 30 seconds; it works sometimes.) Do not be intimidated, though; with care and practice, you will find custards simple to prepare.

TO COAT A MOLD WITH CARAMEL   *Crèmes renversées au caramel,* caramel custards, and flans are baked in molds lined with sugar cooked to the caramel stage. Heat the ingredients to a full rolling boil, stirring gently. When it boils, cover the pan and boil for five minutes (the steam will wash any sugar crystals from the sides of the pan). Remove the cover and wash the sides of the pan with a brush dipped into cold water. Continue to boil over high heat without stirring until the syrup turns golden brown, about 365°F. on a candy thermometer. If it starts to brown on one side of the pan, gently swirl the pan to caramelize the entire mixture. Take care not to get it too dark or the caramel will taste burned. Immediately pour the caramel into the mold. Holding the mold with pot holders, tilt and turn to coat the bottom and about ¼ inch up the sides of the mold. Set aside while you prepare the filling. Do not coat more than ¼ inch up the sides of the mold. If any caramel is above the liquid, it will not dissolve and can act as a hook, making unmolding more difficult, if not impossible.

SAFETY RULES FOR COOKING CARAMEL   Caramel is not only extremely hot but also sticky. It can cause truly painful and possibly disfiguring burns. The rules here are intended to help you to work with caramel safely, not to frighten you. Do not be afraid, just use common sense to create wonderful desserts.

The instructions below teach you to handle caramel safely. Follow them!

1.   Keep everyone out of the way, especially children.

2.   If you should spill any of the molten caramel on you, plunge the affected area under cold running water and keep it there for at least 3 minutes. *Do not try to peel off the caramel.* Let the cold water stop the burning and dissolve the caramel. Yes, the cold will be unpleasant, but a lot less so than an untended burn.

3.   If the caramel should become too dark, do not pour it down the drain until it cools. The hot melted caramel can turn the drain into a form of cannon by overheating the water in the trap and causing it to explode up into the kitchen and onto you. Let the caramel cool to room temperature. Do not worry about the pan.

TO CLEAN A CARAMEL-COATED PAN   No matter how badly the caramel sticks to the pan, these instructions work:
- Soak the pan in water until the sugar dissolves. It may take a day or two, but it *will* dissolve and the pan will be fine.
- Digging at undissolved sugar with can openers, spatulas, or even scrubbing equipment may destroy the pan.
- You can simmer the pan half filled with water to hasten the process.

TO UNMOLD A CARAMEL-LINED DESSERT   Chill the dessert completely. The chilling helps to firm the custard and gives the caramel a chance to dissolve and turn into a sauce. When chilled, run a knife around the outer edge of the mold. If the custard turns freely in the pan, place a serving platter on top of the mold and in one quick movement turn it upside down and lift off the mold. If the custard seems settled in one place in the mold, then dip the mold into a bowl of very hot water for about 30 seconds. Shake the pan lightly and the custard should move in place. Unmold.

A mistake many cooks make when unmolding a dessert or other food is to panic halfway through the process. They cover the mold, start to turn it over, and stop in the middle. Complete the turn and then panic. If you stop in the middle, there is no question that you will create a disaster.

BAKED CUSTARD

3 eggs, lightly beaten	**Pinch of salt**
3 cups milk	**1 teaspoon vanilla**
½ cup sugar	**Ground nutmeg, to taste**

1.   Preheat the oven to 325°F.

2.   In a bowl, mix the eggs, milk, sugar, salt, and vanilla. Strain into 6 custard cups or individual soufflé dishes. Sprinkle the surface with grated nutmeg.

3.   Place in a water bath and bake about 40 minutes, or until done. Remove from the water bath and cool. Chill until cold.

Yields 6 servings

Can be prepared the day before serving.

CRÈME JOSEPHINE BAKER

This adaptation of a recipe by Alice B. Toklas in honor of the great jazz singer is a sophisticated baked custard.

2¼ cups milk	**2 teaspoons kirsch**
2 tablespoons flour	**3 tablespoons Pernod**
3 eggs	**3 bananas, thinly sliced**
3 tablespoons sugar	**Grated rind of 1 lemon**

1.   Preheat the oven to 400°F.

2.   In a blender, blend the milk, flour, eggs, and sugar for 1 minute. Add the kirsch and Pernod and strain into a 1-quart baking dish. Stir in the bananas and the lemon rind.

3.   Bake for 20 minutes, or until it tests done. Chill until cold.

4.   Serve cold or at room temperature.

Yields 6 servings

Can be prepared the day before serving.

NORWEGIAN CUSTARD WITH CHOCOLATE

2 tablespoons apricot jam	**2 cups milk, scalded**
3 eggs	**Shaved chocolate, for**
1 tablespoon sugar	**garnish**
½ teaspoon vanilla	**½ cup heavy cream**

1.   Preheat the oven to 350°F. Spread the jam in the bottom of a 3-cup soufflé dish.

2.   In a bowl, beat 2 eggs and 1 egg yolk with the sugar and the vanilla until creamy. Gradually stir in the hot milk and strain the mixture into the prepared soufflé dish.

3.   Bake in a water bath, covered with foil, for 45 to 50 minutes, or until it tests done. Remove from the water bath and cool. Chill until cold. Sprinkle with chocolate shavings.

4.   Whip the remaining egg white until it holds semifirm peaks. Beat the heavy cream until it holds semifirm peaks. Fold egg white into the cream mixture. Spread over the chocolate shavings and sprinkle with more chocolate, if desired.

Yields 6 servings

Can be prepared the day before serving.

CHOCOLATE CAKE BONNE FEMME

This delicately smooth dessert is more a custard than a cake.

¾ cup Candied Orange Peel, page 38	1 cup butter, softened
8 ounces semisweet chocolate	1 cup superfine sugar
½ cup strong black coffee	5 eggs
	Custard Sauce, page 545

1.   Preheat oven to 250°F. Butter a 5- to 6-cup ring mold.

2.   Chop ½ cup of the candied orange peel. Reserve the remaining strips for garnish.

3.   In a double boiler, melt the chocolate with the coffee. In a mixer, cream the butter and sugar until light and fluffy. Stir the butter mixture into the chocolate and cook until sugar dissolves. Cool 10 minutes.

4.   Beat the eggs to combine and stir one-fourth into the chocolate. Whisk chocolate mixture into the remaining eggs, and stir in the chopped peel. Pour into the ring mold.

5.   Bake for 2 hours, or until it tests done. Cool 10 minutes. Unmold and garnish with the reserved candied peel. Serve with custard sauce.

Yields 8 to 10 servings

Best served warm shortly after baking.

LEMON SPONGE CUSTARD

¾ cup sugar	3 tablespoons flour
2 tablespoons butter, softened	¼ cup lemon juice
2 teaspoons grated lemon rind	1 cup light cream
3 eggs, separated	Pinch of salt
	Whipped cream, for garnish

1. Preheat the oven to 350°F. Butter a 1-quart soufflé dish.

2. In a bowl or a processor, mix the sugar, butter, and lemon rind until blended. Beat in the egg yolks, flour, lemon juice, and light cream.

3. In a clean bowl, beat the egg whites with the salt until almost stiff and fold into the egg yolk mixture.

4. Pour into the prepared dish and bake in a water bath about 1 hour, or until it tests done.

5. Serve hot or cold, garnished with the whipped cream.

Yields 6 servings

Can be prepared the day before serving.

ORANGE CUSTARD

2 cups heavy cream	½ cup sugar
3 eggs, lightly beaten	Pinch of salt
1 cup orange juice	
1½ teaspoons grated orange rind	

1. Preheat the oven to 325°F.

2. In a bowl, mix the cream, eggs, orange juice, rind, sugar, and salt. Strain into six 6-ounce custard cups or individual soufflé dishes. Bake in a water bath about 45 minutes, or until it tests done. Chill until fully set.

Yields 6 servings

Can be prepared the day before serving.

PAPAYA CUSTARD

1½ cups light cream	Grated rind and juice of 1 orange
3 eggs	½ cup toasted coconut, for garnish
1 egg yolk	
1½ cups pureed papaya	1 papaya, peeled and sliced, for garnish
½ teaspoon salt	
¼ cup sugar	

1. Preheat the oven to 325°F.

2. In a bowl, beat the cream, eggs, egg yolk, pureed papaya, salt, sugar, orange rind, and juice until blended. Pour into six 6-ounce custard cups or individual soufflé dishes.

3. Bake in a water bath about 45 minutes, or until it tests done. Chill until fully set.

4. Unmold onto individual plates or a serving platter and garnish with the coconut and papaya slices.

Yields 6 servings

Can be prepared for baking several hours ahead.

BAKED PISTACHIO CUSTARD WITH CUSTARD AND STRAWBERRY SAUCES

2 cups heavy cream	1 cup strawberries
¼ cup peeled pistachios, minced	Juice of 1 lemon
1 cup plus 2 tablespoons sugar	2 cups Custard Sauce, page 545
4 eggs	Strawberry Sauce, page 554

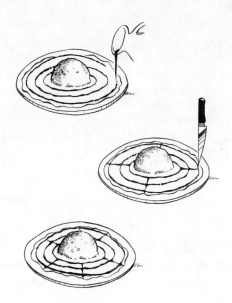

1. Preheat the oven to 350°F.

2. In a saucepan, scald the cream and the pistachios and let steep for 10 minutes.

3. In a bowl, beat ¾ cup of sugar and the eggs until they are thickened and pale in color. Gradually stir in the pistachio-cream mixture and strain into 6 custard cups. Reserve the pistachios.

4. Bake the custards in a water bath about 25 minutes, or until they test done. Cool. Refrigerate until set.

5. Meanwhile, spread the minced pistachios on paper toweling to dry. In a processor, puree the strawberries with the remaining sugar and the lemon juice. Strain.

6. When ready to serve, unmold a chilled custard onto each serving plate. Spoon the custard sauce around each pistachio custard. Put the strawberry sauce into a squirt bottle and pipe two circles of sauce around each pistachio custard in the sauce. Draw the point of a knife through the two circles of sauce to create a design (see illustration). Sprinkle with reserved nuts.

Yields 6 servings

Can be prepared the day before serving.

CARAMEL CUSTARD OR FLAN

Dozens of recipes exist for this ever popular dessert, and almost as many names. It is also known as *crème renversée au caramel* or *crème à la vanille caramelissée.*

4½ cups milk	3 drops lemon juice
1 vanilla bean	4 eggs
1 cup sugar	8 egg yolks
1½ tablespoons water	

1. Preheat the oven to 325°F.

2. In a saucepan, scald the milk and the vanilla bean. Cover and set aside.

3. In a saucepan bring ½ cup of sugar, water, and lemon juice to a boil, stirring gently, until a rich golden brown. Pour into a 9-inch cake pan or 6 custard cups.

4.   In a bowl, beat the eggs, egg yolks, and the remaining sugar until they are thickened and pale. Stirring gently, slowly add the scalded milk. Strain into the prepared pan.

5.   Bake in a water bath for about 30 to 45 minutes, or until it tests done. Refrigerate until cold.

6.   Unmold and serve.

Yields 6 servings

Can be prepared the day before serving.

Variations

• There are many versions of this custard, all based on milk or cream and eggs.
• For a less rich custard, reduce the egg yolks to 2 or use 6 whole eggs.
• For a velvetier effect, substitute half heavy cream or more for the milk.
• Flavor the custard to taste with any favorite liquor, such as rum or Cognac, or with an eau de vie, such as Poire William or kirsch.
• Add a cinnamon stick to the milk when scalding, or stir in 1 teaspoon of ground cinnamon and ¼ teaspoon of nutmeg.
• Add the grated rind of 2 lemons to the milk and omit the vanilla.

Presentations

For most people, most of the time, a simple, unadorned *crème caramel* is more than satisfactory. You can garnish the dessert more elaborately.

• Surround with raspberries, strawberries, or grapes. Serve with whipped cream.
• Unmold onto a plate so the caramel sauce spreads to the borders of the plate. Fill a squirt bottle with Custard Sauce (see page 545) or Chocolate Sauce (see page 540), and squirt 2 circles around the dessert. Draw a knife point through the two sauces to make a design (see page 189).

TIAN AU RHUM (Rum and Milk Custard)

1 cup sugar	3 egg yolks
2 tablespoons water	1 quart milk, scalded
3 eggs	5 tablespoons dark rum

1. Preheat the oven to 350°F.

2. Caramelize ½ cup of sugar and the water. Pour the caramel into a 9-inch cake pan.

3. In a bowl, beat the eggs, egg yolks, and the remaining sugar until thickened and pale. Gradually stir in the hot milk and 4 tablespoons of rum. Strain the custard into the pan.

4. Bake in a water bath for 40 to 50 minutes, or until it tests done. Chill until cold. Run a knife around the sides and unmold onto a platter.

5. If there is any undissolved caramel in the bottom of the pan, place the pan over medium heat. Add the remaining rum and heat, stirring, to dissolve the caramel. Pour it over the dessert.

Yields 6 servings

Can be prepared the day before serving.

DOLCE BONET (Chocolate Amaretti Custard)

½ cup plus ⅓ cup sugar	2½ cups milk
2 tablespoons water	2 tablespoons cocoa
12 amaretti cookies, crushed	1 tablespoon rum
6 eggs	

1. Preheat the oven to 325°F.

2. Caramelize ½ cup of sugar and the water. Pour the caramel into a 9-inch cake pan. Sprinkle one-third of the amaretti crumbs over the caramel.

3. In a bowl, mix the remaining crumbs, remaining sugar, eggs, milk, cocoa, and rum. Strain into the prepared pan. Bake in a water bath for 45 minutes, or until it tests done.

4. Chill until cold. Unmold onto a serving platter.

Yields 6 servings

Can be prepared the day before serving.

CRÈME SAINTE ANNE AU CARAMEL
(Almond Macaroon Custard)

2½ cups milk	1 cup pulverized Macaroons,
1 vanilla bean, split	page 26
1 cup sugar	3 eggs
2 tablespoons water	3 egg yolks

1. Preheat the oven to 325°F.

2. In a saucepan, scald the milk with the vanilla bean. Cover and set aside.

3. Caramelize ½ cup of sugar and the water. Pour the caramel into eight 6-ounce ramekins. Sprinkle the macaroons in the molds.

4. In a bowl, beat the remaining sugar, eggs, and egg yolks until light and foamy. Gradually stir in the scalded milk. Strain the mixture into a 1-quart measuring cup and pour into the molds.

5. Bake in a water bath about 20 to 25 minutes, or until it tests done. Refrigerate until cold. Unmold onto a serving platter.

Yields 8 servings

Can be prepared the day before serving.

GINGER-ORANGE FLAN

1 cup sugar	2 cups heavy cream
¾ cup water	1 cup milk
¾ cup peeled gingerroot,	1 teaspoon grated orange rind
minced	6 eggs

1. Preheat the oven to 325°F.

2. Caramelize ½ cup of sugar and ¼ cup of water. Pour into a 9-inch cake pan.

3. In a small saucepan, simmer the remaining sugar, gingerroot, and water until reduced by half. Stir in the cream, milk, and orange rind and heat until hot, but not boiling.

4. In a bowl, beat the eggs well and gradually stir in the hot cream mixture. Strain the eggs into the caramel-lined pan, pressing on the ginger to extract all the flavor.

5.   Bake in a water bath for 45 minutes, or until it tests done. Refrigerate until fully cold. Unmold onto a serving platter.

Yields 6 servings

Can be prepared the day before serving.

MAPLE CRÈME CARAMEL

1⅓ cups maple syrup	1 cup cream
3 large eggs	2 cups milk, scalded
2 large egg yolks	

1.   Preheat the oven to 350°F.

2.   Cook 1 cup of maple syrup until reduced to ¾ cup, about 10 minutes, stirring often, and pour into 6 ramekins.

3.   In a bowl, beat the eggs, yolks, and cream with remaining syrup. Gradually whisk in the hot milk. Strain into a 1-quart measuring cup and pour into the ramekins.

4.   Bake in a water bath for 30 minutes, or until it tests done. Refrigerate until fully cold. Unmold onto a serving platter.

Yields 6 servings

Can be prepared the day before serving.

FLAN DE NARANJA
(Orange Caramel Custard)

3 navel oranges	2 cups sugar
1 quart milk	¼ cup water
2 cinnamon sticks	6 eggs
1 teaspoon vanilla	2 egg yolks

1.   Preheat the oven to 325°F.

2.   Peel the rind from the orange, without removing the pith, and set aside. Peel the oranges completely, cut into segments, and set aside.

3.   In a saucepan, scald the milk, orange rind, and cinnamon. Remove from the heat, stir in the vanilla, cover, and set aside.

4. Caramelize 1 cup of sugar and the water. Pour into a 9- or 10-inch cake pan.

5. In a large bowl, beat the eggs, egg yolks, and remaining sugar until thickened and pale. Stirring constantly, gradually add the hot milk. Arrange the orange segments over the caramel in the pan. Strain in the custard. Bake in a water bath for 45 minutes, or until it tests done. Refrigerate until cold and unmold.

Yields 6 servings

Can be prepared the day before serving.

NOTE: The orange segments will all float to the surface and be on the bottom when unmolded.

POIRES À LA JOINVILLE
(Poached Pears with Caramel Custard)

This is an elaborate presentation composed of a few simple ingredients.

1 cup sugar	⅛ teaspoon salt
3 tablespoons water	6 Vanilla Poached Pear halves,
1½ cups milk	page 40
1 cup light cream	1 cup heavy cream, whipped,
2-in piece of vanilla bean	for garnish
4 eggs	Candied cherries, for garnish
2 egg yolks	Pistachio nuts, for garnish

1. Preheat the oven to 350°F.

2. Caramelize ¾ cup of sugar and the water. Pour into a 9-inch 6-cup ring mold.

3. In a saucepan, scald the milk and cream with the vanilla bean. In a bowl, beat the eggs, egg yolks, and remaining sugar until they are thickened and pale. Stir in the salt. Gradually stir in the hot cream and strain into the ring mold. Bake in a water bath about 1 hour, or until it tests done. Refrigrate until cold.

4. Unmold onto a serving platter and place the pear halves in the center. Garnish with whipped cream, cherries, and pistachio nuts.

Yields 6 servings

The pears and custard can be prepared the day before serving. Assemble shortly before serving.

PUMPKIN FLAN

Canned pumpkin is suitable for this recipe.

¾ **cup sugar**	**1 cup heavy cream**
2 tablespoons water	**6 eggs**
1 cup pumpkin puree	¼ **teaspoon vanilla**
2 cups milk	

1.   Preheat the oven to 350°F.

2.   Caramelize ½ cup of sugar and the water. Pour into a 9-inch cake pan.

3.   In a bowl, mix the remaining sugar, pumpkin puree, milk, cream, eggs, and vanilla. Stir well and strain into the prepared mold.

4.   Bake in a water bath for about 45 minutes, or until it tests done. Refrigerate until cold. Unmold onto a serving platter.

Yields 6 servings

Can be prepared the day before serving.

Variation

• Flavor the custard with ½ teaspoon of cinnamon, a pinch of ground cloves, a pinch of grated nutmeg, and a pinch of allspice. Serve garnished with a heaping dollop of whipped cream, sweetened and flavored with rum, to taste.

FLAN DE POTIRON
(Rum-Flavored Pumpkin Flan)

1½ **cups milk**	¾ **cup pumpkin puree**
½ **cup heavy cream**	⅓ **cup honey**
Grated rind of 1 lemon	¼ **cup dark rum**
½ **cup plus 2 tablespoons**	¼ **teaspoon salt**
sugar	**3 eggs**
2 tablespoons water	**2 egg yolks**

1.   Preheat the oven to 325°F.

2.   In a saucepan, scald the milk, cream, and lemon rind. Cover and set aside.

3.   Caramelize ½ cup of sugar and the water. Pour into a 9-inch cake pan.

4. In a bowl, beat the pumpkin puree, honey, rum, salt, and remaining sugar. Beat in the eggs and egg yolks. Gradually stir in the hot milk. Strain into the pan.

5. Bake in a water bath about 45 minutes, or until it tests done. Refrigerate until cold. Unmold onto a serving platter.

Yields 6 to 8 servings

Can be prepared the day before serving.

CROSTADE LOMBARDE
(Caramel Flan with Dried Fruit)

This recipe from the Middle Ages tastes just as wonderful without the bone marrow.

¾ **cup pitted prunes, cut into**
  eighths
½ **cup pitted dates, chopped**
¼ **cup dark rum**
1½ **cups sugar**
2 **tablespoons water**
7 **eggs**
5 **egg yolks**

1 **quart milk**
1 **cup heavy cream**
6-in **bone marrow, poached, cut**
  into 1-in pieces, optional
Pinch of salt
Grated lemon rind, for
garnish

1. Preheat the oven to 325°F. In a bowl mix the prunes, dates, and rum and set aside.

2. Caramelize ½ cup of sugar and the water. Pour into a 10-inch cake pan.

3. In another bowl beat the eggs, egg yolks, and the remaining sugar until frothy.

4. In a saucepan, scald the milk and cream. Gradually pour into the egg mixture, whisking constantly. Strain through a fine sieve onto the macerated fruits and mix well. If using, blot the marrow with paper towels to dry it and cut into pea-sized sections. Add to the egg mixture and pour into the prepared mold.

5. Bake in a water bath about 55 minutes, or until it tests done. Refrigerate until cold and unmold onto a serving platter. Sprinkle with grated lemon rind.

Yields 6 servings

Can be prepared the day before serving.

POTS DE CRÈME

This is a delicate custard baked in individual lidded cups in a water bath. Check antique shops or ask your china dealer to order a set for you. Or use ramekins and cover with aluminum foil.

2 cups cream   **6 egg yolks**
1-in piece of vanilla bean
½ cup sugar

1. Preheat the oven to 325°F.

2. In a saucepan, scald the cream with the vanilla bean and sugar; remove from the heat, cover, and cool for 5 minutes. Remove the vanilla bean.

3. In a bowl, beat the egg yolks until lemon-colored and gradually add the cream, stirring constantly. Strain the mixture through a fine sieve into *pots de crème* cups. Let stand for 10 minutes, then scoop all foam from the surface. Cover. Bake in a water bath for about 20 minutes, or until it tests done. Refrigerate until cold and serve.

Yields 6 servings

Can be prepared the day before serving.

Variations

- *Chocolate.* Use ¼ cup of sugar and stir in 4 ounces of melted semisweet chocolate before straining.
- *Coffee.* Omit the vanilla. Dissolve 1 tablespoon of instant espresso powder in 1 tablespoon of hot water and stir into the custard before straining.
- *Orange.* Omit the vanilla and add 1 tablespoon of grated orange rind and 2 tablespoons of orange liqueur to the scalded cream.

Crème Brûlée

Recently *crème brûlée* has become the darling of young chefs. It has a long history and is well and deservedly appreciated. *Crème brûlée* amounts to *crème caramel*. The same ingredients create completely different textures. The dessert consists of a chilled, thick, creamy, stirred custard coated with a layer of brown or white sugar and broiled to caramelize the sugar, and chilled again. During the second chilling the caramel hardens and when served, that topping will break into crispy shards of sugar that partially dissolve in the rich cream.

BAKING DISHES FOR CRÈME BRÛLÉE   Any shallow ovenproof serving dish suits a *crème brûlée*. Use oval gratin pans in copper or porcelain, rectangular or square porcelain or pottery baking dishes, a glass baking dish, or even a soufflé dish. Ideally the cream should be about 1½ inches deep and provide a broad surface area for the sugar topping.

SUGAR TOPPING FOR CRÈME BRÛLÉE   Sift white, light brown, or dark brown sugar and sprinkle evenly over the surface of the cream. The sugar should cover the cream with a ¼-inch layer. Place under a preheated broiler and broil until the sugar melts and starts to bubble. Take care that it does not burn. You may need to lower the dessert from the heat and to move it on the rack to caramelize uniformly. Chill before serving.

CRÈME BRÛLÉE (Burnt Cream)

Burnt cream, the translation of *crème brûlée*, appears on English and a few American menus, but most often the French reigns.

6 egg yolks	**1 teaspoon vanilla**
6 tablespoons sugar	**1 cup light brown sugar,**
2½ cups heavy cream, scalded	**sieved**

1.   In a saucepan, beat the egg yolks and sugar until thickened and pale. Gradually whisk in the hot cream.

2.   Cook over low heat, stirring constantly until the custard is thick enough to coat the back of a spoon. Do not boil. Remove from the heat and stir in the vanilla. Strain into a 1-quart ovenproof serving dish or six 6-ounce souffle dishes. Refrigerate until cold.

3.   No more than a couple of hours before serving, preheat the broiler. Sprinkle the sugar evenly over the custard and brown under the broiler, taking care not to burn the sugar. Refrigerate until cold.

Yields 6 servings

The custard can be prepared the day before serving.

Variations

- *Coffee.* In a small saucepan, dissolve 2 tablespoons of instant coffee in 1 tablespoon of water and stir into the cooked custard. Omit the vanilla.
- *Ginger.* Scald the cream with ⅔ cup of minced gingerroot and let steep for 5 minutes. Strain the cream into the egg yolks.
- *Orange.* Add the grated zest of 2 oranges to the cream before scalding. In a saucepan, reduce ½ cup of orange liqueur and 1 cup of orange juice until it is a sticky liquid, about 3 tablespoons. Stir into the cream and then add to the egg yolks.

CRÈME BRÛLÉE AU POTIRON
(Pumpkin-flavored Crème Brûlée)

2 cups heavy cream	½ teaspoon nutmeg
¾ cup sugar	¼ teaspoon ground cloves
4 eggs	3 tablespoons bourbon or rum
1⅔ cups pumpkin puree	½ cup dark brown sugar,
1½ teaspoons cinnamon	sieved
1 teaspoon ginger	

1. Preheat the oven to 325°F.

2. In a saucepan, heat the cream and sugar, stirring until the sugar dissolves. In a bowl, beat the eggs until pale yellow and beat in the pumpkin, cinnamon, ginger, nutmeg, cloves, and bourbon. Gradually stir in the hot cream and strain into a 5-cup baking dish.

3. Bake in a water bath for 1 hour or until it tests done. Refrigerate until cold.

4. Preheat the broiler. Sprinkle the dark brown sugar evenly over the custard and brown under the broiler, taking care not to burn the sugar. Refrigerate until cold.

Yields 6 servings

The custard can be prepared the day before. Top with the sugar and caramelize only a couple of hours before serving.

Crème Anglaise (English Custard Sauce)

This is a sauce which becomes an integral part of many desserts. In *Oeufs à la Neige* (Snow Eggs), and *Île Flottante* (Floating Island), for instance, the custard serves solely as the sauce for the ingredients, but in Bavarian creams and charlottes, the sauce, with the aid of some gelatin, holds the whipped cream and/or egg whites to create an ethereal dessert of great subtlety.

Because custard is used in so many desserts from fruits to gâteaux, I have placed the recipe for it with the other sauce recipes in Chapter 15. In some of the recipes, however, the sauce is made from milk that is first used to poach part of the dessert. In those cases, the milk is incorporated into those recipes.

Follow the same techniques for making an unbaked or stirred custard. Chapter 15 lists a basic recipe for custard sauce, but the individual recipes here have the quantities and instructions in them. Do not heat the sauce over 180°F. and immediately strain it into a bowl when cooked to prevent overcooking and curdling.

OEUFS À LA NEIGE (Snow Eggs)

Sometimes these are incorrectly called *Île Flottante*, Floating Island. Classically *Île Flottante* is a baked meringue (see page 23). One of the best known of the "nursery desserts" *Oeufs à la Neige*, appears on the most elegant restaurant menus.

4 eggs, separated
1¼ cups sugar
2 cups milk, scalded

1 teaspoon vanilla

1. In a mixer, beat the egg whites until they form soft peaks. Continue beating, adding ¾ cup of sugar slowly. Beat to stiff, unwavering peaks.

2. In a large skillet, bring ¾ inch of water to a simmer. Using two large soup spoons dipped into hot water, shape the egg whites into large eggs and poach in the liquid for 2 minutes on each side. Remove to a paper towel–lined sheet pan and let cool.

3. In a saucepan, beat the egg yolks and the remaining sugar until thickened and pale. Gradually add the milk and cook, stirring constantly, over medium heat until thick enough to coat the back of a spoon. Do not boil.

4.   Stir in the vanilla, strain into a bowl, and refrigerate until cold.

5.   Place the meringues in a large dish and pour the sauce around them.

Yields 6 servings

Can be prepared the day before serving.

NOTE: Many authors suggest poaching the meringues in the milk and then preparing the custard sauce with the same milk. I find the meringues are lighter when poached in water.

Variations

Because the dessert lacks color, many chefs garnish it with a variety of toppings.

• *Caramel.*   Just before serving, caramelize ½ cup of sugar and 2 tablespoons of water. Holding a fork dipped in the caramel high over the dessert, trace lines of caramel back and forth over the surface in a random pattern.
• *Chocolate.*   Sprinkle the top with grated chocolate or cocoa.
• *Fruit.*   Arrange sliced fruits on the custard or scatter berries over the top.

MON RÊVE
(My Dream — Snow Eggs with Chocolate)

The creator of this dessert certainly had luscious dreams.

Oeufs à la Neige, see	**2 tablespoons Praline Powder,**
previous recipe	**page 30**
1½ cups heavy cream	**Kirsch, to taste**
½ cup semisweet chocolate	

1.   Prepare the snow eggs and custard sauce as described in the previous recipe. Melt the chocolate and bring to room temperature.

2.   Whip the cream until stiff and fold in the chocolate and praline powder.

3.   Mound the cream in the center of a deep round platter and shape it into a dome. Arrange the snow eggs around the base.

4.   Stir the kirsch into the custard sauce and pour over all.

Yields 6 to 8 servings

The eggs and custard sauce can be prepared the day before serving. Assemble shortly before serving.

BOULES SUR CHOCOLAT
(Snowballs on Chocolate)

This is *Oeufs à la Neige* on a bed of chocolate custard.

4½ cups milk	8 eggs, separated
4-in piece of vanilla bean	⅔ cup sugar
2¼ cups sugar	⅔ cup cocoa

1. In a skillet, heat the milk, vanilla bean, and ¼ cup of sugar to a simmer.

2. In a mixer, beat the egg whites until they form soft peaks and add the remaining sugar, a few tablespoons at a time, until the meringue holds stiff peaks.

3. With two spoons, shape the egg mixture into ovals and poach in the barely simmering milk about 4 minutes, or until firm, turning once. Transfer to a clean towel-lined pan. Strain the milk and reserve.

4. In a heavy saucepan, beat ⅔ cup sugar, cocoa, and egg yolks together until thick. Slowly stir in the reserved hot milk mixture and cook over medium heat, stirring constantly, until thick enough to coat the back of a spoon. Do not boil. Strain into a bowl. Refrigerate until cold.

5. Pour the sauce into a deep platter, arrange the meringues on top, and serve.

Yields 6 servings

The eggs and sauce can be prepared the day before serving. Assemble shortly before serving.

You can poach the eggs in water if you prefer.

ÎLE FLOTTANTE (Floating Island)

4 large egg whites	Powder, page 30
Pinch of salt	Custard Sauce, page 545
½ cup sugar	Whole toasted blanched
¾ teaspoon vanilla	almonds, for garnish
6 tablespoons Praline	

1. Preheat the oven to 250°F. Butter a 1-quart round mold and sprinkle with sugar.

2. In a large mixer, beat the egg whites and the salt until they form soft peaks. Beat in the sugar, 1 tablespoon at a time, until stiff. Fold in the vanilla and praline powder. Turn into the prepared mold and smooth the surface. Bang the mold once, sharply, on the counter to remove any air pockets.

3. Place in a water bath and bake for 25–35 minutes, or until it is firm. A skewer inserted in the center should come out clean. Refrigerate until cold.

4. Unmold into a deep platter or glass bowl and pour the sauce around it. Garnish with the almonds.

Yields 6 servings

Can be prepared the day before serving.

Bavarian Cream

Bavarian creams have been mentioned in the literature for at least 200 years, though no one seems to know the origin of the name. The most reasonable explanation is that it was a favorite in Bavaria, but *Larousse Gastronomique,* with typical chauvinism, indicates that a French chef working in Bavaria created the dessert. Whoever is responsible deserves our thanks.

Four components comprise Bavarian creams: stirred custard, gelatin, whipped cream, and a flavoring. Soften the gelatin in cold water, dissolve in the hot custard, and cool until near the setting point. Fold in lightly whipped cream with the flavoring, turn into a mold and chill until set. Shortly before serving, unmold the custard and garnish the cream. Here is an opportunity to turn a plain dress into a ballgown. Garnish the dessert with glorious swirls of whipped cream, surround it with pools of fruit sauces, and assemble arrangements of fruits. Embellish a simple vanilla-flavored Bavarian with a ruffle of whipped cream, surround with chocolate sauce, and garnish with pastry boats of caramel-coated strawberries.

See the basic recipes chapter for information on gelatin and whipped cream.

MOLDS   Antique shops as well as gourmet shops carry beautiful molds of copper or tin to mold Bavarian creams. Any metal mold works well, providing it is fully lined with tin or another nonreactive metal. A worn tin-lined or aluminum mold will react with fruits to discolor the cream. Porcelain or pottery molds might seem the perfect solution, but the thickness of the walls make them unsuitable for cold desserts. The thick sides require too much heating and melts the dessert before it will release easily. You can use stainless steel mixing bowls or even plastic storage containers. Remember that once you unmold the dessert, you will garnish it and the original design of the mold becomes secondary.

PREPARING THE MOLD   Many Bavarians require oiling the mold. Use any lightly flavored or flavorless vegetable oil, or almond oil, if available. Use just enough to oil the mold without puddling. Turn the mold upside down to drain the excess oil while you prepare the dessert. Do not use butter because the chilling sets the butter too firmly and you may need to heat the mold too much to melt the butter, and end up melting the Bavarian.

UNMOLDING   Dip the chilled and set dessert into a bowl of very hot water for 10 to 20 seconds. Run the blade of a small knife around the edge and tilt the mold to one side, allowing the Bavarian to pull away from the side and to let some air enter. Place a serving plate on top of the mold and in one quick fluid movement, turn the mold over and place the plate on a counter. Give the mold and platter a firm shake and lift off the mold. If the mold does not release, repeat the shaking. If it is still a bother, cover with a cloth wrung out in very hot water and wrap around the mold for 30 seconds.

PREPARING AHEAD   Serve Bavarians within 12 to 36 hours. They begin to lose their velvety smoothness and lightness if held too long, and the gelatin can cause the cream to become rubbery. You can freeze Bavarians, but they should be served before they are completely thawed. They will not be as velvety.

VANILLA BAVARIAN CREAM

1 cup milk	½ cup sugar
1-in piece of vanilla bean or 1	1 tablespoon gelatin
teaspoon vanilla	2 tablespoons cold water
4 egg yolks	1 cup heavy cream

1. Oil a 3-cup mold.

2. In a saucepan, scald the milk with the vanilla bean and let steep for 10 minutes. In a heavy saucepan, beat the egg yolks with the sugar until they are thickened and pale. Slowly pour the scalded milk into the egg yolks stirring constantly. Cook over low heat, stirring constantly, until smooth and thick enough to coat the back of a spoon. Strain into a bowl and discard the vanilla bean. (If using vanilla extract, add it now.)

3. In a bowl, soften the gelatin in cold water. Stir into the hot custard until dissolved. Refrigerate the custard, covered with plastic wrap, until it is cold and slightly thickened.

4. In a mixer, beat the cream until it forms soft peaks and fold into the custard. Pour into the mold. Chill about 3 hours, or until fully set.

Yields 6 servings

Can be prepared the day before serving. Do not try to prepare further ahead, or the gelatin will make it rubbery.

Variations

- *Liqueur-Flavored.* Omit the vanilla. Substitute a favorite liqueur, to taste. Depending on the liqueur, the Bavarian will require from 2 tablespoons to ¼ cup or more depending on the type.
- *Berry.* Omit the vanilla. Use 2 tablespoons of gelatin. Substitute 2 cups of pureed berries (strained if seedy), adding them to the custard before folding in the cream. For texture, fold in ½ cup of berries just before pouring into the mold.
- *Fruit.* Prepare the Bavarian, using a fruit liqueur if desired, and fold in ½ to 1 cup of diced fruit before pouring into the mold. (Do not use fresh pineapple. It contains an enzyme that prevents gelatin from setting. Therefore, you must either cook the pineapple briefly or use the canned fruit. The briefly cooked pineapple will retain the freshest flavor.)
- *Coffee.* Omit the vanilla. Add 1 tablespoon instant espresso powder, dissolved in 1 tablespoon of hot water, and stir into the hot custard.
- *Chocolate.* Melt 3 ounces of semisweet chocolate in the milk.

GINGER BAVARIAN CREAM

2 tablespoons gelatin	**ginger**
½ cup cold water	**1 teaspoon vanilla**
1 cup hot Custard Sauce,	**2 cups heavy cream, whipped,**
page 545	**sweetened, and flavored with**
3 tablespoons minced	**ginger syrup**
preserved ginger	**Crystallized ginger, minced**
¼ cup syrup from preserved	

1. Oil a 5-cup mold.

2. In a small bowl, soften the gelatin in the water. Stir into the hot custard sauce until dissolved. Stir in the minced ginger, ginger syrup, and vanilla. Refrigerate, stirring occasionally, until slightly thickened.

3. Fold in 2 cups of whipped cream and pour into the mold. Chill until fully set and unmold onto a serving platter. Pipe the remaining whipped cream over and around the dessert and sprinkle with the minced ginger.

Yields 6 servings

Can be prepared the day before. Garnish no more than 2 hours before serving.

ANANAS GEORGETTE
(Pineapple Bavarian Cream)

1 large pineapple	**2 recipes hot Custard Sauce,**
½ cup rum	**page 545**
2 tablespoons gelatin	**4 egg whites**
¼ cup cold water	**1 cup heavy cream, whipped**

1. Cut the core from the center of the pineapple to form a container (see page 55). Reserve the pineapple frond and crush the fruit. In a saucepan, blanch the pineapple shell in boiling water for 2 minutes, drain, and refrigerate until cold.

2. In another saucepan, bring the crushed pineapple and rum to a boil and refrigerate until cold.

3. In a small bowl, soften the gelatin in the cold water. Stir mixture into 3 cups of hot custard sauce until dissolved. (Save remaining sauce for another use.) Refrigerate, stirring occasionally, until slightly thickened.

4. In a bowl, beat the egg whites until almost stiff and fold into the custard. Fold in the whipped cream and then the crushed pineapple. Pour as much as possible into the pineapple mold. Refrigerate until cold. Pour the remaining mixture into oiled individual molds or an oiled 1-quart ring mold and refrigerate until fully set.

5. To serve, arrange the pineapple on a platter and place the frond on top. Arrange the individual molds around the pineapple, or slice the large mold and arrange around the pineapple.

Yields 6 servings

Can be prepared 24 hours before serving.

BAVAROIS PRALINE (Praline Bavarian Cream)

Serve this with a fruit sauce, such as apricot or raspberry, or a kirsch- or orange-flavored chocolate sauce, or just sprinkled lavishly with coarsely crushed praline powder.

1 tablespoon gelatin	3 tablespoons kirsch
2 tablespoons cold water	½ cup Praline Powder, page 30
1½ cups hot Custard Sauce, page 545	1 cup heavy cream, whipped

1. Oil a 3-cup mold.

2. In a small bowl, soften the gelatin in the cold water and stir into the hot custard until the gelatin dissolves. Add the kirsch and praline powder, stirring occasionally. Refrigerate until slightly thickened.

3. Fold in the whipped cream and pour into the mold. Refrigerate until cold. Serve plain or with a sauce of your choice.

Yields 6 servings

Can be prepared 24 hours before serving.

BAVAROISE RUBANÉE AUX FRAMBOISES
(Striped Bavarian Cream with Raspberries)

Striped Bavarians are a favorite dessert. Select one, two, or three flavors and add them to the mold in layers. Try strawberry, vanilla, and apricot, or coffee, chocolate, and vanilla.

2 tablespoons gelatin	pureed, and strained
¼ cup cold water	2 cups heavy cream, whipped
3 cups hot Custard Sauce,	1 cup cold Vanilla Custard
page ••	Sauce, page 545
1 teaspoon vanilla	Whole fresh raspberries, for
20 ounces frozen unsweetened	garnish
raspberries, thawed,	

1. Oil a 3-quart mold.

2. In a bowl, soften the gelatin in the water. Stir the gelatin mixture into the hot custard until dissolved.

3. Divide the custard between 2 bowls. Stir the vanilla into one bowl and half the raspberry puree into the second bowl. Refrigerate until thick and slightly thickened.

4. Fold half of the whipped cream into each bowl.

5. Pour one-third of the raspberry Bavarian into a 3-quart mold and refrigerate for 10 minutes. Keep remainder at room temperature. Add one-third of the vanilla custard and refrigerate 10 minutes more. Repeat the layers and chilling two more times. Refrigerate until fully set.

6. Unmold and garnish with the fresh raspberries. Pass the remaining raspberry puree sauce and cold custard separately, or arrange in a design on the platter (see page 189).

Yields 6 servings

Can be prepared 24 hours before serving.

Variation

• Substitute chocolate- or coffee-flavored Bavarians. Serve with chocolate sauce, coffee-flavored custard sauce, or the vanilla custard and raspberry puree sauce listed above, or any other sauce that complements the flavor of your Bavarian.

BAVAROIS AU KIRSCH ET FRAISES
(Bavarian Cream with Kirsch and Strawberries)

1 tablespoon gelatin	½ cup heavy cream, whipped
2 tablespoons cold water	¼ cup kirsch
1½ cups hot, kirsch-flavored	1 pint strawberries, for
Custard Sauce, page 546	garnish
3 egg whites	

1.   Oil a 1-quart mold.

2.   In a bowl, soften the gelatin in the water. Stir into the hot custard until dissolved. Refrigerate, stirring occasionally, until slightly thickened.

3.   Beat the egg whites until almost stiff and fold into the cooled custard. Fold in the whipped cream and kirsch and pour into the mold. Refrigerate until set.

4.   Unmold onto a serving platter and garnish with the strawberries.

Yields 6 servings

Can be prepared 24 hours before serving.

Chapter 6

CHARLOTTES

A charlotte can be one of two similar but different desserts. The first is a Bavarian cream or a buttercream encased in ladyfingers or cake and the second is a cooked fruit puree encased in a bread-lined mold.

The first version (*Charlotte Russe* is the best-known example) was created by the great chef Antonin Carême, chef to Czar Alexander, the Prince Regent, later George IV of England, and Talleyrand, the renowned diplomat. According to *Larousse Gastronomique,* Carême originally called the dessert *Charlotte Parisienne,* which he prepared as a take-out dessert for the great houses of Paris, just before and after the French Revolution. Apparently he changed the name when he went to work for the czar.

For a *Charlotte Russe,* line a straight-sided mold with ladyfingers, sponge cake slices, or slices of jelly roll and fill with a creamy filling. Originally vanilla-flavored, charlottes now appear in every possible flavor and the creamy filling, once based only on Bavarian cream, may be based on buttercream and whipped cream or even a cold mousse. The unmolded charlotte is garnished with whipped cream, more of the fruit used in the filling, and served with a complementary sauce.

The second version (apple charlotte is the best-known example) dates much earlier. A few basic ingredients, found in most kitchens and standard fare in the kitchens of long ago, combine to make a delicious, nourishing, and eye-appealing dessert. Dip thick bread slices in butter and line a straight-sided mold. Prepare a thick fruit puree; apple is the most common, but pears, bananas, and cranberries are other options. Pile the puree in the center of the mold. Cover with slices of buttered bread and bake to a deep golden brown. The excess juices from the puree soak into the bread while the butter crisps the outside of the bread to form a shell. Allow the cooked charlotte to cool and settle before unmolding. Serve with fruit sauce, ice cream, or whipped cream. If you refrigerate hot charlottes, allow them to come to room temperature before serving. When cold they are far less appealing.

CHARLOTTE MOLDS Gourmet shops sell metal molds specifically designed for charlottes. They have slightly tapering sides with handles. These molds work well for any molded dessert or main course and are extremely useful and well worth the modest expense. But do not allow the lack of a charlotte pan prevent you from making charlottes. Any straight or almost straight-sided mold will do. Soufflé dishes, deep cake pans, and springform pans work especially well for cold charlottes, as do mixing bowls, plastic containers, or even saucepans. Although charlottes traditionally appear in rounded form, there is no reason a loaf pan cannot make a satisfactory mold. Once unmolded, the dessert gets decorated with fruit, whipped cream, sauces, etc. So the mold is of little importance.

Hot charlottes must be baked in an ovenproof mold such as a charlotte mold, deep cake pan, soufflé dish, or glass baking dish. A loaf pan would also work. A springform pan can do in a pinch, if well wrapped in several layers of heavy-duty foil. If it is not wrapped, the juices may leak all over the oven.

Cold Charlottes

TO LINE A MOLD WITH LADYFINGERS Whenever possible make lady-fingers rather than buy them (see recipe on page 21). Most commercial ladyfingers are too spongy and taste like cardboard. Good ladyfingers have a delicate flavor of vanilla, lemon, or perhaps a liqueur and a tender, airy interior within a crispy shell. They absorb a small amount of liquid and yet retain their shape. (They will disintegrate if soaked in too much liquid, or too long.) Ladyfingers freeze well and will keep for several months. They keep at room temperature in a covered container for several weeks. You can still use them even if they have dried out because the moisture from the filling will soften them. Another advantage is that you can shape the ladyfingers to fit your mold. If you must buy them, purchase them from a good bakery rather than accept the tasteless, spongy supermarket offerings.

Lightly oil a charlotte mold, springform pan, or soufflé dish. Line the bottom of the mold with waxed paper, parchment paper, or plastic wrap. Cut the ladyfingers into triangles (see illustration). Arrange the points toward the center. For a perfect fit, cut a 1-inch circle from the center of the points and fill with a 1-inch circle of ladyfinger. Do not worry if they do not fit perfectly; the garnish usually hides any irregularities. Line the remaining ladyfingers around the edge of the pan. I often trim a little slice off one end to give the ladyfingers a straight edge to help them stand. Add the filling and trim any ladyfingers that extend above it. Press the trimmings into the filling. It will be the bottom when you unmold it.

Many recipes suggest dipping the ladyfingers into a liqueur or flavored syrup. Besides adding flavor, this helps to stick them to the sides of the mold. Take care not to soak the ladyfingers or they will disintegrate. Another, safer method is to brush or sprinkle the ladyfingers with the liqueur or syrup once they are in place. A few recipes line only the bottom or only the sides of the mold and sometimes, especially when using a crisp cookie like cats' tongues, the cookies are "glued" to the outside of the charlotte once the filling sets and is unmolded.

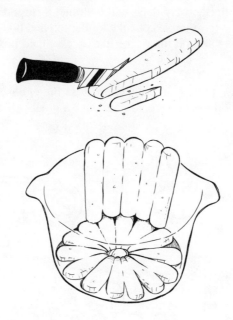

How many ladyfingers? It depends on the ladyfingers. The supermarket variety are about ¾ inch across and 2½ inches long; pastry shop versions may be as much as 2 inches across and 4 to 5 inches long. You will make them a size suited to your mold. I tested the recipes with ladyfingers about 1½ inches across and about 3 inches long. If buying ladyfingers, buy a few extra. They have many uses and you can freeze the excess.

TO LINE A MOLD WITH CAKE   Use sheet cakes made of sponge cake (see page 19) or génoise (see page 20) because they are springy enough to roll and bend to fit the molds. Nutted cakes make delicious tops and bottoms for some charlottes.

Oil and line the bottom of a mold with waxed paper, parchment paper, or plastic wrap, as for ladyfingers. Roll the sponge cake like a jelly roll, after spreading with a suitable filling. Roll from the long side and cut into ¼- to ½-inch thick slices. Arrange cut side down in the bottom and up the sides of the mold. A round mixing bowl, oiled and lined with plastic wrap, allows for a particularly pretty presentation (see illustration).

Another method is to cut a sponge sheet cake in half lengthwise, sandwich with filling, and cut into 1-inch-wide strips. Line a mixing bowl with plastic wrap and arrange the strips cut side down, cutting additional strips to fit. The finished charlotte will look like a striped dome.

Some charlottes have circles of cake for the top and bottom of the mold with strips of cake around the edges like a cake-lined box.

FILLINGS FOR COLD CHARLOTTES   Bavarian cream is the most common, but not the only, filling for cold charlottes. Butter-based creams and mousses in many flavors give cold charlottes a great variety of tastes and

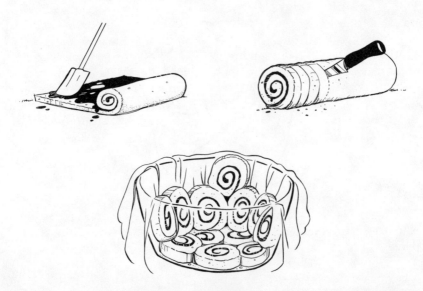

textures. The filling, once set, must be thick enough to support the un-molded dessert. You should be able to cut it into neat slices without it being heavy or dense. Gelatin, butter, and chocolate all help to keep different charlottes upright.

The most important point in preparing fillings for cold charlottes is to have the ingredients at the right consistency. Beat whipped cream and egg whites to the soft peak stage. If they are too stiff, they will deflate when folded into other ingredients. Gelatin mixtures should be slightly thickened, about the consistency of raw egg whites. Then, any heavy ingredients, such as pieces of fruit, will stay in suspension instead of sinking to the bottom. If the gelatin is too liquid, it may settle out of the cream and egg whites and make a gelatin layer, rather than remain fully incorporated.

Baked Charlottes

TO LINE A MOLD WITH BREAD SLICES There are a few differences between a hot and cold charlotte. Do not use a springform pan, unless you wrap the outside with several layers of aluminum foil. Butter the mold with softened butter. The butter helps the bread to stick to the sides of the mold and to crisp during baking. Slice the bread into ½-inch-thick and 2½- to 3-inch-wide slices about 4 inches long. Arrange the slices overlapping in the bottom of mold, or cut triangles to fit the bread to the bottom of the mold. Arrange the remaining slices, upright, and overlapping by at least ½ inch around the edges of the mold. Remove the slices and dip into melted butter. Reline the mold with the buttered bread.

Cook the fruit puree until it will hold its shape in a spoon. If the puree is too soft, the charlotte could collapse when unmolded. Add enough puree to mound slightly in the mold. If you do not have enough, cut the bread ends level after the charlotte cools and before unmolding. Cool the baked charlotte at least 30 minutes before unmolding to allow the puree to settle and thicken. The fruit puree is boiling hot when the charlotte comes from the oven and could cause serious burns if served directly. If you wish to prepare the baked charlotte the day before, bring it to room temperature before serving, or reheat it in a 350°F. oven until the puree registers 140°F. on a thermometer. Let it rest for at least 10 minutes before unmolding.

FRUIT PUREES FOR BAKED CHARLOTTES Almost any fruit that cooks to a thick puree will substitute for the apples, but some fruits are too intensely flavored to be served in large quantities. It would be like eating a jar of jam on a single slice of bread. One method of diminishing the intensity of flavor is to make individual charlottes that provide more bread in relation to the puree.

CHARLOTTE NESSELRODE
(Candied Fruit Charlotte)

This is named for the Russian general.

18–24 Ladyfingers, page 21	**1¼ cup Nesselrode Mix, page 28**
1 tablespoon gelatin	**1 cup heavy cream**
2 tablespoons Cognac, kirsch,	**Whipped cream, for garnish**
or rum	
3 cups hot Custard Sauce,	
page 545	

1.   Lightly oil a 6-cup mold, line the bottom with a circle of waxed paper or parchment paper, and line the bottom and sides of mold with the ladyfingers.

2.   In a bowl, soften the gelatin in the Cognac. Stir the gelatin into the hot custard until dissolved. Refrigerate, stirring occasionally, until slightly thickened.

3.   Fold in 1 cup of Nesselrode mix. Beat the cream until it forms soft peaks and fold into the Nesselrode-custard mixture and pour into the lined mold. Refrigerate until set.

4.   Unmold onto a serving platter and garnish with the whipped cream and the remaining Nesselrode mix.

Yields 6 servings

Can be prepared up to 24 hours before serving.

CHARLOTTE AUX ABRICOTS (Apricot Charlotte)

2 tablespoons gelatin	**1 cup heavy cream, whipped**
1¼ cups cold water	**2 tablespoons kirsch**
1 quart fresh apricots, pitted	**1 (9-in) layer of Génoise,**
2 cups sugar	**flavored with kirsch, page 20**
3 tablespoons light corn	**Whipped cream, for garnish**
syrup	**Apricot slices, for garnish**
Juice of 1 lemon	

1.   In a bowl, soften the gelatin in ¼ cup of the water. In a saucepan simmer the apricots with the sugar, the remaining water, and corn syrup for 15 minutes, or until very soft.

2.   Line the bottom of a 9-inch springform pan with a circle of waxed or parchment paper. Slice the génoise into 2 thin layers. Place 1 layer in the springform pan. Add the apricot mixture and cover with the remaining génoise, pressing gently into place. Refrigerate until set.

3. In a processor, puree the fruit with the lemon juice and the softened gelatin. Refrigerate, stirring occasionally, until slightly thickened.

4. Unmold onto a serving platter. Garnish the charlotte with the whipped cream and the apricots.

5. Fold in the whipped cream and the kirsch.

Yields 8 or more servings

Can be prepared up to 24 hours before serving.

Variation

• If fresh apricots are not available, reconstitute 2 cups of dried apricots in water to cover for 1 hour. Drain, reserving the water. Simmer the apricots in a saucepan with 2 cups of sugar and the reserved water, mixed with enough fresh water to make 1 cup, until tender. Proceed as above.

CHARLOTTE AU CHOCOLAT
(Chocolate Charlotte)

4 ounces semisweet chocolate	1⅓ cups unsweetened cocoa
18–24 Ladyfingers, page 21	1½ cups heavy cream
5 egg yolks	¼ cup confectioners' sugar
¾ cup sugar	2 cups Raspberry Sauce, page 552
9 ounces butter, softened	

1. Melt the chocolate and cool to room temperature.

2. Lightly oil a 6-cup charlotte mold, line the bottom with a circle of waxed or parchment paper and oil the paper. Dust the mold with sugar. Line the bottom and sides with the ladyfingers.

3. In a bowl, beat the egg yolks and the sugar until thickened and pale. In another bowl, cream the butter and the cocoa until smooth. Blend the yolks into the butter mixture and fold in the cooled chocolate.

4.   Whip the cream with the confectioners' sugar until they form soft peaks and fold into the chocolate mixture. Pour into the mold. Refrigerate until set. Trim the ladyfingers, if needed.

5.   Unmold onto a serving platter and serve the sauce on the side, or drizzle over the top.

Yields 6 servings

Can be prepared up to 2 days before serving.

LE RÊVE
(The Dream — Chocolate Charlotte with
Coffee Custard)

18–24 Ladyfingers, page 21	8 ounces semisweet chocolate,
1 cup milk	chopped
1-in piece of vanilla bean	3 tablespoons water
4 tablespoons sugar	½ cup butter
1 egg	Custard Sauce, coffee-
1 egg yolk	flavored, page 546

1.   Line the bottom of a 6-cup charlotte mold with a circle of parchment or waxed paper and line the bottom and sides of the mold with the ladyfingers.

2.   In a saucepan, scald the milk, vanilla bean, and sugar. Cover and let stand for 10 minutes.

3.   In a bowl, beat the egg and the egg yolk until blended. Beat in the hot milk. Return to the pan and cook over medium heat, stirring, until thick enough to coat the back of a spoon. Strain into a bowl.

4.   In a saucepan or microwave, melt the chocolate, water, and butter, stirring as needed. Fold into custard and pour into the mold. Refrigerate about 6 hours, or until set.

5.   Unmold onto a serving dish, and pour the coffee custard around it.

Yields 6 servings

Can be prepared up to 2 days ahead.

CHOCOLATE, COFFEE, AND ORANGE CHARLOTTE

The chocolate stiffens the cream so gelatin is unnecessary.

18–24 Ladyfingers, page 21
2½ tablespoons instant
   espresso powder
¼ cup hot water
8 ounces semisweet
   chocolate, chopped
½ cup butter
½ cup sugar
3 eggs, separated

¼ cup plus 1 tablespoon
   orange liqueur
¼ cup plus 1 tablespoon coffee
   liqueur
1½ cups heavy cream
2 tablespoons confectioners'
   sugar
Shaved chocolate, for
   garnish

1. Lightly oil a 6-cup charlotte mold, line the bottom with a circle of waxed or parchment paper and oil the paper. Dust the mold with sugar. Line the bottom and sides with the ladyfingers. Dissolve the espresso powder in the water.

2. In a saucepan or microwave, melt the chocolate, butter, sugar, and espresso mixture, stirring until smooth. Cool to room temperature.

3. In a bowl, beat the egg yolks to blend. Fold in the cooled chocolate mixture and ¼ cup each of orange and coffee liqueurs. Beat the egg whites until stiff, but not dry, and fold into the chocolate mixture. Beat ¾ cup of cream until it forms soft peaks and fold into the chocolate mixture. Pour into the mold and cover with any extra ladyfingers. Refrigerate until set.

4. Unmold onto platter. Beat the remaining cream until it forms soft peaks, beat in the confectioners' sugar and the remaining orange and coffee liqueurs until stiff. Fill a pastry bag fitted with a #5 open star tip with the whipped cream and pipe rosettes around the dessert. Sprinkle the shaved chocolate over the top.

Yields 6 servings

Can be prepared up to 24 hours before serving.

CHARLOTTE LOUISE (Lemon Charlotte I)

This is a lemon lover's delight — sponge cake layers filled with lemon curd enclosing an airy lemon mousse. For color, surround with fresh cherries or raspberries.

11 × 17-in Sponge Cake, page 19	**2 cups heavy cream**
1 recipe Lemon Curd, page 28	**2 tablespoons grated lemon rind**
1 recipe cold Lemon Soufflé, page 365	**Sugar, to taste**

1.   Line a 4-quart mixing bowl with plastic wrap.

2.   Cut the cake layer in half lengthwise. Spread one half with lemon curd and top with the second layer. Cut the cake into 1-inch-wide strips. They will be 5½ inches long. Line the bowl with the strips of cake, cut sides down. Trim the strips of cake to fit tightly.

3.   Prepare the soufflé and fill the mold. Refrigerate about 3 hours, or until set.

4.   Unmold the cake onto a serving platter. Beat the cream with the lemon rind and sugar until stiff peaks form. Using a pastry bag fitted with a star tip, pipe the whipped cream decoratively over the surface of the mold.

Yields 10 to 12 servings

Can be prepared the day before serving.

LEMON CHARLOTTE II

18–24 Ladyfingers, page 21
¾ cup plus 1 tablespoon
  sugar
3 tablespoons kirsch
¼ cup plus 2 tablespoons
  water
1 tablespoon gelatin
1½ tablespoons grated lemon
  rind

⅔ cup strained lemon juice
4 egg whites
Pinch of salt
1 cup heavy cream, whipped
Whipped cream, for garnish
Grated lemon rind or
  raspberries, for garnish

1. Lightly oil a 6-cup charlotte mold and line with a circle of parchment or waxed paper. Line the bottom and sides of the mold with the ladyfingers, reserving the remaining ladyfingers.

2. In a bowl, stir 1 tablespoon of sugar, the kirsch, and 2 tablespoons of water until the sugar dissolves. Brush over the ladyfingers, reserving 2 tablespoons of syrup.

3. In a small saucepan, soften the gelatin in ¼ cup of cold water. Dissolve over low heat. Stir in the remaining sugar, the lemon rind, and juice. Heat until the sugar dissolves. Pour into a bowl and refrigerate, stirring occasionally, until slightly thickened.

4. In a mixer, beat the egg whites and salt until they form soft peaks. Fold into the gelatin mixture with the 1 cup of heavy cream, whipped. Pour half of the lemon mousse into the ladyfinger-lined mold and top with a layer of remaining ladyfingers. Brush with the reserved kirsch syrup. Add the remaining lemon mousse mixture. Refrigerate 6 hours, or until set.

5. Unmold onto a platter and garnish with whipped cream and grated lemon rind or raspberries.

Yields 6 to 8 servings

Can be prepared 24 hours before serving.

LEMON-BLUEBERRY CHARLOTTE

18–24 Ladyfingers, see page 21	4 eggs, separated
5 tablespoons water	½ teaspoon grated lemon rind
¾ cup plus 1½ tablespoons sugar	1 cup heavy cream, whipped
	2 cups blueberries
¾ cup plus 2 tablespoons lemon juice	2 cups Blueberry Sauce, page 549
1 tablespoon gelatin	

1.   Lightly oil a 6-cup charlotte mold, line the bottom with a circle of waxed or parchment paper and oil the paper. Dust the mold with sugar. Line the bottom and sides with the ladyfingers.

2.   In a small bowl, mix 3 tablespoons of water, 1½ tablespoons of sugar, and 2 tablespoons of lemon juice until the sugar dissolves. Brush the ladyfingers with the lemon syrup.

3.   In a saucepan, soften the gelatin in the remaining water. Beat in the egg yolks, the remaining lemon juice, and ½ cup of sugar. Cook over low heat, stirring until thick enough to coat the back of a spoon. Strain into a bowl and stir in the lemon rind. Refrigerate, stirring occasionally, until slightly thickened.

4.   In a large bowl, beat the egg whites until soft peaks form. Then beat in the remaining sugar until it forms stiff peaks. Fold into the lemon mixture. Fold the whipped cream and the blueberries into the mixture and fill the mold. Refrigerate until set.

5.   Unmold onto a serving platter and serve with the blueberry sauce on the side.

Yields 10 to 12 servings

Can be prepared the day before serving.

PEACH CHARLOTTE

20 Ladyfingers, page 21	1 tablespoons gelatin
6 Vanilla Poached Peach	5 tablespoons water
halves, liquid reserved,	2 cups heavy cream
page 40	Sugar, to taste
3 tablespoons sugar	Vanilla, to taste

1. Line the bottom of a 6-cup charlotte mold with a circle of parchment or waxed paper. Line the bottom and sides of the mold with the ladyfingers.

2. Reserve 1 peach half for garnish. In a processor, puree the remaining peaches with on/off turns and measure. Add enough poaching liquid to make 2 cups. Stir in the sugar. In a small saucepan, soften the gelatin in the water. Stir over low heat until the gelatin dissolves. Stir into the peach puree and refrigerate, stirring occasionally, until slightly thickened.

3. Beat 1 cup of the cream until it forms soft peaks and fold into the puree. Pour into the mold. Refrigerate until set.

4. Unmold the charlotte onto a serving platter. Beat the remaining cream and sweeten with sugar and vanilla to taste. Using a pastry bag fitted with a #5 open star tip, pipe rosettes of whipped cream on the top of the charlotte. Slice the reserved peach half and garnish the charlotte.

Yields 6 servings

Can be prepared up to 24 hours before serving. Do the final assembly just before serving.

Variation

- Substitute 20 Cats' Tongues Cookies for the ladyfingers. Do not line the mold with the cookies. Once set, dip the mold into hot water and unmold onto a serving platter. Spread a thin layer of the whipped cream prepared for garnish around the sides of the charlotte and "glue" the cookies to the cream. Pipe the remaining cream on top of the charlotte.

CHARLOTTE AUX POIRES ET CARAMEL
(Charlotte with Pears and Caramel)

18–24 Ladyfingers, page 21	½ teaspoon vanilla
1 tablespoon gelatin	1 cup heavy cream
¼ cup plus 2 tablespoons cold water	4 Vanilla Poached Pears, page 40
1 recipe hot Custard Sauce, page 545	1 cup Caramel-flavored Custard Sauce, page 545
¾ cup sugar	

1. Lightly butter a 6-cup charlotte mold, line the bottom with a circle of waxed or parchment paper, and dust the mold with sugar. Line the bottom and sides with ladyfingers.

2. Soften the gelatin in ¼ cup of cold water. Stir into the hot custard sauce until dissolved.

3. In a separate saucepan, caramelize the sugar, vanilla, and the remaining water without stirring, until it turns a deep golden brown. Cool to room temperature. Stir into the custard, and refrigerate, stirring occasionally, until slightly thickened.

4. Whip the cream to the soft peak stage and fold into the custard mixture. Dice two pears, fold into the custard, and turn into the prepared mold. Refrigerate until set.

5. Unmold onto a serving platter. Slice remaining pears and garnish charlotte. Serve with sauce.

Yields 6 servings

Can be prepared 24 hours before serving.

CHARLOTTE À LA CHAMBOURIENNE
(Pear Charlotte with Raspberry Sauce I)

24–30 Ladyfingers, page 21	2 cups hot Custard Sauce,
2 Vanilla Poached Pears,	page 545
sliced, page 40	1½ cups heavy cream
2 tablespoons pear eau de vie	¼ cup sugar
1½ teaspoons gelatin	Raspberry Sauce, page 552
¼ cup water	

1. Lightly oil a 6-cup charlotte mold and line the bottom with a circle of waxed or parchment paper. Line the bottom and sides of the mold with the ladyfingers. Dice remaining ladyfingers.

2. In a bowl, macerate the pears in the pear eau de vie.

3. In another bowl, soften the gelatin in the water. Stir into the hot custard sauce until the gelatin dissolves. Refrigerate, stirring occasionally until slightly thickened.

4. In a bowl, beat the cream and the sugar until they form soft peaks and fold into the custard with the pears and the diced ladyfingers. Fill the prepared mold. Refrigerate until set.

5. Unmold onto a serving platter and serve with the raspberry sauce.

Yields 6 to 8 servings

Can be prepared up to 24 hours before serving.

CHARLOTTE AUX POIRES AVEC COULIS DE FRAMBOISES
(Pear Charlotte with Raspberry Sauce II)

2 (10-in) Nutted Génoise	1½ teaspoons gelatin
Layers, page 21	2 cups hot Custard Sauce,
5 Vanilla Poached Pears,	page 545
diced, liquid reserved,	2 egg whites
page 40	1 cup heavy cream
¼ cup plus 2 tablespoons	Raspberry Sauce, page 552
pear eau de vie	

1. Lightly oil a 10-inch springform pan, line with waxed or parchment paper, and sprinkle the bottom of the pan with confectioners' sugar. Place one cake layer in the pan.

2. In a small bowl, mix 2 tablespoons of poaching liquid with 2 tablespoons of pear eau de vie and brush over the cake layer in the pan.

3. In a bowl, soften the gelatin in 2 tablespoons of poaching liquid. Stir into the hot custard sauce until the gelatin dissolves. Refrigerate, stirring occasionally, until slightly thickened.

4. Drain the pears. In a saucepan, reduce the remaining poaching liquid to 2 cups. Cool and reserve. Beat the egg whites until they form soft peaks. Slowly add ⅔ cup of reserved poaching liquid and beat until the mixture forms stiff peaks. Fold into the cooled custard. Beat the cream to the soft peak stage and fold into the custard mixture with the remaining pear eau de vie.

5. Spread half the mixture over the cake in the pan and scatter the diced pears on top. Cover with the remaining custard mixture and the remaining cake layer. Refrigerate until set.

6. Unmold onto a serving platter and sift confectioners' sugar over the top. Serve with the raspberry sauce.

Yields 12 servings

Can be prepared up to 24 hours before serving.

PUMPKIN CHARLOTTE

For a change from the traditional pumpkin pie for the holidays, try this magnificent treat.

⅔ **cup sugar**
½ **cup water**
4 **tablespoons dark rum**
18–24 **Ladyfingers, page 21**
½ **cup gingersnap crumbs**
2 **tablespoons gelatin**
2 **cups hot Custard Sauce,
   prepared with brown sugar,
   page 545**
1 **pound pumpkin puree**

2 **teaspoons grated orange
   rind**
½ **teaspoon cinnamon**
¼ **teaspoon nutmeg**
¼ **teaspoon ginger**
1½ **cups heavy cream**
4 **egg whites**
1 **tablespoon confectioners'
   sugar**

1. Lightly oil the bottom and sides of a 9-inch springform pan.

2. In a saucepan, dissolve the sugar in ¼ cup of water over low heat, cool, and stir in 3 tablespoons of rum. Quickly dip the ladyfingers in the syrup and roll in the gingersnap crumbs. Line the sides of the mold with the ladyfingers.

3. In a bowl, soften the gelatin in the remaining water. Stir the gelatin mixture into the hot custard sauce until dissolved. Stir in the pumpkin, orange rind, cinnamon, nutmeg, and ginger. Refrigerate, stirring occasionally, until slightly thickened.

4. Whip 1 cup of cream with the remaining sugar until it forms soft peaks. Fold into the pumpkin mixture. Beat the egg whites until not quite stiff and fold into the pumpkin mixture. Pour into the prepared mold. Refrigerate until set.

5. Unmold onto a serving platter. Whip the remaining cream to soft peaks and beat in the remaining rum and the confectioners' sugar. Beat until stiff. Using a pastry bag fitted with a #5 open star tip, pipe rosettes of the whipped cream over the top.

Yields 12 servings

Can be prepared up to 24 hours before serving.

CHARLOTTE RUSSE
(Raspberry and Pineapple Charlotte)

Fresh pineapple contains an enzyme that prevents gelatin from setting. Therefore, whenever it is used with gelatin, it must be poached for at least 1 minute to neutralize this enzyme. You may substitute canned pineapple, but it will not taste as fresh.

1½ vanilla syrup cups chopped
    pineapple
1 pound seedless raspberry
    jam
½ cup Cognac or kirsch
2 (10 × 15-in) Sponge Cakes,
    rolled, page 19
2 tablespoons gelatin

¼ cup cold water
3 cups hot Custard Sauce,
    page 545
1½ cups heavy cream
2 teaspoons vanilla
    Apricot Glaze, page 36
    Raspberry Sauce, page 552

1. Poach the pineapple in vanilla syrup for 1 minute (see page 40). Cool.

2. Line a 1½-quart mixing bowl with plastic wrap.

3. In a small saucepan, heat the jam with ¼ cup of Cognac until fluid.

4. Unroll the sponge cakes and spread with the jam. Roll tightly and cut into ½-inch-thick slices. Arrange in the lined bowl, cut side down, pressing the slices as closely together as possible.

5. In a bowl, soften the gelatin in the water. Stir into the hot custard until dissolved. Refrigerate, stirring occasionally, until slightly thickened.

6. Beat the cream until it forms soft peaks. Beat in the vanilla, until it forms stiff peaks. Chill. Fold into the custard mixture with the remaining Cognac and pour into the lined bowl. Refrigerate until almost set.

7. Drain the pineapple well. Press gently into the whipped cream mixture. Refrigerate until set.

8. Unmold and brush the charlotte with the apricot glaze. Garnish with any additional pineapple. Serve the raspberry sauce on the side.

Yields 12 servings

Can be prepared up to 24 hours before serving.

RHUBARB CHARLOTTE

The cats' tongues are crisp cookies that can become soggy if molded with the dessert, so they are "glued" to the outside shortly before serving.

¼ **cup currant jelly**	2 **egg whites**
1 **pound rhubarb, cut into**	¼ **cup sugar**
1-in pieces	1½ **cups heavy cream**
1 **tablespoon gelatin**	12–16 **Cats' Tongues**
¼ **cup water**	

1. Lightly oil a 6-cup charlotte mold or soufflé dish. Line the bottom with a circle of waxed or parchment paper.

2. In a saucepan, heat the currant jelly and rhubarb, stirring occasionally, until the rhubarb disintegrates. Puree in a processor.

3. In a bowl, soften the gelatin in the water. Stir into the hot puree until it dissolves. Refrigerate until slightly thickened.

4. Beat the egg whites until frothy. Add the sugar and beat until the mixture holds stiff peaks. Fold into the rhubarb. Beat 1 cup of cream until it forms soft peaks and fold into the rhubarb mixture. Pour into the prepared mold. Refrigerate until set.

5. Unmold onto a serving platter. In a bowl, whip the remaining cream until stiff and spread around the sides of the charlotte. "Glue" the cats' tongues to the sides of the dessert.

Yields 6 servings

Can be prepared 24 hours before serving.

Variation

• Substitute Ladyfingers (see page 21), for the cookies. Line the bottom and sides of the mold with the ladyfingers before filling.

INDIVIDUAL STRAWBERRY CHARLOTTES

Dariole molds are also called baba molds. They are small metal cups about 2 inches across the base and 3½ inches tall. They also come in other sizes.

1 (10 × 15 in) Sponge Cake, page 19	2 tablespoons orange-flavored liqueur
1 teaspoon gelatin	Red food coloring, optional
2 tablespoons water	Raspberry Cream, page 553, for garnish
1 cup hot orange-flavored Custard Sauce, page 546	12 whole strawberries, for garnish
1 pint strawberries, mashed	
1 cup heavy cream	

1. Lightly oil 12 dariole molds, ramekins, or custard cups. Cut part of the sponge cake into 12 circles large enough to fit the bottoms of the molds. Cut the remaining cake into 6-inch-long strips, wide enough to reach the top of the mold. Fit the cake into the molds.

2. In a bowl, soften the gelatin in the cold water. Stir into the hot custard until it dissolves. Refrigerate, stirring occasionally, until slightly thickened. Fold in the mashed strawberries.

3. In a bowl, whip the cream until it forms soft peaks and fold into the strawberry mixture with the orange liqueur and food coloring, if using. Fill each mold and refrigerate until set.

4.   Unmold onto a serving platter or individual plates and garnish with the raspberry cream and the whole strawberries.

Yields 12 servings

Can be prepared up to 24 hours before serving.

CHARLOTTE MALAKOFF AUX FRAISES
(Strawberry Charlotte Malakoff)

A Malakoff charlotte uses butter for the base instead of a custard sauce. Strawberry, raspberry, and chocolate are the most common flavors, but create your own dessert, using a favorite fruit or flavoring.

24 Ladyfingers, page 21	¼ teaspoon almond extract
⅓ cup plus ½ cup orange liqueur	1⅓ cups finely ground almonds
⅔ cup water	2 cups heavy cream
1 cup unsalted butter, softened	1 quart strawberries, hulled
1 cup sugar	1 cup heavy cream, whipped, sweetened, with sugar and orange liqueur, to taste

1.   Lightly oil a 6-cup charlotte mold and line the bottom with waxed or parchment paper. Line the bottom and sides of the mold with ladyfingers, reserving any extra. In a bowl, mix ⅓ cup of orange liqueur with the water and brush over the ladyfingers. Reserve the remaining orange liqueur mixture.

2.   In a processor or mixer, cream the butter and sugar until pale and fluffy. Beat in the remaining orange liqueur and the almond extract. Beat until the sugar dissolves. Beat in the almonds. In a mixer, whip 2 cups of heavy cream until it forms soft peaks and fold into the butter mixture.

3.   Pour one-third of the filling into the prepared mold. Dip some of the strawberries into the reserved orange liqueur mixture and arrange in a single layer over the filling. Add another third of the filling and top with another layer of liqueur-dipped strawberries. Fill the mold with the remaining filling. Place any remaining ladyfingers over the top of the filling and sprinkle with any remaining liqueur.

4.   Cover the mold with plastic wrap and a plate slightly smaller than the mold. Place a weight, such as a jar of jam, on top of the plate and refrigerate about 4 hours, or until set.

5. Unmold onto a serving platter. Fill a pastry bag fitted with a #5 open star tip with the whipped cream and pipe rosettes on the top and around the base of the charlotte. Place a whole strawberry on top of each rosette.

Yields 6 to 8 servings

Can be prepared up to 2 days in advance. Garnish just before serving.

Variations

• *Chocolate.*   Omit the strawberries. Add 8 ounces of melted semisweet chocolate to the creamed butter before folding in the whipped cream. Use orange, coffee, or almond liqueur. Or select another favorite flavor liqueur. Serve with Raspberry Sauce (see page 552) flavored with framboise, if desired.
• *Coffee.*   Substitute coffee liqueur for the orange liqueur. Omit the strawberries. Toast the almonds for a stronger flavor.
• *Kirsch.*   Substitute kirsch for the orange liqueur.
• *Peach.*   Substitute 4 Vanilla Poached Peaches (see page 40) for the strawberries. Use rum or amaretto instead of the orange liqueur.
• *Raspberry.*   Substitute raspberries for the strawberries. You also may substitute kirsch or framboise for the orange liqueur.

CHIPPOLATA
(South African Tangerine and Ginger Charlotte)

18–24 Ladyfingers, page 21	2 egg whites
½ cup tangerine liqueur	½ cup minced preserved ginger
1 tablespoon gelatin	2 tablespoons confectioners'
¼ cup cold water	sugar
2 cups hot Custard Sauce	1 cup heavy cream, whipped,
flavored with grated	for garnish
tangerine peel, page 546	

1. Lightly oil a 6-cup charlotte mold and line the bottom with a circle of waxed or parchment paper. Line the bottom and sides of the mold with ladyfingers and brush with the liqueur.

2. In a bowl, soften the gelatin in the cold water. Stir the gelatin mixture into the hot custard sauce until dissolved. Refrigerate, stirring occasionally, until slightly thickened.

3. In a bowl, beat the egg whites until stiff and fold into the custard with ¼ cup of minced ginger. Pour into the mold and refrigerate until set.

4. Unmold onto a serving platter and sprinkle with confectioners' sugar. Using a pastry bag fitted with a #5 open star tip, pipe a whipped cream garnish. Garnish with the remaining minced ginger.

Yields 6 servings

Can be prepared the day before serving.

CHARLOTTE MAKRAUER
(Mandarin Orange and Ginger Charlotte with Chocolate Sauce)

I created this dessert for Suzie Makrauer, using her favorite flavors.

11 × 17-in Sponge Cake, page 19
1½ cups Apricot Glaze, page 36
¼ cup orange liqueur
½ cup water
1 recipe Vanilla Bavarian Cream, page 206
½ cup chopped mandarin orange segments
½ cup finely diced preserved ginger
1½ cups heavy cream, whipped, sweetened with sugar and orange liqueur, to taste
1 cup mandarin orange segments, for garnish
Slices of preserved ginger, for garnish
2 cups Chocolate Sauce, page 540

1. Lightly oil a 2-quart charlotte mold or soufflé dish and line the bottom with a circle of waxed or parchment paper.

2. Spread the sponge sheet with the apricot glaze and roll tightly into a long jelly roll. Slice into ¼-inch-thick slices and arrange, cut side down, on the bottom and against the sides of the mold (see page 214).

3. In a bowl, mix the orange liqueur and water and brush over the cake slices.

4. Prepare the Bavarian cream and fold in the chopped mandarin oranges and the ginger. Turn into the mold. Refrigerate until set.

5. Unmold the dessert onto a serving platter. Using a pastry bag fitted with a #5 open star tip, pipe the whipped cream over and around the dessert. Garnish with the mandarin segments and ginger slices. Either pass the chocolate sauce separately or pour around the base of the dessert.

Yields 6 to 8 servings

Can be prepared 24 hours before serving.

CHOCOLATE AND TANGERINE CHARLOTTE

36 **Ladyfingers, page 21**	1 **teaspoon vanilla**
¼ **cup plus 3 tablespoons**	1 **teaspoon butter**
tangerine liqueur	2½ **cups heavy cream**
6 **ounces semisweet**	6 **tangerines, peeled,**
chocolate, melted	**membrane removed, and**
1½ **tablespoons gelatin**	**seeded**
¾ **cup orange juice**	2 **tablespoons confectioners'**
1½ **cups hot Custard Sauce,**	**sugar**
page 545	

1. Lightly oil a 9-inch springform pan and line the bottom with a circle of waxed or parchment paper. Cut the ladyfingers to fit the pan, dip into 2 tablespoons of liqueur, and arrange in the mold. Brush with the melted chocolate.

2. Brush the remaining ladyfingers with the remaining chocolate and refrigerate until set.

3. In a bowl, soften the gelatin in the orange juice. Stir into the hot custard sauce until the gelatin mixture dissolves. Stir in ¼ cup of tangerine liqueur, the vanilla and butter. Refrigerate, stirring occasionally, until slightly thickened.

4. In a bowl, whip 1½ cups of cream and fold into the custard mixture. Spread a ½-inch-thick layer of the custard mixture over the ladyfingers in the bottom of the mold. Cover with a layer of the chocolate-coated ladyfingers. Cover with one-third of the remaining custard mixture and half the tangerine sections. Add half the remaining custard and the remaining tangerines. Add the remaining custard mixture and any remaining ladyfingers. Refrigerate until set.

5. In a bowl, beat the remaining cream with the confectioners' sugar and remaining liqueur until stiff. Fill a pastry bag fitted with a #5 open star tip. Unmold the charlotte onto a serving platter and decorate with the whipped cream.

Yields 12 servings

Can be prepared up to 24 hours before serving.

CHARLOTTE COMTOISE
(Apple Charlotte Comtoise)

Cool at least 30 minutes before serving to settle the apples. If it collapses, it will taste just as good. Use Cortland, Golden Delicious, or Rome Beauty apples for the best results.

½ **cup sugar, plus additional for sprinkling**
1 **pound loaf firm white bread, crusts removed and sliced about ½ in thick**
¼ **pound butter, melted**
6 **large apples, peeled, cored,**
and thinly sliced
½ **teaspoon cinnamon**
6 **tablespoons dry white wine**
2 **tablespoons sherry**
1 **cup heavy cream, whipped, sweetened, and flavored, optional, for garnish**

1.   Preheat the oven to 375°F. Butter a 2-quart charlotte mold or soufflé dish. Sprinkle about 1 tablespoon sugar inside the mold.

2.   Cut the trimmed bread into fingers about 2 inches wide. Dip the bread into the melted butter and roll in the remaining sugar. Line the bottom and sides of the mold with the bread.

3.   Arrange the apple slices in layers in the dish and sprinkle each layer with a little additional sugar and cinnamon. Mound the apples in the center of the mold. Sprinkle the white wine and sherry over the apples.

4.   Bake for about 1 hour, or until the apples soften completely, turn translucent, and appear dry. Rest for 30 minutes and unmold onto a serving platter. Serve warm or at room temperature, garnished with the whipped cream.

Yields 6 servings

Can be prepared up to 2 days ahead. Allow to come to room temperature or reheat in a 350°F. oven before serving.

CHARLOTTE AUX POMMES (Apple Charlotte)

1 cup apricot preserves

6 pounds apples, peeled,
cored, and sliced

1 cup plus 2 tablespoons
sugar

2 teaspoons vanilla

¼ cup plus 3 tablespoons
dark rum

3 tablespoons butter

1 pound firm white bread,
crusts removed and sliced
about ½ in thick

1 cup butter, melted

1 cup heavy cream, whipped,
sweetened, and flavored
with rum, to taste, for
garnish

1. Preheat the oven to 425°F. Sieve ½ cup of preserves and reserve.

2. Place the apples in a heavy saucepan, cover, and simmer over low for 20 minutes, stirring occasionally. Uncover and stir in the unsieved ½ cup of apricot preserves, 1 cup of sugar, the vanilla, ¼ cup of rum, and 3 table- spoons of butter. Raise the heat and boil, stirring often, about 20 minutes, or until the mixture holds its shape in a spoon. (It is important that the apples cook to a thick puree.)

3. Dip the bread slices in the melted butter. Line a 2-quart charlotte mold with these slices.

4. Pour the apple puree into the mold, mounding in the center. Cover the top with remaining buttered bread slices and place the mold on a baking sheet. Bake for 30 minutes, or until the bread is golden. Rest for 30 minutes before unmolding.

5. Unmold the charlotte onto a serving platter. In a saucepan, simmer the reserved sieved apricot preserves, remaining rum, and sugar until lightly thickened. Drizzle over the top of the charlotte. Pass the whipped cream. Serve hot, warm, or cool, but not refrigerated.

Yields 6 servings

Can be prepared up to 2 days ahead. Let come to room temperature or reheat in a 350°F. oven before serving.

Variations

• *Raspberry-Apple.* Serve with a sauce made by melting ½ cup of sieved raspberry jam with ¼ cup of rum and 2 tablespoons of sugar instead of the apricot glaze.

• *Pear.* Substitute pears for the apples. Omit the rum and substitute Poire William.

CHARLOTTE À L'INDIENNE (Banana Charlotte)

1 pound loaf firm white bread, crusts removed, and sliced about ½-in thick	2 tablespoons butter
	1 tablespoon sugar
	1 tablespoon raisins
1 cup plus 3 tablespoons butter	½ cup Apricot Sauce, page 547
	1 tablespoon kirsch
6 bananas, sliced	

1. Preheat the oven to 400°F. Butter a 2-quart charlotte mold. Melt 1 cup of butter. Cut the bread to fit the mold (see page 215), dip the slices into the melted butter, and line the bottom and sides of the mold.

2. In a saucepan, cook the bananas with the remaining butter until hot and stir in the sugar and the raisins. Pour into the prepared mold and bake for 1 hour, or until the bread is golden. Rest for 30 minutes before unmolding.

3. In a saucepan, heat the apricot sauce with the kirsch. When ready to serve, unmold the dessert and pour the apricot sauce over the top. Serve hot, warm, or cool.

Yields 6 servings

Can be prepared up to 2 days before serving. Reheat in a 350°F. oven to serve warm.

HOT INDIVIDUAL CRANBERRY ORANGE CHARLOTTES

1 pound loaf firm white bread, crusts removed, and sliced about ¼ in thick	2 tablespoons grated orange rind
	½ cup orange juice
1 cup butter, melted	1 cup sugar
1 pound whole cranberries	Vanilla ice cream

1. Preheat the oven to 375°F. Cut circles of bread to fit the bottoms of six 6-ounce ramekins and one to two slices to fit around the sides. Dip the bread into the melted butter and place in the ramekins.

2. In a saucepan, simmer the cranberries, orange rind, juice, and sugar about 20 minutes, or until thick enough to hold its shape in a spoon. Spoon the cranberry mixture into the molds, mounding slightly in the center.

3. Bake for 30 minutes, or until the bread is golden. Rest for 30 minutes before unmolding. Serve hot or at room temperature with the ice cream.

Yields 6 servings

Can be prepared up to 2 days ahead. Let come to room temperature or reheat in a 350° oven before serving.

Chapter 7

MOUSSES AND COLD SOUFFLÉS

The light, flavorful airiness of mousses appeals as a first course, main course, side dish, or dessert. Dessert mousses are particularly welcome after a substantial meal because they are light and pretty. They consist of a puree, often fruit, but chocolate is arguably the most popular flavor, lightened with beaten egg whites and/or whipped cream. Gelatin makes some mousses firm enough to stand alone, while others are so delicate that they almost evaporate in the mouth, leaving just an explosion of flavor. The basic preparation is similar to Bavarian creams. With gelatin as the stabilizer, the preparation serves as a mousse, Bavarian cream, charlotte filling, or cold soufflé. Cold soufflés are completely different in preparation and consistency from the hot soufflés found in Chapter 10. They are, essentially, mousses molded in soufflé dishes with a collar for support until set.

The more delicate mousses, prepared with little or no gelatin, must be served in a bowl or dessert dish or other container. Hollowed orange shells, chocolate bowls, or tulip cups make different and interesting containers. Garnish the mousse with whipped cream and grated chocolate, chocolate cutouts, or pieces of fruit.

Cold Soufflés

TO COLLAR A SOUFFLÉ DISH   Lightly oil the inside of a soufflé dish or other straight-sided serving dish. Cut a strip of foil long enough to encircle the mold and overlap by 2 inches. Fold the foil in half lengthwise and lightly oil one side. Wrap the foil, oiled side in, around the outside of the dish,

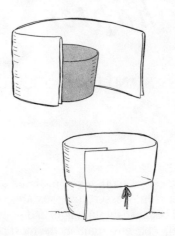

extending it above the rim of the mold. Secure by crimping the top edge, or secure with a paper clip, or tie a string around the mold (see illustration).

Fill the dish at least 1 inch above the mold. It may be as tall as twice the height of the dish. Refrigerate until set. Carefully peel the foil from around the soufflé, using a small knife to release the upper edge without tearing the mousse. Many cooks press cake or cookie crumbs or finely ground nuts into the exposed edge to make it look "baked." Garnish the top of the soufflé with fruit or whipped cream.

TO MAKE A PASTRY SOUFFLÉ SHELL   Preheat the oven to 400°F. Line a souffle dish or other straight-sided mold with foil, leaving a 2-inch overhang. Press the foil into the dish as smoothly as possible. Oil the foil lightly. Roll Pâté Sable, (Sweet Pastry Dough) (see page 386) between sheets of waxed paper to ¼-inch thickness. Peel off the waxed paper, invert the pastry into the dish, and press into the mold evenly. If the pastry should split, simply press a piece of dough into the split, dampening the dough scrap with cold water to make it adhere, if necessary. If the dish is very large, roll the dough in two sections: line half the dish with one section and the other half with the remaining pastry, overlapping slightly. Press to seal, using scraps to fill any holes. Trim the top edge evenly. The sides must be at least ¼ inch thick. Line the inside of the pastry with foil and fill the shell with dried beans or rice.

Bake for 20 minutes. Check to see if the pastry has set and is starting to brown by gently pulling the inner foil away from the side. If the side stands, remove the beans and foil, but if the side starts to give, pat it gently back into place and bake another 5 minutes. Remove the foil and beans and bake until golden. Cool on a rack.

Using the overhanging edge of foil, carefully lift the pastry shell from the soufflé dish and gently peel off the foil. Reline the original mold with clean foil and replace the pastry shell. Wrap a collar around the outside of the mold and fill with the soufflé mixture. Refrigerate until set. Just before serving, carefully remove the foil collar and, with the help of the foil liner, carefully lift the mousse-filled pastry shell out of the soufflé dish. Gently remove the foil and place on a serving platter. Garnish and serve. Serve some shell with the filling. This is the ultimate chiffon pie.

Bake the shell a day or two before using and keep in an airtight container until ready to fill. Do not fill the shell more than 6 hours before serving to prevent the moisture of the filling from softening the shell.

TO MAKE A CHOCOLATE SOUFFLÉ SHELL   Line a soufflé dish or other straight-sided mold with foil or plastic wrap, pressing it firmly into all corners and leaving a 2-inch overhang. Press as smoothly as possible against the sides of the dish. Put the mold into the freezer.

In a double boiler, over low heat, or in a microwave, temper 1 pound of semisweet chocolate until smooth and liquid (see page 9). With a pastry brush, brush the chocolate inside the chilled dish, concentrating on the sides and corners. Refrigerate the dish until the chocolate starts to set. Continue to paint layers until the shell is about ⅛ to ¼ inch thick. Refrigerate until hard.

Carefully remove the shell from the mold and peel off the foil. Cut two sheets of foil or waxed paper long enough to cover the bottom and sides of the mold with a 2-inch overhang. Fold in quarters and arrange the strips in a cross on the bottom and up the sides of the mold. Press the overhang to the outside of the bowl. Wrap a collar over the overhang. Return the shell to the mold and fill with the mousse mixture. Refrigerate until set. Carefully peel off the collar and, using the overhanging ends of the foil, gently lift the shell and mousse from the mold and arrange on a serving platter. The shell can be made up to a week before serving. Because gelatin can become rubbery if made too far ahead, you should not prepare any gelatin-based filling more than 24 hours before serving.

SEMIFREDDO ALLE MANDORLE O ALLE NOCCIOLE
(Almond or Hazelnut Frozen Mousse)

This dessert is particularly delicious and appealing served in a chocolate soufflé shell (see page 241).

2½ cups heavy cream
2 eggs, separated
¾ cup sifted confectioners' sugar

1 cup Praline Powder, made with almonds or hazelnuts page 30
2 tablespoons maraschino liqueur

1.   In a bowl, beat the cream until soft peaks form. In another bowl, beat the egg yolks with ¼ cup of confectioners' sugar until thickened and pale.

2.   In another bowl, beat the egg whites with the remaining sugar until stiff peaks form. Fold the yolks into the whipped cream. Fold in the egg whites, praline powder, and the maraschino liqueur.

3.   Pour into a 6-cup metal mold and freeze until firm. Unmold onto a serving platter and garnish with fresh fruit or more praline powder, if desired.

Yields 6 servings

Can be prepared several days before serving.

APPLE MOUSSE

3 pounds McIntosh apples, peeled, halved, and cored
½ cup sugar
2 tablespoons gelatin
4 tablespoons cold water
2½ tablespoons Calvados or rum

3 eggs, separated
1 egg white
¾ cup heavy cream, whipped
2 cups Apricot Glaze, page 36
1 apple cored, peeled, and sliced, for garnish

1.   Brush a 8 × 4-inch loaf pan with 1 teaspoon of oil. Line the pan with waxed paper and brush the paper with the remaining oil.

2.   In a saucepan, cook the apples and the sugar, covered, over low heat, stirring occasionally, about 35 to 40 minutes, or until tender.

3.   Uncover and simmer until the liquid evaporates, stirring occasionally. Puree in a processor or food mill and strain through a fine sieve. Measure 3½ cups of hot puree.

4. In a small bowl, soften the gelatin in the cold water. Stir the gelatin mixture into the hot puree until it dissolves. Stir in 1½ tablespoons of Calvados and cool to room temperature. Stir in the egg yolks.

5. Beat the egg whites until stiff, but not dry. Fold the egg whites into the puree and fold in the whipped cream. Turn into the prepared pan and refrigerate about 4 hours, or until fully set.

6. Unmold onto a serving platter. In a saucepan, heat the apricot glaze until fluid and cool to room temperature. Brush 3 tablespoons of glaze over the mousse and arrange the apple slices on top. Stir the remaining Calvados into the remaining glaze and brush over the apple slices, letting it drizzle down the sides of the mousse. Refrigerate until set.

Yields 10 to 12 servings

Can be prepared 24 hours before serving.

MOUSSE AUX POMMES AU CALVADOS
(Apple Mousse with Calvados)

2 pounds apples, peeled, cored, and sliced	1 tablespoon gelatin
Grated rind of 1 lemon	Juice of 1 lemon
2 tablespoons brown sugar	4 tablespoons hot water
5 tablespoons apricot jam	½ cup heavy cream, whipped
2 tablespoons butter	¼ cup Calvados
3 eggs	2 oranges, peeled and cut into segments, for garnish
2 egg yolks	1 apple, peeled, cored, and thinly sliced, for garnish
3 tablespoons sugar	

1. In a deep saucepan, simmer the apples, lemon rind, brown sugar, and 2 tablespoons of jam about 20 minutes, or until it forms a thick puree. Stir in the butter. Cool.

2. In a mixer, beat the eggs, egg yolks, and sugar until thickened and pale.

3. In a small saucepan, soften the gelatin in the lemon juice. Add 1 tablespoon of hot water to dissolve the gelatin, stirring over low heat, if necessary. Stir the gelatin into the egg mixture and fold into the apple puree.

4. Fold in the whipped cream and the Calvados. Pour into six 6-ounce cups or a large bowl and refrigerate until set.

5.   Arrange the orange segments and apple slices on top of each mousse. In a small saucepan, simmer the remaining jam with the remaining water until slightly thickened. Brush over the fruit. Refrigerate until set.

Yields 6 servings

Can be prepared the day before serving.

APPLE MOUSSE BRITTANY STYLE

5 apples, peeled, cored, and sliced	**1 teaspoon cornstarch**
¼ cup apricot preserves	**1½ cups milk, scalded**
½ teaspoon cinnamon	**1 tablespoon gelatin**
¼ teaspoon grated lemon rind	**1 tablespoon water**
** Pinch of nutmeg**	**1 cup heavy cream**
4 egg yolks	**1 teaspoon vanilla**
¾ cup sugar	** Apricot Sauce, page 547**

1.   In a large saucepan, cook the apples, apricot preserves, cinnamon, lemon rind, and nutmeg over low heat until very soft, stirring. Puree in a processor and cool.

2.   In a saucepan, beat the egg yolks, sugar, and cornstarch until thickened and pale. Gradually stir in the milk and cook, stirring, until thick enough to coat the back of a spoon.

3.   In a small bowl, soften the gelatin in the water. Stir into the custard until dissolved. Refrigerate, stirring occasionally, until slightly thickened.

4.   In another bowl, whip the cream and the vanilla until they form soft peaks and fold into the custard. Fold in the apple puree and pour into a 6-cup mold. Refrigerate until set.

5.   Shortly before serving, unmold onto a serving platter and surround with the apricot sauce.

Yields 6 to 8 servings

Can be prepared up to 24 hours before serving.

MOUSSE DE POMMES À LA BÉNÉDICTINE
(Apple Mousse with Bénédictine)

½ cup sugar	5 egg whites
1 tablespoon water	3 tablespoons Bénédictine plus
2 pounds apples, peeled,	additional to taste, see Note
cored, and sliced	2 cups heavy cream
1 cup confectioners' sugar	Sugar, to taste

1. Preheat the oven to 400°F.

2. In a small saucepan, caramelize the sugar and water. Pour the caramel into the bottom of a 6-cup charlotte mold or soufflé dish.

3. In a covered saucepan, simmer the apples in ⅓ cup of confectioners' sugar until tender. Puree in a processor. If the mixture is very thin, return to the saucepan and cook, over high heat, stirring until most of the liquid evaporates. Cool.

4. In a mixer, beat the egg whites until they form soft peaks. Beat in the remaining confectioners' sugar until it forms stiff peaks. Fold into the apple puree with the Bénédictine and pour into the prepared mold.

5. Cover with foil and bake in a water bath for 40 minutes, or until it tests done. Refrigerate for at least 4 hours. Whip the cream and flavor to taste with sugar and Bénédictine. Pass the whipped cream with the mousse.

Yields 6 servings

Can be prepared the day before serving.

NOTE: This recipe is similar to *Île Flottante*, (Floating Island) (see page 204). If desired, unmold onto a deep serving platter and serve surrounded with custard sauce flavored with Bénédictine.

Variations

• Substitute a favorite liqueur for the Bénédictine. Pernod, Kümmel, or Chartreuse are interesting, different choices from the more usual orange or rum flavors.

BANANA MOUSSE

1 tablespoon gelatin	4 bananas
1 cup orange juice	1 cup heavy cream
2 tablespoons lemon juice	¾ cup confectioners' sugar
¼ cup boiling water	

1.   In a small saucepan, soften the gelatin in the orange and lemon juices. Add the water and stir over low heat until dissolved. In a processor, puree the bananas with the gelatin mixture. Refrigerate, stirring occasionally, until slightly thickened.

2.   Whip the cream with the confectioners' sugar until soft peaks form. Fold into the banana mixture. Spoon into a serving bowl and refrigerate about 3 hours, or until set.

Yields 6 servings

Can be prepared up to 24 hours before serving.

MOUSSE DE BANANES AU CHOCOLAT BLANC
(Banana Mousse with White Chocolate)

⅓ cup golden raisins	2 tablespoons lemon juice
¼ cup dark rum	1 tablespoon gelatin
½ pound white chocolate, chopped	2 tablespoons water
	¾ cup sweetened condensed milk
4 bananas, cut into ½-inch slices	½ cup heavy cream

1.   In a small bowl, macerate the raisins in the rum for 2 hours.

2.   Melt the chocolate and cool to room temperature.

3.   In a processor, puree the bananas and lemon juice and pour into a bowl. In a small saucepan, soften the gelatin in the water. Stir over low heat, until the gelatin dissolves. Mix the gelatin into the banana mixture and stir in the milk, melted chocolate, raisins, and any remaining rum.

4.   Beat the cream until soft peaks form and fold into the banana mixture. Spoon into eight to ten 6-ounce ramekins, custard cups, or dessert dishes. Refrigerate until set.

Yields 8 to 10 servings

Can be prepared up to 24 hours before serving.

Chocolate Mousse

Chocolate is the favorite mousse flavor. It makes strong men weep and perfectly decent ladies sell their souls. Writers have extolled its virtues while praising its sensuality. For some, chocolate mousse is a smooth, pudding-like mixture lightened with whipped cream, while for others, the mousse is a deep, dark, intensely flavored chocolate essence, lightened with egg whites. Which is the best? The one you like. For direct eating from a dessert glass, I find the whipped cream makes for a lighter dessert. When the mousse acts as a filling or frosting for desserts, use the deeper, denser version. Flavor the mousse with a favorite liqueur, ground nuts, or praline.

See pages 6–9 for a discussion of the types of chocolate suitable for mousses and tips on melting chocolate.

MOUSSE AU CHOCOLAT I (Chocolate Mousse)

4 **eggs, separated**	2 **tablespoons orange liqueur**
4 **ounces semisweet**	½ **cup heavy cream, whipped,**
chocolate	**sweetened and flavored, to**
2 **tablespoons butter softened**	**taste with orange liqueur, for**
	garnish

1.   Melt the chocolate and cool to room temperature.

2.   In a bowl, stir the egg yolks into the chocolate with the softened butter until smooth. Stir in the orange liqueur.

3.   Beat the egg whites until soft peaks form and fold into the chocolate mixture. Spoon into six 6-ounce ramekins or a 36-ounce cup dessert bowl. Chill for at least 4 hours.

4.   Using a pastry bag fitted with a #5 open star tip, pipe rosettes of whipped cream on top of the mousse.

Yields 6 servings

Can be prepared the day before serving.

Variations

- *Liqueur-Flavored.*   Substitute kirsch, maraschino liqueur, framboise, Poire William, amaretto, rum, Cognac or other favorite liqueur for the orange liqueur.
- *Cinnamon-Flavored.*   Omit the orange liqueur and add ¼ teaspoon of ground cinnamon.
- *Rum-and-Raisin-Flavored.*   Omit the orange liqueur. In a small bowl, macerate ½ cup of raisins in ¼ cup of rum for 2 hours and fold into the mousse with the egg whites.
- *Coffee-Flavored.*   Omit the orange liqueur and add 1 tablespoon of instant espresso powder, dissolved in 2 tablespoons of hot water.
- *Mint-Flavored.*   Omit the orange liqueur and add ½ teaspoon of peppermint extract.
- *Nut-Flavored Mousse.*   Substitute Cognac or rum for the orange liqueur and fold in ½ cup of ground toasted almonds, walnuts, pecans, or hazelnuts.

MOUSSE AU CHOCOLAT II
(Chocolate Mousse II)

6 ounces semisweet chocolate	**2 teaspoons vanilla**
	Pinch of salt
2 tablespoons water	**¾ cup heavy cream**
4 eggs, separated	**1½ teaspoons sugar**

1.   Melt the chocolate with the salt and the water. Remove from the heat and cool slightly.

2.   In a bowl, beat the egg yolks until light in color and stir in the melted chocolate with the vanilla. In another bowl, beat the egg whites until soft peaks form. Fold into the chocolate mixture.

3.   In a bowl, beat ½ cup of cream until soft peaks form and fold into the mousse. Spoon into a serving bowl or six individual bowls and refrigerate for at least 2 hours, or until set.

4.   Shortly before serving, beat the remaining cream until soft peaks form. Beat in the sugar and beat until almost firm. Either pipe rosettes or use a spoon to drop dollops of cream onto the mousse.

Yields 6 servings

Can be prepared the day before serving.

NOTE: Flavor with any of the suggestions for Mousse au Chocolat I, above.

CHOCOLATE MOUSSE FOR FILLINGS

This is a particularly dense and flavorful mousse that makes a fabulous filling for various gâteaux. It is also delicious on its own.

11 ounces semisweet chocolate	5 egg yolks
	8 (1¼ cups) egg whites
¾ cup butter, cut into pieces	3½ tablespoons sugar

1. Melt the chocolate. Stir in the butter until smooth. Allow the mixture to cool completely. It should be about as thick as mayonnaise. Stir in the egg yolks, one at a time.

2. In a mixer, beat the egg whites until soft peaks form. Beat in the sugar, 1 tablespoon at a time, and continue beating until they form almost-stiff peaks. Fold into the chocolate mixture. Refrigerate until needed.

Yields 1 Quart

Can be prepared the day before serving.

NOTE: To use as a filling, prepare no more than 30 minutes before using.

Suggested Serving

To serve plain, spoon into bowls. Garnish with additional mousse piped through a star tip, sprinkle with chocolate shavings, dust with cocoa, or top with a dollop of whipped cream.

CHOCOLATE WALNUT MOUSSE

7 ounces semisweet chocolate	3 tablespoons sugar
	½ cup Cognac
½ cup milk	1½ cups heavy cream, whipped
2 teaspoons gelatin	½ cup chopped toasted walnuts
2 tablespoons cold water	½ teaspoon instant coffee
2 eggs, separated	Walnut halves, for garnish
Pinch of salt	

1. Melt 6 ounces of chocolate in the milk, stirring occasionally, until smooth. Remove from the heat.

2. In a small saucepan, soften the gelatin in the cold water. Heat over low heat, stirring until the gelatin dissolves. Stir into the chocolate mixture.

3.   In a bowl, beat the egg yolks until thickened and pale. Stir into the chocolate and cook, stirring, over low heat, until the mixture thickens slightly. Do not boil. Cool to room temperature.

4.   Beat the egg whites with the salt until soft peaks form. Beat in the sugar and continue to beat until stiff peaks form.

5.   Stir the Cognac into the cooled chocolate mixture and fold in the egg whites, 1 cup of whipped cream, and the nuts. Spoon into a 6-cup serving bowl. Refrigerate until set.

6.   Melt the remaining chocolate and fold into the remaining whipped cream with the instant coffee. Using a pastry bag fitted with a #5 open star tip, pipe rosettes of whipped cream on top of the mousse. Garnish with walnut halves.

Yields 6 servings

Can be prepared the day before serving.

SPUMA DI CIOCCOLATA
(Italian Chocolate Mousse)

6 ounces semisweet	**¼ cup strong espresso**
chocolate	**2 tablespoons rum**
4 eggs, separated	**⅔ cup heavy cream**
2 teaspoons sugar	

1.   Melt the chocolate and cool to room temperature.

2.   In a bowl, beat the egg yolks with the sugar until thickened and pale. Mix in the chocolate, espresso, and rum.

3.   Whip the cream until stiff peaks form and fold into the chocolate mixture.

4.   Beat the egg whites until stiff peaks form and fold into the chocolate mixture. Spoon into 6 parfait glasses. If desired, garnish with additional whipped cream.

Yields 6 servings

Can be prepared the day before.

FRESH FIG MOUSSE

½ cup plus 2 tablespoons
  sugar
⅓ cup water
1½ in piece of vanilla bean,
  split
3 (2-inch) strips lemon peel
5 large, ripe, fresh figs,
  stemmed
1 tablespoon gelatin

2 tablespoons lemon juice
¾ cup chilled Pastry Cream,
  page 26
½ cup heavy cream, whipped
½ teaspoon vanilla
2 egg whites
Pinch of salt

1. In a saucepan, boil the sugar, water, vanilla bean, and lemon peel until the sugar dissolves. Poach the figs in the syrup for 3 minutes.

2. In a small bowl, soften the gelatin in the lemon juice. Remove 1 fig from the poaching liquid and reserve. Add the softened gelatin to the remaining figs and stir until it dissolves. Puree the figs and the poaching liquid in a processor and cool.

3. Fold the pastry cream into the fig puree and refrigerate, covered, until slightly thickened. Fold in the whipped cream and vanilla.

4. Beat the egg whites with the salt until soft peaks form. Fold into the fig mixture and pour into a serving bowl. Refrigerate about 2 hours, or until set. Garnish with the reserved fig.

Yields 6 servings

Can be prepared 24 hours before serving.

GINGER MOUSSE

1 tablespoon gelatin
¼ cup cold water
2 cups evaporated milk,
  scalded
4 eggs, separated

½ cup sugar
Pinch of salt
½ cup rum
1 cup minced crystallized
  ginger

1. In a small bowl, soften the gelatin in the water. Stir the gelatin into the hot milk until dissolved.

2. In a saucepan, beat the egg yolks and the sugar until thickened and pale. Gradually stir in the hot milk and cook the mixture over low heat, stirring, until it is thick enough to coat the back of a spoon. Refrigerate until slightly thickened.

3. Beat the egg whites with the salt until soft peaks form. Fold into the custard mixture with the rum and the ginger. Pour into six 6-ounce dessert dishes. Refrigerate at least 2 hours, or until set.

Yields 6 servings

Can be prepared up to 24 hours before serving.

SOUFFLÉ FROID DES ÎLES (Cold Island Soufflé)

The flavors of the islands—ginger, rum, and nutmeg—permeate this mousse.

3 **cups cold milk**	¼ **cup chopped crystallized**
4 **tablespoons gelatin**	**ginger**
½ **cup plus 6 tablespoons**	⅔ **cup heavy cream**
sugar	½ **cup cake crumbs, for garnish**
1 **teaspoon grated nutmeg**	1 **cup heavy cream, whipped,**
1 **tablespoon grated**	**sweetened, and flavored with**
gingerroot	**rum, to taste**
4 **teaspoons cornstarch**	**Strips of crystallized ginger**
2 **tablespoons dark rum**	**for garnish**
3 **eggs, separated**	

1. Collar and lightly oil a 1-quart soufflé dish (see page 240).

2. In a 1½-quart saucepan, mix the milk, gelatin, and ½ cup of sugar. Let stand until the gelatin softens. Cook over medium heat, stirring, until the gelatin dissolves. Stir in the nutmeg and gingerroot.

3. In a small bowl, mix the cornstarch and rum and stir into the simmering milk. Cook, stirring, until the mixture thickens.

4. Beat in the egg yolks, strain, and cool. Fold in the chopped crystallized ginger.

5. Beat the egg whites with 4 tablespoons sugar until stiff, but not dry, and fold into the egg yolk mixture. Beat the cream with the remaining sugar until soft peaks form and fold into the mousse.

6. Pour into the soufflé dish and refrigerate about 3 hours or until set. If desired, press cake crumbs into the side of the soufflé. Garnish with rum-flavored whipped cream and strips of crystalized ginger.

Yields 6 servings

Can be prepared 24 hours before serving.

COPPETTE ALLE NOCCIOLE (Hazelnut Mousse)

Serve with Raspberry or Strawberry Sauce, if desired.

3 eggs, separated	4 ounces ground and toasted
⅓ cup sugar	hazelnuts
1 tablespoon gelatin	3 tablespoons Cognac
2 tablespoons water	1 cup heavy cream

1.   In a bowl, beat the egg yolks with the sugar until thickened and pale.

2.   In a small saucepan, soften the gelatin in the water. Stirring continually, dissolve over low heat. Stir into the egg yolks with the hazelnuts and Cognac.

3.   Beat the egg whites until soft peaks form and fold into the nut mixture. Beat the cream until soft peaks form and fold into the nut mixture. Turn into six 6-ounce custard cups or 1 large bowl and refrigerate about 4 hours, or until set.

Yields 6 servings

Can be prepared up to 24 hours before serving.

MOUSSE DE KIWI (Kiwi Mousse)

3 eggs	¼ teaspoon vanilla
¾ cup sugar	3 kiwi, peeled and minced
⅓ cup orange liqueur	1 kiwi, peeled and sliced, for
2 cups heavy cream	garnish

1.   In a double boiler over hot, but not boiling water, or a saucepan over direct heat, cook the eggs, ½ cup of sugar, and 4 tablespoons of orange liqueur, beating with an electric mixer, until thickened to the consistency of mayonnaise. Remove from the heat and continue to beat until cooled.

2.   In a bowl, beat the cream until soft peaks form. Beat in the remaining sugar and the vanilla and beat until stiff. Fold in the minced kiwi and the remaining orange liqueur. Fold into the egg mixture. Pour into sherbet glasses and refrigerate at least 30 minutes, or until set. Garnish with the kiwi slices.

Yields 8 to 10 servings

Can be prepared up to 12 hours before serving.

COLD LEMON SOUFFLÉ

Serve with Raspberry or Blueberry sauce.

4 **eggs**	**lemon**
3 **egg yolks**	1 **cup heavy cream, whipped**
¼ **cup sugar**	1 **cup heavy cream, whipped,**
2 **tablespoons gelatin**	**sweetened and flavored, to**
½ **cup lemon juice**	**taste with vanilla**
Grated rind of 1 large	

1.   Collar and lightly oil a ¾-quart soufflé dish (see page 240).

2.   In a bowl, beat the eggs, egg yolks, and sugar until the mixture is thickened and pale.

3.   In a small saucepan, soften the gelatin in the lemon juice and heat over low heat. Stir until the gelatin dissolves. Beat into the egg yolk mixture and strain. Fold in the lemon rind and the unflavored whipped cream. Pour into the soufflé dish and refrigerate until set.

4.   Carefully remove the collar. Using a pastry bag fitted with a star tip, garnish with rosettes of the sweetened and flavored whipped cream.

Yields 6 to 8 servings

Can be prepared 24 hours before serving.

Variations

• *Lime.*   Substitute ½ cup of lime juice for the lemon rind and juice.
• *Lemon-Blueberry.*   In a saucepan, cook 1 pint of blueberries with ½ cup of sugar until the juices flow. Refrigerate until cold. Pour a layer of mousse into a glass bowl, add a layer of blueberries, and keep filling the bowl, alternating the mousse and berries.

MOUSSE AU CITRON (Lemon Wine Custard)

10 eggs, separated	**Grated rind of 1 lemon**
2½ cups dry white wine	**⅔ cup sugar**
Juice of 4 lemons	

1. In a saucepan, over medium heat, cook the egg yolks, wine, lemon juice, lemon rind, and sugar. Stir until the custard is thick enough to coat the back of a spoon. Refrigerate until cold.

2. Beat the egg whites until stiff, but not dry, and fold into the custard. Pour into a large glass bowl and refrigerate, covered, until set.

Yields 8 servings

Can be prepared up to 12 hours before serving.

COLD LEMON SOUFFLÉ WITH RASPBERRY SAUCE

¾ cup plus 1 tablespoon sugar	**3 egg whites**
½ cup lemon juice	**1½ cups heavy cream**
½ cup butter	**1 teaspoon vanilla**
7 egg yolks	**½ cup Candied Lemon Rind, page 38, for garnish**
1 tablespoon grated lemon rind	**1½ cups Raspberry Sauce, page 552**

1. Collar and lightly oil a ¾-quart soufflé dish (see page 240).

2. In a saucepan, cook ¾ cup of sugar, lemon juice, butter, egg yolks, and lemon rind over medium heat until thickened. Remove from the heat and refrigerate until cold.

3. In a bowl, using an electric mixer, whip the egg whites until soft peaks form and fold into the cooled lemon mixture.

4. Beat 1 cup of heavy cream until soft peaks form and beat in the remaining sugar and the vanilla. Beat until stiff peaks form. Fold into the lemon mixture and pour into the soufflé dish. Refrigerate until set.

5. Beat the remaining cream and sugar to taste until they form stiff peaks. Garnish the soufflé with the whipped cream and candied rind. Pass the sauce separately.

Yields 6 servings

Can be prepared up to 24 hours before serving.

COLD LIME SOUFFLÉ

1 tablespoon gelatin	¼ cup water
1 cup strained lime juice	1 cup evaporated milk
4 eggs, separated	¼ cup grated lime rind
1½ cups sugar	Pinch of salt
1 tablespoon cornstarch	½ cup grated coconut, for garnish

1. In a small bowl, soften the gelatin in the lime juice.

2. In a saucepan, beat the egg yolks and sugar until thickened and pale.

3. Stir the cornstarch and the water until smooth and add to the egg yolk mixture. Stir in the evaporated milk and the softened gelatin. Cook over low heat, stirring until thickened and smooth. Stir in the grated rind and refrigerate until slightly thickened.

4. Beat the egg whites and salt until soft peaks form. Fold into the custard. Spoon into six 6-ounce serving dishes and refrigerate until set.

5. In a 325°F. oven, toast the coconut until golden (see page 10). Sprinkle the coconut over the top of the mousse.

Yields 6 servings

Can be prepared up to 24 hours before serving.

RUM PUMPKIN MOUSSE

2 tablespoons gelatin	1 teaspoon cinnamon
½ cup dark rum	½ teaspoon ginger
4 eggs, separated	¼ teaspoon nutmeg
1 cup sugar	1⅔ cups pumpkin puree
Pinch of salt	1½ cups heavy cream
¾ cup milk	½ cup chopped toasted walnuts, for garnish

1. Collar and lightly oil a 4-cup soufflé dish (see page 240).

2. In a small bowl, soften the gelatin in the rum. In a saucepan, beat the egg yolks, ½ cup of sugar, and salt until thickened and pale. Add the milk and the gelatin mixture and cook until the mixture is thick enough to coat the back of a spoon. Beat in the cinnamon, ginger, nutmeg, and pumpkin. Refrigerate until almost ready to set.

3. Beat the egg whites until they form soft peaks and fold into the pumpkin mixture. Beat 1 cup of cream to form soft peaks and fold into the mousse. Pour into the soufflé dish and refrigerate 3 hours, or until set.

4. Remove the collar. Beat the remaining cream until stiff peaks form and pipe around the top of the dessert. Garnish with the walnuts.

Yields 8 to 10 servings

Can be prepared up to 24 hours before serving.

MOUSSE À L'ORANGE (Orange Mousse)

3 eggs	½ cup heavy cream, whipped
2 egg yolks	2 oranges peeled and cut into
½ cup sugar	segments, for garnish
Grated rind and juice of	3 tablespoons Currant Glaze,
1 large orange	page 36
2 tablespoons gelatin	

1. In a bowl, beat the eggs, egg yolks, and sugar until thickened and pale. Stir in the orange rind.

2. In a small saucepan, soften the gelatin in the orange juice. Heat, stirring, until the gelatin dissolves. Stir into the egg mixture and fold in the whipped cream. Pour into 6 custard cups and refrigerate about 4 hours, or until set.

3. Arrange the orange segments on the mousse and brush with the glaze.

Yields 6 servings

Can be prepared 24 hours before serving.

MOUSSE AU COINTREAU
(Orange Mousse with Cointreau)

5 eggs, separated	¼ cup orange juice
¾ cup plus 2 tablespoons sugar	1 tablespoon grated orange rind
1 cup milk, scalded	1 teaspoon vanilla
⅓ cup Cointreau	1 cup heavy cream, whipped
3 tablespoons Cognac	2 cups raspberries, for garnish
1 tablespoon gelatin	

1.   In a saucepan, beat the egg yolks with ¾ cup of sugar until thickened and pale. Gradually stir in the milk, Cointreau, and Cognac. Cook, stirring, until the mixture is thick enough to coat the back of a spoon.

2.   In a small bowl, soften the gelatin in the orange juice. Stir into the hot custard until the gelatin dissolves. Stir in the orange rind and vanilla. Refrigerate, stirring occasionally, until slightly thickened.

3.   Using an electric mixer, beat the egg whites until soft peaks form and fold into the custard. Fold the whipped cream into the mousse and turn into a serving bowl. Refrigerate until set.

4.   Just before serving, toss the raspberries with the remaining sugar and scatter over the top of the mousse.

Yields 6 servings

Can be prepared up to 24 hours before serving.

Variations

• Substitute blueberries, pitted cherries, or strawberries for the raspberries.

PEACH-AND-BLUEBERRY MOUSSE

Accompany with Blueberry or Raspberry Sauce.

3 pounds peaches, peeled and diced
Juice of 1 lemon
Sugar to taste
3 tablespoons gelatin
½ cup cold water
5 egg yolks

½ cup sugar
1½ cups milk, scalded
1 teaspoon vanilla
2 tablespoons peach brandy
1 pint blueberries
1 cup heavy cream, whipped

1. In a processor or blender, puree all but 1 cup of diced peaches with half of the lemon juice. Sprinkle the remaining lemon juice over the reserved peaches and set aside. Sweeten the puree with the sugar to taste.

2. In a bowl, soften the gelatin in the water. In a saucepan, beat the egg yolks with ½ cup of sugar until thickened and pale. Gradually stir in the hot milk and the vanilla. Cook, stirring, until thick enough to coat the back of a spoon.

3.   Stir in the gelatin until it dissolves and strain the mixture into a bowl. Stir in the peach puree and brandy. Refrigerate, stirring occasionally, until slightly thickened. Fold in the reserved diced peaches, the blueberries, and whipped cream. Pour into a serving bowl and refrigerate until set.

Yields 8 to 10 servings

Can be prepared up to 24 hours before serving.

PEAR MOUSSE WITH CURRANT SAUCE

Black currants in syrup are available in gourmet shops.

5 **Vanilla Poached Pears,**	¾ **cup heavy cream, whipped**
halved and cored, page 40	48 **ounces black currants in**
1 **tablespoon gelatin**	**syrup**
2 **tablespoons water**	6 **fresh pears, peeled and**
¼ **cup pear eau de vie**	**cored**
	Mint leaves, for garnish

1.   Drain the poached pears, reserving the syrup. Finely dice enough pears to make ½ cup and reserve. In a processor, puree the remaining pears.

2.   In a bowl, soften the gelatin in the water. Stir the gelatin mixture into 1 tablespoon of hot pear poaching liquid until dissolved. Stir into the pear puree with the reserved diced pears. Cool to room temperature. Stir in the pear eau de vie and fold in the whipped cream. Pour into six 6-ounce custard cups or ramekins and refrigerate until set.

3.   In a processor, puree all but 1 tablespoon of currants in syrup and pour into a saucepan. Poach the fresh pears in the currant puree until tender. Drain the pears, reserving the puree, and refrigerate until cold.

4.   When ready to serve, mound the currant puree on individual plates and place a poached pear on one side of each plate. Unmold a mousse next to each pear and garnish with the mint leaves and reserved tablespoon of currants.

Yields 6 servings

Can be prepared up to 24 hours before serving.

PRUNE ARMAGNAC MOUSSE

8 ounces pitted prunes
½ cup water
7 tablespoons Armagnac,
    plus additional to taste
2 tablespoons gelatin
4 egg yolks
10 tablespoons sugar

¾ cup sour cream
6 egg whites
12 pitted prunes soaked in
    Armagnac, for garnish
½ cup heavy cream, whipped,
    sweetened, and flavored with
    Armagnac, to taste for
    garnish

1.   In a saucepan, simmer the 8 ounces of prunes with ¼ cup of water and 4 tablespoons of Armagnac until the prunes soften and absorb most of the liquid. Cool to room temperature.

2.   In a small saucepan, soften the gelatin in the remaining water. Dissolve over low heat, stirring. In a processor, puree the prunes and cooking liquid with the egg yolks and 6 tablespoons of sugar. Blend in the gelatin, remaining Armagnac, and sour cream.

3.   Beat the egg whites until they form soft peaks and beat in the remaining sugar to form stiff peaks. Fold into the prune mixture and turn into a 6- to 7-cup mold. Refrigerate until set.

4.   Unmold onto a serving platter and serve garnished with the Armagnac-soaked prunes and whipped cream.

Yields 6 servings

Can be prepared up to 24 hours before serving.

COLD LIQUOR-FLAVORED SOUFFLÉ

For variety, you can substitute any favorite liquor for the rum.

4 eggs, separated
½ cup sugar
1 tablespoon cornstarch
¼ cup plus 2 tablespoons cold
    water
1 cup light cream
1 tablespoon gelatin
½ teaspoon vanilla

½ cup dark rum
Pinch of salt
1 cup heavy cream, whipped,
    sweetened, and flavored with
    rum, to taste
8 Chocolate Wedges, page 42,
    for garnish

1.   Collar and slightly oil a 3-cup soufflé dish (see page 240).

2.   In a saucepan, beat the egg yolks with the sugar until they are thickened and pale. Stir in the cornstarch, 2 tablespoons of water and cream. Cook, stirring, until thickened and smooth.

3.   In a small bowl, soften the gelatin in the remaining water. Stir into the hot custard until the gelatin dissolves. Stir in the vanilla and rum. Refrigerate until slightly thickened.

4.   Beat the egg whites until they form soft peaks and fold into the custard mixture. Turn into the soufflé dish and refrigerate until set.

5.   Shortly before serving, using a pastry bag with a #5 open star tip, pipe 8 rows of whipped cream from the center to the edge in spoke fashion. Place a chocolate wedge, slanted, against each row of cream. Pipe a rosette of cream in the center of the mousse on top of the points of the wedges.

Yields 8 servings

Can be prepared up to 24 hours before serving.

Variation

• Omit the chocolate wedges, pipe the cream in a lattice, and serve with Chocolate Sauce (see page 540).

RASPBERRY MACAROON MOUSSE

This is one of the best desserts ever. Although often served frozen, it is equally good, if not better, when assembled and served within a few hours. For a spectacular garnish, top with a Chocolate Butterfly (see page 45).

1 **quart raspberries**	1 **quart heavy cream, whipped**
1 **cup sugar**	½ **cup cream, whipped,**
1 **cup crushed amaretti**	**sweetened, and flavored with**
cookies	**framboise, to taste**
Pinch of salt	**Whole raspberries, for**
½ **cup framboise**	**garnish**

1.   In a processor, puree the raspberries. Press through a sieve into a large bowl. Discard the seeds. Stir the sugar into the puree.

2. In a small bowl, mix the cookie crumbs with the salt and framboise and fold into the puree. Fold the unflavored whipped cream into the puree and pour into a crystal bowl. Freeze for at least 6 hours or refrigerate for up to 12 hours.

3. Garnish the dessert with the cream and whole raspberries.

Yields 8 to 10 servings

Can be frozen for a month.

Variations

• Substitute two 16-ounce packages of frozen unsweetened raspberries for the fresh. Thaw them before pureeing. If the frozen raspberries are in syrup, use four 10-ounce packages.
• Substitute Almond Macaroons (see page 26), for the amaretti cookies.

MOUSSE AUX FRAMBOISES (Raspberry Mousse)

1 cup sugar	2 tablespoons gelatin
1½ cups water	3 egg whites
2½ cups raspberries	1 cup heavy cream, whipped

1. In a saucepan, boil the sugar and 1 cup of water to 250°F. Add 2 cups of raspberries. Cook until soft and press through a sieve, discarding the seeds.

2. In a small bowl, soften the gelatin in the remaining water. Stir into the hot raspberry puree until the gelatin dissolves. Refrigerate until slightly thickened.

3. Beat the egg whites until soft peaks form and fold into the puree. Fold half of the cream into the raspberry mixture. Spoon into six 6-ounce dessert glasses or a large bowl. Refrigerate about 2 hours, or until set.

4. Shortly before serving, using a pastry bag with a #5 star tip, pipe the remaining whipped cream over the mousse, and garnish with the remaining raspberries.

Yields 6 servings

Can be prepared up to 24 hours before serving.

MOUSSE AUX FRAISES (Strawberry Mousse)

1 pint strawberries
½ cup sugar
1 teaspoon lemon juice
2 egg whites

1¼ cups heavy cream
6 strawberries, sliced, for garnish

1.   In a processor, puree the strawberries with the sugar and the lemon juice. Pour into a large bowl.

2.   In a bowl, beat the egg whites until soft peaks form. In another bowl, beat the cream until soft peaks form. Fold the egg whites and whipped cream into the puree.

3.   Pour into a serving bowl or six 6-ounce dessert glasses and refrigerate for at least 2 hours or until set. Garnish with the strawberry slices.

Yields 6 servings

Can be prepared up to 24 hours before serving.

STRAWBERRY MOUSSE WITH COINTREAU

1 pint strawberries, crushed
1 cup confectioners' sugar, sifted
1 pint whole strawberries
1 tablespoon gelatin

⅓ cup Cointreau, plus additional to taste
3 cups heavy cream, whipped, and sweetened, and flavored with Cointreau, to taste

1.   In a bowl, sprinkle the crushed berries with the sugar and mix until the sugar dissolves. Reserve 6 to 8 of the prettiest whole strawberries for a garnish. Cut the remaining berries in half.

2.   In a small saucepan, soften the gelatin in the Cointreau. Cook, stirring until the gelatin dissolves. Cool to room temperature. Stir into the fruit puree with the halved strawberries. Refrigerate until slightly thickened.

3.   Beat 2 cups of cream until soft peaks form and fold into the strawberry mixture. Pour into a 1½ quart decorative mold. Refrigerate about 4 hours, or until set.

4.   Unmold the mousse onto a serving platter. Beat the remaining cream until stiff peaks form. Garnish the dessert with the whipped cream and the reserved berries.

Yields 6 servings

Can be prepared up to 24 hours before serving.

STRAWBERRY RHUBARB MOUSSE

1¼ pounds chopped rhubarb
1 cup sliced strawberries
1 cup sugar
2 tablespoons kirsch

1 tablespoon gelatin
4 tablespoons cold water
2 cups heavy cream

1. In a saucepan, simmer the rhubarb, strawberries, and sugar until the rhubarb softens, about 20 minutes. Pour two-thirds of the mixture into a blender and puree with the kirsch.

2. In a small saucepan, soften the gelatin in the cold water. Cook over low heat until the gelatin dissolves. Stir into the rhubarb puree. Stir in the remaining fruit mixture. Refrigerate, stirring occasionally, until slightly thickened.

3. Whip the cream until stiff and fold into the rhubarb mixture. Turn into a serving bowl or eight 6-ounce dishes. Refrigerate until set.

Yields 8 to 10 servings

Can be prepared up to 24 hours before serving.

WALNUT-HONEY MOUSSE

1 tablespoon gelatin
¼ cup plus 3 tablespoons
water
⅔ cup sugar
4 eggs separated
4 egg yolks
½ cup chopped walnuts
⅓ cup honey

4 egg whites
2 cups heavy cream
1 cup heavy cream, whipped
and sweetened to taste, for
garnish
Chopped toasted walnuts,
for garnish

1. In a small saucepan, soften the gelatin in ¼ cup of water. Cook, stirring, until the gelatin dissolves.

2. In another small saucepan, heat the sugar with the remaining water until the sugar dissolves. Increase the heat and boil 5 minutes. Meanwhile, in a bowl, beat the egg yolks until lemon-colored. Gradually beat in the hot sugar syrup in a slow, steady stream. Beat until thickened and pale. Fold in the walnuts, honey, and the dissolved gelatin.

3. Using clean beaters, beat the egg whites until stiff, but not dry, and fold into the mousse. Beat the cream until soft peaks form and fold into the mousse. Divide among 6 goblets or turn into a large soufflé dish and refrigerate until set. Garnish with whipped cream and toasted walnuts.

Yields 6 servings

Can be prepared up to 24 hours before serving.

Chapter 8

Frozen Desserts

A frozen dessert may be as simple as whipped cream and lemon flavoring folded together, or as elaborate as several flavors of ice cream or sherbet, garnished with fruits, sauces, and whipped cream, surrounded with chocolate cutouts. Ice cream is easily the favorite dessert of Americans at any time of the year. Many chefs create picture-pretty plates with a variety of sorbets surrounded with an assortment of fruits, or they stack crisp cookies with ice cream in impossible-to-eat towers. The overly conscientious prefer to make their ice creams, sherbets, and sorbets using one of the many machines, from wooden-barreled, hand-cranked, salt-and-ice machines to sleek, modern, countertop machines that prepare the ice cream almost without effort. In the interests of space, I have chosen not to include recipes for making ice creams, sherbets, or sorbets, because premium ice creams are readily available. Ice cream machines are expensive considering their limited use and, if you do buy a machine, it will come with a fine collection of recipes and instructions.

When selecting ice cream, sample several brands to make sure that the brand you are using is the best available in your area. The ice cream should have a high butterfat content, superior flavor, and a moderate amount of air. *Ice cream should be creamy.* Sorbets must be freshly made; use sherbet unless you have a reliable supplier. They should just melt in the mouth without any hard, icy parts. Sherbet's consistency is somewhere between that of sorbet and ice cream—not as creamy as the latter one and yet creamier than the former. There are many good brands.

Some ice cream manufacturers add vegetable gums and beat in as much air as possible to create volume. When packed into a mold, a quart is much less than a quart. Even with quality ice cream you will lose some volume, but it should be small. In many areas, small local firms produce fine-quality ice cream that is often extraordinarily better than the national brands.

FROZEN YOGURT   With current attitudes about diet and health, there are many people who substitute frozen yogurt, or ice milk, for ice cream. You can prepare these desserts with these products but they will lack flavor and quality. If you cannot eat ice cream, you probably should not be eating frozen yogurt or ice milk. The difference in calories is not great and the flavor and texture difference is enormous. Try one of the wonderful fruit desserts in Chapters 3, 4, and 6, and save the ice cream dessert for when you can enjoy the real thing instead of a not-so-cheap imitation.

There are two major ice cream preparations: coupes and bombes.

Coupes

Coupe is French for "cup," and in this instance, English for "ice cream sundae." Place a scoop of ice cream in a serving dish and garnish. Use whipped cream, chocolate, other decorations, or cookies with sauce and you have a coupe. Anyone can prepare a coupe; no dessert, apart from an unpeeled apple, is simpler. The one problem with coupes for the host or hostess is that at the end of the dinner, when most of us would prefer to sit back and enjoy the praise for producing a grand meal, we have to go to the kitchen and arrange the individual dessert glasses on the counter, then fill them with ice cream, top with fruit, coat with a sauce, decorate with whipped cream, and possibly add a decoration to that. When you present your effort your guests say, "How lovely, sundaes." After all that effort, the praise is lukewarm at best. For a more enthusiastic reception from your guests, serve a dramatically presented bombe.

Bombes

Bombes are layers of ice cream packed into large molds, often with a mousse-like mixture in the center. The garnishes are the same as those used for coupes. Instead of going through the same steps repeatedly, you only need do them once. When you present a platter topped with a large beautifully decorated dessert the guests will *ooh* and *aah!* The plaudits will make the rafters ring—more evidence of how important presentation is for good food.

With a little thought, you can serve any coupe as a bombe and vice versa. If the bombe has a mousse-like filling and several ice cream flavors, instead of lining small molds, place separate small scoops of each flavor in the serving dishes.

Because the desserts are frozen, there is a temptation to prepare the desserts, including the garnishes, and keep them in the freezer until shortly before serving. Sometimes, this is a satisfactory technique, but more often it is detrimental. Fruits freeze to an unappealing hardness and whipped cream is not as light. Whenever possible, save the garnishing until shortly before serving. Unmold a well-frozen bombe a few hours before serving, decorate, and store in the refrigerator to allow the ice cream to temper and become far more pleasing to eat. You can keep the filled mold in the freezer for up to a month without a loss of quality, just let it temper before serving.

Once you understand the principles of bombes and coupes, you can create many exciting variations. Although the ice cream is always cold, you can use warm sauces, such as in Coupe Nectarine Sultane, Cherries Jubilee, or Bananas Foster, to provide an interesting counterpoint. The recipes here give you many ready-made ideas. Once you are familiar with the technique, use them to give vent to your imagination to create desserts to suit your needs.

TO LINE A MOLD WITH ICE CREAM Whenever possible use a metal mold. Fancy or plain molds are traditional and true bombe molds look like howitzer shells and often have a small knob that screws into the top of the mold. When it is time to unmold, unscrew the knob and let air break the vacuum to allow easier unmolding. The next best choice is a slightly flexible plastic container, such as the half-gallon containers in which some ice cream is sold. Allow the ice cream to temper in the refrigerator for 2 to 3 hours, or at room temperature for 30 minutes, before attempting to scoop and pack into the mold. If using more than one flavor, make a 1-inch outer layer and freeze for about 30 minutes. Add the remaining flavors and freeze a layer at a time until you fill the mold. Cover securely and freeze until solid. The mold can be prepared up to a month before using.

For a large group of people, prepare a single large mold instead of several smaller molds. You may not have a single mold to serve 50 or more, but if you use a variety of different-sized molds such as a 12-inch round cake pan, a 9-inch round cake pan and perhaps a 7-inch round bowl, you can unmold and stack them like a wedding cake. If you are nervous about your tower of molds toppling, run a wooden dowel through the center. Garnish the whole dessert with the appropriate sauce and other garnishes. When you carry this into the room guests will gasp.

FRUITS BEATRICE

Spun sugar gives a mysterious airy finish to many desserts. It is tricky to prepare and should be served immediately. The dessert will be as delicious, if not as fantastic, without it.

1 quart raspberry sherbet, softened

3 cups fresh fruits or berries Sauce Riche flavored with anisette, page 547

Spun Sugar, page 37, for garnish

Crystallized violets, for garnish

1. Pack the raspberry sherbet into a mold and freeze until firm.

2. Unmold onto a serving platter and surround with the fruit. Coat the fruit with some of the sauce and surround the dessert with a halo of spun sugar. Garnish the dessert with the crystallized violets. Pass the remaining sauce.

Yields 6 to 8 servings

Can be prepared for garnishing several days before serving.

BOMBE DE LA RÉVOLUTION FRANÇAISE

1½ quarts strawberry ice cream

1½ cups White Chocolate Sauce, page 542

Fresh blueberries and sliced strawberries, for garnish

1. Pack the ice cream into a mold and freeze until firm.

2. Unmold the ice cream onto a platter, ladle some sauce over the ice cream, and surround with the fruit. Pass the remaining sauce.

Yields 6 to 8 servings

Can be prepared for garnishing up to a month before serving.

COUPE ST. ANDRÉ (Mixed Fruit Sundae)

12 maraschino cherries	½ orange, peeled, membrane
1 pear	removed, diced
1 slice pineapple, diced	1 teaspoon lemon juice
½ banana, diced	2 tablespoons sugar
1 peach, diced	6 scoops vanilla ice cream
	6 peach slices, for garnish

1.   Dice 6 cherries and reserve the remainder.

2.   In a bowl, macerate the diced cherries, pear, pineapple, banana, peach, and orange in the lemon juice and sugar for at least 5 minutes, and as long as 3 hours.

3.   Divide the fruit among 6 dessert glasses and top with a scoop of ice cream. Garnish with the peach slices and whole cherries.

Yields 6 servings

Serve immediately.

BOMBE CLO-CLO

1 cup glacéed chestnut pieces	for garnish
¼ cup maraschino liqueur	1 cup heavy cream
1 quart vanilla ice cream,	1 cup Strawberry Puree,
softened	page 29
6 whole glacéed chestnuts,	

1.   In a small bowl, macerate the chestnut pieces in the maraschino liqueur for at least 4 hours. Drain the chestnuts and fold into the ice cream. Pack into a 1-quart mold. Freeze until firm.

2.   Unmold the ice cream onto a serving platter and decorate with the whole chestnuts. Beat the cream until stiff and fold in the strawberry puree. Spoon around the base of the mold. (The cream is too soft to pipe.)

Yields 6 to 8 servings

GELATO AGLI AMARETTI (Bombe with Amaretti)

You may substitute 1½-inch Almond Macaroons (see page 26), for the amaretti cookies.

16 amaretti cookies, ground	1 pint vanilla ice cream,
5 tablespoons espresso	softened
1 tablespoon espresso coffee	6 amaretti cookies, for garnish
beans, ground	1 tablespoon rum

1. In a bowl, mix the amaretti crumbs, espresso, and ground beans until moistened.

2. Pack a 3-cup dome- or melon-shaped mold with two-thirds of the ice cream, leaving the center hollow, and fill the center with the amaretti mixture. Cover with the rest of the ice cream. Freeze for several hours, or until firm.

3. Unmold the dessert onto a platter. Dip the remaining amaretti into the rum and press into the sides of the bombe.

Yields 6 servings

Can be prepared for garnishing up to 1 month before serving.

BOMBE LILLIAN

1 quart lemon sherbet,	Kirsch to taste
softened	1 cup Apricot Sauce, page 547
1 pineapple, peeled, cored,	½ cup toasted almonds, for
and diced	garnish
1 cup seedless grapes	

1. Pack the sherbet into a 1-quart mold and freeze until serving time.

2. In a bowl, macerate the pineapple and grapes in the kirsch for at least 1 hour.

3. Unmold the sherbet onto a platter and surround with the fruit. Pour the apricot sauce over all and sprinkle with the almonds.

Yields 6 to 8 servings

Can be prepared for garnishing up to 1 month before serving.

BOMBE AUX MYRTILLES
(Lemon-Blueberry Bombe)

1 quart vanilla ice cream, softened	page 549
1 quart lemon sherbet, softened	1 cup heavy cream, whipped, sweetened, and flavored with vanilla or myrtilles liqueur, for garnish
Blueberry Cassis Sauce,	

1. Pack the vanilla ice cream into a 2-quart mold, leaving the center hollow. Freeze for 30 minutes. Pack the center of the mold with the lemon sherbet and freeze 3 hours, or until firm.

2. Unmold onto a serving platter and surround with the sauce. Decorate with the whipped cream piped through a pastry bag.

Yields 8 to 10 servings

Can be prepared for garnishing up to 1 month before serving.

CERISES LOS ANGELES
(Cherries in Orange Sherbet)

6 scoops orange sherbet	Sauce Parisienne, page 547
1½ cups Cherry Compote, page 77	Crystallized violets, for garnish

Place the sherbet in individual dessert glasses. Surround with the cherries. Spoon the sauce on top and garnish with the violets.

Yields 6 servings

Serve immediately.

Variation

• *Cherries Pompadour.* Substitute 1 cup of heavy cream, whipped and flavored to taste with sugar and kirsch, for the Sauce Parisienne.

CERISES MONTE CARLO
(Cherries in Liqueur and Orange Sherbet)

1½ cups Cherry Compote, page 77	6 scoops tangerine or orange sherbet
1 tablespoon maraschino liqueur	1 cup heavy cream, whipped

1. Macerate the cherries in the liqueur for 12 hours.

2. Spoon the fruit into 6 individual serving dishes and top with the sherbet. Pipe the whipped cream through a pastry bag, fitted with a large tip.

Yields 6 servings

Serve immediately.

CERISES DES GOURMETS
(Cherry and Pineapple Sundaes)

6 scoops pineapple sherbet	1 tablespoon prunelle liqueur
1½ cups Cherry Compote, page 77	Sauce à la Ritz, page 546

Place the sherbet in 6 dessert dishes, cover with the cherries, and sprinkle with the liqueur. Spoon the sauce over all.

Yields 6 servings

Serve immediately.

CERISES LAURETTE
(Cherries with Raspberry Sherbet)

6 scoops raspberry sherbet	sweetened, and flavored with
1½ cups Cherry Compote, page 77	kirsch, to taste, for garnish
Sauce Cardinale, page 554	Spun Sugar, page 37,
1 cup heavy cream, whipped,	for garnish

Place the sherbet in 6 dessert dishes. Spoon the cherries on top and coat with the Sauce Cardinale. Decorate with the whipped cream and surround with the spun sugar, if desired.

Yields 6 servings

Serve immediately.

BOMBE EDNA MAY
(Cherry Bombe with Raspberry Sauce)

1 **quart vanilla ice cream,**	1 **cup heavy cream, whipped**
softened	**and sweetened**
2 **cups Cherry Compote, page**	¼ **cup Raspberry Puree, page**
77	**29**

1.   Pack the ice cream into a 1-quart mold and freeze until firm.

2.   Unmold onto a platter and surround with the cherries. Fold the whipped cream and raspberry puree together and spoon over the dessert. (The cream will be too soft to pipe.)

Yields 6 servings

Can be prepared for garnishing up to 1 month before serving.

COUPE GERMAINE (Cherry and Chestnut Sundae)

Chestnut puree is available from gourmet shops. Be sure to buy sweetened puree.

1½ **cups pitted cherries**	**puree**
1 **tablespoon kirsch**	1 **cup heavy cream, whipped**
6 **scoops vanilla ice cream**	**and sweetened to taste,**
1 **cup sweetened chestnut**	**for garnish**

1.   Macerate the cherries in the kirsch for at least 30 minutes.

2.   Place the ice cream in 6 individual dishes and surround with the cherries. Press the chestnut puree through a ricer onto the ice cream. Garnish with the whipped cream piped through a pastry bag.

Yields 6 servings

Serve immediately.

CHOCOLATE CHESTNUT BOMBE

1 quart chocolate ice cream, softened	**1 tablespoon confectioners' sugar**
1 pound sweetened chestnut puree	**¼ teaspoon vanilla**
2 egg whites	**Marrons glacés or crystallized violets, for**
2 cups heavy cream	**garnish**

1.   Press the ice cream into a 1½-quart mold, leaving the center hollow. Freeze for at least 20 minutes.

2.   Scrape the chestnut puree into a bowl and whisk until smooth. Beat 1 egg white until stiff, but not dry. Whip 1¼ cups of cream until soft peaks form. Fold into the chestnut puree. Fold in the beaten egg white. Pour into the ice cream-lined mold, cover with a sheet of foil and freeze until firm. Unmold onto a serving platter.

3.   Whisk the remaining egg white until stiff, but not dry. Whip the remaining cream to stiff peaks, with the sugar and vanilla. Fold the egg white into the cream. Pipe the whipped cream over the bombe and garnish with marrons glacés or violets.

Yields 6 servings

The bombe can be prepared for garnishing up to 1 month before serving.

BOMBE BOSOMWORTH

1 pint double chocolate ice cream, softened	**page 29**
1 pint raspberry sherbet, softened	**1 tablespoon framboise**
1 cup Raspberry Puree,	**1 recipe Custard Sauce, page 545**

1.   Line a 1-quart metal mold with the chocolate ice cream. Fill the center with the sherbet and freeze until firm.

2.   In a bowl, mix the raspberry puree with the framboise.

3.   When ready to serve, unmold the bombe onto a platter and pour the custard sauce around the base. Put the raspberry sauce into a plastic squirt bottle and pipe designs around the base of the dessert (page 189).

Yields 6 servings

Can be prepared for garnishing up to 1 month before serving.

GELATO SPAZZACAMINO
(Chimney Sweep Ice Cream)

This simple, but extraordinary dessert is an Italian favorite.

6 scoops vanilla ice cream	**2 tablespoons ground espresso**
3 tablespoons scotch	**coffee beans, for garnish,**
	see Note

Put the ice cream into 6 individual serving dishes. Pour the scotch over the top and sprinkle with the coffee grounds.

Yields 6 servings

Serve immediately.

NOTE: Grind the coffee beans as finely as possible in a coffee grinder. They provide texture and flavor.

Variation

• Substitute coffee or chocolate ice cream for the vanilla ice cream and bourbon, rum, or Cognac for the scotch.

FROZEN CRANBERRY-CASSIS MOUSSE

5 cups cranberries	**1 cup heavy cream**
4 eggs, separated	**½ cup sugar**
4 egg yolks	**¼ cup water**
⅓ plus ¼ cup crème de cassis	**1 tablespoon cornstarch**

1. In a saucepan, simmer cranberries in water to cover for 10 minutes. Drain and reserve juice.

2. In a saucepan, beat the egg yolks until thickened. Stir in 1 cup reserved cranberry juice and beat until blended. Cook, over medium heat, until thick enough to coat the back of a spoon. Do not boil. Cool.

3.   Fold 4 cups of cooked cranberries into the custard and blend well. Refrigerate until the mixture is slightly thickened. Stir in ⅓ cup of crème de cassis and mix well.

4.   Beat the cream until it forms soft peaks and fold into the cranberry custard mixture. With clean beaters, beat the egg whites until stiff, and fold into the cranberry mixture. Pour into a 2½-quart mold. Freeze until firm.

5.   In a saucepan, bring the reserved cranberries to a simmer. In a bowl, mix the water and the cornstarch, and stir into the hot cranberries. Cook, stirring, until thickened. Remove from the heat. Cool and stir in the remaining crème de cassis.

6.   Unmold the mousse and serve with the sauce on the side.

Yields 8 to 10 servings

Can be prepared up to 1 month before serving.

BOMBE PALM SPRINGS

1 quart vanilla ice cream, softened	**sweetened and flavored with Cognac, for garnish**
4 ounces dates, chopped	**Chocolate Palm Trees,**
¼ cup Cognac	**page 44, for garnish**
1 cup heavy cream, whipped,	

1.   Pack the ice cream into a 1-quart mold and freeze until firm.

2.   In a bowl, macerate the dates in the Cognac for at least 3 hours and up to 6 months.

3.   Unmold the ice cream onto a serving platter, garnish with the dates and decorate with the whipped cream piped through a pastry bag.

Yields 6 servings

Can be prepared for garnishing several days before serving.

FROZEN LEMON SOUFFLÉ

6 eggs, separated
6 egg yolks
1¾ cups plus 2 teaspoons
   sugar
¾ cup lemon juice
Grated rind of 1 lemon

½ cup heavy cream
1 cup heavy cream, whipped
   and sweetened, for garnish
Crystallized violets, for
garnish

1. In a large bowl, beat the egg yolks and 1½ cups of sugar until thickened and pale. Add the lemon juice and place the bowl over a pan of boiling water. Do not let the water touch the bottom of the bowl. Beat constantly until the mixture is thick, smooth, creamy, and tripled in volume. Fold in the grated rind. Refrigerate until slightly thickened.

2. Collar a 1-quart soufflé dish and lightly oil the dish and the collar, (see page 240). Beat the cream with 2 teaspoons of sugar until it forms soft peaks. Fold into the egg-lemon mixture.

3. With clean beaters, beat the egg whites until soft peaks form. Beat in the remaining ¼ cup of sugar and beat until they form stiff peaks. Fold into the lemon mixture and pour into the prepared mold. Freeze until firm.

4. When ready to serve, remove the collar, and garnish with the violets and the whipped cream piped through a pastry bag.

Yields 6 to 8 servings

Can be prepared for garnishing up to 1 month before serving.

FROZEN LEMON CREAM IN LEMON SHELLS

See page 51 for information on how to prepare the shells.

1 cup sugar
1 cup milk

1 cup heavy cream
8 lemons

1. In a bowl, dissolve the sugar in the milk and heavy cream. Pour into an ice cube tray or a loaf pan, and freeze until mushy.

2. Grate the rind of 2 of the lemons and squeeze the juice. Stir into the mushy cream mixture and beat well. Freeze for 2 hours.

3. Cut a slice off the tops of the remaining 6 lemons and scoop out the pulp to make shells. Cut a thin slice off the bottom of each lemon shell to prevent it from rolling. Using a pastry bag fitted with a large plain tip, pipe the frozen cream mixture into the lemon shells. Arrange the cutoff lids askew, and freeze the assembled dessert until firm.

Yields 6 servings

Can be prepared up to 1 month before serving.

Store the unfilled shells in the freezer for up to 1 month, if needed.

FROZEN LIME SOUFFLÉ

1 cup plus 2 tablespoons sugar	½ cup lime juice
¼ cup water	3 cups heavy cream
7 egg yolks	Candied Lime Rind, page 38, for garnish

1. Collar a 1-quart or six 6-ounce soufflé dishes and lightly oil the collar and dishes (see page 240).

2. In a saucepan, cook 1 cup of sugar and the water until the mixture registers 240°F.

3. In a mixer beat the egg yolks until pale. While beating, pour the sugar syrup in a slow steady stream. Beat until cool and tripled in volume. Add the lime juice. Beat 2 cups of heavy cream to soft peaks and fold into the lime-egg mixture. Pour into the serving dish. Freeze about 6 hours, or until firm.

4. Whip the remaining cream until stiff peaks form. Using a pastry bag, fitted with a #5 star tip, pipe rosettes of whipped cream. Decorate with candied lime rind.

Yields 6 servings

Can be prepared up to 1 month before serving. Keep covered with plastic wrap or foil once set.

COUPE NECTARINE SULTANE

6 scoops pistachio ice cream	Sabayon Sauce flavored with kirsch, page 544
6 Vanilla Poached Nectarines, halved, page 40	Chopped pistachio nuts, for garnish

Arrange the ice cream in six dessert dishes. Top with the nectarines and pour the sabayon sauce over the fruit. Sprinkle the nuts on top.

Yields 6 servings

Serve immediately.

BOMBE GRIMALDI
(Tangerine and Pineapple Bombe)

1 quart tangerine or orange sherbet, softened	Sugar, to taste
1 pineapple, peeled, cored, and diced	1 cup heavy cream, whipped and sweetened, for garnish
2 tablespoons kirsch	Crystallized violets, for garnish

1.   Pack the sherbet into a 1-quart mold and freeze 3 hours or until firm.

2.   Macerate the pineapple in the kirsch for 1 hour. Sweeten to taste with sugar.

3.   Unmold the sherbet onto a serving platter. Put the pineapple into the center and around the mold. Using a pastry bag fitted with a #5 star tip, pipe the whipped cream around the dessert. Garnish with the violets.

Yields 6 to 8 servings

Can be prepared for garnishing several days ahead.

FUJIYAMA
(Orange and Vanilla Ice Cream Dessert)

1 (8-in) Orange-flavored Génoise layer, page 21	1 pint orange sherbet, softened
½ cup orange liqueur	1 cup heavy cream, whipped to soft peaks
1 pint vanilla ice cream, softened	Orange slices, for garnish

1.   Place the génoise on a serving platter. Sprinkle the cake with ¼ cup of liqueur and cover with alternating scoops of ice cream and sherbet, piling them into a pyramid.

2.   Fold the remaining orange liqueur into the whipped cream and drizzle over the ice cream. Garnish the dessert with the orange slices.

Yields 6 to 8 servings

Serve immediately.

Variation

• Pack a 1-quart peaked decorative mold with the vanilla ice cream and fill the center with the orange sherbet. Refrigerate until firm. Prepare a Grand Marnier Sauce (see page 545), and fold the whipped cream into it. Omit the remaining orange liqueur. Drizzle the sauce over the ice cream.

BOMBE EUNICE (Orange-Walnut Bombe)

Eunice Ehrlich gave me the recipe for the sauce, which then inspired the dessert.

1 quart vanilla ice cream, softened	3 oranges, peeled and sliced, for garnish
1 pint orange sherbet, softened	1 recipe Eunice's Walnut Orange Sauce, page 552
1 pint maple walnut ice cream, softened	1 cup heavy cream, whipped, sweetened, and flavored to taste, for garnish

1.   In a mold, pack the vanilla ice cream, leaving the center hollow. Freeze for 30 minutes. Pack in the orange sherbet, leaving the center hollow and freeze 30 minutes longer. Pack the maple walnut ice cream into the center of the mold and freeze until firm.

2.   When ready to serve, unmold the ice cream onto a platter and surround with orange slices. Coat with some of the sauce. Using a pastry bag, pipe on the whipped cream. Pass the remaining sauce separately.

Yield 8 to 10 servings

Can be prepared for garnishing up to 1 month before serving.

COUPE À L'ORANGE AU CHOCOLAT
(Orange Sherbet with Oranges
and Chocolate Sauce)

3 oranges, peeled and sectioned	Bittersweet Chocolate Sauce, page 541
⅓ cup orange liqueur	1 tablespoon grated orange rind, for garnish
6 scoops orange sherbet	

1. Macerate the orange sections in the liqueur for 1 hour.

2. Scoop the sherbet into 6 dishes, surround with the orange sections, and coat with the chocolate sauce. Sprinkle with the grated orange rind.

Yields 6 servings

Serve immediately.

ORANGE SHELLS GLACÉ

9 navel oranges	whipped and sweetened
1 cup sugar	2 teaspoons vanilla
6 egg yolks	2 tablespoons lemon juice
2 cups heavy cream,	4 teaspoons grated lemon rind

1. Slice the tops off 8 of the oranges, scoop out the pulp reserving any juice, and set the shells aside. Grate the rind from the remaining orange.

2. Measure ¾ cup of the juice from the oranges into a saucepan. (Use the remaining fruit for another purpose.) Add the sugar and boil until the mixture reaches 220°F.

3. In another saucepan, beat the egg yolks until thickened and pale. Slowly beat in the hot syrup and cook, over medium heat, beating constantly, until the consistency of mayonnaise. Remove from the heat, place in a sink of cold water, and continue to beat until cold.

4. Fold in the whipped cream, vanilla, lemon juice, lemon rind, and orange rind into the mixture.

5. Spoon into the reserved orange shells, cover with the tops of the oranges, and freeze until firm.

Yields 8 servings

Can be prepared up to 1 month before serving.

MOUSSE GLACÉ GRAND MARNIER
(Frozen Grand Marnier Mousse)

2 egg whites	1 cup heavy cream, whipped
Pinch of salt	and sweetened
⅓ cup sugar	Raspberry or Strawberry
¼ cup Grand Marnier	Sauce, pages 552, 554

1. Beat the egg whites with the salt until they form soft peaks. Beat in the sugar, 1 tablespoon at a time, until the whites are stiff and shiny.

2. Fold the Grand Marnier into the whipped cream and fold into the egg white mixture. Pour into a 1-quart mold and freeze at least 2 hours, or until firm. Unmold and serve with the berry sauce of your choice.

Yields 4 to 6 servings

Can be prepared for garnishing up to 1 month before serving.

FROZEN PEACH-MASCARPONE SOUFFLÉ

2½ pounds unpeeled peaches,	4 egg whites
quartered and pitted	1 cup mascarpone
1¼ teaspoons lemon juice	1 peach, peeled and sliced, for
⅛ teaspoon vanilla	garnish
1 cup sugar	2 tablespoons lemon juice
½ cup water	2 cups fruit sauce

1. Line a 2½-quart soufflé dish with plastic wrap as smoothly as possible.

2. In a processor, puree the peaches and 1 teaspoon of lemon juice until smooth. Transfer to a saucepan, add the vanilla, and simmer, stirring often, about 40 minutes, or until reduced by half. Press through a sieve and cool.

3. In a small saucepan, boil the sugar, remaining lemon juice and the water until the mixture reaches 240°F.

4. In a bowl, beat the egg whites until frothy. Slowly pour in the hot syrup. Beat until the meringue is stiff and cool to the touch. Whisk the mascarpone into the peach puree and lightly fold in one-fourth of the meringue. Fold into the remaining meringue and pour into the soufflé dish.

5. Freeze for at least 6 hours, until firm. Unmold, garnish with peach slices dipped in the lemon juice, and serve with blueberry, raspberry, or strawberry sauce.

Yields 10 servings

Can be prepared for garnishing up to 1 month before serving

PEACH-RASPBERRY BOMBE

2 (9-in) Nutted Génoise
layers, page 21

4 tablespoons plus ½
teaspoon framboise

1 quart raspberry ice cream,
softened

1 pint peach ice cream,
softened

1½ cups heavy cream

¼ cup plus 1 tablespoon
confectioners' sugar

¼ teaspoon almond extract

2 peaches, peeled, pitted, and
sliced

½ cup ground toasted almonds

Fresh whole raspberries, for
garnish

1. Cut the génoise layers in half horizontally. Sprinkle each layer with 1 tablespoon of framboise. Place one layer in a springform pan and spread with half of the raspberry ice cream. Add another cake layer and spread with the peach ice cream. Add another cake layer and spread with the remaining raspberry ice cream. Add the final cake layer and press down lightly. Cover and freeze at least 2 hours, or until firm.

2. About 1 hour before serving, remove the sides of the pan. Beat the cream until it forms soft peaks and beat in ¼ cup of sugar and the almond extract. Beat until stiff peaks form. Spread a thin layer evenly over the top of the cake. Put the remainder into a pastry bag fitted with a #5 open star tip and pipe a border.

3. Sprinkle the sliced peaches with the remaining framboise and confectioners' sugar and macerate for 10 minutes. Arrange the peaches on top of the bombe and press the almonds into the sides of the bombe. Garnish with the raspberries.

Yields 8 to 10 servings

Can be prepared for garnishing up to 1 month before serving.

PÊCHES MELBA (Peach Melba)

6 scoops vanilla ice cream
6 cold Vanilla Poached
Peaches, halved, page 40

1½ cups Raspberry Sauce, page
552

Place a scoop of ice cream in each dessert dish and top with 2 peach halves and coat with the raspberry sauce.

Yields 6 servings

Serve immediately.

BOMBE MASCOTTE (Peach and Kirsch Bombe)

1 pint peach ice cream,
softened
3 tablespoons kirsch
½ pint vanilla ice cream,
softened

6 peaches, pitted and sliced
1 cup heavy cream, whipped,
sweetened, and flavored with
kirsch to taste, for garnish

1. Pack the ice cream into a 1½-pint mold leaving the center hollow. Freeze for 30 minutes. Beat in 2 tablespoons of kirsch into the vanilla ice cream. Pack into the center of the mold and freeze at least 2 hours, or until firm.

2. Macerate the peaches in the remaining kirsch for 1 hour.

3. Unmold the ice cream onto a platter and surround with the peaches. Decorate with the whipped cream.

Yields 6 servings

Can be prepared for garnishing up to 1 month before serving.

POIRES BELLES DIJONNAISES
(Raspberry and Pear Bombe)

1 quart raspberry sherbet,
softened
6 cold Vanilla Poached Pears,
page 40
Sauce Riche, page 547

Crystallized violets, for
garnish
Spun Sugar, page 37, for
garnish

Fill a 1-quart ring mold with the sherbet and freeze until firm. Unmold the sherbet onto a serving platter and place the cold pears in the center. Pour some of the sauce over the pears and garnish with the violets and spun sugar. Pass the remaining sauce separately.

Yields 6 servings

Can be prepared for garnishing up to 1 month before serving.

POIRES GERALDINE FARRAR
(Pear-and-Orange-Sherbet Sundae)

> 6 cold Vanilla Poached Pears, halved and cored, page 40
> 6 scoops orange sherbet
> Apricot Sauce, page 547

> 1 cup heavy cream, whipped and sweetened, to taste
> Crystallized violets, for garnish

1. Arrange two pear halves in individual dessert dishes and top with a scoop of sherbet.

2. Mask the pears with the apricot sauce and garnish the dessert with the whipped cream and candied violets.

Yields 6 servings

Serve immediately.

POIRES BELLE HÉLÈNE
(Pear-and-Fudge-Sauce Sundaes)

> 6 cold Vanilla Poached Pears, halved and cored, page 40
> 6 scoops vanilla ice cream

> Fudge Sauce, page 540
> 1 cup heavy cream, whipped and sweetened to taste, for garnish

Arrange the pear halves in dessert dishes and top with a scoop of ice cream. Spoon on the sauce and garnish with the whipped cream.

Yields 6 servings

Serve immediately.

ANANAS GLACÉ À LA BOURBONNAISE
(Pineapple Ice Cream Mold)

1 pineapple cut as a container, page 55	3 tablespoons sugar
4 tablespoons rum	1 quart rum-flavored ice cream, softened

1.   Dice the flesh from the pineapple and macerate in 3 tablespoons of rum and 2 tablespoons of the sugar for 2 hours.

2.   Sprinkle the inside of the pineapple shell with the remaining rum and 1 tablespoon of sugar. Fill the shell with alternating layers of ice cream and diced pineapple. Freeze for 2 hours, until firm. Place the frond on top and serve.

Yields 6 servings

Do not freeze for more than 4 hours, or the fruit will freeze, making the dessert less than pleasant to eat.

BOMBE MAYERLING

1½ quarts vanilla ice cream, softened	2 cups diced pineapple, for garnish
1 (9-in) Génoise layer, page 20	1 cup heavy cream, whipped, sweetened, and flavored to taste with orange liqueur, for garnish
Orange liqueur, to taste	

1.   Pack the ice cream into a 1½-quart mold and freeze until firm.

2.   Place the cake layer on a serving dish and sprinkle generously with the orange liqueur. Unmold the ice cream onto the cake and garnish with the pineapple and the whipped cream.

Yields 6 to 8 servings

Can be prepared for garnishing up to 1 month before serving.

BOMBE JAMAÏQUE
(Coffee Ice Cream with Pineapple)

1 quart coffee ice cream,
softened
2 cups cubed pineapple,
drained
2 tablespoons dark rum

1 cup heavy cream, whipped
and sweetened, for garnish
Candied coffee beans, for
garnish

1. Pack the ice cream into a 1-quart mold and freeze 3 hours, or until firm.

2. In a bowl, macerate the pineapple in the rum for at least 1 hour. Drain.

3. To serve, unmold the ice cream onto a platter and surround with drained pineapple.

4. Fold 2 tablespoons of macerating liquid into the cream and, using a pastry bag, pipe onto the bombe. Garnish with the coffee beans.

Yields 6 servings

Can be prepared for garnishing up to 1 month before serving.

BOMBE DE RÊVE DE BÉBÉ
(Baby's Dream Bombe)

1 pint pineapple sherbet,
softened
1 pint raspberry sherbet,
softened
1 pint strawberries, hulled
½ cup orange juice, flavored

with orange liqueur, to taste
Sugar, to taste
1 cup heavy cream, whipped
and sweetened, for garnish
Crystallized violets, for
garnish

1. Line a 1-quart mold with the pineapple sherbet, leaving the center hollow. Fill the hollow with the raspberry sherbet and freeze until firm.

2. In a bowl, macerate the strawberries in the orange juice mixture for 2 hours. Add sugar, to taste.

3. Unmold the ice cream onto a platter and surround with the strawberries. Pipe the cream through a pastry bag, and garnish with the violets.

Yields 6 servings

Can be prepared for garnishing up to 1 month before serving.

FROZEN PUMPKIN MOUSSE

¾ cup sugar
¾ cup water
3 egg whites
Pinch of salt
½ cup pumpkin puree
⅛ teaspoon cinnamon

⅛ teaspoon ginger
⅛ teaspoon nutmeg
2 cups heavy cream
Sugar, to taste
1–2 tablespoons rum

1.   In a saucepan, boil the sugar and water until the mixture reaches 238°F.

2.   Beat the egg whites until foamy. Add the salt and beat until soft peaks form. While beating, add the syrup in a slow, steady stream. Continue beating until the mixture cools. Fold in the pumpkin, cinnamon, ginger, and nutmeg.

3.   Beat 1 cup of cream until it forms soft peaks, and fold into the pumpkin mixture.

4.   Pour into a 1½-quart mold and freeze for at least 4 hours or until firm. Unmold the mousse onto a serving platter. Whip the remaining cream until stiff peaks form, flavoring with the sugar and rum to taste. Using a pastry bag fitted with a #6 star tip, pipe whipped cream over the dessert.

Yields 6 servings

Can be prepared for garnishing up to 1 month before serving.

RASPBERRY BOMBE

3 pints raspberry sherbet, softened
¾ cup plus 1 teaspoon sugar
¼ cup water
4 egg yolks
1 tablespoon grated orange rind

1¼ cups heavy cream
¼ cup orange liqueur
3 cups raspberries, for garnish
½ cup heavy cream, whipped and sweetened, for garnish
Mint leaves, for garnish

1.   Line the bottom and sides of a 2-quart mold with the sherbet. Freeze, for 30 minutes.

2.   In a saucepan, boil ¾ cup of sugar with the water until it reaches 238°F.

3. In a mixer, beat the egg yolks until light in color. While beating, add the syrup in a slow, steady stream. Continue to beat until the mixture cools to room temperature. Refrigerate, covered, until cold.

4. In a small bowl, mash the orange rind and the remaining sugar. Whip the 1¼ of cups cream until it forms soft peaks and fold in the orange rind and liqueur. Fold into the chilled egg yolk mixture. Pour into the mold and freeze, covered overnight.

5. Unmold onto a serving platter and garnish with the raspberries, whipped cream, and mint leaves.

Yields 10 to 12 servings

Can be prepared for garnishing up to 1 month before serving.

FROZEN RASPBERRY TORTE

24 Ladyfingers, page 21	**1 teaspoon light corn syrup**
20 ounces frozen unsweetened	**3 egg whites**
raspberries, thawed	**2 tablespoons kirsch**
1¼ cups sugar plus additional,	**2 cups heavy cream**
to taste	**Whole raspberries, for**
⅓ cup water	**garnish**

1. Line the sides of a 9-inch springform pan with the ladyfingers and set aside. In a processor, puree the raspberries, press through a sieve. There should be 2 cups of puree. Add sugar to taste.

2. In a saucepan, boil 1¼ cups of sugar, the water, and corn syrup until the mixture reaches 238°F.

3. In a mixer, beat the egg whites until they form soft peaks. While beating, add the hot syrup in a slow, steady stream. Beat until the mixture cools. Beat in the puree and kirsch.

4. Whip the cream until it forms soft peaks and fold into the mousse mixture. Turn into the prepared pan. Freeze until firm. Unmold and garnish with whole raspberries.

Yields 12 servings

Can be prepared for garnishing up to 1 month before serving.

Variation

• Substitute 1 (9-inch) Nutted Génoise layer (see page 21) for the ladyfingers. Cut the cake into 2 layers and place 1 layer in the bottom of a 9-inch springform pan. Add the mousse mixture, cover with the remaining cake layer and freeze until firm. Serve garnished with whipped cream and raspberries, or coat with Chocolate Glaze (see page 35).

LE PAVÉ AUX FRAMBOISES
(Frozen Raspberry Dessert)

1¼ cups sugar

2 cups water

4 egg yolks

2⅓ cups raspberries

⅓ cup lemon juice

1 cup heavy cream, whipped

and sweetened

1 cup framboise

20 Ladyfingers, page 21

1⅓ cups heavy cream, whipped and sweetened, for garnish

1. In a saucepan, boil ¾ cup of sugar and 1 cup of water until it reaches 250°F.

2. In a mixer, beat the egg yolks until thickened and pale. While beating, add the syrup in a slow, steady stream. Continue beating until the mixture is cool.

3. Sieve 1 cup of raspberries and discard the seeds. Flavor the puree with the lemon juice and fold in the whipped cream. Fold into the egg yolk mixture.

4. In a saucepan, boil the remaining sugar and water until the sugar dissolves. Cool 5 minutes and stir in the framboise.

5. In a 2-quart loaf pan, spread a layer of the raspberry mixture. Cover with a layer of ladyfingers dipped in the framboise syrup and continue layering the ingredients, ending with the raspberry mixture. Freeze until firm.

6. Unmold onto a serving platter and garnish with the remaining raspberries and the whipped cream.

Yields 6 to 8 servings

Can be prepared for garnishing up to 6 hours before serving.

FRAISES DE JEANNE GRANIER
(Strawberry and Orange Sherbet Sundaes)

⅓ cup sugar
¼ cup water
¼ cup orange juice
3 egg yolks
5 tablespoons orange liqueur

1 cup heavy cream, whipped
and sweetened
1 quart strawberries, hulled
and halved
8 scoops orange sherbet

1. In a saucepan, cook the sugar, water, and orange juice until the mixture reaches 238°F.

2. In a mixer, beat the egg yolks until thickened and pale. While beating, add the syrup in a slow, steady stream, beating constantly. Continue beating until the mixture is cool and thickened. Refrigerate until cold.

3. Fold in 3 tablespoons of orange liqueur and the whipped cream. Refrigerate the sauce until ready to serve.

4. In a bowl, macerate the strawberries with the remaining orange liqueur for up to 4 hours.

5. Arrange the sherbet in 6 dessert glasses, surround with the strawberries, and spoon the sauce over the top.

Yields 8 servings

Serve immediately.

FROZEN STRAWBERRY SOUFFLÉ

6 eggs, separated
3 cups sugar
2 cups Strawberry Puree,
page 29
½ cup orange liqueur
⅓ cup orange juice

3½ cups heavy cream
½ cup chopped walnuts or
pistachios, for garnish
Whole strawberries
Raspberry Sauce, page 552

1. Collar a 1½-quart soufflé dish and lightly oil the collar and dish, (see page 240).

2. In a saucepan, beat the egg yolks and 2 cups of sugar until thickened and pale. Stir in ½ cup of the strawberry puree. Cook over low heat, stirring constantly, until thick enough to coat the back of a spoon. Remove from the heat, stir in the liqueur, and cool.

3. In a small saucepan, heat the remaining cup of sugar and orange juice over medium heat, stirring until the sugar dissolves. Raise the heat and cook, without stirring, until the mixture reaches 250°F.

4. In a mixer beat the egg whites until soft peaks form. While beating, add the syrup in a slow, steady stream. Continue beating until they form stiff peaks.

5. Whip 3 cups of cream and fold into the mixture. Fold in the remaining strawberry puree. Pour into the soufflé dish and freeze until firm. When ready to serve, remove the collar and press the chopped nuts around the exposed edge of the soufflé. Whip the remaining cream until it forms firm peaks. Using a pastry bag fitted with a #6 open star tip, garnish the dessert with the whipped cream, and the strawberries. Pass the raspberry sauce.

Yields 12 servings

Can be prepared for garnishing up to 1 month before serving.

BOMBE ALHAMBRA
(Strawberry–Mandarin Orange Bombe)

1 **quart vanilla ice cream, softened**	2 **tablespoons kirsch**
1 **pint strawberry ice cream, softened**	1 **cup heavy cream**
	Sugar, to taste
1 **quart strawberries, hulled, for garnish**	2 **cups Sauce Riche, flavored with mandarin liqueur, page 547**

1. Pack a 1½-quart mold with the vanilla ice cream leaving the center hollow. Freeze for 30 minutes. Fill the center with the strawberry ice cream. Freeze until firm.

2. In a bowl, macerate the strawberries in the kirsch for up to 2 hours.

3. When ready to serve, unmold the ice cream onto a platter. Whip the cream until soft peaks form and flavor with sugar to taste. Garnish the bombe with whipped cream and strawberries. Pour some sauce over the berries and serve the remainder on the side.

Yields 6 servings

Can be prepared for garnishing up to 1 month before serving.

BOMBE TEIXEIRA (Coffee Ice Cream, Raspberry Sauce, and Strawberries)

I created this dessert for Eugene Teixeira, a marathon runner who loves ice cream.

1 quart coffee ice cream, softened	3 tablespoons kirsch
	1 pint strawberries
1½ cups Raspberry Sauce, page 552	1 cup heavy cream, for garnish
	1 tablespoon sugar

1. Pack the ice cream into a 1-quart mold and freeze until firm.

2. In a bowl, mix the raspberry sauce and 2 tablespoons of kirsch, and set aside.

3. When ready to serve, unmold the ice cream onto a platter, and surround with the strawberries. In a bowl, whip the cream with the sugar and the remaining kirsch. Garnish the dessert with the sweetened cream. Spoon some sauce over the berries and pass the remainder.

Yields 6 servings

Can be prepared for garnishing up to 1 month before serving.

FROZEN PUDDING

This old-fashioned dessert amounts to homemade ice cream. The flavors are sophisticated and delicious. You may garnish the unmolded pudding with whipped cream and additional brandy-soaked fruits.

1½ cups chopped candied fruits, see Note	2 eggs
	2½ cups milk, scalded
Brandy	2 cups heavy cream
1 cup sugar	½ cup rum
⅛ teaspoon salt	

1. In a bowl, cover the fruits with brandy and let macerate for several hours.

2. In a saucepan or a double boiler, beat the sugar, salt, and eggs until thickened and pale. Gradually stir in the scalded milk and cook, stirring over simmering water, until the custard is thick enough to coat the back of a spoon. Strain into a bowl, cover with plastic wrap, and chill until cold.

3.   In a mixer, beat 1 cup of the cream until it forms soft peaks and fold into the custard with the rum. Fill a decorative mold with alternating layers of cream and 1 cup of brandied fruits. Cover the mold tightly and freeze until firm.

4.   Unmold, whip the remaining cream, and garnish the pudding with the cream and remaining brandied fruits.

Yields 6 to 8 servings

Can be prepared for garnishing up to 1 month before serving.

NOTE: Nesselrode Mix (see page 28) is suitable for the candied fruits in brandy.

Chapter 9

PUDDINGS

Puddings, (a graceless name, not even helped by the French *pouding*), offer a wide range of dessert styles from dense, fruit-laden, liqueur-soaked Christmas plum puddings to the ethereal *Pouding aux Liqueurs.* The very stodginess of the name brings thoughts of *Tom Brown's School Days,* dreary school lunchrooms, and bleak cafeterias. But puddings provide great pleasure when properly prepared. They can recall warm memories of the best times of childhood. Caring grandmothers, loving aunts, and all that is warm and wonderful about childhood come to the fore, as clearly to each of us as the memories of madeleines to Proust. A hot pudding just removed from the steamer makes a cold, raw November day in New England endurable. Perfectly made puddings appear in the best dining rooms and at the most *luxe* of establishments. Recently, top chefs vied to create the best bread pudding.

In English and American cookery, there are a slew of desserts with a variety of names indicating similar preparations: crisps, cobblers, slumps, crumbles, etc., all mean fruit baked by itself, over a crust, or under some sort of topping. I have chosen to place them in this section because they seem to fit with puddings more than with any other form of dessert. As with almost all fruit desserts, you may exchange one fruit for another, especially if they are similar in type: pears for apples, strawberries for raspberries, etc.

Perception and memory are the enemies of puddings. Faces sink into despair at the mention of rice pudding. The disappointment is palpable with dreary memories of cafeteria offerings. Once diners taste good rice pudding, the faces glow with appreciation of the eggs, milk, cream, and seasonings used to make this rich yet delicate delight. Try *Riz à la Maltaise* (orange-flavored rice pudding) or one of the other versions here to learn just how wonderful rice pudding is. Rice pudding does not need to be hard pellets in a gluey mass dotted with a few hard raisins and a dusting of old and flavorless cinnamon.

Serve puddings hot, warm, at room temperature, or cold, depending on the type. As with so many cold foods, "cold" should never be refrigerator cold. Let refrigerated puddings warm to almost room temperature so the flavors can blossom.

VANILLA AND CHOCOLATE PUDDINGS   For many people pudding means the chocolate or vanilla pudding mixes. These additive-loaded mixes usually taste dreadful. The theory is that they are quickly and easily prepared, a reason that seldom is in the interest of flavor, and, as in so many instances, unnecessary since you can prepare the puddings quickly. They do take a little while to chill. Pastry cream, or Crème Pâtissière, is the base of these puddings. For the basic recipe and a list of other flavor possibilities, see pages 26–27.

DOUBLE CHOCOLATE CUSTARD PUDDING

1 quart plus ½ cup milk	10 ounces semisweet chocolate,
1 cup sugar	grated
6 tablespoons cornstarch	2 tablespoons dark rum
¼ cup cocoa, sifted	2 tablespoons vanilla
2 eggs	Heavy cream, whipped,
4 egg yolks	sweetened, and flavored to
¼ cup butter	taste, for garnish

1.   In a saucepan bring the 1 quart of milk and ½ cup of sugar to a boil. In a large bowl, mix the remaining sugar, cornstarch, cocoa, milk, eggs, and egg yolks until smooth.

2.   Gradually beat in the hot milk. Return to the saucepan and cook over low heat, stirring, until the mixture comes to a boil and thickens. Remove from the heat and stir in the grated chocolate, butter, rum, and vanilla until smooth.

3. Pour into 6 serving dishes. Refrigerate until cold and top with lightly beaten whipped cream, if desired.

Yields 6 servings

Can be prepared the day before serving.

NOTE: A skin will form on the surface of the cooked pudding if left uncovered. Cover securely with plastic wrap or dot lightly with the end of a stick of butter.

RØD GRØD
(Molded Red Fruit Pudding)

This cornstarch-thickened pudding is somewhat firmer than custard puddings.

1 pint strawberries, crushed	¼ cup cornstarch
1 pint raspberries, crushed	½ cup water
½ cup sugar, or to taste	1 cup Custard Sauce, page 545
Pinch of salt	

1. In a saucepan, bring the strawberries, raspberries, and sugar to a boil, stirring. Strain through a fine sieve and discard the seeds. Return the puree to the saucepan and stir in the salt.

2. In a small bowl, mix the cornstarch and water and stir into the puree. Simmer the puree for 1 minute and pour into a 1-quart mold.

3. Chill for 4 hours, or until fully set. Unmold onto a serving platter and serve with the custard sauce.

Yields 6 servings

Can be prepared the day before serving.

Bread Pudding

Bread pudding has had a remarkable renaissance. Many chefs in the finest restaurants have used their skills to produce the richest, silkiest of puddings with the implication that a sainted grandmother handed out the original recipe, or that they were "improving" her recipe, often proving that more is less. Bread pudding is indeed a simple dessert that can easily hold its own against the most complex dishes. It is simplicity itself to prepare. It is really little more than French toast, *pain perdu,* baked as a whole rather than drained and sautéed.

BREAD PUDDING

This pudding is delicious by itself, or enhance the pudding with Lemon, Vanilla, or Hard sauce.

5 cups stale French or Italian bread cubes with crusts, see Note	1¼ teaspoons cinnamon
	¼ cup butter, melted
	2 cups milk
3 large eggs	½ cup raisins or currants
1¼ cups sugar	Lightly whipped heavy
1½ teaspoons vanilla	cream, for garnish
1¼ teaspoons nutmeg	

1.   In a 9 × 13-inch baking dish, scatter the bread cubes.

2.   In a bowl, mix the eggs, sugar, vanilla, nutmeg, cinnamon, butter, and milk. Pour over the bread and sprinkle with the raisins. Let stand for 20 minutes; press the bread to help it absorb the liquid. Let stand another 20 minutes; press the bread again. Preheat the oven to 350°F.

3.   Bake for 45 minutes to 1 hour, or until the custard sets. If the top becomes too brown, cover with a sheet of foil after 45 minutes. Serve warm or at room temperature with the whipped cream, if desired.

Yields 6 servings

NOTE: Almost any stale bread can suit, use white, whole wheat, or even pumpernickel.

BLUEBERRY BREAD PUDDING

4 slices white bread, crusts removed and cubed	sugar
	1 quart blueberries
½ cup butter	1 cup heavy cream
⅔ cup plus 2 tablespoons	½ teaspoon cinnamon

1.   In a skillet, sauté the bread cubes in the butter until golden and crisp. Add ⅔ cup of sugar and stir to coat the croutons.

2. When ready to serve, reheat the croutons, add the berries, and cook until the juices start to flow.

3. In a bowl, whip the cream until it forms soft peaks. Add the remaining sugar and the cinnamon and beat until stiff peaks form. Place in a serving dish and refrigerate until the pudding is ready to serve.

4. Serve the pudding immediately, with the whipped cream on the side.

Yields 6 servings

Toasted bread and whipped cream can be prepared several hours ahead.

COLD BLUEBERRY BREAD PUDDING

1 quart blueberries	4 tablespoons butter
1 cup sugar	1 pound loaf sliced white
1 teaspoon cinnamon	bread, crusts removed
¼ teaspoon salt	Hard Sauce, page 543, or
1 cup water	Custard Sauce, page 545

1. In a 2-quart saucepan, simmer the blueberries, sugar, cinnamon, salt, and water for 10 minutes.

2. Butter the bread slices and cut into ½-inch cubes. Spread a thin layer of hot blueberries on the bottom of a 1½-quart soufflé dish or six 6-ounce ramekins or custard cups. Fill with bread cubes, press down, and add more blueberry mixture. Keep filling and pressing until the bread soaks up all the juices.

3. Refrigerate at least 2 hours. Serve cold with the sauce on the side.

Yields 6 servings

Can be prepared 2 days before serving.

CAPIROTADA
(Mexican Bread Pudding with Cheese)

1 quart water	sliced
2 cups brown sugar	1 cup raisins
2-in piece stick cinnamon	1 cup chopped blanched
1 clove	almonds
6 slices toast, cubed	½ pound Monterey Jack cheese,
3 apples, peeled, cored, and	grated

1. Preheat the oven to 350°F. Butter a 9 × 13-inch baking dish.

2. In a saucepan, simmer the water, sugar, cinnamon, and clove for 5 minutes, or until it is of a thin, syrupy consistency. Strain and discard the spices.

3. Arrange half of the toast cubes in the baking dish. Add a layer of half of the apples, raisins, almonds, and cheese. Repeat, using the remaining ingredients. Pour the syrup over the top and bake for 30 minutes, or until golden and bubbling. Serve hot.

Yields 6 servings

Can be prepared for baking several hours ahead.

GINGER-RUM BREAD PUDDING

3 eggs	1 tablespoon dark rum
½ cup sugar	3 cups milk
¼ teaspoon salt	4 slices buttered toast, cut in
¼ teaspoon ginger	1-in cubes
¼ teaspoon cinnamon	

1. Preheat the oven to 375°F. Butter an 8- or 9-inch baking dish.

2. In a bowl, beat the eggs, sugar, salt, ginger, cinnamon, rum, and milk until blended. Add the toast. Pour into the baking dish and let stand for 20 minutes.

3. Bake in a water bath for about 45 minutes, or until it tests done. Serve warm.

Yields 6 servings

Can be prepared for baking several hours ahead.

Variations

• Substitute 1 teaspoon of vanilla for the ginger and rum and add ½ cup of raisins.
• Add the grated rind of 1 orange and substitute the juice of 1 orange for the ginger and rum.

BUDINO DI PANE CARAMELLATO
(Glazed Bread Pudding)

½ cup raisins	2 cups milk
½ cup plus ⅓ cup sugar	2 tablespoons flour
2 tablespoons water	¼ cup pine nuts, toasted
2½ cups stale bread cubes,	2 eggs, separated
crustless and lightly toasted	1 egg yolk
½ cup butter	¼ cup rum

1.   Preheat the oven to 375°F. In a bowl, pour warm water over the raisins to cover. Set aside.

2.   In a saucepan, caramelize ½ cup of sugar and the water until deep golden brown (see page 5). Pour into a 2-quart mold.

3.   In a bowl, mix the bread, remaining sugar, and butter. In a saucepan, bring the milk to a boil and immediately pour over the bread. Set aside until cool.

4.   With a spoon or whisk, beat the bread mixture until smooth.

5.   Drain the raisins and dredge in the flour. Shake off any excess. Stir into the bread mixture with the pine nuts and egg yolks.

6.   Beat the egg whites until they form soft peaks and fold into the bread mixture. Pour into the prepared pan.

7.   Bake in a water bath for 1 hour. Lower the heat to 300°F. and bake 15 minutes longer, or until golden.

8.   Remove from the oven, pierce the top randomly with a toothpick, and pour on 2 tablespoons of the rum. After the pudding absorbs the rum, unmold onto a serving platter, and pour the remaining rum over the top. Serve warm or at room temperature.

Yields 6 servings

Can be prepared for baking several hours ahead.

CHOCOLATE BREAD PUDDING

½ pound semisweet chocolate	1 cup milk
12 slices bread or brioche,	1 cup sugar
crusts removed	5 eggs
1 cup butter, melted	1 teaspoon Vanilla
3 cups heavy cream	Custard Sauce, page 545

1.   Preheat the oven to 425°F.

2.   Melt the chocolate and cool to room temperature.

3.   Brush the bread with butter and toast in the oven until light golden brown. Arrange the slices, slightly overlapping, in a 9 × 13-inch baking dish.

4.   In a saucepan, scald the cream and the milk. Stir in the sugar until dissolved. In a bowl, beat the eggs, and slowly stir in the hot milk. Gradually stir the mixture into the melted chocolate with the vanilla. Pour the custard over the bread and soak for 1 hour, pressing the bread every 20 minutes to help it absorb the liquid.

5.   Lower the oven to 325°F. Place the pudding in a water bath, cover with foil, and bake for 1 hour and 45 minutes, or until the bread absorbs the liquid. Serve warm with the custard sauce, if desired.

Yields 6 servings

Can be prepared for baking several hours ahead.

PEAR BREAD PUDDING WITH CARAMEL-BOURBON SAUCE

1¾ pounds Bartlett pears,	2 cups milk
peeled, cored, and sliced	¾ cup bourbon
2 tablespoons lemon juice	1 teaspoon vanilla
1 cup red wine	Pinch of salt
1 cup sugar	5 eggs
4 teaspoons cinnamon	4 cups ½-in bread cubes
4 teaspoons nutmeg	Caramel Sauce, page 539

1.   In a bowl, toss the pears with the lemon juice. In a saucepan, bring the wine, ½ cup of sugar, 2 teaspoons of cinnamon, and 2 teaspoons of nutmeg to a simmer. Add the pears and poach 5 minutes, or until just tender. Transfer the pears to a bowl. Reduce the liquid to a thin, syrupy consistency and return the pears to the saucepan.

2. In another saucepan, scald the milk and add the remaining sugar, ½ cup of bourbon, vanilla, salt, and the remaining cinnamon and nutmeg. In a medium bowl, beat the eggs to combine and gradually beat in the scalded milk mixture.

3. Place the bread cubes in a 9-inch square baking dish and add the custard. Gently press the bread to help absorb the liquid and let stand for 20 minutes. Press the bread cubes again. Preheat the oven to 325°F.

4. Place in a water bath and bake 20 minutes. Arrange the pears on top and bake 25 minutes longer, or until the pudding sets. Serve the warm pudding with the sauce on the side.

5. Prepare Custard Sauce and stir in remaining bourbon.

Yields 6 servings

Can be prepared for baking several hours ahead.

Pudding Cakes

Pudding cakes create their own sauce. The ingredients, often mixed in the baking pan, separate while baking to become a cake and a sauce. They are always better when served warm.

MOCHA WALNUT PUDDING CAKE

1 cup flour	½ cup milk
1¼ cups sugar	¼ cup butter, melted
7 tablespoons cocoa	1 teaspoon vanilla
2 teaspoons baking powder	1 tablespoon rum
1 teaspoon instant coffee powder	½ cup dark brown sugar
¼ teaspoon salt	1 cup hot water
Pinch of cinnamon	1 cup heavy cream, whipped
1 cup chopped walnuts	to soft peaks and sweetened,
	for garnish

1. Preheat the oven to 350°F.

2. In a bowl, mix the flour, ¾ cup of sugar, 3 tablespoons of cocoa, baking powder, coffee powder, salt, cinnamon, and walnuts. In another bowl, mix the milk, butter, vanilla, and rum. Pour over the flour mixture and mix until combined. Spread in an 8-inch baking dish.

3. Mix the remaining sugar, brown sugar, and the remaining cocoa in a small bowl and sprinkle over the batter. Pour on the hot water but do not stir.

4. Bake about 40 minutes, or until the top glazes and turns dark brown. Cool 1 hour and serve with whipped cream if desired.

Yields 8 servings

Prepare and serve.

WARM CHOCOLATE PUDDING CAKE

5½ ounces bittersweet chocolate	⅔ cup sugar
11 tablespoons butter	5 tablespoons flour
3 eggs	Ice cream or heavy cream,
3 egg yolks	whipped and sweetened, for garnish

1. Preheat the oven to 325°F. Butter and flour six 6-ounce custard cups.

2. Melt the chocolate and the butter. Remove from the heat.

3. In an electric mixer, beat the eggs, egg yolks, and sugar about 10 minutes, or until thickened and pale. Beat in the flour and the chocolate mixture and continue to beat until thick and glossy. Divide among the prepared cups.

4. Bake about 12 minutes, or until set around the edges, but the center moves slightly. Cool for 5 minutes. Unmold and serve with ice cream or whipped cream.

Yields 6 servings

Prepare and serve.

Steamed Puddings

Steamed puddings are a blessing. Usually, you can prepare them days and sometimes weeks ahead. If you choose to freeze them, resteaming does no harm. Many make a delicious breakfast bread, toasted, if desired, or just reheated—a far better choice to my taste than some other breakfast options.

PUDDING MOLDS   Any porcelain, pottery, or metal container serves as a pudding mold. Use mixing bowls, charlotte molds, or any other container that is the right size for your needs. Traditionally, pudding molds are made of tin, porcelain, pottery, or copper. The tin molds often have covers held in place with "bail handles." The molds can be plain or elaborately designed to give the pudding a fancy shape. Scour gourmet and antique shops for molds with lions couchant, floral arrangements, or handsome geometric designs. Whatever the shape or material, butter the inside of the mold well, including the lid if it has one. Fill the mold no more than three-quarters full to allow for expansion. Cover with a sheet of buttered waxed paper or parchment, and seal with the cover or a sheet of aluminum foil tied in place with twine.

Pottery bowls often have a lip around the outer edge to which you can tie a cheesecloth or towel handle. Reaching into a steaming kettle with a pair of pot holders is extremely awkward. *Remember that steam can cause a severe burn.*

TO MAKE A CLOTH HANDLE FOR A PUDDING MOLD   Cover the mold with the buttered paper and cut a square of cheesecloth twice as wide as the opening, or use a kitchen towel. Center the cloth over the filled pudding

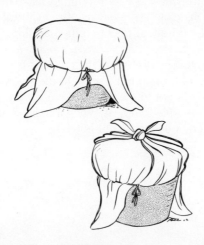

mold. Tie a string around the mold, over the towel, and under the lip of the mold. Bring the opposite corners of the cloth back up over the top and tie securely (see illustration). The knot of fabric on top of the mold serves as a handle, allowing you to get a firm grip on the mold to remove it from the steam, or more safely, to insert the prongs of a kitchen fork into the handle to remove it. After removing the cover, be sure to allow the steam to escape before you reach in to remove the pudding. Keep the cooked pudding in the steamer until ready to serve, or prepare a day or more ahead and reheat in the steamer. Many steamed puddings respond to curing to allow the flavors to meld and to enrich the flavor with the addition of a good brandy or rum soak.

TO SET UP A STEAMING KETTLE   Any pot deep enough to cover the pudding mold will do. I have found no need to use a bottom rack, but do so if you wish. Add enough water to come at least 1 inch up the sides of the mold and bring to a simmer. Add the mold, cover, and steam as long as required. If the pudding steams for a long period, be sure to check the water level and add more boiling water as needed.

TO CURE A PUDDING   Plum pudding, probably the most common steamed pudding, develops its special flavor from curing in cloths soaked in liqueur. Other puddings filled with dense fruit mixtures also benefit from a period of curing. Unmold the steamed pudding and cool. Saturate a piece of cheesecloth, sheeting, or a linen towel in the liqueur of choice, such as Cognac, rum, or orange liqueur. Wrap the cloth around the pudding and then wrap the package in foil and put into an airtight container. (The tin from last year's fruitcake does nicely.) Store in a cool, dry place for at least a week. A month is better, and some prefer to make the pudding in the early fall to let the flavors truly develop. Some families make theirs as much as a year ahead. Resoak the cloth every few months, as the alcohol evaporates, leaving the flavor of the liqueur to enrich the pudding.

TO REHEAT A STEAMED PUDDING   If the pudding is served on the same day, leave it in the mold and put it back into the steamer until a skewer inserted in the center is hot to the touch. If prepared ahead, unmold the pudding and wrap it in foil. To reheat, place it in a colander or on a rack, *over,* not *in* the water, and steam until hot.

GRAHAM PUDDING

1 egg
1 cup molasses
1 cup milk
1 cup flour
1 cup whole wheat flour
1 teaspoon baking soda
1 teaspoon salt

1 cup chopped raisins
¼ cup butter, softened
½ cup sugar
2 eggs, separated
½ cup heavy cream, whipped
  and sweetened
1 teaspoon vanilla

1. Butter a 1½-quart steamed pudding mold and set up a kettle for steaming the pudding (see page 308).

2. In a bowl, beat the egg and stir in the molasses and the milk.

3. In another bowl, mix the flour, whole wheat flour, baking soda, and salt and fold into the molasses mixture with the raisins. Stir in the egg-milk mixture. Pour into the prepared mold and steam for 2½ to 3 hours.

4. Just before serving, in a small bowl, cream the butter and sugar. Beat in the egg yolks. Using clean beaters, beat the egg whites until stiff and fold into the butter mixture with the whipped cream and the vanilla. Unmold the pudding onto a serving platter. Serve the sauce with the warm pudding.

Yields 8 servings

Can be steamed a day ahead or frozen.

CSARDA (Hungarian Walnut Pudding)

½ cup milk
7 tablespoons butter
¾ cup flour
5 eggs, separated
1 teaspoon vanilla

½ cup sugar
1 cup Praline Powder, made
  with walnuts, page 30
1 cup heavy cream, whipped
  and sweetened, for garnish

1. Butter a 1½-quart soufflé dish and set up a kettle for steaming the pudding (see page 308).

2. In a saucepan, bring the milk and butter to a boil and lower the heat. Add the flour, all at once, and cook, stirring, until the mixture pulls away from the sides of the pan. Remove from the heat and beat in the egg yolks, one at a time. Mix in the vanilla and transfer to a large bowl.

3. Beat the egg whites until they form soft peaks. Gradually add the sugar and beat until stiff peaks form. Fold half of the egg whites into the pudding to lighten it. Fold in the remaining whites and all but 2 tablespoons of the walnut praline.

4. Pour into the soufflé dish and cover with foil. Steam in a water bath for 2 hours.

5. Unmold onto a serving plate. Sprinkle with the remaining praline and serve warm with the whipped cream if desired.

Yields 8 servings

Can be reheated.

MOHR IM HEMD (Moor in a Shirt)

This European favorite is named for the "Turk's head" mold, towering over a ruff of whipped cream.

4 ounces unsweetened chocolate	9 eggs plus 4 egg yolks
8 slices white bread	¾ cup blanched ground almonds
2¾ cups heavy cream	¾ cup sugar
⅔ cup butter, softened	½ cup confectioners' sugar

1. Butter a 2 quart steamed pudding mold, preferably a tall one, and set up a kettle for steaming the pudding, adding enough water to come halfway up the side of the mold (see page 308).

2. Melt the chocolate and bring to room temperature.

3. In a bowl, soak the bread in ¾ cup of cream for at least 10 minutes. In a mixing bowl, cream the butter. Add the soaked bread and cream. Beat in the eggs, egg yolks, almonds, and sugar. Beat in the melted chocolate.

4. Pour the mixture into the mold, cover and seal. Steam for 1½ hours, adding more water if needed.

5. Beat the remaining cream until it forms soft peaks. Add the confectioners' sugar and beat until stiff peaks form. Refrigerate until needed. Unmold the pudding onto a platter and, using a pastry bag fitted with a #8 open star tip, pipe swirls of whipped cream around the base to look like a ruffled shirt.

Yields 12 servings

Can be prepared and reheated in the mold before serving.

STEAMED COCONUT FUDGE PUDDING

4 ounces semisweet chocolate, chopped	1 cup sweetened flaked coconut
¼ cup butter	½ cup dark brown sugar
½ cup canned unsweetened coconut cream	¼ cup flour
3 eggs, separated	1 teaspoon baking powder
1 tablespoon plus 1½ teaspoons vanilla	⅛ teaspoon salt
22 chocolate wafer cookies, crumbled	2 tablespoons sugar
¾ cup macadamia nuts, chopped	¾ cup heavy cream
	3 tablespoons confectioners' sugar
	3 tablespoons sour cream

1. Butter a 2½-quart steamed pudding mold and set up a kettle for steaming the pudding (see page 308).

2. Melt the chocolate and the butter. Remove from the heat and whisk in the coconut cream, egg yolks, and 1 tablespoon of vanilla. In a bowl, mix the cookie crumbs, nuts, ¾ cup of coconut, brown sugar, flour, baking powder, and salt. Stir in the chocolate mixture.

3. In another bowl, beat the egg whites until they hold soft peaks. Beat in 2 tablespoons of sugar until the whites hold stiff peaks. Fold into the chocolate mixture.

4. Pour into the mold. Cover and steam about 2 hours. Remove and cool 5 minutes.

5. Whip the cream to soft peaks with the remaining sugar and fold in the sour cream and the vanilla. Unmold the pudding onto a serving platter and serve hot, sprinkled with the remaining coconut. Pass the whipped cream.

Yields 8 servings

Can be reheated.

STEAMED CARROT PUDDING

1 cup brown sugar	½ teaspoon nutmeg
½ cup butter, softened	½ cup Candied Orange Rind,
1 egg	page 39
1 cup coarse bread crumbs	1 cup golden raisins
½ cup flour	1 cup grated raw carrot
1 teaspoon baking powder	1 cup grated raw potato
1 teaspoon baking soda	1 cup peeled, chopped tart
¾ teaspoon salt	apple
1 teaspoon cinnamon	Hard or Foamy Sauce, page
½ teaspoon allspice	543

1.   Butter a 1½ quart steamed pudding mold. Set up a kettle for steaming (see page 308).

2.   In a bowl, cream the sugar and the butter until light and fluffy. Beat in the egg.

3.   In another bowl, mix the bread crumbs, flour, baking powder, baking soda, salt, cinnamon, allspice, and nutmeg. Stir into the butter mixture with the orange rind, raisins, carrot, potato, and apple.

4.   Pour into the mold. Cover and steam for 4 hours. Unmold onto a serving platter. Serve with hard sauce or foamy sauce.

Yields 6 to 8 servings

Can be reheated.

STEAMED CHUTNEY PUDDING

1 cup flour	gooseberry chutney
½ teaspoon baking soda	⅓ cup chopped walnuts
½ cup butter, softened	Confectioners' sugar, for
½ cup dark brown sugar	garnish
2 eggs	Orange Rum Hard Sauce,
⅓ cup peach, pear, or	page 544

1.   Butter and flour a 4-cup steamed pudding mold and set up a kettle to steam the pudding (see page 308).

2.   Sift the flour and baking soda together.

3.   In a bowl, cream the butter and sugar until light and fluffy. Stir the eggs, chutney, and walnuts into the butter mixture with the flour mixture.

4.   Pour into the mold and cover. Steam for 1½ hours. Cool for 15 minutes and unmold onto a serving plate.

5.   Sprinkle with confectioners' sugar. Serve the pudding with the hard sauce on the side.

Yields 6 servings

Can be reheated.

CRANBERRY PUDDING

1½ cups sifted flour	1 egg, lightly beaten
½ teaspoon salt	1 teaspoon vanilla
1 tablespoon baking powder	1 cup chopped cranberries
½ cup butter, softened	⅔ cup milk
¾ cup sugar	Heavy cream, whipped and sweetened, for garnish

1.   Butter a 1-quart steamed pudding mold and set up a kettle to steam the pudding (see page 308). In a bowl, mix the flour, salt, and baking powder.

2.   In another bowl, cream the butter and sugar until fluffy. Beat in the egg and vanilla. Stir in the cranberries. Add the flour mixture alternately with the milk and stir until blended.

3.   Pour into the mold and cover tightly. Steam 1 to 1½ hours, or until it tests done. Unmold onto a serving plate. Serve with whipped cream, if desired.

Yields 6 servings

Can be reheated.

STEAMED LEMON PUDDING

1 cup sifted dry bread crumbs	1 lemon
6 tablespoons sugar	2 cups milk
Juice and grated rind of	2 eggs, separated
	Heavy cream, optional

1. Butter and flour a 1 quart pudding mold and set up a kettle to steam the pudding (see page 308).

2. In a large bowl, combine the bread crumbs and the sugar. Stir in the lemon juice, rind, and milk, and beat in the egg yolks.

3. Beat the egg whites until stiff and fold into the mixture. Turn into the prepared mold. Cover and steam for 3 hours. Unmold onto a serving platter. Serve hot with heavy cream, if desired.

Yields 6 servings

Can be reheated.

LEMON-ALMOND PUDDING WITH MAPLE-MADEIRA SABAYON SAUCE

1 cup fresh bread crumbs	**rind**
½ pound sliced almonds, finely ground	**2 tablespoons lemon juice**
	4 eggs
1 cup plus 3 tablespoons sugar	**1 tablespoon kirsch**
	5 egg yolks
1¼ cups milk, scalded	**¼ cup maple syrup**
½ cup tawny port	**¾ cup Madeira wine**
1 teaspoon baking powder	**¾ cup heavy cream, whipped**
2 teaspoons grated lemon	**to soft peaks, and sweetened**

1. Butter a 2 quart pudding mold or a soufflé dish and dust with 3 tablespoons of bread crumbs. Set up a kettle to steam the pudding (see page 308).

2. In a bowl, mix the remaining bread crumbs, almonds, 1 cup sugar, milk, port, and baking powder, and let stand for 10 minutes. In a small bowl, beat the lemon rind, lemon juice, eggs, and kirsch. Stir into the almond mixture and pour into the mold.

3. Cover and steam for 3 hours. Cool slightly and unmold the pudding onto a serving plate.

4. In a bowl, mix the egg yolks, sugar, maple syrup, and wine over hot water and beat until foamy and slightly thickened. Place over cold water and continue to beat until the sauce is cold. Fold in the whipped cream. Serve the pudding warm with the sauce.

Yields 8 servings

Steam the pudding ahead and reheat. The Maple-Madeira Sabayon sauce will keep overnight if necessary.

PEAR AND ALMOND STEAMED PUDDING

4 **Vanilla Poached Pears, peeled, halved, and cored, poaching liquid reserved**	¼ **pound almond paste**
1 **whole vanilla bean**	3 **eggs**
1¼ **cups sugar**	1 **teaspoon almond extract**
½ **cup butter, softened**	1¾ **cups cake flour**
	2 **teaspoons baking powder**
	2 **egg whites**

1. Preheat the oven to 350°F. Butter and lightly flour 2 quart pudding mold and set up a kettle for steaming (see page 308).

2. Remove the pears from the syrup and puree them. Remove half of the puree and reserve. Transfer the remaining puree to a bowl. Add 1 cup of the poaching liquid to the remaining puree and scrape in the seeds from the vanilla bean. Stir and refrigerate the pear sauce until ready to serve.

3. In a bowl, cream 1 cup of sugar, butter, and almond paste until smooth. Add the eggs, almond extract, and reserved pear puree to the butter mixture and mix until smooth.

4. In another bowl, mix the flour and baking powder. Stir into the butter mixture gradually.

5. Using clean beaters, beat the egg whites with the remaining sugar until stiff peaks form. Fold into the batter. Pour the batter into the pudding mold. Cover and steam for 2 hours. Unmold onto a serving plate and serve with the pear sauce.

Yields 8 to 10 servings

Can be reheated.

STEAMED PEACH PUDDING

¼ cup butter, softened	4½ teaspoons baking powder
½ cup sugar	½ cup milk
1 egg	1 teaspoon almond extract
1½ cups flour	1 cup diced dried peaches
½ teaspoon salt	Lemon Sauce, page 550

1. Butter a 1½ quart steamed pudding mold and set up a kettle for steaming the pudding (see page 308).

2. In a processor, cream the butter and the sugar. Add the egg and mix well.

3. In a bowl, mix the flour, salt, and baking powder and add to the butter mixture. Add the milk and almond extract and process for 30 seconds or until just moistened. Add the peaches with on/off turns.

4. Pour into the mold and cover. Steam for 1 hour. Unmold onto a serving plate. Serve with lemon sauce.

Yields 6 servings

Can be reheated.

KING GEORGE'S CHRISTMAS PUDDING

This sensational plum pudding is rich, flavorful, and loaded with fruits. In Olde England, raisins were called "plums," so do not let the lack of them disturb you. I sometimes add a pound of pitted chopped prunes. Plan to prepare it at least a month before serving. Several months ahead is even better.

1 pound raisins	3½ cups flour
10 ounces currants	1½ teaspoons nutmeg
6 ounces pitted dates	1 tablespoon salt
4 ounces chopped Candied Lemon Rind, page 39	4 teaspoons cinnamon
4 ounces chopped Candied Orange Rind, page 39	1½ teaspoons ginger
1 cup Cognac	1 teaspoon ground cloves
1½ pounds shredded suet	½ teaspoon mace
1 pound brown sugar	8 eggs
1 pound fresh bread crumbs	1 cup milk, approximately
	Cognac or rum, for soaking
	Hard Sauce, page 543

1. Butter four 1-quart pudding molds and set up a kettle for steaming (see page 308). In a bowl, macerate the raisins, currants, dates, lemon rind, and orange rind in the Cognac for 2 hours.

2. In a large bowl, mix the suet, sugar, bread crumbs, flour, nutmeg, salt, cinnamon, ginger, cloves, and mace.

3. In another bowl, beat the eggs with the milk and stir in the dry ingredients. Add enough milk to form a heavy batter that drops from a spoon. Stir in the macerated fruits and liquid. Cover and refrigerate overnight.

4. When ready to steam, bring the pudding to room temperature and beat well. Fill the molds no more than two-thirds full. Cover and steam the puddings for 5 hours. Cool and unmold.

5. Wrap in sheeting or several layers of cheesecloth soaked in Cognac or rum. Wrap in foil and store in a cool area for at least 1 month. If storing longer, remoisten the cloth covering about once a month.

6. To serve, steam the pudding for at least 1 hour, or until hot, and serve flamed with brandy. Pass the hard sauce.

Yields 4 1-quart puddings, 6–8 servings each

Can be prepared several months before serving.

NOTE: One-pound coffee tins make suitable molds if you do not have enough pudding molds.

Baked Puddings

Many puddings are baked in the oven, sometimes in a water bath. I have put other baked desserts, loosely classified as puddings, such as crumbles, pan dowdies, etc., in a separate section, (see page 328).

LA FLAMUSSE AUX POMMES
(Baked Apple Pudding)

This is a close relative of Clafouti (see page 322).

2 tablespoons butter	1 tablespoon flour
8 large apples, peeled, cored,	2 cups milk
and thickly sliced	3 tablespoons sugar
4 eggs	2 tablespoons dark rum

1.   Preheat the oven to 350°F. Butter a 12-inch gratin dish.

2.   In a skillet, heat the butter and sauté the apples slices until tender.

3.   In a bowl, beat the eggs. Blend in the flour, milk, sugar, and rum. Fold in the apple slices. Pour into the prepared dish and bake for 30 to 45 minutes, or until set. Serve warm.

Yields 6 servings

Can be prepared for baking several hours ahead.

Variation

• Dip the apple slices in a crêpe batter, spread them on buttered cabbage leaves, and bake. The leaves disappear, leaving an extraordinary flavor.

SWISS PUDDING

2 pounds Cortland apples, peeled and sliced	1 quart dried bread crumbs
¼ cup sugar	⅔ cup brown sugar
Grated rind of 1 lemon	½ cup butter
½ teaspoon cinnamon	Cold heavy cream or Custard Sauce, page 545
2 tablespoons water	

1.   Preheat the oven to 350°F. In a saucepan, simmer the apples, sugar, lemon rind, cinnamon, and water until the apples are tender.

2.   In a bowl, mix the bread crumbs and brown sugar. In a 1½ quart baking dish, layer the apples and bread crumb mixture, ending with the bread crumbs. Dot the top with the butter.

3.   Bake 25 to 30 minutes, or until browned. Serve hot or warm with cold heavy cream or custard sauce, passed separately.

Yields 6 servings

Can be reheated.

BONDEPIGE MED SLØR
(Veiled Country Lass)

There are many versions of this popular Danish dessert, but this is my favorite. The bread crumbs represent a tanned farm girl and the cream, of course, is the veil. Far-fetched? Perhaps, but none of this affects the delicious result.

10 tablespoons butter	semisweet chocolate
3 cups dark rye pumpernickel bread crumbs	2½ cups applesauce
3 tablespoons sugar	1 cup heavy cream
2 tablespoons grated	2–3 tablespoons raspberry jam, for garnish

1.   Preheat the oven to 375°F. Lightly butter a 4-cup soufflé dish.

2.   In a skillet, cook 8 tablespoons of butter, the bread crumbs, and the sugar over low heat until the mixture browns evenly and the crumbs become dry and crisp. Remove from the heat and stir in the chocolate until it is melted.

3.   Cover the bottom of the mold with ½ inch of crumbs and spoon on a thick layer of applesauce; continue to layer, ending with the crumbs. Dot with the remaining butter and bake for 25 minutes. Cool to room temperature.

4.   Shortly before serving, beat the cream to soft peaks and spoon over the pudding. Garnish with dabs of jam.

Yields 6 servings

Can be prepared the day before.

DIPLOMATE AUX BANANES (Banana Pudding)

¼ **cup golden raisins**	6 **bananas, sliced**
3 **cups milk**	6 **tablespoons sugar**
½ **cup rum**	3 **egg yolks**
18–24 **Ladyfingers, page 21**	

1.   Preheat the oven to 350°F. In a small bowl, soak the raisins in enough warm water to cover for 20 minutes. Drain well.

2.   In another bowl, mix 1 cup of milk and the rum. Dip the ladyfingers into the milk-rum mixture and use to line the bottom and sides of a 1 quart charlotte mold or soufflé dish.

3.   Place a layer of banana slices in the mold and top with a scattering of raisins and another layer of moistened ladyfingers. Continue to layer the ingredients, ending with the ladyfingers.

4.   In a saucepan, scald the remaining milk with the sugar. In a bowl, beat the egg yolks until well-mixed and gradually stir in the hot milk. Pour the mixture into the mold and let stand for 30 minutes.

5.   Bake the pudding in a water bath for 45 minutes. Remove from the water bath. Cool to lukewarm before unmolding.

Yields 6 servings

Can be prepared the day before and served at room temperature.

BLUEBERRY BUTTERMILK PUDDING

½ cup butter, softened
1 cup sugar
3 eggs
½ teaspoon salt
1½ cups flour
2 teaspoons baking powder

1 teaspoon nutmeg
½ cup buttermilk
½ teaspoon baking soda
2 cups blueberries, see Note
Hard Sauce, page 543

1. Preheat the oven to 350°F. Butter a 5-cup baking dish.

2. In a processor, cream the butter and the sugar. Add the eggs and salt. Add the flour, baking powder, nutmeg, buttermilk, and baking soda and incorporate with on/off turns.

3. Pour into a bowl and fold in the blueberries. Pour into the baking dish and bake for 30 minutes, or until it tests done. Serve warm with hard sauce, if desired.

Yields 6 servings

Prepare and serve.

NOTE: If using frozen blueberries, do not thaw; the juices can turn the batter an unappealing blue.

STICKY TOFFEE PUDDING

1 cup flour
1 teaspoon baking powder
¾ cup pitted dates, finely
  chopped
1 teaspoon baking soda
1 teaspoon vanilla
1¼ cups boiling water
7 tablespoons butter,

softened
¾ cup sugar
1 egg
⅓ cup brown sugar
2 tablespoons heavy cream
1 cup heavy cream, whipped,
  sweetened, and flavored with
  vanilla, to taste, for garnish

1. Preheat the oven to 350°F. Butter an 8-inch gratin dish.

2. Sift the flour and baking powder together.

3. In a bowl, mix the dates, baking soda, vanilla, and boiling water.

4. In a bowl, cream 4 tablespoons of butter and the sugar until light and fluffy. Beat in the egg and the flour mixture. Mix in the date mixture and beat well.

5. Pour into the baking dish and bake 35 to 40 minutes, or until set and browned on top. Cool on a wire rack.

6. Preheat the broiler. In a saucepan, heat the remaining butter, brown sugar, and heavy cream, stirring until thickened. Remove from the heat and pour over the top of the pudding.

7. Broil about 1 minute, or until bubbling. Serve hot or warm, with whipped cream, if desired.

Yields 6 servings

Can be prepared several hours ahead.

CLAFOUTI (Cherry Pancake Pudding)

Clafouti is a custard-like pudding baked with fruit, usually cherries, but apricots or plums are also superb. In France, they often leave the pits in the fruit, but for your teeth's sake, pit them!

1 pound cherries, apricots, or plums, pitted	1 cup milk, scalded
1½ tablespoons flour	¾ teaspoon vanilla
Pinch of salt	2 tablespoons eau de vie (such as kirsch) or Armagnac, see
2 tablespoons sugar	page 14
2 eggs	Confectioners' sugar, for
1 egg yolk	garnish

1. Preheat the oven to 350°F. Butter an 8-inch gratin and arrange the fruit in a single layer.

2. In a bowl, mix the flour, salt, and sugar. In another bowl, combine the eggs, egg yolk, and milk, and stir into the flour mixture until blended. Add the vanilla and kirsch and strain over the fruit.

3. Bake for 40 minutes, or until set. Serve warm or at room temperature sprinkled with confectioners' sugar.

Yields 6 servings

Can be prepared several hours ahead.

BOULE DE NEIGE (Snowball)

When served, the pudding should look like a snowball completely covered by the cream.

10 ounces semisweet
chocolate, chopped
¾ cup coffee
1¼ cups butter, softened
1 cup sugar

4 large eggs
2 cups heavy cream, whipped
and sweetened
Crystallized violet, for
garnish

1. Preheat the oven to 350°F. Line a 1½ quart ovenproof bowl with foil.

2. Melt the chocolate with the coffee. Add the butter and sugar, and stir until smooth and the sugar dissolves. Remove from the heat. Beat in the eggs and strain into the prepared bowl.

3. Bake in a water bath about 1¼ hours, or until a crust forms. Cool to room temperature. Press down on the edges to even the surface as it cools. Cover and refrigerate at least 12 hours.

4. Unmold onto a platter and remove the foil. Using a pastry bag fitted with a #5 star tip, pipe stars of whipped cream over the top of the pudding to cover the surface completely. Garnish with a crystallized violet, if desired.

Yields 10 to 12 servings

Can be prepared the day before serving.

BAKED CHOCOLATE AND HAZELNUT PUDDINGS

7 ounces semisweet
chocolate
1 cup hazelnuts, skinned
1 cup flour
1 cup croissant or bread
crumbs

1 cup butter, softened
8 eggs, separated
Custard Sauce, page 545
Strawberries, raspberries,
etc., for garnish

1. Preheat the oven to 350°F. Butter six 6-ounce ramekins or custard cups.

2. Melt the chocolate and cool to room temperature.

3. In a processor, chop the hazelnuts with the flour and crumbs until the consistency of coarse meal. Set aside.

3.   In the processor, cream the butter. Add the egg yolks, hazelnut mixture, and chocolate, and process until combined. Transfer to a bowl.

4.   In a mixer, beat the egg whites until stiff peaks form, and fold into the chocolate mixture. Fill the ramekins.

5.   Bake in a water bath for 40 minutes, or until it tests done. Serve with custard sauce and any berries of choice.

Yield 6 servings

Can be prepared the day before serving.

INDIAN PUDDING

This longtime New England favorite, for some at least, is an acquired taste.

2 eggs	**¼ teaspoon salt**
6 cups milk	**1 cup yellow cornmeal**
½ cup dark molasses	**¼ cup butter**
¼ cup sugar	**Vanilla ice cream or whipped**
¼ teaspoon baking soda	**heavy cream**

1.   Preheat the oven to 350°F. Butter a 2 quart soufflé dish.

2.   In a saucepan, beat the eggs, and mix in 4 cups of milk, molasses, sugar, baking soda, and salt. Bring to a simmer over medium heat, stirring.

3.   Slowly sprinkle the cornmeal into the simmering milk, so the simmering does not stop, stirring constantly with a wire whisk until thickened and smooth. Cook, uncovered, until the mixture is thick enough to hold its shape in a spoon.

4.   Beat in the butter until melted and remove from the heat. Whisk in the remaining milk. Pour the pudding into the prepared dish and bake for 1 hour. Lower the oven to 300°F. and bake for 4 hours longer, or until the top is firm.

5.   Serve hot from the baking dish with vanilla ice cream or whipped cream.

Yields 6 servings

Can be reheated. The long, slow cooking is necessary to attain the proper texture. Fortunately, while it is baking you can do anything else you wish.

Variations

- Flavor the pudding with 1 teaspoon of ground ginger and 1 teaspoon of ground cinnamon, if desired.
- Flavor the whipped cream with sugar and ground ginger.

MILLAS AUX PRUNEAUX (Prune Pudding)

1 pound dried, pitted prunes	3 large eggs
3 tablespoons Armagnac	3 tablespoons flour
5 tablespoons sugar	2 cups milk

1. Two days before preparing, in a bowl macerate the prunes in the Armagnac at room temperature.

2. Preheat the oven to 375°F. Butter and flour a 10½-inch ceramic quiche dish.

3. Add 1 tablespoon of sugar to the prunes, mix gently, and arrange in a single layer in the dish.

4. In a bowl, beat the eggs with 3 tablespoons of sugar and beat in the flour. Pour over the prunes and bake for 45 minutes, or until bubbly and brown. Sprinkle with the remaining sugar. Allow to cool to lukewarm and serve.

Yields 6 servings

Can be prepared for baking several hours ahead.

COTTAGE PUDDING

This delicious, gentle dessert is really a cake served with a sauce (lemon is my favorite) over the top. Try fruit or chocolate sauce for a change.

¼ cup butter, softened	2¼ cups flour
⅔ cup sugar	4 teaspoons baking powder
1 egg	½ teaspoon salt
1 cup milk	1½ cups Lemon Sauce, page 550

1. Preheat the oven to 350°F. Butter an 8-inch square baking pan.

2. In a processor, cream the butter and sugar. Add the egg and process until combined.

3. Add the milk, flour, baking powder, and salt with on/off turns, scraping down the sides as needed. Turn into the pan and bake for 35 minutes, or until it tests done.

4. Serve warm with the sauce.

Yields 8 servings

Can be prepared ahead, but is best served warm.

POUDING AU CHOMEUR (Poor Man's Pudding)

2 **cups dark brown sugar**	¼ **teaspoon salt**
2 **cups water**	¾ **cup sugar**
2 **cups plus 1 tablespoon flour**	¼ **cup butter, melted**
1 **teaspoon vanilla**	1 **cup milk**
4 **teaspoons baking powder**	**Heavy cream, whipped and sweetened, for garnish**

1. Preheat the oven to 350°F. Lightly butter a 9 × 13-inch baking pan.

2. In a saucepan, cook the sugar, water, 1 tablespoon of flour, and vanilla until the sugar dissolves. Bring to a boil and cook, stirring, until slightly thickened, about 5 minutes. Pour the syrup into the prepared pan.

3. In a bowl, mix the remaining flour, baking powder, and salt. In another bowl, blend the sugar and butter and add to the dry ingredients alternately with the milk to form a sticky, thick batter. Drop onto the syrup in the pan.

4. Bake until golden, about 35 minutes, or until it tests done. Serve warm or cool with whipped cream.

Yields 12 to 14 servings

Can be prepared ahead.

BUDINO DI RICOTTA (Ricotta Pudding)

2½ cups ricotta cheese, sieved
⅓ cup almond paste
6 tablespoons butter, melted
4 eggs, separated
2 tablespoons rum
½ cup minced mixed glacéed fruits
Grated rind of 1 lemon
½ cup flour

¾ cup confectioners' sugar
½ teaspoon cinnamon
5–6 canned pineapple rings, drained and halved, for garnish
1 cup heavy cream, whipped, sweetened, and flavored with vanilla, for garnish

1. Preheat the oven to 350°F. Butter a 1½ quart fluted mold.

2. In a bowl, mix the cheese, almond paste, butter, egg yolks, rum, glacéed fruit, and lemon rind. Sift the flour, ½ cup of confectioners' sugar, and cinnamon together. Stir into the cheese mixture.

3. Beat the egg whites until stiff but not dry and stir one-fourth of them into the cheese mixture to lighten. Gently fold in the remaining egg whites. Fill the mold and bake for 30 minutes, or until it tests done.

4. Unmold and serve hot or cold, dusted with the remaining confectioners' sugar and surrounded with the pineapple halves. Pass the whipped cream.

Yields 6 servings

Can be prepared ahead.

FLAMRI
(Semolina Pudding with Two Fruit Sauces)

1⅓ cups dry white wine
1 strip lemon rind
½ vanilla bean
1⅓ cups water
1 cup semolina flour
¾ cup sugar

Pinch of salt
1 egg
1 egg yolk
6 egg whites
Raspberry Sauce, page 552
Apricot Sauce, page 547

1. Preheat the oven to 325°F. Butter a 6-cup ring mold.

2.   In a saucepan, combine the wine, lemon rind, vanilla bean, and water. Bring to a boil, cover, turn off the heat, and let steep for 15 minutes.

3.   Remove the rind and vanilla bean. Bring the wine mixture to a boil.

4.   Gradually whisk in the semolina, stirring vigorously to prevent lumps. Reduce the heat to low and cook, stirring, about 5 minutes, or until thick and smooth. Remove from the heat and cool, stirring for 5–10 minutes.

5.   Add the sugar and salt and beat until smooth. Beat in the egg and egg yolk. Beat the egg whites until stiff, but not dry, peaks form. Fold into the semolina mixture and pour into the prepared mold. Bake in a water bath for 40 minutes, or until set.

6.   Remove from the water bath and cool about 45 minutes. Unmold and serve at room temperature, drizzled with the sauces.

Yields 6 servings

Can be prepared the day before.

Betties, Buckles, Cobblers, Pan Dowdies, Crisps, Crumbles, Grunts, and Slumps

This extraordinary selection of names describes a whole series of fruit desserts with toppings. The toppings may be crumbs, streusel mixtures, batters, or doughs. Or, the fruit may be layered with another ingredient. Although similar, there are differences, and here is a brief description of the various desserts. The recipes that follow are basic suggestions for creating this type of pudding. You may substitute different fruits for different effects. Remember that the fruit ought to be of a similar type for the greatest success. Berries for berries, orchard fruits for orchard fruits, etc. Plums cooked with sugar make a large amount of syrup, so they also can be used for grunts, just like berries.

BETTIES   Slice the fruit and layer with buttered bread crumbs.

BUCKLES   Sprinkle the fruit over a dough base and let the dough "buckle" up through the fruit during the baking.

COBBLERS AND PAN DOWDIES   These are the same dessert. Place the fruit in the bottom of a baking dish and the rolled dough on top.

CRISPS AND CRUMBLES   These are much the same; place the fruit in a baking dish and top with a crumbled mixture of butter, flour and/or oats, sugar, and possibly spices, scattered over the fruit.

GRUNTS   Perhaps these are the least well known of this type of dessert. Drop a batter onto simmering fruit to make dumplings.

SLUMPS   A batter on top of the fruit "slumps" into it while it bakes.

PEAR BROWN BETTY

8 slices white bread
½ cup butter, melted
1½ cups sugar
Pinch nutmeg
¾ teaspoon cinnamon
12 pears, peeled and sliced

Grated rind and juice of 1 lemon
2 cups hard cider or apple juice
Heavy cream or whipped cream

1.   Preheat the oven to 375°F. Butter a 9 × 13-inch baking dish.

2.   In a processor, make coarse crumbs from the bread and toss with the butter.

3.   In a bowl combine the sugar, nutmeg, and cinnamon. In another bowl, toss the pears with the lemon juice and rind and half of the sugar mixture.

4.   Sprinkle the baking dish with some of the sugar mixture and arrange half the pears in the dish. Sprinkle with ½ cup of bread crumbs and some more of the sugar mixture. Top with remaining pears and pour the cider over the pears. Top with the remaining crumbs and sugar mixture.

5.   Cover with foil and bake for 45 minutes. Uncover and bake about 15 minutes, or until golden. Serve warm with cream or whipped cream.

Yields 6 servings

Can be prepared ahead and reheated.

BLUEBERRY BUCKLE

1 quart blueberries	2 teaspoons baking soda
Sugar, to taste	1 cup buttermilk
1½ cup butter, softened	½ cup dark brown sugar
⅓ cup plus ½ cup sugar	½ cup toasted pecans, chopped
1 egg	½ teaspoon nutmeg
3 cups flour	¼ teaspoon ginger

1.   Preheat the oven to 350°F. Butter and flour an 13 × 9-inch square baking dish.

2.   In a bowl, mix the blueberries with sugar, to taste.

3.   In an electric mixer, cream 1 cup of butter and ⅓ cup of sugar until light and fluffy. Beat in the egg. In another bowl, mix 2 cups of flour and the baking soda. Stir the dry ingredients, alternately with the buttermilk, into the creamed butter. Spread in the baking dish and cover with the blueberries.

4.   In a bowl, mix the flour, sugar, dark brown sugar, pecans, butter, nutmeg, and ginger until crumbly. Sprinkle over the berries. Bake about 1 hour, or until browned on top and the cake is firm.

Yields 6 servings

Can be prepared ahead and served hot, warm, or at room temperature.

PEAR COBBLER

5 cups peeled, ½-inch-thick pear slices	¾ teaspoon salt
2½ tablespoons Poire William	¼ cup toasted almonds, finely ground
1 tablespoon lemon juice	1 teaspoon baking powder
¾ cup plus 5½ tablespoons sugar	½ cup chilled butter, cut into pieces
1¼ cups plus 2½ tablespoons flour	⅓ cup milk
1 teaspoon grated lemon rind	1 egg

1.   Preheat the oven to 400°F. Butter a 2 quart soufflé dish. Dust with sugar.

2.   In a large bowl, toss the pears with the Poire William and lemon juice.

Place in the soufflé dish. In the bowl mix ¾ cup of sugar, 1¼ cups of flour, lemon rind, and salt together and sprinkle over the pears. Bake for 20 minutes.

3. In a clean bowl, mix the remaining flour, almonds, 3 tablespoons of sugar, baking powder, and salt. Cut in the butter until the mixture resembles coarse meal. Add the milk and egg and stir until combined. Drop the batter over the hot pears in large spoonfuls. Sprinkle with the remaining sugar. Bake about 20 minutes, or until golden and the juices bubble. Cool 15 minutes.

Yields 8 servings

Can be prepared ahead and served hot, warm, or at room temperature.

PURPLE PLUM COBBLER

1½ **pounds plums, pitted and quartered**
¾ **cup plus 1 tablespoon sugar**
2 **tablespoons orange liqueur**
1 **tablespoon orange juice**
¼ **teaspoon cinnamon**
¼ **cup butter, chilled and cut into pieces, plus 1**
tablespoon
¼ **cup pecan pieces**
1 **cup flour**
1½ **teaspoons baking powder**
¼ **teaspoon salt**
⅓ **cup milk**
1 **egg yolk**
Heavy cream, optional

1. Preheat the oven to 375°F. Butter a 2½ quart porcelain quiche dish or baking dish.

2. In a bowl, mix the plums, ¾ cup of sugar, orange liqueur, orange juice, cinnamon, and 1 tablespoon of butter together. Arrange in the dish.

3. In a processor, finely chop the nuts with the sugar. Blend in the flour, baking powder, and salt. Add the remaining butter with on/off turns. Add the milk and yolk, and blend until the dough just comes together.

4. Gather the dough into a flat cake and pat into a 9½-inch circle. Place on top of the fruit and crimp the edges, leaving a ½-inch border of fruit exposed. With a sharp knife, cut slits through the dough in several places.

5. Bake about 40 minutes, or until the filling bubbles and the top is golden. Serve with cream, if desired.

Yields 6 servings

Can be prepared ahead and served hot, warm, or at room temperature.

PEACH PANDOWDY

For a delicious change, this decidedly Southern version has cornbread rather than the more customary biscuit topping.

4 cups peeled, sliced peaches	**¼ teaspoon baking soda**
⅓ cup plus 3 tablespoons	**½ teaspoon salt**
sugar	**1 egg, lightly beaten**
2 teaspoons lemon juice	**½ cup buttermilk**
¼ teaspoon nutmeg	**2 tablespoons butter, melted**
Pinch of cinnamon	**1½ tablespoons dark brown**
1 cup cornmeal	**sugar**
1½ teaspoons baking powder	

1.   Preheat the oven to 350°F. In a bowl, mix the peaches, ⅓ cup of sugar, lemon juice, nutmeg, and cinnamon. Arrange the peaches in a shallow baking dish.

2.   In a bowl, mix the cornmeal, baking powder, baking soda, salt, and remaining sugar. Stir in the egg, buttermilk, and 1 tablespoon of melted butter. Pour evenly over the peaches.

3.   Bake about 30 minutes, or until it tests done. Remove from the oven.

4.   Preheat the broiler. Brush the top of the pandowdy with the remaining melted butter and press the brown sugar through a sieve over the top. Broil until the sugar melts.

Yields 6 servings

Can be prepared ahead and served hot, warm, or at room temperature.

APPLE CRISP

6 tart apples, peeled, cored,	**¾ cup sifted flour**
and sliced	**Pinch of salt**
1 cup sugar	**5 tablespoons butter**
¼ teaspoon ground cloves	**¼ cup chopped walnuts**
½ teaspoon cinnamon	**Whipped cream or ice cream**
2 teaspoons lemon juice	

1.   Preheat the oven to 350°F. Butter a 1½ quart casserole or soufflé dish.

2. In a bowl, mix the apples, ½ cup of sugar, cloves, cinnamon, and lemon juice. Place in the soufflé dish.

3. In another bowl, mix the remaining ½ cup of sugar, flour, salt, and butter. Work the mixture with your fingertips until it is the consistency of coarse meal. Add the nuts and sprinkle the mixture over the apples.

4. Bake for 45 minutes, or until the apples are tender and the crust browns. Serve warm or cold with whipped cream or ice cream.

Yields 6 servings

Can be prepared ahead and reheated.

Variations

• Substitute pecans for walnuts, or stir ½ cup of sliced almonds into the apple mixture.
• Flavor the apples with the grated rind of an orange or add 2 tablespoons of minced crystallized ginger.

PASTEL DE MANZANA (Apple Mint Crisp)

1 cup sugar
1 cup flour
½ teaspoon baking powder
1 egg
1 tablespoon dried mint leaves

1 tablespoon cinnamon
4 tart apples, peeled, cored, and sliced
1 cup heavy cream, whipped and sweetened

1. Preheat the oven to 350°F. Butter an 8-inch square baking pan.

2. In a processor, mix the sugar, flour, and baking powder. Add the egg and process until the mixture resembles coarse meal.

3. In another bowl, mix the mint and cinnamon together. Add the apples and toss until evenly coated. Place apples in the baking pan and sprinkle with the flour mixture.

4. Bake for 45 minutes, or until the topping is crusty. Let cool to room temperature and serve with the whipped cream.

Yields 6 servings

Can be prepared ahead and reheated.

PEAR AND APPLE CRISP

4 large McIntosh apples, peeled and sliced	1 teaspoon baking powder
2 Comice pears, peeled and sliced	¼ teaspoon salt
	⅓ cup butter, cut into pieces
½ cup plus ½ teaspoon sugar	1 egg, lightly beaten
½ teaspoon cinnamon	½ cup walnuts, toasted and cooled
¼ teaspoon nutmeg	3 tablespoons quick-cooking oatmeal
Grated rind of 1 lemon	
1 cup flour	Heavy cream or ice cream

1.   Preheat the oven to 375°F. Lightly butter a 10-inch shallow baking dish.

2.   In a bowl, mix the apples, pears, ½ teaspoon of sugar, cinnamon, nutmeg, and lemon rind. Spread the fruits evenly in the baking dish.

3.   In a bowl, stir the flour, baking powder, salt, and the remaining sugar together. With your fingertips, crumble the butter into the flour mixture until it resembles coarse meal. With a fork, stir in the egg and continue cutting into the mixture to form coarse crumbs. Stir in the nuts and oatmeal, and sprinkle over the fruit.

4.   Bake for 30 minutes, or until the fruit is tender and the top browns. Let settle for 10 minutes. Serve with heavy cream or ice cream.

Yields 6 servings

Best served hot, but can be reheated.

PLUM-HAZELNUT CRISP

3 pounds red plums, pitted and thickly sliced	¾ cup rolled oats
9 tablespoons sugar	⅔ cup light brown sugar
½ cup plus 1½ tablespoons flour	Pinch of salt
	½ cup butter, cut into pieces
¾ teaspoon vanilla	½ cup toasted hazelnuts, skinned
¼–½ teaspoon cinnamon, to taste	Ice cream

1. Preheat the oven to 375° F. Butter a 2- to 2½-quart baking dish with 3-inch sides.

2. In a bowl, macerate the plums, sugar, ½ cup of flour, vanilla, and cinnamon to taste for 30 minutes, stirring occasionally.

3. In a processor, combine the oats, brown sugar, remaining flour, cinnamon, and salt, and process with on/off turns. Add the butter with on/off turns until the mixture resembles coarse meal. Add the hazelnuts and chop coarsely.

4. Stir the plum mixture and place in the baking dish. Sprinkle with the topping and bake for 45 minutes, or until brown and bubbly. Serve with ice cream, if desired.

Yields 6 servings

Can be prepared ahead and reheated. Serve hot, warm, or at room temperature.

RHUBARB CRISP

6 cups sliced rhubarb	grated nutmeg
Grated rind and juice of 1	2 tablespoons butter, melted
lemon	¼ cup dark brown sugar
¼ cup sugar	1 teaspoon cinnamon
1 cup plus 2 tablespoons	¼ cup quick-cooking oatmeal
flour	¼ cup butter, chilled and cut
¼ teaspoon plus a pinch of	into pieces

1. Preheat the oven to 400°F. Butter a 2 quart baking dish.

2. In a bowl, toss the rhubarb with the lemon rind and juice, sugar, 2 tablespoons flour, ¼ teaspoon nutmeg, and melted butter, and place in the baking dish.

3. In a bowl, stir together the remaining flour, brown sugar, cinnamon, remaining nutmeg, and oatmeal. With your fingertips, crumble the chilled butter into the flour mixture until it resembles coarse meal. Scatter over the fruit.

4. Bake for 35 to 40 minutes, or until the mixture is bubbling at the edges and golden on top. Let settle 10 minutes and serve warm.

Yields 6 servings

Can be prepared ahead and reheated.

BLUEBERRY CRUMBLE I

This old New England favorite works as well with rhubarb, apples, raspberries, pears, and peaches.

1 quart blueberries
2 teaspoons lemon juice
⅓ cup sugar
⅓ cup dark brown sugar
4 tablespoons butter, cut into

pieces
½ cup flour
1¼ cups quick-cooking oats
Yogurt, sour cream, or heavy cream

1. Preheat the oven to 350°F. Butter an 8-inch baking pan.

2. Place the berries in the pan and sprinkle with lemon juice and sugar.

3. In a bowl, mix the brown sugar, butter, flour, and oats with your fingertips until the mixture resembles crumbs. Sprinkle evenly over the blueberries.

4. Bake for 40 minutes, or until the topping is golden and the blueberries bubble around the edges. Serve with yogurt, sour cream, or heavy cream.

Yields 6 servings

Can be prepared ahead and reheated. Serve hot, warm, or at room temperature.

BLUEBERRY CRUMBLE II

Another version of this luscious dessert.

1 pint blueberries
1 tablespoon lemon juice
¼ teaspoon cinnamon
¼ teaspoon allspice
½ cup butter, cut into pieces

1 cup flour
1 cup sugar
Heavy cream, ice cream, or sour cream

1. Preheat the oven to 375°F.

2. In a 1-quart baking dish, mix the blueberries, lemon juice, cinnamon, and allspice.

3. In a bowl, cut the butter into the flour until the mixture resembles coarse meal. Stir in the sugar and spread over the blueberries.

4. Bake for 40 minutes, or until the topping is crisp and brown and the fruit is bubbling hot. Serve with heavy cream, ice cream, or sour cream.

Yields 6 servings

Can be prepared ahead and reheated. Serve hot, warm, or cold.

PEACH AND BOURBON CRUMBLE

1½ **pounds very ripe peaches, peeled and sliced, see Note**	¼ **cup chopped walnuts**
1½ **tablespoons bourbon**	1 **tablespoon plus 1 teaspoon flour**
2 **teaspoons lemon juice**	¼ **teaspoon mace**
6 **tablespoons light brown sugar**	¼ **cup butter, cut into pieces**
	Heavy cream, optional

1. Preheat the broiler.

2. In a 12-inch gratin dish, toss the peaches with the bourbon and lemon juice.

3. In a processor combine the sugar, walnuts, flour, and mace with on/off turns. Add the butter and process until the mixture resembles coarse meal. Sprinkle over the peaches and broil 6 inches from the heat source until the topping browns. Serve with cream, if desired.

Yields 6 servings

Can be prepared ahead and reheated. Serve hot, warm, or at room temperature.

NOTE: If the peaches are not that ripe, bake the crumble in a 350°F. oven for 10 minutes, or until the fruit is tender. If the top is not browned, then brown under the broiler.

BLUEBERRY GRUNT

1 **cup flour**	1 **pint blueberries**
2 **teaspoons baking powder**	1 **cup water**
¼ **teaspoon salt**	½ **cup sugar**
½ **cup light cream**	1 **cup heavy cream**

1. In a bowl, mix the flour, baking powder, and salt. Briskly stir in the cream to make a batter.

338 The Book of Great Desserts

2. In a deep, 12-inch nonreactive skillet or wide saucepan, bring the blueberries, water, and sugar to a boil and simmer 1 minute.

3. Drop the batter into the pan by the tablespoonful, spacing about 1 inch apart.

4. Cover and simmer, without removing the lid, for 20 minutes. To test: a skewer inserted into a dumpling will come out clean. Serve the dumplings in bowls surrounded by the blueberries. Pass the cream separately.

Yields 6 servings

Serve immediately.

BLUEBERRY SLUMP

1 quart blueberries	½ teaspoon vanilla
1 cup sugar	Vanilla ice cream or 1 cup
1 cup flour	heavy cream, whipped,
1½ teaspoons baking powder	sweetened, and flavored with
Pinch of salt	¼ teaspoon vanilla, or to
2 tablespoons butter	taste
¾ cup milk	

1. Preheat the oven to 375°F. Butter a 2 quart baking dish.

2. In a bowl, mix the blueberries with ¾ cup of sugar and pour into the dish.

3. In another bowl, toss the flour, baking powder, salt, and remaining sugar with a fork or wire whisk.

4. In a small saucepan, melt the butter in the milk over low heat. Add the vanilla and stir into the flour mixture to make a thick batter. Spread the batter over the blueberries and bake for 45 minutes, or until browned.

5. Cool 5 minutes and spoon onto plates. Serve with vanilla ice cream or vanilla-flavored whipped cream.

Yields 6 servings

Can be prepared ahead and reheated. Serve hot, warm, or at room temperature.

Rice Puddings

Rice pudding ranks among the most maligned puddings. Childhood memories bring thoughts of undercooked rice, or gooey masses speckled with hard raisins and dusted with copious amounts of poor-quality cinnamon. Rice pudding, when well made, is one of the finest desserts. The rice grains become meltingly soft, are held in a delicious custard, and delicately flavored with an appropriate spice.

Select short-grain rice that will cook to a truly soft consistency. Long-grain rice does not produce the desired consistency and converted rice retains too much of its shape and texture, even after long cooking, to make a delicate pudding. (For baking and testing, see pages 17–18.)

CRÈME RENVERSÉE AU RIZ ET AUX POMMES (Rice and Apple Caramel Custard)

½ cup short-grain rice, washed and drained	1 large cooking apple, peeled, cored, and sliced
2 cups milk	¼ cup butter, softened
¼ teaspoon salt	¼ cup Calvados
1 cup sugar	3 egg yolks, beaten
2 tablespoons water	

1. Preheat the oven to 325°F.

2. In a saucepan, simmer the rice, milk, and salt, covered, over low heat, for 30 minutes, or until the rice is very tender and has absorbed all but half of the milk. Remove from the heat and cool.

3. In a small saucepan, caramelize ½ cup of sugar and the water, (see page 5). Pour into a 1-quart soufflé dish or charlotte mold.

4. In a skillet, sauté the apple slices in 2 tablespoons of butter until tender. Add the Calvados and ignite. Let the flames subside.

5. In a bowl, cream the remaining butter and beat in ½ cup of sugar. Beat in the egg yolks and stir in the rice mixture. Add half the rice to the prepared mold, cover with the apples, and then the remaining rice.

6. Place the mold in a hot water bath and bake for 30 minutes, or until it tests done. Remove from the water bath. Let stand for 30 minutes.

7. Unmold onto a serving dish and serve warm or cool. To serve cold, refrigerate in the mold.

Yields 6 servings

Can be prepared the day before serving.

RIZ À LA MALTAISE
(Orange-Flavored Rice Pudding)

⅔ cup rice

2 cups milk

1½ tablespoons gelatin

⅓ cup cold water

  Grated rind and juice of 1

  orange

½ cup minced Candied Orange

Rind, page 39

1 tablespoon orange liqueur

⅔ cup sugar

2 cups heavy cream, whipped

  Peeled orange segments, for

  garnish

  Orange Apricot Sauce,

  page 547

1. In a covered saucepan, simmer the rice and the milk until the rice absorbs the milk and becomes tender.

2. In a small bowl, soften the gelatin in the water. Stir into the hot rice with the orange juice, fresh and candied rind, orange liqueur, and sugar. Cool completely. Fold in the whipped cream.

3. Pour into a 6-cup mold and refrigerate at least 2 hours, or until set. Unmold onto a serving platter and decorate with orange segments. Serve the sauce on the side, if desired.

Yields 6 servings

Can be prepared the day before and unmolded shortly before serving.

POIRES À L'IMPERIALE
(Rice Pudding with Pears)

2 teaspoons gelatin	2 cups cooked white rice
¼ cup cold water	½ cup mixed glacéed fruits
½ cup sugar	1 cup heavy cream
4 egg yolks	6 Vanilla Poached Pear halves,
Pinch of salt	page 40
1 cup milk	2 tablespoons kirsch
1½ teaspoons vanilla	½ cup currant jelly, melted

1.   Lightly oil an 8-inch round cake pan. In a small bowl, soften the gelatin in the water.

2.   In a saucepan, cook the sugar, egg yolks, salt, and milk, stirring over medium heat, until the mixture is thick enough to coat the back of a spoon. Stir in the vanilla, rice, glacéed fruits, and softened gelatin. Refrigerate until the mixture begins to thicken.

3.   Whip ½ cup of heavy cream until it forms soft peaks. Fold into the rice.

4.   Turn into the cake pan and refrigerate at least 2 hours, or until firm. Unmold onto a platter. Arrange the pears on top of the rice.

5.   In a small bowl, whip the remaining cream. Flavor with the kirsch, and pile in the center of the pears. Brush the pears with the melted currant jelly and refrigerate until ready to serve.

Yields 6 servings

Can be prepared the day before serving.

Variations

• *Ananas à l'imperiale* (Pineapple Rice Pudding).   Substitute diced fresh pineapple macerated in kirsch, to taste, for the pears.
• *Condé.*   A condé is a poached fruit of choice served on a base of rice pudding. Prepare as for the Rice Pudding with Pears, omitting the glacéed fruits. Pack into the cake pan. When set, unmold onto a serving platter and top with poached plums, pears, peaches, apricots, etc.

$\mathscr{C}hapter$ 10

CRÊPES, OMELETS, AND SOUFFLÉS

Crêpes, omelets, and soufflés, three stars of the French culinary firmament, are the mainstays of the French housewife. When money is scarce, use one of these to act as a budget stretcher to provide delicious food inexpensively without ever looking frugal.

All three have the ability to use leftovers with great skill and élan. Leftover poached pears? Dice them and fold them inside a crêpe, top with some of the poaching syrup, heat, and *voilà*. Some extra apples? Sauté them in a little butter, sweeten with sugar, and use to fill an omelet, or just use some bottled applesauce if pressed for time. A luscious *velours au chocolat* in the refrigerator, but alas, only enough for one? Make a soufflé, dice the *velours*, fold it in, and once again, heaven on earth.

Crêpes

Just a few years ago, crêpes were the *ne plus ultra* of desserts. Crêpes Suzette still is the code for elegance, chic, and *savoir-faire*. Crêpes may have lost some of their cachet, but none of their quality. They are still a delectable, easily prepared, and readily available dessert.

Serve crêpes saturated with a favorite liquor, aflame or not, filled with fruits, pastry cream, or whipped cream, soufflé mixtures or combinations of these. Serve them rolled, folded, or stacked into a cake.

As ethereal as crêpes are, they are still substantial. Serve 1 or 2 filled crêpes, or perhaps 3 unfilled crêpes for each serving. Serve crêpes after a light meal, or for an evening coffee and dessert party. They may be too much after a large dinner.

CRÊPE BATTER   Dessert crêpes must be very thin. The batter should be about the consistency of heavy cream. Make the easily prepared batter in a food processor, blender, or by hand. In the machines, it is possible to add all the ingredients and process until combined. If preparing by hand, mix all the dry ingredients, gradually work in the liquid ingredients slowly to form a paste and then slowly whisk in the remaining liquid to form a smooth batter. If lumps should form, do not be concerned. Let it stand for an hour or longer to give the starch granules an opportunity to swell. Strain before using and make a practice crêpe. If it is too thick, add a little extra liquid.

TO SEASON A CRÊPE OR OMELET PAN   Strictly speaking, an omelet pan is 5 to 7 inches across the bottom with rounded sides that gently curve away from the bottom. The traditional black steel crêpe pan has straight sides that slope away from the bottom of the pan. Today, most chefs are more likely to use an aluminum omelet pan. It suits both purposes. Many cooks prefer to use a nonstick pan. Unless the pan has a nonstick finish, it must be seasoned before using to prevent the crêpes from sticking and again after every washing with soap and water.

Pour about ½ inch of unflavored vegetable oil in the pan and place over the lowest heat for about an hour or until the pan and the oil are very hot. Turn off the heat and cool completely. Pour off the oil. (Save it to use for sautéing or deep frying.) Wipe the pan with paper toweling. After each use, wipe the cooled pan with paper toweling and salt if there is any food stuck to the pan. With regular use, you need never wash the pan, but if you do not make crêpes and omelets often, then it is better to wash it in warm, soapy water and dry well. You can then use the pan for other foods and reseason it before making crêpes or omelets, a great help if space is scarce.

TO COOK AND FLIP CRÊPES   There are at least two schools of thought on how to cook crêpes. One is to use a small amount of butter for each crêpe and to flip the crêpe in the air to turn it; the other is to use just enough butter to keep the crêpe from sticking and to use a long thin, flexible metal spatula to turn each crêpe.

Which is the correct way? There isn't one. The method that works best for you is the method to use. I prefer the second method.

Method I. Heat about ½ teaspoon of butter in a hot pan, swirling to coat the pan fully. Add about ¼ cup of batter and swirl to spread evenly. Cook over high heat until the edges start to brown. Shake the pan to loosen the crêpe or use a long, thin, flexible metal spatula to loosen the edges while shaking the pan. With a flip of the wrist, toss the crêpe into the air, letting the uncooked side land on the bottom of the pan. Cook until browned and turn out onto a sheet of waxed paper. Add more butter to the pan and repeat.

NOTE: To practice flipping crêpes, place a matchbook in the pan opposite the handle. Give the handle a tug toward yourself, making a circular upward motion. Catch the matchbook with the opposite side facing up. Once you get the knack, you can toss crêpes, mushrooms, or other foods like a professional.

Method II. Heat a crêpe pan until hot. Add about ½ teaspoon of butter to the pan and swirl to coat the bottom of the pan. Pour in about ¼ cup of batter, swirl to coat the pan evenly, and cook 10 seconds. Tilt the excess batter into the bowl. Do not worry, the crêpe clings to the pan unless there is too much butter. Return the pan to the heat and cook until the edges start to brown. With a long, thin, flexible metal spatula, loosen the edges of the crêpe, slide the spatula under the crêpe and turn it. Cook until lightly browned on the second side. Invert the crêpe onto a sheet of waxed paper. Continue making crêpes, buttering the pan only when needed.

With a little practice you can cook two, three, or four crêpes at a time, using several burners. Heat the pans, butter if needed, and add the batter to each pan. Return to the first pan, flip the crêpe, and continue with the others. Turn out the first pan, refill, and continue with the other pans. You will soon develop a rhythm that will allow you to prepare dozens of crêpes quickly. Stack them in groups of three to 12 and wrap securely. Freeze until needed. It is best to freeze the crêpes in small amounts so you can select the amount you need for any specific occasion.

FILLING THE CRÊPE You have many options for placing your filling. All have different benefits for both cooking needs and final presentation.

Rolling. Place a tablespoon or two of the filling on each crêpe, roll into logs, and arrange seam side down in an ovenproof serving dish.

Folding. Fold the crêpes in half and in half again to make a triangle. Lift one section and spoon in the filling. (Soufflé mixtures make wonderful fillings this way.) Arrange on a baking sheet and heat, or if using a soufflé, cook until puffed and golden.

Stacking. Spread the filling mixture on a flat crêpe arranged in an ovenproof serving dish. Top with another crêpe and spread on more filling; continue, using all the filling, and finish with a crêpe (see illustration). Brush with butter and bake until heated through. Use a skewer inserted into the center to test the temperature.

Flambéing—Final Presentation. Flaming foods with liquor not only provides a certain excitement in the dining room, it burns off the raw alcohol leaving the flavor. To flambé successfully the liquor should be warm, but do not boil. As soon as you pour it over the food, hold a lighted match to the liquor. The vapors will catch fire. Be careful to keep your face away from the flame, but be sure to watch what you are doing to prevent a fire. If you feel comfortable with this technique, try lighting the match before the liquor is poured, and flame the dessert immediately. The fumes will have less time to travel and float about the room creating a hazard.

CRÊPES FINES SUCRÉES
(Dessert Crêpes)

Select a liqueur to complement the filling. If preparing crêpes for an unspec- ified future use, use rum or Cognac. The liqueur tenderizes the batter, but you can substitute milk or water.

¾–1¼ cups cold water	1½ cups flour, sifted
¾ cup milk	5 tablespoons butter, melted
3 egg yolks	1 tablespoon sugar
3 tablespoons liqueur (rum, Cognac etc.)	Butter, for cooking

1. In a blender or processor, blend the water, milk, egg yolks, liqueur, flour, butter, and sugar until smooth. Strain into a bowl.

2. You can use the batter at once, or for a more delicate crêpe, let it rest for 1 to 2 hours.

Yields about 24 crêpes

NOTE: This batter may need as much as another ½ cup of cold water to get the right consistency. It is better to have it too thick, to start. It should be about as thick as *heavy* cream. Test-cook a crêpe and add more liquid, a tablespoon at a time as needed.

Alternate Method

To prepare the batter by hand, put the flour into a bowl, and work in the egg yolks and liqueur to make a thick, pasty mixture. Slowly work in the milk and water until the mixture is a smooth, thin liquid. Stir in the butter and sugar. Strain into a bowl. Let rest for an hour before cooking.

Variations

- *Lemon.* Add 1 teaspoon of grated lemon rind to the batter.
- *Tangerine.* Add 3 tablespoons of tangerine liqueur and the grated rind of 1 tangerine to the batter.

APPLE CRÊPES WITH GINGER

3 tablespoons butter	5 tablespoons Calvados or
4 apples, peeled, cored, and	Cognac
sliced	¾ cup apricot preserves
2 tablespoons sugar	Nutmeg, to taste
2 tablespoons minced	12 Dessert Crêpes, page 346
crystallized ginger	¼ cup dark rum

1. Preheat the oven to 300°F.

2. In a skillet, heat the butter, and sauté the apples and sugar over medium heat, shaking the pan, until the apples brown and the sugar caramelizes. Add the ginger, 2 tablespoons of Calvados, and the apricot preserves. Simmer 2 minutes and sprinkle with the nutmeg.

3. Fill each crêpe with the apples. Roll. Place in a buttered ovenproof serving dish and reheat in the oven until hot.

4. In a small saucepan, heat the rum and the remaining Calvados and pour over the hot crêpes. Carefully ignite the crêpes at the table.

Yields 6 servings

Can be prepared for reheating several hours before serving.

Variations

• *Orange-flavored Apple Crêpes.* Omit the ginger, Calvados, apricot preserves, and rum. Add ½ cup of raisins, grated rind of 1 orange, and ¼ cup of Grand Marnier to the apples. Make a sauce by simmering the juice of ½ a lemon, juice of 1 orange, ⅓ cup of dark rum, and ¼ teaspoon of groundginger for 3 minutes. Pour over the crêpes just before reheating.

• *Apple Crêpes with Caramel Sauce.* Omit the ginger, Calvados, apricot preserves, nutmeg, and rum. Fill the crêpes with the sautéed apples and arrange in an ovenproof serving dish. Make a sauce by cooking 1 cup of sugar and ¼ cup of water until it turns golden brown. Stir in ¾ cup of heavy cream and ½ cup of maple syrup and simmer until lightly thickened, about 5 minutes. Pour over the crêpes and sprinkle with ½ cup of toasted sliced almonds.

GÂTEAU DE CRÊPES À LA NORMANDE
(Normandy Apple Cake)

4–5 cups Cortland apples, sliced	**½ cup butter, melted**
⅓ cup sugar, plus additional for sprinkling	**12 Dessert Crêpes, page 346**
	6–8 stale Almond Macaroons, crushed, page 26
	Calvados, to taste

1. Preheat the oven to 350°F.

2. Spread the apples in a 9 × 13-inch baking pan and sprinkle with the sugar and ¼ cup of butter. Bake about 15 minutes, or until tender.

3. Place one crêpe flat in the center of a buttered ovenproof serving dish, spread with a layer of apples, and sprinkle with some of the macaroon crumbs, the remaining butter, and Calvados. Continue to layer the ingredients to make a cake, ending with a crêpe. Sprinkle the top with sugar, macaroon crumbs, and Calvados.

4. About 30 minutes before serving, preheat the oven to 375°F. Bake until heated. Test the temperature by inserting a metal skewer or small knife into the center of the cake for 30 seconds and then feel the skewer to test the temperature.

Yields 6 servings

Can be prepared the day before and heated just before serving.

BANANA CRÊPES WITH RUM SAUCE

4 bananas, sliced	Pinch of nutmeg
9 tablespoons butter	12 Dessert Crêpes, page 346
¼ cup brown sugar	8 tablespoons sugar
2 teaspoons grated orange rind	½ cup orange juice
¼ teaspoon ginger	⅓ cup dark rum
	Vanilla ice cream, optional

1.   Preheat the oven to 325°F.

2.   In a skillet, sauté the bananas in 3 tablespoons of butter and the brown sugar until well coated. Add 1 teaspoon of orange rind, ginger, and nutmeg.

3.   Fill the crêpes with the banana mixture and arrange in a buttered ovenproof serving dish.

4.   In the skillet, cook the remaining butter and sugar until the sugar just starts to caramelize. Add the orange juice and bring to a boil. Add the remaining orange rind and rum and pour over the crêpes.

5.   Bake until heated through. Serve with ice cream on the side, if desired.

Yields 6 servings

Can be prepared for baking several hours ahead.

BERRY AND CHEESE–FILLED CRÊPES

3 tablespoons heavy cream	2½ cups fresh berries, see Note
2 egg yolks	12 Dessert Crêpes, page 346
3 tablespoons sugar	½ cup berry jam
6 ounces cream cheese, softened	⅔ cup red wine

1.   Preheat the oven to 325°F. In a bowl, beat the cream, egg yolks, sugar, and cream cheese together. Fold in 2 cups of the berries.

2.   Fill the crêpes and arrange in an ovenproof dish. In a saucepan, simmer the jam and wine for 5 minutes and spoon over the crêpes.

3.   Bake until heated through, about 15 minutes. Serve garnished with remaining berries.

Yields 6 servings

Can be prepared for heating several hours ahead.

NOTE: If berries are large, cut into halves, quarters, or slices. Use strawberries, raspberries, blackberries, blueberries, or a combination of berries.

Variation

• Substitute cherries, or cut-up plums or peaches for the berries.

CRÊPES WITH LEMON SOUFFLÉ

6 eggs, separated	¼ cup lemon juice
Pinch of salt	16 Dessert Crepes, page 346
¾ cup sugar	2–3 tablespoons confectioners'
2 tablespoons grated lemon	sugar
rind	⅓ cup Cointreau

1.   Preheat the oven to 400°F. Butter 2 large ovenproof platters.

2.   Beat the egg whites with the salt until stiff, but not dry, peaks form.

3.   In a bowl, beat the egg yolks with the sugar until thickened and pale. Beat in the lemon rind and juice. Fold in the egg whites and spoon ¼ cup of the mixture onto each crêpe. Fold into quarters (see illustration). Arrange on the platters and bake until puffed and set, about 7 minutes.

4.   Dust with the confectioners' sugar. Pour the Cointreau over the crêpes and ignite the crêpes.

Yields 8 servings

Can be prepared for baking up to 1 hour before serving.

LEMON CUSTARD–FILLED CRÊPES

6 egg yolks	2 tablespoons grated lemon
⅔ plus ¾ cup sugar	rind
¼ cup cornstarch	12 Dessert Crepes, page 346
2 cups milk, scalded	6 tablespoons butter
1 teaspoon vanilla	⅔ cup lemon juice

1. Preheat the oven to 325°F.

2. In a bowl, beat the egg yolks and ⅔ cup of sugar until thickened and pale. Stir in the cornstarch. Stir the hot milk into the egg yolk mixture gradually. In a saucepan, cook, stirring, over medium heat, until thickened and smooth. It must come to a boil. Strain into a bowl. Add the vanilla and 1 tablespoon of lemon rind.

3. Fill the crêpes with the custard and arrange in a buttered, ovenproof serving dish.

4. In a saucepan, cook the butter and the remaining sugar over low heat until the butter melts. Stir in the lemon juice and simmer until the sugar dissolves. Spoon the sauce over the crêpes and sprinkle with the remaining grated lemon zest. Bake until hot, about 10 to 15 minutes.

Yields 6 servings

Can be prepared for saucing and baking the day before.

CRÊPES GIL BLAS

Why the 17th-century scoundrel of French literature gets credit for this dessert is not clear. Perhaps their exceptional taste is as outrageous as the personality of this roguish character. These are extraordinarily rich and one per serving may suffice.

¼ **cup butter, softened**
1 **cup confectioners' sugar**
  Pinch of salt
½ **teaspoon grated lemon rind**
¼ **cup light cream**

1 **teaspoon kirsch**
6 **Lemon Dessert Crêpes, page 346**
  Strawberry Sauce, page 554

1. Preheat the oven to 350°F. In a processor, cream the butter, sugar, and salt until very smooth. With the machine running, add the lemon rind and enough cream to make a fluffy mixture. Add the kirsch.

2. Place a tablespoon of the mixture on each crêpe and roll.

3. Arrange the crêpes on an ovenproof serving platter and bake 5 minutes, or until heated. Pass the sauce.

Yields 6 servings

The filling and crêpes can be prepared the day before. Reheat the crêpes, wrapped, in a microwave, or 300°F. oven, before filling.

CRÊPES AUX MANDARINES
(Crêpes with Tangerine Liqueur)

Grated rind and juice of 1	**liqueur**
tangerine, plus additional	**½ cup butter**
teaspoon of grated rind	**12–16 Tangerine Dessert Crêpes,**
4 tablespoons tangerine	**page 346**

1.   Preheat the oven to 375°F.

2.   In a processor, cream the butter with the tangerine rind and juice. Add the liqueur. Place 1 tablespoon of the butter mixture in each crêpe and fold into quarters. Place in an ovenproof baking dish and bake for 10 minutes, or until hot.

Yields 6 to 8 servings

Can be prepared for baking several hours ahead.

CRÊPES AU MOCHA (Mocha-flavored Crêpes with Rum-flavored Whipped Cream)

2 cups flour	**2 eggs**
2 tablespoons sugar	**2 egg yolks**
Pinch of salt	**2 cups milk**
2 tablespoons grated	**2 tablespoons butter, melted**
semisweet chocolate	**1 cup heavy cream**
2 tablespoons instant coffee	**1 tablespoon rum**
powder	**Sugar, to taste**

1.   In a bowl, mix the flour, sugar, salt, chocolate, and coffee. Stir in the eggs and egg yolks. Add the milk gradually to form a smooth mixture as thick as heavy cream. Add the melted butter. Allow to rest for 2 hours.

2.   Cook the crêpes (see page 344), and cool.

3.   Whip the cream until soft peaks form. Flavor with the rum and sugar to taste. Fill the crêpes with the whipped cream and serve.

Yields 8 to 12 servings

You can prepare the crêpes and filling ahead and freeze.

CRÊPES SOUFFLÉ AUX ORANGE
(Crêpes Filled with Orange Soufflé)

24 Dessert Crepes, page 346	Sugar
1 recipe Orange Soufflé, page 365	3 tablespoons orange liqueur
	Apricot Sauce, page 547, optional

1. Preheat the oven to 400°F.

2. Place a crêpe on a baking sheet, place a generous tablespoon of the soufflé mixture on top, and fold into quarters. Continue with the remaining crêpes and soufflé mixture. Sprinkle the crêpes with sugar.

3. Bake 10 minutes, or until puffed and golden.

4. Remove to a serving platter and, if desired, flambé with the orange liqueur. Serve the sauce on the side.

Yield 6 to 8 servings

Can be prepared for baking several hours ahead.

CRÊPES SUZETTE
(Crêpes in Orange Butter and Liqueur)

¾ cup butter	1 teaspoon grated lemon rind
¾ cup sugar	Lemon juice, to taste
¾ cup orange juice	12 Dessert Crêpes, page 346
Grated rind of 1 orange	¼ cup Grand Marnier
	2 tablespoons Cognac

1. In a saucepan, melt the butter and cook with the sugar, stirring, until it starts to turn golden. Add the orange juice and bring to a boil. Add the orange and lemon rinds with the lemon juice, to taste.

2. Transfer to a skillet or a chafing dish. Fold the crêpes into quarters and heat in the sauce, soaking them completely.

3. Add the Grand Marnier and Cognac, and ignite, spooning the flaming juice over the crêpes. Serve immediately.

Yields 6 servings

Can be prepared ahead and reheated.

CRÊPES AUX POIRES AUX GINGEMBRE
(Pear-filled Crêpes with Ginger)

1 cup sugar	¼ cup chopped crystallized
¼ cup water	ginger
3 pears, peeled, cored, and	12 Dessert Crêpes, page 346
sliced	2 cups hot Custard Sauce,
½ teaspoon vanilla	page 545

1.   In a skillet, caramelize the sugar and water (see page 5).

2.   Carefully add the pear slices, vanilla, and ginger to the hot caramel. Simmer until the pears are tender and the syrup thickens.

3.   Fill the crêpes with the warm pear mixture and arrange on serving plates. Spoon the custard sauce over the crêpes and serve.

Yields 8 to 12 servings

Prepare the pear mixture the day before and reheat if desired.

CRÊPES AUX POIRES AU CRÈME PÂTISSIÈRE
(Crêpes with Pears and Pastry Cream)

2 Vanilla Poached Pears, page	⅓ cup orange juice
40	⅓ cup apricot liqueur
1 cup Pastry Cream, page 26	¼ cup Cognac
12 Dessert Crêpes,	2 tablespoons strained apricot
page 346	preserves
6 tablespoons butter	Lemon juice, to taste
⅓ cup sugar	Grated rind of 1 lime

1.   Preheat the oven to 325°F.

2.   Dice the pears and fold into the pastry cream. Fill the crêpes with the mixture and arrange in an ovenproof serving dish.

3.   In a saucepan, cook the butter and sugar, stirring, until golden in color. Beat in the orange juice, apricot liqueur, Cognac, apricot preserves, and lemon juice to taste. Spoon over the crêpes.

4. Bake until heated. Sprinkle with the grated lime rind and serve.

Yields 6 servings

Can be prepared for baking several hours ahead.

Omelets

Dessert omelets are a wonderful, easily prepared finish to a small family meal and make a perfect sweet after a soup-and-bread supper or a salad and meatless pasta dish. They may also make an ethereal ending to a major dinner.

There are 4 basic types of dessert omelets: the traditional folded French omelet, the *omelette soufflée*, the frittata, and the Baked Alaska or *omelet en surprise.*

OMELET PANS   For information on omelet pans and seasoning them, see the description of crêpe pans on page 344.

FRENCH DESSERT OMELET   To prepare the French dessert omelet follow these steps: Break the eggs into a bowl and season with a pinch of salt and sugar to taste. Beat about 40 vigorous strokes with a fork. Place the omelet pan over high heat and preheat until very hot. Add 1 tablespoon of butter and let it melt until it is foamy and starts to turn golden brown. It should smell nut-like.

Pour in the egg and let set about 5 seconds. Hold the fork with the tines horizontal to the pan and stir the eggs while shaking the pan back and forth with your other hand. (The object is to keep the egg mixture moving so that it does not stick.) As the omelet begins to set, pull its sides toward the center and lift the edges to let the uncooked egg flow underneath.

When the center is almost set, but still moist, place the filling in a line across the center. Tilt the pan up and back toward the handle using the sloping sides of the pan and a fork to help turn a third of the omelet over the filling. Put the pan on the side of the stove top and place the palm of your hand under the handle with your thumb pointing away from you. Grasp the handle firmly. In one fluid movement, tilt the pan in the opposite direction to fold the omelet into thirds. Turn the omelet onto a plate in a neat, yellow oval. Sprinkle the omelet with confectioners' sugar and garnish with some of the filling. Serve at once. (Try not to brown the omelet because that changes the flavor. Of course there *are* people who believe any omelet is not cooked

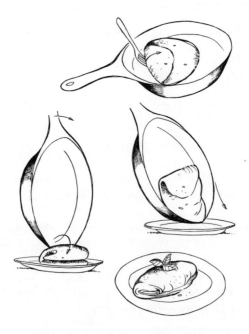

unless it is brown; you may wish to brown it for them.)

It takes about 30 seconds to prepare these omelets so you can serve 6 people in a matter of minutes. A 3-egg omelet can be divided among two persons easily, but do not try to make larger omelets, they take too long to cook and are not as delicate.

THE SOUFFLÉED OMELET   Beat the yolks with the sugar until they become thickened and pale. Beat the whites until stiff, but not dry. Fold both together with the flavoring and bake in a skillet with a heatproof handle, a gratin pan, or a baking dish. Usually, you heat the mixture on top of the stove before baking to a puffy lightness. Bake and serve it in the same dish, or it will deflate when you try to transfer it. Serve the omelet immediately after baking.

This is not a problem for the professional, since the waiter can place the order 10 minutes or so before serving. For the home cook, beat the egg yolks and flavoring before dinner and just before serving the salad, beat the egg whites and fold into the egg yolks. Let it bake while eating the salad. Or, place it to bake after the salad course so guests can relax before the des-sert course. Remember, dining should be leisurely. A few minutes between courses is a pleasure, not a disaster.

FRITTATAS   These omelets are especially popular in Spain and Italy. Mix the ingredients including the eggs, sugar, and fruit together and pour into a hot, buttered skillet. Cook the mixture over moderate heat until the bottom browns lightly. Slip the frittata onto a plate and turn over into the pan to brown on the second side. Cut frittatas into wedges to serve.

THE OMELET SURPRISE   These are not really omelets but one or more flavors of ice cream or fruit topped with a meringue then browned quickly in the oven. Although cooks are often hesitant to prepare these, there is no reason to fear. The meringue acts as insulation protecting the ice cream from melting.

The classic omelet surprise is a layer of cake, topped with a block of ice cream, and decorated with meringue. You also can fill orange or lemon shells with ice cream, freeze them until firm and garnish with the meringue before broiling to brown the tops. Another method of presenting this type of dessert is to place a layer of cake in a small clay flowerpot, pack in the ice cream and garnish the top with the meringue. Brown under the broiler and insert a real flower in the center.

Do not let the piped meringue wait too long before browning or the meringue will start to break down. Ideally, bake just before serving, to give the diner a sensation of hot and cold. You may not be up to this after a long meal. You can prepare and bake the meringue earlier in the day or even a day or two before and keep it frozen. Let it mellow in the refrigerator for an hour or two before serving.

OMELETTE NORMANDE (Normandy Apple Omelet)

Substitute any orchard fruit such as peaches, pears, plums, or pitted cherries for the apples. Pineapple and berries are also succulent.

2 apples, peeled, cored, and chopped	**½ teaspoon vanilla**
3 tablespoons sugar, plus extra for glazing	**3 tablespoons Calvados**
2½ tablespoons butter	**4 eggs**
	2 teaspoons water
	Pinch of salt

1.   Preheat the broiler.

2.   In a skillet, sauté the apples in 1½ tablespoons of sugar, 1½ tablespoons of butter, and the vanilla until very soft. Add 1 tablespoon of Calvados.

3. In a bowl, beat the eggs, the remaining 1½ tablespoons sugar, the water, and salt.

4. Heat an omelet pan and melt the remaining butter. When the bubbles start to subside, add the egg mixture.

5. Prepare a French Dessert Omelet (see page 355). When almost set, place the apple mixture in the center, fold and turn onto a ovenproof platter. Sprinkle the omelet with the sugar and glaze under the broiler.

6. In a small saucepan, warm the remaining Calvados, pour over the omelet at the table, and ignite. Serve immediately.

Yields 2 to 3 servings

Cannot be prepared ahead.

FRITTATA CON MELE
(Flat Open Omelet with Apples)

2½ tablespoons flour	Grated rind of 1 lemon
Pinch of salt	2 apples, peeled and thinly
½ cup milk	sliced
2 eggs, beaten	2–3 tablespoons butter
4 teaspoons sugar	Confectioners' sugar

1. In a bowl, make a thin, smooth batter with the flour, salt, and milk. Beat in the eggs, sugar, and lemon rind, and mix well. Fold the apples into the batter.

2. In an 8-inch skillet, melt 2 tablespoons of butter and cook over medium heat until the omelet is golden brown on the bottom. Invert onto a hot plate and slide the omelet back into the pan to brown the other side. Add more butter to the skillet, if needed.

3. Slide out onto a platter and sprinkle with the confectioners' sugar. Serve immediately, cut into wedges.

Yields 2 to 4 servings

APRICOT AND KÜMMEL OMELET

2 tablespoons kümmel	2 teaspoons sugar
½ cup apricot preserves	2 tablespoons butter
6 eggs	1 teaspoon confectioners'
½ teaspoon salt	sugar

1. Preheat the broiler.

2. In a small bowl, mix the kümmel and apricot preserves, and set aside.

3. Using the instructions for a French Dessert Omelet (page 355), make two omelets. Fill them with the apricot mixture.

4. Sprinkle each omelet with ½ teaspoon of confectioners' sugar and glaze under the broiler. Serve immediately.

Yields 2 to 4 servings

OMELETTE SOUFFLÉE
(Dessert Omelet Soufflé)

8 eggs, separated	**¼ teaspoon salt**
1 cup sugar	**2 tablespoons Clarified Butter,**
Flavoring, see Variations	**page 4**

1. Preheat the oven to 425°F.

2. In a bowl, beat the egg yolks with ½ cup of sugar until thickened and pale. Beat in the flavoring.

3. In a separate bowl, with clean beaters, beat the egg whites with the salt until they form soft peaks. Add the remaining sugar, 1 tablespoon at a time, and beat until the egg whites form stiff and glossy peaks. Fold into the egg yolk mixture.

4. In a deep, 10-inch skillet with an ovenproof handle, melt the butter. Remove from the heat and spread ¾ of the batter in the skillet, smoothing the surface. Put the remaining mixture into a pastry bag fitted with a #6B tip and pipe rosettes and swirls over the soufflé. Or, if desired, you can just swirl the mixture with a spoon.

5. Place over low heat and cook for 3 minutes, or until the bottom starts to set. Transfer to the oven and bake 8 minutes, or until the top is firm and golden brown. Serve immediately.

Yields 6 to 8 servings

Do not attempt to prepare the omelet ahead.

Variations

• *Nut.* Fold ½–¾ cup of ground nuts of your choice into the batter. Hazelnuts, toasted almonds, and walnuts are all favorites.

- *Chopped Fruit.*   Use ½–¾ cup of chopped fresh fruit, such as strawberries, raspberries, or pears. You can enhance the flavor by macerating the fruit in a complementary liqueur such as framboise, kirsch, or rum for 20 minutes before folding into the batter.
- *Vanilla.*   Fold 1 teaspoon of vanilla into the batter.
- *Orange.*   Fold 1 tablespoon of grated orange rind and 2 tablespoons of orange-flavored liqueur into the batter.
- *Lemon.*   Fold 1 tablespoon of grated lemon rind and 2 tablespoons of lemon juice into the batter.
- *Salzburg Omelet Soufflé.*   Fold 1 tablespoon of grated lemon rind or 1 tablespoon of rum into the batter and spoon the mixture into a large oval gratin dish, dropping the mixture in 3 distinct mounds. Bake until puffed and browned, and serve with Strawberry Sauce, (see page 554).

OMELETTE EN SURPRISE VALBERGE
(Fruit-filled Baked Omelet)

The surprise in this omelet is that it's more like an omelet soufflé.

1 **orange, sliced**	**additional, for glazing**
1 **banana, sliced**	8 **eggs, separated**
5 **tablespoons butter**	2 **tablespoons Cointreau**
2 **teaspoons sugar plus**	¼ **cup Cognac or rum**

1.   Preheat the broiler.

2.   In a skillet, heat the orange and banana slices in 3 tablespoons of butter and 2 teaspoons of sugar until warmed. Set aside.

3.   In a bowl, whisk the egg yolks until frothy. In another bowl, beat the egg whites until very stiff peaks form. Fold the whites into the yolks and add the sugar, to taste.

4.   In a large omelet pan, heat the remaining butter and add the egg mixture. Spoon the Cointreau over all and cook until the omelet puffs and sets, but is still moist. Place the heated fruit slices and their juices in the center and fold over.

5.   Place on a hot platter, sprinkle with sugar, and glaze under the broiler. Flambé with the Cognac and serve immediately.

Yields 6 to 8 servings

Cannot be prepared ahead.

KAISERSCHMARRN
(Kaiser's Omelet)

Reputed to have been the favorite dessert of Emperor Franz Josef of Austria, this slightly strange preparation is delicious.

⅔ **cup raisins**	**4 eggs, separated**
¼ **cup Cognac**	**2 cups milk**
½ **cup sugar**	**6 tablespoons butter**
1 **cup flour**	**Confectioners' sugar**

1. Preheat the oven to 350°F. Butter a 9 × 11-inch baking dish.

2. In a small bowl, macerate the raisins in the Cognac for 20 minutes.

3. In a bowl, stir ¼ cup of sugar and the flour together. Gently and slowly stir the egg yolks and milk into the dry ingredients until smooth.

4. In another bowl, beat the egg whites until stiff peaks form and fold them into the batter. Pour into the baking dish and bake for 10 to 15 minutes, or until golden. Use two forks to tear the cooked omelet into small pieces.

5. In a skillet, melt the butter and sauté the omelet pieces with the raisins and the remaining sugar until lightly coated and heated. Serve immediately with confectioners' sugar sprinkled over the top.

Yields 6 servings

Can be prepared for the final reheating several hours ahead.

OMELETTE EN SURPRISE (Baked Alaska)

If desired, serve with a strawberry or other fruit sauce. You can make the meringue without the egg yolk enrichment if you prefer. Just beat the egg whites with 3 tablespoons of sugar until stiff but not dry.

1 **quart ice cream, softened**	⅔ **cup sugar**
1 **(8-inch) Sponge Cake or**	1 **tablespoon kirsch or other**
Génoise cake layer, pages	**liqueur**
19 and 20	3 **egg whites**
3 **eggs, separated**	**Pinch of salt**

1. Pack the ice cream into a mold 1 inch smaller in diameter than the cake layer. Freeze at least 4 hours, or until very hard.

2.   Preheat the oven to 425°F.

3.   In a bowl, beat the egg yolks with ½ cup of sugar and the kirsch until thick and lemon-colored.

4.   Using clean beaters, beat the egg whites with 1 tablespoon of sugar and the salt until stiff but not dry peaks form. Fold the egg whites into the egg yolk mixture.

5.   Place the cake layer on an ovenproof serving dish. If desired, sprinkle with some of the liqueur used to flavor the meringue. Unmold the ice cream onto the cake, centering it.

6.   Fill a pastry bag fitted with a #5 open star tip with the meringue, and pipe it over the ice cream, being sure to cover it completely. Sprinkle the top with the remaining sugar.

7.   Bake until golden, about 6 minutes, watching carefully. Serve immediately or return to the freezer.

Yields 6 to 8 servings

Can be kept frozen for several days; let temper in the refrigerator for at least 1 hour before serving.

Soufflés

Many authors describe soufflés as fraught with danger and difficulty when the truth is they are simple to prepare and, with a little precaution, almost mistake proof. A soufflé has three basic components: a thick base (usually a white sauce, sweetened for a dessert soufflé, a pastry cream, or a thick fruit puree), a flavoring, and beaten egg whites. The recipes for whips (see Chapter 4), if baked, would produce soufflé-like results.

BASE   The most common bases for dessert soufflés are a thick, sweetened cream sauce or pastry cream. Because the creams are made with flour, it is necessary to boil them for about 2 minutes to cook the starch in order to remove any floury taste. Once cooked, allow the cream to cool for 5 minutes before adding the egg yolks and the flavoring. Use liqueur, grated orange or lemon rind, vanilla extract, and/or fruit purees to flavor the soufflé.

BEATING EGG WHITES   Proper beating of the egg whites is the most critical point in preparing a soufflé. Beat the whites, preferably with a little sugar, until they have reached their full volume, but are not stiff or dry. Adding some of the sugar in the recipe to the egg whites helps to prevent overbeating. The goal is to beat the whites until they mound with soft peaks when you lift the beater. If you do not beat them enough they will not be able to "lift" the soufflé, and if you overbeat them, they will deflate as you try to fold them into the base.

FOLDING EGG WHITES   It takes a little practice to learn to fold egg whites or other light ingredients into a stiffer mixture. First, gently mix about one-fourth of the beaten egg whites into the base. Do not worry about deflating these whites; the object is to loosen and lighten the base mixture. Place the remaining egg whites on top of the base and fold them in as follows: Using a large rubber spatula, cut down through the center of the mixture, then, holding the spatula firmly, twist your wrist and bring the spatula up along the outside of the bowl, turning your hand over onto the mixture. Repeat, giving the bowl a slight turn every time you fold the batter. Once you have circled the bowl, the mixture should be almost fully blended. If needed, continue around the bowl until the ingredients are folded together. A few streaks of white are acceptable and preferable to overfolding.

FLAVORING SOUFFLÉS   You may flavor the base with vanilla, grated orange or lemon zest, and orange or lemon juice. Liqueurs give a particularly subtle and delicate flavor to soufflés. Plan on about 2 tablespoons for each six servings. You can turn fruit purees into the base before adding the egg whites, or use purees in place of the base, as in Soufflé Chambord. Add a complementary liqueur for added punch. Grated nuts especially in company with a nut-flavored liqueur, Cognac, or rum flavor some soufflés. Or, prepare a soufflé of choice, and brush ladyfingers or macaroons with a complementary liqueur. Put one-third of the soufflé mixture in the dish, top with a layer of ladyfingers, then another third of soufflé, and another layer of ladyfingers. Finish with soufflé. You can divide the soufflé mixture, flavor each half differently, and fill the dish alternately with spoonsful of each flavor.

SOUFFLÉ DISHES   Soufflé dishes are flat-bottomed, straight-sided porcelain molds. Charlotte molds or any other straight-sided molds work as well. The only requirement is that the mold look good enough to present at the table.

Preparing a Soufflé Dish. If the soufflé mixture is thin, it is wise to put a collar on this dish. Butter a soufflé dish and sprinkle with sugar. Cut a strip of foil or parchment paper long enough to encircle the dish and overlap with a 2-inch extension above the rim. Pin, crimp, or tie the foil or paper in place. Butter and sugar the inside of the foil above the soufflé dish. Carefully remove the collar before serving.

BAKING THE SOUFFLÉ   Scrape the soufflé mixture into the dish and, with your thumb, wipe around the inside edge of the dish about 1 inch deep. This pushes the soufflé away from the sides of the dish and helps it to rise.

   Bake the soufflé on the bottom rack of the oven as close to the heat source as possible. Dessert soufflés generally bake at 375°F. to 400°F. for 18 to 20 minutes. The interior of the soufflé should be almost runny when served. The runny center provides a sauce and dessert all in one. Some people prefer a soufflé that is more fully cooked, almost to the point of being cake-like.

   A soufflé, once baked, will not wait for your guests; serve it immediately. This is not as unnerving as it sounds. You can prepare the soufflé for the oven several hours ahead and keep it in a draft-free area, including the refrigerator. Or, prepare the base, flavoring, and the soufflé dish. Place the egg whites in the mixer (they will beat better if at room temperature). Just before you serve the salad, beat the egg whites, fold them into the base and bake. The baking time is brief, brief enough to let you prepare it after the salad and to give your guests a respite before the next course.

SOUFFLÉ À LA VANILLE (Vanilla Soufflé)

½ cup milk	1½ tablespoons flour
(1-in) piece vanilla bean, or	5 eggs, separated
1 teaspoon vanilla extract	¼ cup plus 4 tablespoons sugar
2 tablespoons butter	1 egg white

1.   Preheat the oven to 400°F. Butter a 1-quart soufflé dish and sprinkle with sugar.

2.   In a saucepan, scald the milk and vanilla bean, if using. Remove from the heat and steep for 10 minutes.

3.   In a 1-quart saucepan, melt the butter. To create a roux, add the flour and cook until the mixture just starts to turn golden. Stir the milk into the roux and cook, stirring, until thick and smooth. Boil, stirring constantly, for 2 minutes. Remove from the heat and discard the vanilla bean, or stir in the vanilla extract. Cool 5 minutes.

4. Beat the egg yolks and 3 tablespoons of the sugar into the sauce.

5. In a bowl, beat the egg whites with the remaining sugar until stiff enough to hold soft peaks. Fold into the sauce and pour into the soufflé dish.

6. Bake on the bottom shelf of the oven for 18 to 20 minutes, or until puffed and browned.

Yields 4 to 6 servings

Can be prepared for baking several hours ahead.

Variations

- *Chocolate.* Stir 1½ ounces of grated semisweet chocolate into the hot base before adding the egg yolks.
- *Coffee.* Add 2 tablespoons of double-strength coffee with the egg yolks.
- *Ginger.* Add ½ tablespoon of grated gingerroot and 2 tablespoons of minced crystallized ginger with the egg yolks.
- *Lemon.* Omit the vanilla and add the grated rind of 1 lemon and the juice of ½ lemon with the egg yolks.
- *Liqueur.* Omit the vanilla and add 2–4 tablespoons of liqueur with the egg yolks. For added flavor, dip 5 or 6 ladyfingers in the liqueur. Ladle half the soufflé mixture into the dish, cover with ladyfingers and cover with the remaining soufflé.
- *Nut.* Add ¾ cup of ground almonds, hazelnuts, pecans, or walnuts with the egg yolks. Serve with rum-flavored whipped cream.
- *Orange.* Omit the vanilla and add the grated rind of 1 orange, 2 table-spoons of orange juice, and 1 tablespoon of orange liqueur with the egg yolks.
- *Palmyra (Anisette and kirsch-flavored).* Omit the vanilla and add 2 table-spoons anisette with the eggs. Turn one-third of the soufflé mixture into the dish. Soak 5 ladyfingers in 3 tablespoons of anisette and place on top of the soufflé, add another third of the soufflé, dip 5 more ladyfingers into 3 tablespoons of kirsch, place on top of the soufflé, and cover with the remaining soufflé mixture.

APPLE-MACAROON SOUFFLÉ

1 cup Apple Puree, page 28	6 tablespoons sugar
½ cup Almond Macaroon crumbs, page 26	3 eggs, separated
	Confectioners' sugar
2 tablespoons Cognac	1 cup heavy cream, whipped,
6 tablespoons butter, softened	sweetened and flavored with Cognac

1.   Preheat the oven to 375°F. Butter a 1-quart soufflé dish and sprinkle with sugar.

2.   In a bowl, mix the apple puree, macaroon crumbs, and Cognac.

3.   In another bowl, cream the butter and sugar until light and fluffy. Stir in the egg yolks and fold into the apple mixture.

4.   Using clean beaters, beat the whites until stiff, but not dry and fold into the apple mixture.

5.   Pour into the soufflé dish and bake for 20 minutes, or until puffed and golden.

6.   Sprinkle with the confectioners' sugar and serve immediately. Pass the cream separately.

Yields 4 to 6 servings

Best if prepared and baked.

ANTONIN CARÊME'S APPLE SOUFFLÉ

Carême was chef to the Prince Regent of England, the Rothschilds, the Czar of Russia, and Talleyrand. This soufflé cooks longer than others to firm the meringue.

3 cups sliced apples	1 cup water
2 cups confectioners' sugar	9 egg whites
Grated rind of 1 lemon	

1.   Preheat the oven to 350°F. Butter a 2-quart soufflé dish and sprinkle with sugar.

2.   In a large saucepan, cook the apples with 1 cup of confectioners' sugar, the lemon rind, and water until the apples are tender and dry, but not burned.

3. In a bowl, beat the egg whites until they hold soft peaks. Beat in the remaining confectioners' sugar until the mixture is very stiff. Fold into the apples and pour into the soufflé dish. Bake for 40 minutes.

Yields 8 servings

HAZELNUSS AUFLAUF (Hazelnut Soufflé)

This soufflé is baked in a water bath for a different consistency from other soufflés.

5 eggs, separated	**3 tablespoons butter**
¼ cup sugar	**2 tablespoons dark rum**
¼ cup flour	**1 egg white**
Pinch of salt	**1 cup coffee ice cream,**
1 cup milk, scalded	**softened**
1 cup skinned hazelnuts,	**½ cup heavy cream, whipped**
ground	**and sweetened to taste**

1. Preheat the oven to 325°F. Butter a 1-quart soufflé dish and sprinkle with sugar.

2. In a saucepan, beat the egg yolks and sugar until they are thickened and pale. Add the flour and salt and beat well. Gradually stir in the scalded milk and cook, stirring, over medium heat, until the mixture comes to a boil and is thick and smooth. Boil, stirring, for 2 minutes. Remove from the heat and cool the pastry cream for 5 minutes.

3. In a small skillet, sauté the hazelnuts in the butter until golden. Add 1 tablespoon of rum and cool. Add the hazelnuts to the pastry cream.

4. In a mixer, beat the egg whites until stiff peaks form, and fold into the hazelnut mixture. Pour into the soufflé dish and bake in a water bath for 45 minutes, or until puffed and golden.

5. Meanwhile, beat the softened ice cream with the remaining rum and fold in the whipped cream. Serve with the soufflé.

Yields 4 to 6 servings

Can be prepared for baking several hours ahead.

ORANGE SOUFFLÉ IN ORANGE CUPS

6 large navel oranges	**¼ cup orange liqueur**
½ cup Almond Macaroon crumbs, page 26	**1 recipe Orange Soufflé, page 365**

1.   Preheat the oven to 400°F.

2.   Grate the rind from the top third of each orange and reserve. Cut off the tops and discard. Hollow the oranges reserving the pulp for another use. If necessary, cut a thin slice from the bottom of each orange so the shells stand upright.

3.   In a small bowl, soak the macaroon crumbs in the orange liqueur. Fold 2 tablespoons of grated rind and all of the macaroon mixture into the soufflé base before folding in the egg whites.

4.   Fill the orange cases and bake for 10 to 12 minutes, or until puffed and brown.

Yields 6 servings

Can be prepared for baking several hours ahead.

SOUFFLÉ AUX POIRES (Pear Soufflé)

3 Vanilla Poached Pears, quartered, page 40	**4 egg whites**
1½ teaspoons Poire William	**Pinch of salt**
2 eggs, separated	**¼ cup sugar**

1.   Preheat the oven to 425°F. Butter a ¾-quart soufflé dish and sprinkle with sugar.

2.   In a processor, puree the pears with the Poire William. Add the egg yolks.

3.   In a mixer, beat the egg whites with the salt and the sugar until almost stiff and fold into the pear puree. Pour into the soufflé dish and bake for 18 to 20 minutes, or until puffed and golden brown.

Yields 4 to 6 servings

Best if prepared and baked.

SOUFFLÉ AUX FRAISE CHAMBORD
(Strawberry Soufflé Chambord)

In the 40s & 50s, the Café Chambord was one of New York's finest restaurants. Even then, diners wanted healthful, fat-free desserts.

1 pound fresh strawberries,	**3 tablespoons kirsch**
hulled	**6 egg whites**
½ cup sugar	**½ cup confectioners' sugar**

1. Preheat the oven to 375°F. Butter a 1-quart soufflé dish and sprinkle with sugar.

2. In a processor, puree the strawberries with the sugar and kirsch. In a mixer, beat the egg whites until stiff, but not dry, peaks form, with the confectioners' sugar.

3. Fold into the puree and turn into the prepared dish. Bake for 20 minutes, or until puffed and golden brown.

Yields 4 to 6 servings

For the nondieter, serve with Custard Sauce (see page 545).

Chapter 11

FRITTERS AND BEIGNETS

Fritters or beignets are foods dipped in batter, coated with bread crumbs, wrapped in short pastry, or mixed into cream puff pastry and deep fried. Cook them just before serving for the best flavor. If they stand, they lose quality quickly and if they cool, they become even less appealing. The exception is fried cream puff pastries, but even those are better eaten as soon as they are cooked. Fortunately they take no more than minutes to cook and they can be readied for cooking well ahead of time. Occasionally, cooked fritters get dusted with confectioners' sugar and glazed under the broiler.

Deep Frying Fritters

Faultless deep frying is the result of the right oil heated to the correct temperature. Whenever possible use a thermometer. If necessary, you can test the temperature by frying a 1-inch cube of bread. It will brown in 50 to 55 seconds at 375°F., the customary temperature for fritters.

Select an unflavored oil such as soybean, corn, peanut, or canola oil. Fill a heavy pot no more than half full. If you use more than that the oil may bubble up and over the sides and catch fire. When deep frying, it is wise to have a large box of salt or baking soda at hand to douse any fire. *Never use water on a grease fire.*

Heat the oil over moderate heat to 375°F. Do not add too many fritters at one time, because the temperature will lower too much, causing the food to absorb the oil, rather than set up a crisp crust. After the first batch, let the fat return to 375°F. before adding a second batch. Drain the golden brown fritters on paper towels and serve immediately.

You can reuse the oil several times as long as you do not overheat it. You can tell when the oil needs to be changed; it will cease to turn the food golden brown. When cooking the last pieces, make sure the temperature is correct and fry the food. If it no longer turns golden readily, discard the oil.

Cool any good oil, strain, and keep in a cool, dry place for the next occasion. In warm weather or a warm house, store it in the refrigerator.

PÂTE À FRIRE POUR BEIGNETS DE FRUITS (Fritter Batter for Fruits)

This is the basic batter used for many fruit fritter recipes. You may substitute water or milk for the beer, but the result will not be as light and delicate.

½ cup flour	1 egg
¼ teaspoon salt	½ cup beer
1 tablespoon butter, melted	1 egg white

1. In a processor, mix the flour and salt together. Add the butter and the egg and process to a stiff dough. With the machine running, slowly add the beer, and process until the batter is smooth and the consistency of heavy cream. Let stand in a warm place for 1 to 2 hours.

2. Just before using, whip the egg white until stiff peaks form and fold into the batter.

Yields enough batter for 8 to 12 servings

Can be prepared the day before.

NOTE: Occasionally the batter will not adhere to the fruit because it is too moist. In this case, dry the fruit on paper towels and dust lightly with flour before dipping into the batter.

You can prepare the batter in a blender or by hand.

BEIGNETS DE FRUITS (Fruit Fritters)

Select almost any favorite fruit, prepare it, and cut into wedges or rings. This makes a simple, delicious treat.

2 cups fresh fruit	Fritter Batter for Fruits, see
Sugar, to taste	page 372
Kirsch, orange, or other	Confectioners' sugar,
liqueur	optional
Oil, for deep frying	Fruit sauce of choice,
	optional, (see Chapter 15)

1. Prepare the fruit and cut into bite-sized pieces. In a bowl, macerate in the sugar and the liqueur for at least 30 minutes and up to 3 hours.

2. Heat the oil to 375°F.

3. Dip the fruit into the batter and deep fry until puffed and golden. Drain on paper towels. Serve plain, dusted with confectioners' sugar, or with a favorite fruit sauce.

Yields 6 servings

Cannot be prepared ahead.

NOTE: The liqueur is not mandatory, but it can make a difference. Use just enough to flavor the fruit without overpowering it. If the batter does not adhere to the fruit, dry the pieces on paper towels and dredge in flour before dipping in the batter.

BEIGNETS DE PRUNEAUX À LA PROVENÇALE (Provençale Prune Fritters)

1 pound pitted prunes	Fritter Batter for Fruits,
2 cups hot, weak tea	page 372
1 cup light rum	⅓ cup sugar
Oil, for deep frying	⅓ cup cocoa

1. In a bowl, soak the prunes in the tea for several hours. Drain and soak in the rum for 1 hour or longer.

2. Heat the oil to 375°F.

3. Drain the prunes, dip in the batter, and deep fry until golden. Drain on paper towels.

4. In a small bowl, mix the sugar and the cocoa. Roll the warm fritters in the mixture. Serve immediately.

Yields 8 to 10 servings

Cannot be prepared ahead.

BEIGNETS D'ANANAS (Pineapple Fritters)

1 pineapple, peeled, cored, and thinly sliced	**Fritter Batter for Fruits, page 372**
½ cup dark rum	**Sugar, to taste**
1 cup apricot jam	**1 cup raspberry jam, melted**
Oil, for deep frying	

1. In a bowl, macerate the pineapple slices in the rum for 1 hour.

2. Sandwich the pineapple slices with the apricot jam.

3. Heat the oil to 375°F.

4. Dip the fritters into the batter and deep fry until golden. Drain and sprinkle with sugar. Serve on a warmed platter and pass the warm raspberry jam.

Yields 6 servings

Cannot be prepared ahead.

PANER À L'ANGLAISE (English or Bread Crumb Coating)

Use this egg-and-bread coating for fruit fritters. Although you can coat the fruit just before serving, it is better to let them dry before frying so they do not become soggy.

Flour, as needed
2 eggs, lightly beaten
2 cups fresh bread crumbs, see Note

1. In 3 separate containers, place the flour, eggs, and bread crumbs.

2. Dip the fruit into the flour, roll in the egg, and then roll in the bread crumbs.

3. Dry on a wire rack until ready to fry. Coat the fruit up to 6 hours before frying. See page 371 for frying directions.

Yields enough batter for 8 to 12 servings

NOTE: Bread crumbs should be made from bread that is 2 to 3 days old, but not hard or stale. Remove the crusts and crumble the bread in a processor or blender. They will make a light crisp coating instead of the heavier coating from dried stale bread crumbs. Remove the crust from the bread, or it will darken further, possibly giving the fritters a speckled look.

FRIED BANANAS AND RUM

6 small bananas, cut into 1-in pieces	2 cups fresh bread crumbs
3 tablespoons light rum	Oil, for deep frying
1 egg, lightly beaten	Apricot Sauce, page 547

1. In a bowl, macerate the bananas in the rum for 45 minutes. Drain.

2. Dip the bananas into the egg and roll in the bread crumbs. Dry on a wire rack for at least 30 minutes, refrigerated.

3. Heat the oil to 375°F.

4. Deep fry the fritters until golden. Drain. Serve with the Apricot Sauce on the side.

Yields 6 servings

Can be prepared for frying several hours ahead.

APRICOT-RICE CROQUETTES

½ cup long-grain rice	1 cup apricot jam
1½ cups milk	1 cup flour
1 vanilla bean, split	2 eggs beaten
¼ cup sugar	2 cups fresh bread crumbs
Pinch of salt	Oil, for deep frying
3 egg yolks	Apricot Sauce, page 547

1. Preheat the oven to 300°F.

2. In a saucepan, bring the rice and cold water, to cover, to a boil. Drain the rice, rinse under warm water, and drain again. Return to the pan.

3. In a saucepan, scald the milk, vanilla bean, sugar, and salt. Strain over the rice and simmer, covered, until the milk is absorbed. Discard the vanilla bean. Transfer the rice to a bowl, beat in the egg yolks, and cool, covered.

4. Shape the rice mixture into 1½-inch balls and poke a hole in the center of each ball. Using a pastry bag, pipe apricot jam into the hole in each ball. Pinch the opening closed and reshape into a ball.

5. In three separate containers, place the flour, whole eggs, and bread crumbs. Roll the rice balls in the flour, eggs, and bread crumbs, and let dry on a wire rack.

6. Heat the oil to 375°F. Fry the croquettes until golden; drain on paper towels. Serve the apricot sauce on the side.

Yields 6 servings

Can be prepared the day before cooking.

NOTE: This is a good way to use leftover Rice Pudding (see page 339). Use 1½ cup of rice pudding to replace the rice, milk, vanilla bean, sugar, salt, and egg yolks.

SOUPIRS DE NONNE (Fried Puff Balls)

The polite translation for this dessert is "nun's sighs."

1 cup water	**4 eggs**
⅓ cup butter	**Oil, for deep frying**
½ tablespoon sugar	**Confectioners' sugar**
Pinch of salt	**Fruit sauce of choice,**
1 teaspoon grated lemon rind	**Chapter 15**
1 cup flour	

1. In a saucepan, bring the water, butter, sugar, salt, and lemon rind to a full, rolling boil. Add the flour, all at once, and cook, stirring vigorously, until the mixture forms a ball and starts to coat the bottom of the pan. Remove from the heat and allow to cool for 4 to 5 minutes.

2. Beat in the eggs, one at a time, until fully incorporated, or put the paste into a processor, add the eggs all at once, and process until combined.

3. Heat the oil to 375°F. Using two spoons, drop spoonsful of the dough into the hot oil. Cook until puffed and golden. Drain and sprinkle with confectioners' sugar. Serve the sauce separately.

Yields 10 to 12 servings

Can be prepared several hours before frying.

Chapter 12

PIES AND TARTS

Pie is the favorite American dessert. It symbolizes comfort, home, well-being, happiness, and patriotism. Real men do not eat quiche, but they thrive on pie, especially apple. Pies filled with fall fruits, summer berries, custards, and purees all provide delicious eating and secret thoughts of midnight snacking.

Pies are divided into two major types: two-crust and open-face or tart. You may need to slice two-crust pies to reveal the filling, but open-faced pies or tarts clearly show their contents, unless a froth of whipped cream or meringue conceals it. A peek-a-boo lattice crust offers an alternative somewhere in between.

This chapter is organized according to the type of pastry—flaky, sandtorte, puff, and crumb crusts, followed by the various fillings of fruits, creams, custards, and chiffons. Many of the fillings make superb individual tarts, *barquettes,* or turnovers. In most cases, this is indicated at the end of each recipe and in a few instances it is the recipe.

PANS AND MOLDS   Pies and tarts can be round, square, rectangular, or, in some cases, free-form. Of the many possible pie molds, the more common are the standard round, slope-sided pie pan; the traditional round, square, or rectangular, straight-sided fluted tart pan (with or without a removable bottom); and flan rings. Flan rings are about 1 inch high and can be round, rectangular, square, or even heart-shaped.

ROLLING PINS   There are two types of rolling pins: the French pin and the roller bearing pin. The French pin resembles a log: Maneuver it over the pastry with your palms, fingers held out straight. Many bakers insist that this gives them greater control and that they can "feel" the pastry better. The roller bearing pin has handles to allow you to roll it smoothly over the pastry, without the (to my mind) awkward movements required with the French pin. Whichever you select, it should be at least 18 inches long and heavy. A smaller pin requires twice as much rolling and a lot more effort. These factors can cause you to overwork the dough. A longer pin allows you to make just a few passes to make the dough large enough to fit the pan.

TO ROLL PASTRY   Do not attempt to roll the pastry into a circle, as it stretches and toughens the dough. Think of the dough with a warp and a woof. Roll the pastry, as a square or rectangle, from the middle forward and middle back several times. Turn the pastry so the longer side faces you and repeat until the square is larger than the pie pan and as thin as desired. The shape of the pan does not matter. Always roll as a square to avoid pulling the dough in too many directions and toughening it.

TO TRANSFER PASTRY TO THE PIE PAN   Roll the pastry around the rolling pin, lift it over the edge of the pie pan, and unroll. Or, fold the pastry in half and, with one fluid movement, move the pastry so the fold is across half the pie pan and unfold it. Once the pastry is spread across the pan, lift the sides of the dough into the pan to cover the interior surface. Do not press and stretch the dough. If it is stretched, it will shrink during the baking. Once the dough is in place, trim the edges to fit the pan and flute the edge, if desired.

Pie and Tart Shells

TWO-CRUST PIES   Roll two-thirds of the dough into a square and place in the pie pan, lift and press the dough to fill the corners, and trim the edges. Add the filling and roll the remaining third large enough to cover the top of the pie. It is not unusual to have a thicker top crust than bottom. Press the dough to the edge of the pie pan, crimp to seal, and cut off any excess dough. Use a paring knife to cut a simple V, or stencil out a flower or an apple to provide steam vents. Or, prick out the children's names. Before baking, brush the top with an egg wash, and, for a more professional look, sprinkle with sugar to give the finished pie sparkle.

LATTICE CRUST   Lattice crusts enhance many pies. To prepare: Roll a one-third of the dough into a 9-inch square. With a crimped pastry wheel cut ½-

inch-wide strips. Line a cookie sheet, without sides, with waxed paper and lay half the strips of pastry parallel at 1-inch intervals. Fold every other strip in half away from you. Place one long strip horizontally over the center of the unfolded strips. Bring the folded strips back over the horizontal strip and fold the strips that lie under the horizontal strip away from you. Add another horizontal strip 1 inch from the first. Repeat to make a lattice and refrigerate on the baking sheet. When ready to put on the pie, slide the chilled pastry from the waxed paper onto the pie and cut the edges to fit.

OPEN-FACED TART SHELLS   Roll the sheet of dough large enough to line the pan. Lift into the pan. Then lift the dough onto the bottom and up the sides of the pan without stretching the dough. To provide extra support to the sides, trim the dough even with the outside bottom edge of the pan. Fold over inside the pan and press the edges to secure. The dough makes a thick, rope-like upper edge. Mark this "rope" with the back of a knife or the tines of a fork.

Blond. Refers to partially baked shells that will be cooked further once the filling is added. Prick the bottom of the uncooked shell with the tines of a fork. Cover with foil and fill with dried beans or pie weights. Bake about 15 minutes and carefully draw part of the foil from one side of the pan. If the side stays in place, remove the foil and beans, and bake until the crust just starts to turn golden.

Brown. Refers to fully baked shells that have cold fillings added to them. Follow the instructions for blond, as above, and bake until golden brown.

TO MAKE A FLAN RING   Flan rings are available from gourmet shops, but you can make a reasonable substitute. Fold a length of foil, as long as needed and about 1-inch wide. Shape the strip of foil into a square, rectangle, etc., and secure with a paper clip. Place the flan ring on a lightly buttered baking sheet, line with pastry, and bake. When ready to serve, slide the tart and the ring onto a serving platter and lift off the ring.

TO MAKE A TART SHELL WITHOUT A PAN OR MOLD   You can shape both flaky and puff pastry without a pan. Roll the pastry about ¼ inch thick, and cut into the desired shape. If using flaky pastry, lightly grease the pan. If using puff pastry, rinse the baking sheet under cold water but do not dry it; the steam helps the pastry to rise. Turn the cut pastry onto the baking sheet and brush a 1-inch border of cold water. Cut 1-inch-wide strips of pastry and arrange around the edge to make a box-like case. Brush the rim with egg

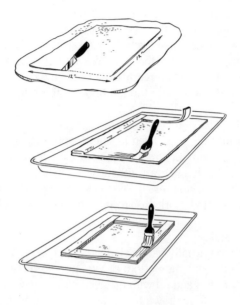

wash, (see page 383), without dribbling over the side; if it does, it will act as an anchor and hold the pastry to the baking sheet, preventing it from rising. Use the point of a paring knife to cut a crosshatch design into the egg wash. Prick the bottom of the pastry shell with a fork. Bake filled with fruit as an open-faced tart or bake empty and fill after baking.

TURNOVERS   Roll the flaky or puff pastry ⅛ to ¼ inch thick and cut into 3- to 7-inch circles, squares, or rectangles. Place 1 teaspoon to 2 tablespoons of filling in the center of each circle. Moisten the edges and fold one side over the filling to form a half-circle, triangle, rectangle, or square. Press the edges to seal with your fingertips or with the tines of a fork. Prick the tops of the pastries to allow the steam to escape. Brush with egg wash and bake at 400°F. about 20 minutes, or until golden. Do not try to stuff the turnovers, or the filling will ooze out during baking.

TARTLET OR BARQUETTE PASTRY SHELLS   Use 2- to 3-inch tartlet molds. On a counter, arrange the molds in a rectangle or square with the edges touching. Roll the pastry ⅛ inch thick and large enough to cover the group of molds. Lift the pastry onto the molds and let "rest" into position for about 3 minutes. With a small ball of extra dough, press the pastry into each mold. Roll a rolling pin over the molds, letting the edges of the molds cut the pastry to fit. (See illustration.)

Stack two pastry-lined molds with one empty mold on top and arrange on a baking sheet. Cover the assembled molds with another baking sheet and weight with half a brick or a heavy ovenproof pot. Bake at 375°F. about 25 minutes, or until set and golden.

To Roll Scraps of Dough. Both flaky pastry and puff pastry consist of layers of dough between layers of fat. To maintain these layers, prevent over-working of the dough, and to keep the resulting pastries flaky, do not roll the scraps into a ball. Neatly pile them on top of each other and roll the pile of scraps. Unless you are very forceful, the second round should be almost as tender as the first.

Egg Wash, or Dorure. A *dorure,* or wash, is a gilding for pastry. In bread baking it can be as simple as salted water. For dessert pastries, use milk, cream, or egg, alone or in combination. Egg yolk and heavy cream give the deepest, richest sheen. For most purposes, a whole egg mixed with a tablespoon of milk will serve.

Pastry Doughs

There are four principal crusts used for pies and tarts. *Pâte brisée,* flaky pastry, works for all types of pies and tarts, including barquettes and turnovers. *Pâte sablée,* or sandtorte pastry, makes crisp shells for open-faced fruit tarts or barquettes, but is too crumbly for two-crust pies. *Pâte feuilletée,* or classic puff pastry, works for open tarts or turnovers. It is not recommended for two-crust pies, because the filling weighs down the pastry. Cookie or graham cracker crumb crusts are used for open-faced pies with cream-based fillings. Select the right pastry for the type of pie or tart you are preparing to increase your chances of success.

Pies and tarts sometimes cause fear and trepidation among even the most experienced cooks. Improperly made pastry can turn a delight into a soggy, leaden mass with a crust that could sink a battleship. Pastry making is not difficult but it does require patience and attention. For the truly fearful, concentrate your first attempts on open-faced pies prepared with *pâte sablée,* sandtorte pastry. This cookie dough crust is virtually impossible to ruin and should instill confidence in you. Or, resort to one of the excellent frozen products available in most markets.

With the exception of *pâte sablée,* the major point in preparing pastry is to handle it as little as possible. Work quickly and lightly and do not worry if during much of the preparation it looks less than perfect; remember, it is the result that is important.

Pâte Brisée, or Flaky Pastry

There are two methods of preparing this pastry: the traditional hand method and a processor method.

To Prepare Pâte Brisée by Hand. Put the flour into a bowl and work in the fats with your fingertips, not the palms of your hands. Be sure to keep the flour between your fingers and the fats as you crumble them together. Or use a pair of crossed knives or a wire pastry blender until the fat-flour mixture forms into pieces the size of peas. (The large pieces of fat make the pastry flakier.) Dissolve the salt in the water and add most, but not all, to the flour. Add the remaining water if needed. The dough will be crumbly and messy; do not try to make it smooth. Turn onto the counter and, starting at the edge farthest from you, with the heel of your hand, smear the dough in ¼- to ½-cup portions about 8 inches across the counter. With a pastry scraper, push the dough into a flat cake about 5 inches square. Wrap in waxed paper or put into a plastic bag and chill about 20 minutes. Do not shape the pastry into a ball since the first step in rolling is to flatten it.

To prepare *pâte brisée* by processor, (see page 385).

Pastry for Custard Pies. Because the liquid of a custard can make a soggy crust, crumble the fat into the flour until the consistency resembles coarse meal rather than small peas. This provides a firmer pastry to withstand the moisture.

PÂTE BRISÉE I (Flaky Pastry—Hand Method)

The butter gives the pastry flavor and the lard provides flakiness. If necessary you can substitute vegetable shortening, but the flavor and texture will not be the same.

3½ cups flour	into 1-in pieces
1¼ cups cold butter, cut into	2 teaspoons salt
1-in pieces	¼ teaspoon sugar
5 tablespoons cold lard, cut	1 cup ice water

1. Put the flour into a bowl. Using your fingertips, a pastry blender, or two knives, cut the butter and the lard into the flour until the size of small peas.

2. In a measuring cup, mix the salt and sugar. Add about ¾ cup of the water and mix to combine. With a spoon or fork, pull the sides of the fat-flour mixture just to the center. Give the bowl a slight turn and repeat, pulling the dough together rather than stirring until the dough is just moistened. Add more water if required until the mixture is crumbly and just holds together. Do not add too much water and do not stir into a compact mass.

3. Turn the pastry onto a board in a pile. It will look messy. With the heel of your hand, starting at the far edge of the dough, smear about ¼ to ½ cup of dough at a time about 8 inches across the counter. With a pastry scraper gather the dough into a flat cake about 5 inches square and wrap in waxed paper, plastic wrap, or put into a plastic bag. Refrigerate at least 20 minutes.

Yields enough for 4 to 6 (8- to 9-inch) open tarts, 2 to 3 (9-inch) two-crust pies, or 36 to 72 turnovers

Can be frozen before or after shaping and baking. May be divided into smaller portions for freezing.

Variation

- For custard-filled pies and tarts, cut the butter and lard into the flour until it resembles coarse meal rather than the size of a pea. This provides a firmer pastry to withstand the moisture.

PÂTE BRISÉE II
(Flaky Pastry—Food Processor Method)

1½ cups flour
8 tablespoons cold butter, cut into 1-in pieces
4 tablespoons cold lard, cut into 1-in pieces
3½ tablespoons cold water
1 teaspoon salt

1. In a processor, combine the flour, butter, and lard, and process with on/off turns until the size of peas.

2. In a cup, mix the water and the salt. With the machine running, add the water and process until the mixture is moistened and starts to form clumps.

3. Place the dough on a counter and gather into a flat cake. Wrap in waxed paper or plastic wrap, or put into a plastic bag. Refrigerate for 20 minutes.

Yields enough for 1 (10-inch) open tart shell, 1 (8-inch) two-crust pie, or about 24 (3-inch) barquettes or tartlets

Pâte Sablée, or Sandtorte Pastry

Sandtorte pastry is more like a sugar cookie dough than a pie dough. It is crisp, rather than flaky. It is almost impossible to ruin. Put all the ingredients into a bowl and work with your hand until the dough becomes waxy and no longer sticks to your hand, or put all the ingredients in a processor and process until it almost forms a ball. Shape the dough into a flat cake and chill for about 20 minutes. If you chill it too long you will have trouble rolling, so let it stand at room temperature until it is pliable. It is often easier to roll between sheets of waxed paper or parchment. But even if the dough should tear, do not worry, you can just press it into the pan until evenly thick.

PÂTE SABLÉE (Sandtorte Pastry)

The egg yolks make a crisper, more crumbly dough. Using the whole egg, or substituting egg whites makes the dough more cake-like.

½ cup butter
¼ cup sugar
2 egg yolks or 1 whole egg

1½ cups flour
1 teaspoon baking powder

1. In a bowl, mix the butter, sugar, eggs, flour, and baking powder. With your hands, work the pastry until it feels waxy, holds together, and no longer sticks to your hands.

2. Shape into a flat cake and wrap in waxed paper. Chill for about 20 minutes.

Yields 1 (9- to 10-inch) open tart shell

Can be shaped and frozen before or after baking.

Food Processor Method

Put the butter, sugar, egg yolks, flour, and baking powder into the processor and process until the mixture forms a ball on top of the blades. Remove, shape into a flat cake, and wrap in waxed paper. Chill for about 20 minutes.

Variations

- Add ½ cup of ground walnuts, pecans, or hazelnuts with the flour.
- Add 1 tablespoon of grated lemon rind with the flour.

Pastry for Barquettes

Although flaky pastry and sandtorte pastry make excellent barquettes and tartlets, this formula is specifically designed for barquettes. It creates a crisp, delicate shell suitable for both sweet and savory fillings.

BARQUETTE PASTRY

3 **scant cups flour**	1 **cup sour cream**
1½ **cups cold butter, cut into**	
pieces	

1. In a bowl, with your fingertips, a pastry blender, or two knives, crumble the flour and butter together until the consistency of coarse meal.

2. Stir in the sour cream and shape into a flat cake. Refrigerate for 20 minutes.

Yields about 50 (3-inch) tartlets or barquettes

Can be prepared ahead and frozen before or after shaping or baking.

NOTE: Barquettes are sometimes called "pastry boats" and are typically oval whereas tartlets are generally round.

Pâte Feuilleté or Classic Puff Pastry

Unquestionably, this is the most difficult pastry to make properly. It is time-consuming and exacting. When prepared correctly the results are superb; incorrectly done, it will develop the gluten to make it tough and unappealing. Many qualified bakers have trouble and often never master the technique of puff pastry, so, when you do, feel proud. You can, by following the instructions below, become proficient at this pastry.

Bake this pastry on metal baking sheets run under cold water. It provides the steam needed to give the pastry lift.

PÂTE FEUILLETÉ (Classic Puff Pastry)

2 cups cold butter   **2 teaspoons salt**
4 cups flour
1 cup ice water

1.   In a bowl, work ½ cup of butter into the flour with your fingertips until it resembles coarse meal.

2.   Mix the water and salt and add just enough to make a medium-firm dough. *Do not beat.* Work quickly and lightly. Turn the dough onto a counter. It should be a crumbly mass.

3.   With a pastry scraper or broad-bladed putty knife, pick up the dough and press it onto itself about 8 to 10 times, going around the edges. Use the blade to cut through the dough repeatedly to incorporate the ingredients without kneading and developing the gluten. The process should take no more than 2 minutes. The dough will still be crumbly. With the pastry scraper, put the dough into a plastic bag. Gently press the dough into a flat 5-inch square and refrigerate about 20 minutes.

4.   In another plastic bag, work the remaining butter until it is a pliable, waxy mass. Work quickly and do not let the butter get too warm. Shape it into a 5-inch square and refrigerate until it is the same consistency as the pastry, about 20 minutes.

5.   Place the pastry on a lightly floured board and roll into an 8-inch square. It may look messy, even crumbly. Place the square of butter on top of the pastry with the corners of the butter pointing toward the sides of the

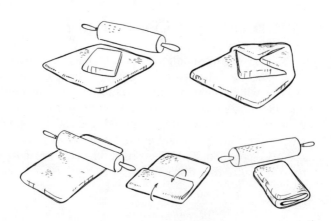

pastry. Pick up 2 corners of pastry and wrap over the butter, pressing the edges together. Continue to enclose the butter, pinching the edges to seal. (See illustration.)

6.   With a lightly floured rolling pin, roll the pastry into a 12 × 20-inch rectangle. Fold into thirds, brushing off any excess flour, and roll again into a 12 × 20-inch rectangle. Fold in thirds again, thus completing two turns, and return to the plastic bag. Refrigerate for 40 minutes.

7.   If the pastry is too firm to roll easily, bang it with the side of the rolling pin until it starts to soften and move on itself. Roll into a 12 × 20-inch rectangle and fold in thirds. Repeat the process and refrigerate 40 minutes. Repeat the rolling and folding twice and refrigerate 2 hours before shaping.

Yields about 2½ pounds

Store in the refrigerator for 2 days or freeze for up to 6 months.

NOTE: Puff pastry will start to turn gray after 3 or more days in the refrigerator. The color is not appealing, but the only effect to the pastry is that it does not puff quite as much. I prefer to keep it frozen and thaw in the refrigerator when I need it.

SHAPING PUFF PASTRY   Unlike most other pastries, puff pastry is baked without a mold or pan. The baker cuts and arranges the pastry to make the cases needed for a specific filling.

Round Tart Shells. Roll a portion of the pastry ⅛ inch thick and cut two circles to the desired size. With a pie pan, pot lid, or another form 1 inch smaller than the pastry circle, cut out the center of one of the circles. On a moistened baking sheet, invert the uncut circle onto the pan. (Turning it over allows for more even rising.) Brush the edge of the circle with water. Using a cookie sheet without sides, lift the outer ring from the cut pastry circle and slip it onto the uncut circle, matching the sides. Press together lightly. Brush the ring with egg wash and refrigerate 5 minutes. Brush again with egg wash and refrigerate for 10 minutes. With a paring knife, cut hatch marks through the egg wash on the ring. Bake at 400°F. until puffed, crisp, and golden. May be made in any size. Use 2- to 3-inch shells for tartlets.

Square or Rectangular Tart Shells. Roll the pastry ⅛ inch thick. Using a ruler as a guide, cut a base the desired size. Invert the shape onto a moistened baking sheet. Moisten about 1 inch of the edge all around the base with water. Using the ruler, cut two 1-inch strips as long as the longest sides and arrange on the moistened edges of the base. Cut two strips to fit the shorter sides and place between the long strips. Brush the top of the strips with egg wash and refrigerate for 5 minutes. Brush again with egg wash and refrigerate for 10 minutes. With a paring knife, cut hatch marks through the egg wash on the sides. Bake at 400°F. until puffed, crisp, and golden.

Diamond-shaped Cases. Roll the pastry ⅛-inch-thick. With a ruler, cut 5-inch squares and invert onto a moistened baking sheet. With a sharp paring knife, starting ½ inch from one corner, cut a ½-inch-wide border to within ½ inch of the next corner, cutting to release the corner. Cut down to the next corner within ¾ inch of the next corner. Starting at the opposite side of the corner, *without cutting through this corner,* cut to the third corner, releasing the pastry at this corner. Cut up to the fourth corner, *without cutting through the corner.* You will have a square of pastry with two opposite corners still attached to the base and two opposite corners released from the base. Brush a ½-inch border of the base with cold water. Carefully lift one of the free corners over the base and lay it on its opposite corner. Repeat with the opposite corner. The pastry will have a ½-inch border on the base with twisted points at opposite corners.

Phyllo

Phyllo dough is a second cousin of *pâte feuilletée,* or puff pastry. With puff pastry, the baker rolls and folds the dough and butter together to make, literally, hundreds of layers of butter and dough. With phyllo, the baker pulls and stretches the dough to tissue-paper thinness, and then cuts and stacks it. When ready to prepare the recipe for bakery, the baker spreads butter between each layer.

Making phyllo dough itself is an art which most of us leave to the professional phyllo dough maker, and buy the dough from local suppliers. In areas where there is a large Middle Eastern population, the fresh dough is available from bakeries; in other areas we must rely on the frozen phyllo found in most supermarkets.

Phyllo dough requires careful handling to reach perfection. If using frozen dough, thaw it in the refrigerator overnight. When ready to use, unwrap the dough, place on a counter, and cover with sheets of waxed paper. Cover the paper with a cloth wrung out in warm water. The cloth provides enough humidity to prevent the dough from drying out, making it impossible to use. Phyllo dough dries out very quickly if not kept covered. Recover the stack with the waxed paper and the towel, when you are working with individual sheets.

To use the pastry, remove one sheet from the stack and place on a counter. Brush the sheet with melted butter, using a soft pastry brush (goose feather brushes, available from gourmet shops, are the best), taking care not to tear the pastry. Cover with another sheet of pastry and brush again. Add the filling and shape according to the directions in the particular recipe.

Fruit fillings for pies are particularly suited for use in phyllo.

Crumb Crust

Graham crackers, gingersnaps, vanilla or chocolate wafers, zwieback, stale or fresh cake or bread—including pumpernickel bread—all make crisp, delicious pie shells. Break the graham crackers, cookies, cake, or bread into small pieces and pulverize them in a blender or processor. For evenness you can sift the crumbs through a coarse sieve or a colander. Adjust the sugar and seasonings, if any, to suit your taste.

CRUMB CRUST

2 cups fine crumbs	Pinch of salt
½ cup butter, melted	Ground cinnamon or
3 tablespoons sugar	nutmeg, to taste

1. Preheat the oven to 325°F. Lightly butter a 9-inch pie pan.

2. In a bowl, mix the crumbs, butter, sugar, salt, and spice. Stir until the crumbs are evenly coated.

3. Press the crumbs evenly over the bottom and sides of the pie pan. Refrigerate for 15 minutes.

4. Bake the crust for 10 minutes, or until crisp and dry to the touch. Cool the crust before adding the filling.

Yields 1 (9-inch) pie shell

Can be prepared several days ahead.

APPLE PIE

As American as. . . . Of course, there are many versions of apple pie, some of which are listed below. But, this is the version to serve at Thanksgiving.

Flaky Pastry for 9-in, two-crust pie, page 384
2 pounds apples, sliced
1¼–1½ cups sugar
Pinch of salt
¾ teaspoon cinnamon
½ teaspoon nutmeg

2 tablespoons flour
2 tablespoons molasses
1–2 tablespoons butter
Milk or Egg Wash, optional, page 383
Sugar, optional

1.   Preheat the oven to 375°F. Line a 9-inch pie pan with pastry.

2.   Place the apples in a large bowl. In another bowl, mix the sugar, salt, cinnamon, nutmeg, flour, and molasses. Sprinkle over the apples and mix gently. Fill the pie shell, dot with the butter, and moisten the edges of the pastry.

3.   Cover the pie with the remaining dough and trim to fit. Crimp the edges to seal and cut steam vents.

4.   Brush the crust with milk or egg wash and sprinkle with sugar, if desired. Bake for 30 to 40 minutes, or until the apples are tender and the crust is golden.

Yields 6 to 8 servings

Can be prepared the day before or frozen.

Variations

• Omit the molasses and add 1 teaspoon of grated lemon rind and 1 tablespoon of lemon juice.
• Substitute brown sugar for the white sugar.
• Omit the molasses and add 2 tablespoons of grated orange rind.
• Omit the molasses and add ½ cup of raisins soaked in brandy to cover for 5 minutes. Add the brandy.
• Omit the molasses and add ½ cup of heavy cream and 2 tablespoons of kirsch.

- *Mincemeat*. Substitute 2 to 3 of cups mincemeat (see page 27) for the apple filling. This is particularly attractive with a lattice crust. Of course you do not need the flour, salt, and sugar for the filling.
- *Peach*. Substitute peaches for apples. Add 2 tablespoons of rum, if desired.

CROUSTADE DE POMMES OU POIRES
(Apples or Pears in Phyllo Dough)

You can substitute peaches or apricots for the apples or pears.

2½ pounds apples or pears, peeled, cored and thinly sliced	1 tablespoon orange flower water, see Note
½ cup sugar	9–10 phyllo sheets
¼ cup Armagnac, plus more for topping	½ cup butter, melted
	Confectioners' sugar

1.   Brush a 10-inch cake pan with some butter. In a bowl, mix the fruit, sugar, Armangnac, and orange flower water. Let macerate for 2 to 12 hours.

2.   Preheat the oven to 400°F. Drain the fruit, reserving the liquid.

3.   Spread a sheet of phyllo with butter and fold in half lengthwise. Place 1 end in the center of the pan, letting the other end overhang the side of the pan. Continue with the remaining sheets, overlapping them to line the pan completely. Sprinkle with some of the reserved liquid. Pile the fruit in the center and lift the last sheet of phyllo up and over the fruit, give the sheet a twist, and open it over the top, like a flower. (See illustration.) Continue with

the remaining leaves. Sprinkle more of the liquid over the top of the phyllo "flower" in the center of the pie.

4. Bake 12 minutes, lower the heat to 350°F., and bake 20 to 35 minutes longer, or until golden brown.

5. Remove to a wire rack and cool. Loosen the sides of the pastry from the pan with a sharp knife and gently remove from the pan. Sprinkle with additional Armagnac and the confectioners' sugar. Serve warm or cold.

Yields 8 to 10 servings

Best served the same day.

NOTE: Orange flower water is available from pharmacies, Middle Eastern markets, and gourmet shops.

TO MAKE UNMOLDING EASIER: Fold a sheet of aluminum foil 10 inches long into a 3-inch-wide strip. Wrap the strip around the outside of a 10-inch cake pan. Place on a lightly buttered baking sheet. With a paper clip, secure the foil. Remove the cake pan and shape the pie within the foil. Once backed and lightly cooled, you can lift the pie with a cookie sheet (without sides) as a spatula.

BLUEBERRY PIE

During the season, Down-Mainers know of no other pie.

Flaky Pastry for 9-in two-crust pie, page 384
2½ cups blueberries
¼ cup flour or 2 tablespoons cornstarch
Pinch of salt
½ cup sugar
Milk or Egg Wash, optional, page 383
Additional sugar, optional

1. Preheat the oven to 400°F. Line a 9-inch pie pan with pastry.

2. In a bowl, mix the blueberries with the flour, salt, and sugar. Fill the pastry shell and moisten the edges of the pastry. Roll a cover for the pie and put over the top. Trim the edges and crimp to seal. Cut steam vents. Brush with milk or egg wash and sprinkle with sugar, if desired.

3. Bake about 30 minutes, or until golden brown.

Yields 6 to 8 servings

Can be prepared the day before or frozen.

NOTE: Bake juicy fruit or berry pies on a cookie sheet to catch any drips.

Variations

- Substitute frozen berries for fresh.
- Add 2 teaspoons of grated lemon rind and 1 tablespoon of lemon juice.
- Omit half of the sugar and add ¼ cup of molasses.
- Season the pie with ¼ teaspoon of nutmeg or mace.
- Bake with a lattice crust (see page 380).
- *Deep Dish Blueberry*. In a deep pie dish, arrange the berries, mixed with sugar and flour, or cornstarch. Roll a piece of dough to fit the top and place over the blueberries, pinching the dough to the sides of the dish. Bake for about 30 minutes, or until the crust is golden. Serve with whipped cream or vanilla ice cream, if desired.
- *Cherry*. Substitute 1 quart of pitted sour cherries for the blueberries and add sugar, to taste.
- *Cranberry*. Substitute 1 quart of cranberries for the blueberries and increase the sugar to taste.

RHUBARB PIE

Flaky Pastry for 9-in two-crust pie, page 384
1 quart rhubarb, cut in 1-in pieces
2 cups sugar
2 tablespoons flour

1. Preheat the oven to 400°F. Line a 9-inch pie pan with two-thirds of the pastry.

2. In a bowl, toss the rhubarb, sugar, and flour and turn into the pie shell. Moisten the edges of the pastry.

3. Roll out the remaining pastry to cover the pie. Place on top and crimp and seal the edges. Cut a steam vent. Bake for 40 minutes, or until golden.

Yields 6 to 8 servings

Can be prepared a day ahead or frozen.

Variation

• *Strawberry Rhubarb.* Substitute 2 cups of sliced strawberries for 2 cups of the rhubarb and reduce the sugar to 1 cup.

Tarts

For tarts, roll the flaky or sandtorte pastry (see page 380) to fit the pie or tart pan. Lift the pastry into place and gently press onto the bottom and up the sides. Take care not to stretch the dough. Trim the edges and add the filling if directed. Bake until done. For unfilled tarts, see page 381. Fill tart shells with fruits, custards, creams, or chiffons.

CARAMELIZED ALMOND TART

To cut some of the sweet, rich flavor of this dessert serve with ice cream or whipped cream flavored with vanilla.

¾ cup heavy cream
¾ cup sugar
¼ teaspoon almond extract
1 tablespoons almond liqueur

1 cup sliced almonds, toasted
1 (9-in) Sandtorte Pastry tart shell, baked blond, page 386

1. Preheat the oven to 400°F.

2. In a bowl, mix the cream, sugar, almond extract, almond liqueur, and almonds and pour into the tart shell.

3. Bake about 30 minutes, or until the filling bubbles and is golden.

Yields 8 to 10 servings

Can be prepared the day before or frozen.

TARTE AUX POMMES (Apple Tart)

Juice of 2 lemons
1 teaspoon vanilla
3 pounds apples, peeled, cored, and thinly sliced
Grated rind of 1 lemon

½ cup raisins
½–1 cup sugar, to taste
1 (9-in) Flaky Pastry tart shell, unbaked, page 384
½ cup Apricot Glaze, page 36

1. Place a rack in the lowest position of the oven and preheat to 350°F. In a bowl, mix the juice of 1 lemon, the vanilla, and enough apple slices to cover the tart shell with overlapping slices and add water to cover. Set aside.

2. In a saucepan, cook the remaining apples, the remaining lemon juice, grated lemon rind, and ½ cup water, covered, until the apples begin to steam. Stir gently and cook, uncovered, until tender, mashing coarsely with a fork. Stir in the raisins and sugar to taste. Cool.

3. Fill the tart shell with the applesauce. Drain the apple slices and arrange in concentric circles over the applesauce. Bake for 1 hour, or until the crust is golden brown. Cool and brush with apricot glaze.

Yields 6 to 8 servings

Best served the same day.

TARTE DES DEMOISELLES TATIN
(Caramelized Apple Tart)

Of the several versions of this recipe, this is my favorite. Plan to serve it warm.

4 pounds apples, peeled, cored, and sliced	**1 (9-in) circle of Flaky Pastry, page 384**
⅓ plus ½ cup sugar	**Confectioners' sugar, optional**
1 teaspoon cinnamon, optional	**Heavy cream, whipped, sweetened, and flavored with rum, optional**
2 tablespoons butter, softened	
6 tablespoons butter, melted	

1. Place a rack in the lowest position of the oven and preheat to 375°F.

2. In a bowl, toss the apples, ⅓ cup of sugar, and cinnamon.

3. In a 9-inch black cast-iron skillet, spread the butter and sprinkle with ¼ cup of sugar. Cook until sugar starts to turn golden. Add one-third of the apples and sprinkle with 2 tablespoons of melted butter. Repeat two more times, using the remaining apples and melted butter. Sprinkle with the remaining sugar.

4.   Place the pastry circle on top, letting the edges of the pastry fall inside of the skillet. Cut several steam vents. Bake the tart for 45 minutes, or until the liquid is a thick, brown syrup. If the top browns too soon, cover with a sheet of foil. Remove from the oven and cool for at least 10 minutes.

5.   Place a serving dish over the skillet and turn over. Let the apples fall out of the pan. They should be a medium caramel color. If not, sprinkle with confectioners' sugar and brown under the broiler. Serve warm with the whipped cream, if desired.

Yields 6 to 8 servings

Best served within a few hours.

NOTE: If necessary, leave the tart in its baking pan until shortly before serving and reheat over low heat to aid in unmolding.

Variation

• For a different effect, substitute peeled, cored, and halved apples, standing on end.

TARTE AU YAOURT ET BLEUETS D'ABITIBI
(Blueberry-Yogurt Tart from Quebec)

1 cup ricotta	page 386
⅔ cup yogurt	½ cup warm Apricot Glaze,
⅔ cup sugar	page 36
3 eggs	2 cups blueberries
2 teaspoons flour	Confectioners' sugar
1 tablespoon lemon juice	Shredded lemon rind, for
1 (9-in) Sandtorte Pastry tart	garnish
shell, baked blond,	

1.   Preheat the oven to 350°F.

2.   In a bowl, mix the ricotta, yogurt, sugar, eggs, flour, and lemon juice. Pour into the partially cooked tart shell and bake about 40 minutes, or until the filling sets. Cool.

3.   Brush the warm glaze over the filling and cover with blueberries. Sprinkle the berries with the confectioners' sugar and garnish with the lemon rind, if desired.

Yields 8 servings

Prepare and serve on the same day.

BLUEBERRY-LEMON CURD TART

1 (10-in) Sandtorte Pastry	page 551
tart shell, baked brown,	1 quart blueberries
page 386	Sugar
1½ cups cold Lemon Curd,	

Fill the tart shell with the cold lemon curd and mound the blueberries on top. Sprinkle with sugar and serve within a few hours.

Yields 6 to 8 servings

CHOCOLATE CHUNK PECAN PIE

2 cups pecans, toasted and
   chopped
6 ounces semisweet
   chocolate, chopped
¾ cup butter, softened
1 cup brown sugar
5 eggs
¾ cup light corn syrup
3 tablespoons flour
2 tablespoons coffee liqueur

2 tablespoons molasses
1½ teaspoons vanilla
½ teaspoon salt
1 (10-in) deep Flaky or
   Sandtorte Pastry tart shell,
   baked blond, page 386
   Coffee ice cream or heavy
   cream, whipped, sweetened,
   and flavored with coffee
   liqueur, optional

1.   Preheat the oven to 375°F.

2.   In a bowl, mix the pecans and chocolate.

3.   In a mixer, cream the butter and sugar until light and fluffy. Add the eggs, one at a time, beating well after each addition. Add the corn syrup, flour, liqueur, molassses, vanilla, and salt, stirring until smooth. Fold in the pecans and chocolate and pour into the pastry shell.

4.   Bake about 1 hour, or until the sides are set, but center is still moist.

5.   Serve warm or at room temperature with coffee ice cream or whipped cream flavored with coffee liqueur.

Yields 8 to 10 servings

Can be prepared the day before or frozen.

GRAPE TARTLETS

3 cups green grapes
9 tablespoons sugar
6 (3-in) Flaky or Sandtorte
   Pastry tartlet, or barquette

shells, unbaked, pages
384–387
3 egg whites
½ cup ground almonds

1.   Preheat the oven to 350°F.

2.   In a bowl, toss the grapes with 3 tablespoons of sugar and fill the tart shells. Bake 15 minutes.

3.   Meanwhile, in a bowl, beat the egg whites with the remaining sugar to stiff peaks. Fold in the almonds. Mound or pipe the meringue over the grapes and bake for 8 to 10 minutes, or until golden. Serve warm or at room temperature.

Yields 6 tartlets

Best served the same day.

LEMON CURD TARTS

2 cups cold Lemon Curd, page •••	1 cup heavy cream, whipped, sweetened and flavored, to
12 (3-in) Sandtorte Pastry tartlets or barquettes, baked brown, page 386	taste, for garnish Crystallized violets, for garnish

Spoon the lemon curd into the tart shells and garnish with rosettes of whipped cream and individual candied violets.

Yields 12 tartlets

Prepare filling and shells ahead and fill just before serving.

NOTE: You can prepare this as one large tart if you desire.

LEMON MERINGUE PIE

You can fill a lemon meringue pie with lemon curd, but it will not cut into neat slices. The cornstarch in this recipe makes the filling firm enough to slice.

1½ cups sugar	½ cup lemon juice
⅓ cup plus 1 tablespoon cornstarch	1 (9-in) Flaky Pastry pie shell, baked brown, page 384
3 egg yolks	3 egg whites
1½ cups water	¼ teaspoon cream of tartar
3 tablespoons butter	⅓ cup sugar
1 tablespoon grated lemon rind	½ teaspoon vanilla

1.   Preheat the oven to 400°F.

2.   In a saucepan, mix the sugar and the cornstarch, and stir in the egg yolks and the water. Place over medium heat and cook, stirring, until the mixture comes to a boil. Boil 1 minute. Remove from the heat and stir in the butter, lemon rind, and juice. Pour the hot filling into the prepared shell and spread evenly.

3.   Using an electric mixer, beat the egg whites and cream of tartar until they form soft peaks. Slowly beat in the sugar and beat to stiff glossy peaks. Beat in the vanilla.

4.   Heap the meringue on the filling and spread over the pie with a rubber spatula, swirling and lifting to give the meringue peaks. Spread the meringue so it attaches to the crust to cover the filling completely. Bake for 20 minutes, or until delicately browned.

Yields 6 to 8 servings

Best served the same day.

NOTE: If any of the filling is exposed the meringue will shrink and may weep.

Variation

• *Lime Meringue.* Omit 1 tablespoon of cornstarch, the butter, lemon rind, and juice, and add 2 teaspoons of grated lime rind and ¼ cup of lime juice.

ORANGE MERINGUE PIE

1⅓ cups sugar	1 tablespoon grated orange
3 tablespoons cornstarch	rind
3 eggs, separated	1 (9-in) Flaky Pastry pie shell,
1 cup orange juice	baked brown, page 384
½ cup water	¼ teaspoon cream of tartar
3 tablespoons butter	½ teaspoon vanilla
1 tablespoon lemon juice	

1.   Preheat the oven to 400°F.

2.   In a saucepan, mix 1 cup of sugar, the cornstarch, egg yolks, orange juice, and water and cook, over medium heat, stirring, until the mixture comes to a boil. Cook, stirring, 1 minute, and remove from the heat. Stir in the butter, lemon juice, and orange rind. Pour into the prepared pie shell.

3. In a mixer, beat the egg whites and cream of tartar until they form soft peaks. Slowly beat in the remaining sugar and beat until stiff, glossy peaks form. Beat in the vanilla and spread over the filling, being sure to cover the filling completely and that the meringue touches the crust at all sides.

4. Bake about 20 minutes, or until golden.

Yields 6 to 8 servings

Best served the same day.

NOTE: If any of the filling is exposed, the meringue will shrink and may weep.

ORANGE-ALMOND TART

1 (9-in) Flaky Pastry tart	minced, page 39
shell, unbaked, page 384	1 teaspoon almond extract
½ cup orange marmalade	Apricot Glaze, page 36
4 eggs	Heavy cream, whipped,
⅔ cup sugar	sweetened, for garnish
4 ounces ground almonds	Grated rind of 1 orange,
⅓ cup Candied Orange Rind,	optional

1. Preheat the oven to 350°F. Freeze the pie sheel until firm. Spread the orange marmalade over the bottom of the tart shell.

2. In a bowl, mix the eggs, sugar, almonds, candied orange rind, and almond extract. Pour into the tart shell.

3. Bake about 25 minutes, or until set and nicely browned. Brush the top with apricot glaze and cool.

4. Fold the whipped cream and orange rind together, and serve on the side.

Yields 6 to 8 servings

Can be prepared the day before.

LA TARTE CHAUDE AUX POIRES (Hot Pear Tart)

1 (10-in) round Puff Pastry
tart shell, unbaked, page
388
4–5 pears, peeled, halved,

cored, and sliced, see Note
6 tablespoons sugar
5 tablespoons butter

1.   Preheat the oven to 400°F.

2.   Prick the bottom of the shell with a fork. Arrange the pear slices neatly on the pastry, sprinkle with the sugar, and dot with the butter. Bake for 30 minutes, or until the pastry is golden and crisp. Serve at room temperature.

Yields 6 servings

Best served the same day.

NOTE: Halve the pears and place on a cutting board, cut side down. Cut thin slices across the pear and press gently to fan them.

PEAR KUCHEN

1½ cups flour
½ cup cold butter, cut into
   pieces
½ cup plus 3 tablespoons
   heavy cream
3 tablespoons brown sugar
½ teaspoon ginger
¼ teaspoon nutmeg

¼ teaspoon salt
¾ cup sugar
3 egg yolks
1 teaspoon lemon juice
1 teaspoon vanilla
3 pears, peeled, cored, and
   sliced
1 cup heavy cream, optional

1.   Preheat the oven to 350°F. Butter a 9-inch tart pan.

2.   In a processor, blend 1¼ cups of flour, butter, 3 tablespoons of cream, 1 teaspoon of brown sugar, the ginger, nutmeg, and salt with on/off turns until the mixture resembles coarse meal. Transfer ½ cup of the mixture to a small bowl and stir in the remaining brown sugar. Set aside.

3.   Press the remaining mixture into the bottom and up the sides of the tart pan and bake until lightly browned, about 20 minutes. Cool. Lower the heat to 325°F.

4.   In the processor, blend the sugar, the remaining cream, the remaining flour, egg yolks, lemon juice, and vanilla. Pour into the tart shell and arrange the pears on top. Sprinkle with the reserved crumb mixture.

5.   Bake about 45 minutes, or until set. Cool for 20 minutes before removing the sides of the pan. Serve warm or at room temperature with the heavy cream served separately.

Yields 6 to 8 servings

Best served the same day.

UPSIDE DOWN PEAR TART
(Tarte Aux Poires Renversée)

This is a tarte tatin (see page 397) made with pears and red wine.

7 firm pears, peeled, halved, and cored	**2½ cups red wine, approximately**
½ cup sugar	**1 (9-in) circle Flaky Pastry, page 384**
½ teaspoon cinnamon	

1.   In a 9-inch black cast-iron skillet, place the pear halves, cored side up with the pear points toward the center. Fill any spaces with split pear halves, tips pointing out. Sprinkle the sugar and cinnamon over the pears, and add enough red wine to cover.

2.   Simmer over direct heat until the pears are tender. (This can take up to an hour, depending on the pear.)

3.   Place a lid firmly against the pears to keep them in position and pour all the juices into a saucepan. Reduce over high heat to ½ cup of syrupy liquid. Drizzle over the pears.

4.   Preheat the oven to 375°F.

5.   Roll the pastry large enough to cover the top of the skillet and place over the pears, (See illustration.) The pastry can come up to the edge or meet over the top, as shown. Cut several steam vents. Bake for 40 minutes, or until the pastry is golden. Cool for 5 minutes. Place a serving dish over the skillet, turn over the dessert, and lift off the pan. If necessary, push the pears back into position with a spatula.

Yields 8 to 10 servings

Best served the same day.

ALMOND-PEAR TART

⅓ cup butter, softened	1 (10-in) Flaky Pastry tart
⅓ cup sugar	shell, unbaked, page 384
1 egg	4 pears, peeled, halved, cored,
1 egg yolk	and sliced
½ cup ground almonds	½ cup sugar
2 tablespoons flour	½ cup Apricot Glaze, page 36
2 teaspoons kirsch	

1.   Preheat the oven to 400°F.

2.   In a processor, cream the butter and sugar until fluffy. Add the egg and egg yolk and process until combined. Add the almonds, flour, and kirsch with on/off turns, and pour into the tart shell.

3.   Arrange the pears on top, pressing into the filling. Bake 15 minutes, or until the dough starts to brown. Lower the heat to 350°F. and bake 20 minutes longer. Sprinkle the tart with sugar and bake, until the sugar melts and starts to caramelize, about 10 minutes. Cool and brush with apricot glaze. Serve at room temperature.

Yields 10 to 12 servings

Can be prepared the day before or frozen.

PEAR AND GINGER TART

8 pears, peeled, cored, and
  sliced
⅔ cup sugar
¾ teaspoon ginger
½ cup water

1 (9-in) Sandtorte Pastry tart
  shell, unbaked, page 386
⅓ cup apricot preserves
Heavy cream, whipped

1. Preheat the oven to 400°F.

2. In a saucepan, simmer the pears, sugar, ginger, and water until the pears are tender but firm. Refrigerate until cold.

3. Drain the pears, reserving the liquid, and arrange in the tart shell.

4. In a saucepan, simmer ¼ cup of poaching liquid with the preserves for 1 minute, and strain. Brush the fruit with some of the glaze.

5. Bake for 30 minutes, or until tender. Remove from the oven and brush with remaining glaze and serve warm. Pass the whipped cream, if desired.

Yields 6 to 8 servings

Best served the same day.

PLUM TART

Substitute almost any fruit for the plums. Serve with whipped cream or cold heavy cream, if desired.

¾ cup blanched almonds
⅓ cup sugar
1 egg
2 tablespoons butter
1 teaspoon vanilla
¼ teaspoon almond extract
1 teaspoon grated lemon rind

1 (9-in) Flaky or Sandtorte
  Pastry tart shell, unbaked,
  pages 384–386
24 plums, halved and pitted
1 cup currant jelly
2 tablespoons port

1. Preheat the oven to 350°F. In a processor, grind the almonds and the sugar to a fine powder. (Do not turn into a paste.)

2. Add the egg, butter, vanilla, almond extract, and lemon rind, and process until mixed. Spread in the tart shell. Arrange the plums on top, cut side down. Bake for 1 hour. Cool.

3. In a small saucepan, melt the jelly and port, stirring until smooth. Brush the glaze over the plums. Serve the tart warm or at room temperature.

Yields 6 to 8 servings

Best served the same day.

PLUM PHYLLO TURNOVERS

½ cup plus 1 tablespoon honey	¼ teaspoon ground cloves
⅓ cup water	1 tablespoon arrowroot or cornstarch
2 slices lemon peel	3 tablespoons cold water
1 cinnamon stick	12 sheets of phyllo dough
2 pounds plums, pitted and quartered	1 cup butter, melted
½ teaspoon cinnamon	1 cup heavy cream, whipped

1. In a saucepan, simmer ½ cup of honey, water, lemon peel, and cinnamon stick for 5 minutes. Add the plums, ground cinnamon, and cloves and simmer 30 minutes or until thickened.

2. Preheat the oven to 375°F.

3. In a bowl, mix the arrowroot with the cold water, and stir into the honey mixture. Simmer until thickened and clear. Remove from the heat and cool.

4. Place the phyllo on a counter, brush one sheet with butter, and cut into 3-inch-wide strips. Place a generous teaspoon of filling at one end of the pastry, pick up one corner and fold it over the filling, aligning the short edge with one of the long edges to form a triangle. Pick up the uppermost point and fold it straight down to form a triangle again, as if folding the American flag. (See illustration.) Continue folding until you reach the end of the strip. Place the turnover, seam-side down, on a baking sheet. Brush with butter. Repeat with each strip.

5. Bake 25 to 30 minutes, or until puffed and golden. Cool at least 5 minutes. Serve warm with the whipped cream and flavored with the honey.

Yields about 36 turnovers

Can be prepared ahead and frozen before or after baking.

Variation

• Substitute flaky or puff pastry for the phyllo. Roll the pastry about ⅛ inch

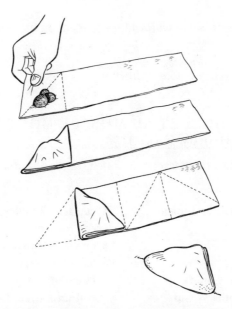

thick. Cut into circles or squares, and brush the edges with cold water. Fill with a teaspoon of filling, and fold to form half circles or triangles. Brush with an egg wash. Cut a steam vent into each turnover.

SHOOFLY PIE

1 cup flour	⅓ cup dark molasses
½ cup light brown sugar	1 (9-in) Flaky Pastry pie shell,
¼ cup vegetable shortening	unbaked, page 384
1 teaspoon baking soda	Heavy cream, whipped and
1 cup boiling water	sweetened, optional
⅔ cup light corn syrup	

1. Preheat the oven to 375°F.

2. In a bowl, crumble the flour, sugar, and shortening until the mixture resembles coarse meal.

3. In a deep bowl, dissolve the soda in the boiling water and add the corn syrup and the molasses. Stir to blend. Pour into the pie shell and sprinkle the flour mixture over the top.

4. Bake the pie for 10 minutes. Lower the heat to 350°F. and bake 25 minutes longer, or until the filling does not quiver when the pan is moved. DO NOT OVERBAKE.

5. Cool to lukewarm. Serve with whipped cream on the side, if desired.

Yields 6 to 8 servings

Can be prepared the day before or frozen.

GÂTEAU AUX NOIX ET AU MIEL DE MONTAGNE (Walnut and Honey Cake)

This is one of my favorite desserts. It is rich, intense, and a tiny amount satisfies.

⅓ **recipe Flaky Pastry I, page 384**

1½ **cups sugar**

½ **cup water**

3½ **cups chopped walnuts**

14 **tablespoons plus ¼ cup butter, softened**

1 **cup less 2 tablespoons milk**

⅓ **cup honey**

6 **ounces semisweet chocolate**

¾ **teaspoon vegetable oil**

Pinch of salt

Walnut halves, for garnish

1. Preheat the oven to 425°F.

2. Roll ⅔ of the dough into a 12½-inch circle and line an 11-inch tart pan, letting the excess dough hang over the sides. Refrigerate until firm. Roll the reserved dough into an 11-inch circle, put on a baking sheet, and refrigerate until firm.

3. In a deep skillet, boil the sugar and water to a light caramel color (see page 5). Add the chopped walnuts, 14 tablespoons of butter, and milk and simmer, stirring for 15 minutes. Stir in the honey.

4. Pour the nut mixture into the chilled shell and fold the overhang over the mixture. Brush the overhang with water and immediately cover with the circle of dough. Press to seal the edges. Cut a steam vent in the center of the pastry.

5. Bake on the lowest rack of the oven for 20 minutes or until browned. Cool at least 4 hours. Unmold onto a pastry rack.

6. Melt the chocolate with the remaining butter and the vegetable oil. Season with the salt and stir until smooth. Spread evenly over the top and sides of the cake. Decorate with the walnut halves.

Yields 8 to 10 servings

Refrigerate until serving time, or freeze. Let come to room temperature before serving.

Cream-filled Tarts

Cream filling can be whipped cream, sour cream, pastry cream, or a buttercream.

If the pastry is to be filled and served within 30 minutes, any pastry shell will work, but if it must wait for several hours or longer before serving, use sandtorte pastry or a crumb crust because they will not become soggy. The recipes have suggested pastry shells but select the shell you prefer.

Be sure to brush lemon juice on bananas, peaches, and other fruits that darken when exposed to the air, before putting on the glaze. Top the cream filling with fruit. Single fruits such as strawberries, raspberries, or grapes are perhaps the most common toppings. But you can create a jewel-like tart by arranging overlapping slices of banana on one side of the shell, filling the curve with a fan of peach slices, and using kiwi and berries to fill in the remaining spaces. In winter, try using orange slices for a refreshing flavor, or poached pears. The glaze brushed over the fruit should complement the color of the fruit: currant glaze on red fruits and apricot glaze on light fruits.

TARTE AUX FRUITS I (Fruit Tart I)

Use one fruit such as raspberries or blueberries, or an assortment of fruits such as banana slices brushed with lemon juice, orange slices, strawberries, peaches, grapes, etc.

½ cup butter, softened	brown, page 386
½ cup sugar	2 cups fruit or berries, see
¼ cup orange liqueur	above
⅛ teaspoon almond extract	¼ cup Apricot or Currant
1 cup ground almonds	Glaze, page 36
1 cup heavy cream, whipped	Chopped pistachio nuts or
1 (9- to 10-in) Sandtorte	almonds, toasted, optional,
Pastry tart shell, baked	for garnish

1. In a processor or mixer, cream the butter and sugar for 3 to 4 minutes, or until pale and fluffy. Add the orange liqueur and almond extract. Beat until the sugar is almost completely dissolved. Beat in the almonds. If using a processor, scrape the mixture into a large bowl. Fold in the cream and chill for about 20 minutes, or until ready to fill the tart.

2. Spread the filling in the tart shell. Arrange the fruit or berries of your choice over the filling. Brush the fruit with the glaze.

3. If desired, sprinkle the outside edge of the tart with chopped pistachio nuts or toasted almonds.

Yields 6 to 8 servings

Best served the same day.

TARTE AUX FRUITS II (Fruit Tart II)

I am partial to the previous recipe because I created it. Here is a more common one.

2 cups Pastry Cream, made with cornstarch, page 26	fruits, or a combination, page 411
1 (9-in) Sandtorte Pastry tart shell, baked brown, page 386	Currant or Apricot Glaze, page 36
2–3 cups berries, grapes, sliced	Chopped pistachio nuts or sliced almonds, optional

Spread the pastry cream in the tart shell. Arrange the fruit on top and brush with the glaze. If desired, sprinkle the outside edge with chopped pistachio nuts or sliced almonds.

Yields 6 to 8 servings

Best served the same day.

BARQUETTES OU TARTELETTES AUX FRUITS (Pastry Boats or Tartlets with Fruits)

12 (3-in) Flaky or Puff Pastry barquettes or tartlets, baked brown, pages 384, 388	with kirsch
	1 pint strawberries or other fruit
1 cup heavy cream, whipped, sweetened, and flavored	Confectioners' sugar, for garnish

Just before serving, using a pastry bag, pipe the whipped cream through a #6 open star tip, into the shells. Arrange the berries on top and dust with the sugar.

Yields 12 barquettes or tartlets

Best served within an hour.

Variation

• Puff Pastry Boats   Preheat the oven to 425°F. Roll a half recipe of puff pastry until ⅛-inch thick. Cut into 4-inch ovals, brush with egg wash, and sprinkle with sugar. Place on a dampened baking sheet and bake until puffed and golden. Cool. Cut the ovals in half horizontally, put the cream and strawberries on the bottom half, and top with the lid. Serve decorated with a sliced strawberry or a stripe of confectioners' sugar.

To stripe the confectioners' sugar, line the pastries side-by-side. Lay a strip of waxed paper over one end of the pastries and another strip over the other, leaving a ½-inch opening. Sift the confectioners' sugar over the top and carefully remove the paper.

KEY LIME PIE

Key limes are tarter than, and not as green as the Persian limes usually available in most markets. The juice is available bottled in specialty stores.

4 **egg yolks**	**Crumb Crust, page 391**
14-ounce can sweetened	2 **cups heavy cream, whipped,**
condensed milk	**sweetened, and flavored with**
½ **cup key lime juice**	**vanilla, for garnish**
½ **teaspoon cream of tartar**	**Candied Lime Slices, page**
1 **(9-in) Graham Cracker**	**38, optional, for garnish**

1.   Preheat the oven to 325°F.

2.   In a mixer, beat egg yolks until thickened and pale. Add the condensed milk and mix on low speed. Add half of the lime juice and the cream of tartar and then the remaining juice, mixing well after each addition. Pour into the pie crust.

3.   Bake 10 to 15 minutes, or until the center is firm and dry to the touch. Refrigerate for 3 hours.

4.   Garnish with whipped cream and candied lime slices.

Yields 6 to 8 servings

Best served the same day, or frozen.

Best served the same day, or frozen.

PEACH CREAM PIE

8 large whole peaches	2 cups heavy cream
4 tablespoons lemon juice	1 (10-in) Flaky Pastry pie
2 tablespoons gelatin	shell, baked brown, page
2 tablespoons orange liqueur	384
¼ cup sugar	

1.   Peel and stone 5 peaches and puree in a processor.

2.   In a bowl, mix the peach puree with 2 tablespoons of lemon juice, then pour into a fine sieve set over another bowl. Drain for 20 minutes.

3.   In a saucepan, soften the gelatin in ½ cup of the drained peach juice. Heat over low heat, stirring until dissolved. Stir into the peach puree, with the orange liqueur and the sugar.

4.   In a cold bowl, whip the cream until it forms soft peaks and fold into the puree.

5.   Spoon into the pie shell and chill for 4 to 6 hours, or until set. Just before serving peel and slice the remaining peaches and toss with the remaining lemon juice. Arrange the sliced peaches on top.

Yields 8 to 10 servings

Best served the same day. Can be prepared to the point of garnishing about 6 hours before serving.

NOTE: Change the fruit to suit your needs or use whatever is fresh and wonderful in the market. Plan on 4 cups of puree fruit—strawberries, pears, raspberries, apples, or blackberries—and substitute a suitably flavored liqueur.

TARTE FEUILLETÉE À L'ANANAS
(Pineapple Tart)

1 (12-in) square Puff Pastry tart shell, baked, brown, page 388	1 pineapple, peeled, cored, and sliced
1 cup rum-flavored Pastry Cream, page 27	Candied cherries, for garnish
	⅓ cup Apricot Glaze, page 36

Spread the puff pastry tart shell with the pastry cream. Arrange the pineapple slices on the pastry cream and garnish with the cherries. Brush with the glaze and serve.

Yields 10 to 12 servings

Prepare no more than 3 hours before serving.

RASPBERRY CREAM TART

2 cups raspberries	2 eggs
¼ cup sugar	½ cup ground almonds
1 (9-in) Sandtorte Pastry tart	¾ cup confectioners' sugar
shell, baked blond, page	2 cups heavy cream
386	1 tablespoon framboise

1. Preheat the oven to 350°F.

2. In a bowl, mix the raspberries with 2 tablespoons of sugar and place in the tart shell.

3. In another bowl, beat the eggs, almonds, confectioners' sugar, and 1 cup of cream. Pour into the tart shell. Bake for 30 minutes, or until set and lightly browned. Cool.

4. Whip the remaining cream with the remaining sugar and the framboise. Pass separately.

Yields 6 to 8 servings

Best served the same day.

VANILLA CREAM PIE

⅔ cup sugar	vanilla
¼ cup cornstarch	1 (9-in) Flaky Pastry pie shell
½ teaspoon salt	or Crumb Crust, baked
3 cups milk	brown, pages 384, 391
4 egg yolks	2 cups heavy cream, whipped
2 tablespoons butter	and sweetened, for garnish
1 tablespoon plus 1 teaspoon	

1. In a saucepan, with a wire whisk, blend the sugar, cornstarch, and salt. Stir in the milk and the egg yolks. Cook, stirring, over medium heat until the mixture thickens. Boil, stirring, 1 minute. Remove from the heat and whisk in the butter and vanilla.

2.   Pour into the prepared shell and press a sheet of waxed paper or plastic wrap directly onto the filling. (The paper prevents a skin from forming on the filling.) Refrigerate at least 2 hours, or until cold.

3.   Top the pie with the cream, piped through a pastry bag fitted with a #6 open star tip, if desired.

Yields 6 to 8 servings

Best served the same day.

Variations

- *Chocolate Cream.* Increase the sugar to 1½ cups and cornstarch to ⅓ cup. Add 2 ounces of chopped unsweetened chocolate with the milk and omit the butter.
- *Banana Cream.* Prepare the vanilla cream and strain into a bowl. Press a sheet of waxed paper or plastic onto the cream and cool. Slice 2 large bananas into the pie shell and cover with the cooled cream.
- *Coconut Cream.* Prepare the vanilla cream and decrease the vanilla to 2 teaspoons. Stir in ¾ cup toasted flaked coconut, and sprinkle the finished pie with ¼ cup of toasted flaked coconut.

Custard Pies

To test for doneness, insert a knife halfway between the center and the edge of the pie. It should come out clean. The center will finish cooking as the pie cools. If cooked until done in the center, it can overcook and curdle as it cools. See page 384 for special instructions about crusts for custard pies.

MARLBOROUGH PIE

2 **cups finely shredded apples**	2 **tablespoons dark rum**
½ **cup raisins or currants**	¼ **teaspoon nutmeg**
½ **cup heavy cream**	**Pinch of salt**
3 **eggs**	1 **(10-in) Flaky Pastry pie**
⅓ **cup light brown sugar**	**shell, unbaked, page 384**

1.   Preheat the oven to 450°F.

2.   In a bowl, mix the apples, raisins, cream, eggs, sugar, rum, nutmeg, and salt. Pour into the prepared shell.

3. Bake 15 minutes. Lower the heat to 325°F. and bake about 30 minutes, or until set. Serve warm or at room temperature.

Yields 6 to 8 servings

Best served the same day.

CARROT CUSTARD CREAM PIE

1 large carrot, boiled, cut into pieces	3 eggs, lightly beaten
¼ cup sugar	1 pint light cream
1 teaspoon grated orange rind	2 tablespoons brandy
¼ teaspoon nutmeg	1 (9-in) Flaky Pastry pie shell, unbaked, page 384

1. Preheat the oven to 350°F.

2. In a processor, puree the carrot. Add the sugar, orange rind, nutmeg, and eggs and process to combine. Add the cream and brandy. Process again. Pour into the pie shell.

3. Bake for 10 minutes. Lower the heat to 325°F. and bake for about 25 minutes longer, or until the center is firm.

Yields 8 to 10 servings

Best served the same day.

FRENCH CHERRY CUSTARD TART

1 pound cherries, pitted	½ cup sugar
1 (9-in) Sandtorte Pastry tart shell, unbaked, page 386	¾ cup heavy cream
	1 egg yolk

1. Preheat to 425°F.

2. Arrange the cherries in the pastry shell in 1 layer. Sprinkle with the sugar.

3. In a bowl, beat the cream and the egg yolk until blended. Pour over the cherries. Bake on the middle rack of the oven for 20 minutes. Lower the heat to 350°F. and bake 15 to 20 minutes longer, or until the pastry is done and the custard tests done.

Yields 6 to 8 servings

Best served the same day.

CUSTARD PIE

4 eggs
⅔ cup sugar
½ teaspoon salt
¼ teaspoon nutmeg

2⅔ cups milk
1 teaspoon vanilla
1 (9-in) Flaky Pastry pie shell,
  unbaked, page 384

1. Preheat the oven to 450°F.

2. In a bowl, beat the eggs until blended and stir in the sugar, salt, nutmeg, milk, and vanilla. Pour into the prepared pie shell.

3. Bake for 20 minutes. Lower the temperature to 350°F. and bake 15 minutes longer, or until it tests done. Cool to lukewarm before serving.

Yields 6 to 8 servings

Best served the same day.

CROSTATA DI PERE AL CIOCCOLATO
(Chocolate Pear Tart)

¾ cup butter
1½ cups flour
3 eggs
½ plus ⅓ cup sugar
½ cup cocoa
2 tablespoons orange

marmalade or raspberry
  preserves
2 pears, peeled, quartered,
  and cored
3½ ounces semisweet chocolate
¼ cup butter

1. Preheat the oven to 350°F. In a bowl or in a processor, knead ½ cup of butter, flour, 1 egg, ½ cup of sugar, and cocoa into a dough.

2. Roll the dough into a 10-inch square and place in an 8-inch tart pan. Trim and crimp the edges, and brush the shell with the marmalade. Arrange the pears in the tart shell.

3. Melt the chocolate and the remaining butter. Remove from the heat.

4. Separate 2 eggs in a bowl. Beat the egg whites until stiff peaks form.

5. In another bowl, whisk the egg yolks and remaining sugar together and add the melted chocolate. Fold in the whites. Spoon the mixture over the pears and bake for about 40 minutes, or until the fruit is tender and the topping is set. Cool.

Yields 6 to 8 servings

Best served the same day.

PUMPKIN PIE

1 cup pumpkin puree	ginger, optional
3 eggs	¼ cup Cognac, optional
1 cup heavy cream	⅛ teaspoon mace, optional
⅛ teaspoon salt	1 (9-in) Flaky Pastry pie shell,
⅓ cup sugar	baked blond, page 384
½ teaspoon cinnamon	Heavy cream, whipped,
⅛ teaspoon ground cloves	sweetened, and flavored with
¼ cup minced crystallized	Cognac, optional

1. Preheat the oven to 375°F.

2. In a bowl, mix the pumpkin, eggs, cream, salt, sugar, cinnamon, cloves, ginger, Cognac, and mace. Pour into the pie shell and bake about 35 minutes, or until just set. Serve with Cognac-flavored, sweetened whipped cream, if desired.

Yields 6 to 8 servings

Can be prepared the day before or frozen.

TARTE À LA RHUBARBE
(Normandy Rhubarb Tart)

1 (10-in) Flaky Pastry tart	sugar
shell, unbaked, page 384	2 eggs
4 cups rhubarb cut in ¼-in	½ cup heavy cream
pieces	2 tablespoons butter, melted
¼ cup plus 2 tablespoons	Pinch of cinnamon

1. Preheat the oven to 350°F.

2.   Place the rhubarb in the pastry shell and sprinkle with the sugar. Bake 20 minutes.

3.   Meanwhile, in a bowl, mix the eggs, cream, butter, and cinnamon together. Pour the custard mixture over the baked rhubarb and bake 25 minutes longer, or until the custard tests done. Serve at room temperature.

Yields 8 to 10 servings

Best served the same day.

TARTE À LA RHUBARBE DAUPHINE
(Rhubarb Tart Dauphine)

1½ **pounds rhubarb, chopped**   2 **eggs**
  1 **(8-in) Flaky Pastry tart**   2 **tablespoons flour**
      shell, unbaked, page 384   ¼ **cup confectioners' sugar,**
  ¼ **cup heavy cream**   **plus additional for garnish**

1.   Preheat the oven to 400°F.

2.   Place the rhubarb in the tart shell.

3.   In a bowl, mix the cream, eggs, flour, and ¼ cup confectioners' sugar. Pour over the rhubarb. Bake for 35 minutes, or until set. Remove from the oven and sprinkle with confectioners' sugar.

Yields 6 to 8 servings

Best served the same day.

Chiffon Pies

These are the showstoppers of the pie world. Towering fillings as light as air, created by folding egg whites and sometimes whipped cream into a base stabilized with gelatin, contained in delicate pastry shells.

To thicken the base, use cornstarch with fruits, eggs with chocolate and pumpkin, and egg and cornstarch with lemon.

Gelatin stabilizes the filling, making it possible to mound it in the shell and, once set, to cut into neat slices. Gelatin is always unflavored, unless a flavor is specified. Because there is less gelatin per spoonful in flavored gelatin, substituting a flavored gelatin may prevent the dessert from setting properly. It is necessary to soften the gelatin in a liquid before heating to melt. Adding the gelatin to hot liquid directly will cause it to melt unevenly and can cause it to clump.

BRANDIED DATE CHIFFON PIE

1 cup dates, pitted and chopped	¼ cup sugar
½ cup brandy	Pinch of salt
1 tablespoon gelatin	1¾ cups heavy cream
¼ cup water	1 (9-in) Flaky Pastry pie shell, baked brown, page 384
1¼ cups milk	Sugar, to taste
2 eggs, separated	Brandy, to taste

1.   In a small bowl, soak the dates in the brandy overnight.

2.   In a bowl, soften the gelatin in the water.

3.   In a saucepan, cook the milk, egg yolks, sugar, and salt until thick enough to coat the back of a spoon, stirring constantly. Stir in the softened gelatin until dissolved. Cool and refrigerate until the custard is slightly thickened.

4.   Whip ¾ cup of cream in a bowl. In another bowl, beat the egg whites until stiff peaks form.

5.   Fold the egg whites, then the dates, and finally the cream into the custard mixture, and refrigerate until it is firm enough to mound slightly when dropped from a spoon. Pour into the pie shell and refrigerate for 1 hour.

6.   Meanwhile, whip the remaining cream. Sweeten with sugar and flavor with brandy to taste.

Yields 6 to 8 servings

Can be prepared the day before serving.

CHOCOLATE CHIFFON PIE

1 tablespoon gelatin	1½ cups heavy cream
1 cup sugar	1 (9-in) Graham Cracker or
½ teaspooon salt	Chocolate Wafer Crumb
1⅓ cups water	Crust, baked, page 391
2 ounces chocolate	¼ cup confectioners' sugar
3 eggs, separated	Chocolate Curls or Shavings,
2 teaspoons vanilla	page 42, for garnish

1.   In a saucepan, mix the gelatin, ½ cup of sugar, salt, water, and choco-late. Let stand 3 minutes to soften the gelatin, then place over low heat and cook, stirring, until the chocolate melts and the gelatin dissolves. Remove from the heat.

2.   Whisk in the egg yolks, return to the heat, and cook, stirring constantly, just until the mixture comes to a boil. Remove from the heat and place in a bowl of ice water. Refrigerate, stirring occasionally, until the mixture mounds when dropped from a spoon. Stir in 1 teaspoon of vanilla.

3.   In a mixer, beat the egg whites until they form soft peaks. Beat in the remaining sugar, a tablespoon at a time, and beat until stiff and glossy peaks form. Fold into the chocolate mixture. Beat ½ cup of the heavy cream until it holds soft peaks. Fold into the filling and pour it into the pie shell. Refriger-ate for 1 hour.

4.   Meanwhile, beat the remaining cream with the remaining vanilla until it starts to thicken. Sprinkle with the confectioners' sugar and beat until stiff peaks form. Using a pastry bag fitted with a #5 open star tip, or with a spatula, decorate the top of the pie with the cream and garnish with the chocolate curls.

Yields 6 to 8 servings

Can be prepared the day before or frozen.

COFFEE CHIFFON PIE

3 eggs, separated
1¼ cups sugar
3 tablespoons instant coffee granules
1 tablespoon gelatin
½ teaspoon salt
1½ cups milk

1 teaspoon vanilla
1½ cups heavy cream
1 (9-in) chocolate Crumb Crust or Flaky Pastry pie shell, baked, pages 391, 384
1 teaspoon rum

1. In a saucepan, mix the egg yolks, ½ cup of sugar, the coffee, gelatin, salt, and milk. Let stand 3 minutes to soften gelatin. Cook, over medium heat, stirring constantly, just until it reaches a boil. Remove from the heat and stir in the vanilla. Immediately place the pan in a bowl of ice water to stop the cooking. Refrigerate, stirring occasionally, until the mixture is thick enough to mound when dropped from a spoon.

2. In a mixer, beat the egg whites until foamy. Beat in ½ cup of sugar, 1 tablespoon at a time, until stiff peaks form, and fold into the coffee mixture.

3. In another bowl, beat ½ cup of cream until stiff peaks form, fold into the coffee mixture, and pile into the pie shell. Refrigerate for 1 hour.

4. Beat the remaining cream, sugar, and rum until stiff peaks form. Decorate the pie with the cream.

Yields 6 to 8 servings

Can be prepared the day before or frozen.

Variation

• *Liqueur-flavored.* Omit the coffee and stir 3 tablespoons of liqueur into the cooked custard.

LEMON CHIFFON PIE

4 eggs, separated
1 cup sugar
1 tablespoon gelatin
⅔ cup water
⅓ cup lemon juice
1 tablespoon grated lemon rind

1 (9-in) Flaky Pastry or Graham Cracker Crumb Crust, baked brown, pages 384, 391
1 cup heavy cream, whipped, sweetened, and flavored with vanilla, for garnish

1. In a saucepan, cook the egg yolks, ½ cup of sugar, the gelatin, water, and lemon juice over medium heat, stirring constantly just until the mixture boils. Stir in the lemon rind and place the pan in a bowl of ice water. Refrigerate, stirring occasionally, until the mixture is just thick enough to mound when dropped from a spoon.

2. Beat the egg whites until foamy and beat in the remaining sugar, 1 tablespoon at a time, until stiff peaks form. Fold into the lemon mixture and pile into the pie shell. Refrigerate several hours, or until set. Garnish with the whipped cream.

Yields 6 to 8 servings

Can be prepared the day before or frozen.

RASPBERRY CHIFFON PIE

Substitute pureed strawberries, peaches, or other favorite fruit for the raspberries, with a complementary liqueur.

1 tablespoon gelatin	1 (9-in) Sandtorte Pastry or
¼ cup framboise	Crumb Crust pie shell,
3 eggs, separated	baked brown, pages 386, 391
⅔ cup sugar	1½ cups heavy cream, whipped,
Pinch of salt	sweetened, and flavored with
1½ tablespoons lemon juice	framboise, for garnish
½ cup Raspberry Puree, page	1½ cups fresh raspberries, for
29	garnish
1 cup heavy cream	

1. In a saucepan, soften the gelatin in the framboise. Dissolve over low heat, stirring.

2. Beat the egg yolks with the sugar and salt until pale. Beat in the lemon juice and raspberry puree.

3. In a saucepan, cook over medium heat, stirring, until the mixture thickens. Remove from the heat and place in a bowl of ice water. Refrigerate, stirring occasionally, until the mixture is thick enough to mound when dropped from a spoon.

4. Using clean beaters, beat the egg whites until almost stiff and fold into the raspberry mixture. In the same bowl, beat the heavy cream until almost stiff and fold into the raspberry mixture.

5. Pile into the shell and refrigerate for 1 hour. Garnish with the whipped cream and raspberries.

Yields 6 to 8 servings

Can be prepared the day before or frozen.

Chapter 13

GÂTEAUX, TORTEN, AND CHOCOLATE DESSERTS

Here are the drop-dead, show-stopping, no-holds-barred efforts of the pastry cook. These desserts make us forget calories. Fortunately, a thin slice is often enough because they are so good they immediately satisfy both the eye and the taste buds.

These desserts often look complicated and would seem to require great skill and hours of arduous labor, but most are easily prepared. It is practice that gives them the professional look. They are combinations of a few basic preparations. Sponge cakes, nutted meringue layers, chocolate cutouts, buttercreams, and grated nuts can all be prepared ahead. And, because most of them freeze perfectly, it is possible to do much of the work well ahead to be prepared for that emergency gala. Also the icings enclose the cakes completely, and prevent the cake from turning stale, allowing you to prepare them several days before serving. Once assembled, most gâteaux (cakes), with the exception of those with meringue layers, freeze well.

There is no true definition of what a gâteau or torte is. It may be as simple as a whipped cream-covered sponge layer garnished with fresh fruit, or as elaborate as a combination of génoise, nutted layers, and cream puffs seasoned with fruit or liqueur syrups, filled with pastry cream, whipped cream, or buttercream, and decorated with fruits, nuts, chocolate, or various glazes.

Gâteaux are often big desserts. Plan your meal and make the dessert the star. Better still, invite guests for dessert and coffee and show off. For those less willing to indulge, add a mélange of fruits with some cookies to complete your dessert table. Serve a dessert wine or not-too-dry Champagne or perhaps an assortment of liqueur-flavored coffees or teas as well as a full-bodied, plain coffee and tea. Avoid coffees and teas flavored with spices or nuts, unless the flavors complement your dessert. Or, serve them as additional beverages—perhaps as desserts in their own right.

Some chocolate desserts are so special that I have placed them in a separate section at the end of this chapter. They are rich, intense, and delectable. Usually they are not very difficult to prepare, many can be made at least a day ahead, and most freeze well. Do not be concerned with names, there are probably dozens of "Deaths by Chocolate" or "Chocolate Decadences." No chef can claim these as hers alone. As with so many other culinary creations, when the time is right, and the stars are in alignment, many people come up with the same or very similar ideas.

Equipment

Even the most elaborate of torten requires only a few ordinary pieces of equipment—some cake pans, parchment or waxed paper, a pastry bag, and some pastry tips.

CAKE PANS   Most of the cakes require round pans. Select 9-inch pans with 2-inch sides to start your collection. You will want to add 8-inch pans later. Some desserts, charlottes, and many cheesecake recipes require a springform pan. Again, 9-inch is the most common size. Later you may want to add an 8- or 10-inch pan. Sheet or jelly roll pans are essential for every kitchen. They are not only important for baking but also have many uses for general cooking. Select sturdy, heavy tin or aluminum pans to avoid warping for even baking. For the recipes here you will need 10 × 15-inch and 11 × 17-inch sheet or jelly roll pans. They are available in many supermarkets and hardware stores.

PARCHMENT OR WAXED PAPER   Most professional cooks prefer parchment paper. They can purchase it in sheets cut to fit their sheet pans or cut into 8-, 9-, or 10-inch circles. The home cook may not find these readily available. Call a local bakery or bakery supply company, or try the gourmet mail order houses. Parchment paper is easy to use and sometimes allows you to omit buttering and flouring the pans. In almost every instance, waxed paper will serve as a suitable substitute.

To cut a paper circle to fit a specific pan, tear off a sheet large enough to cover the pan. Fold the sheet in half and in half again and keep folding to make a long, narrow triangle. Hold the tip of the triangle at the center of the pan and, with scissors, cut off the excess paper at the outside edge of the pan. Unfold and place in the pan. For a tube pan, cut the point where it meets the edge of the tube opening.

CARDBOARD ROUNDS   Professional bakers serve cakes on cardboard rounds slightly smaller than the cake. The rounds allow the icer to glaze the cakes evenly and simplifies moving the cakes. The cardboard rounds are available from bakery supply companies. If you only need one or two, cut them from a cardboard box and cover with aluminum foil.

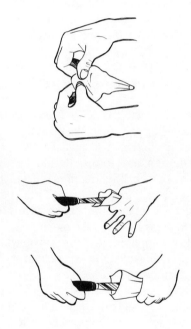

PASTRY BAGS AND TIPS   One of the most useful tools for the pastry cook is the pastry bag. Pastry bags make so many jobs easy and quick, although they seem to instill fear in the uninitiated. Select larger rather than smaller bags. I suggest 14-, 16-, and 18-inch bags for most uses. For the work in this book, you will not need many small bags for many different colors of icing. The cakes use the same icing to decorate the whole cake. If you are using a pastry bag (and I hope you will) to pipe meringues, cookies, or ladyfingers, it makes sense to have a bag that holds as much of the mixture as possible instead of constantly having to refill. Select supple cotton or Dacron bags. Stiff plastic bags make the piping awkward and difficult.

A paper cone is invaluable to pipe thin lines of chocolate over cakes. You can buy them ready-made, or make one by cutting a triangle of parchment or waxed paper. Place the triangle on a board, with the point toward you and the long side opposite the point, lift the left hand point and roll it so it meets the point facing you and repeat with the right hand point to form a cone. Work the points to tighten up the end of the cone and when it is tight, crimp the side to hold in place. Fill the cone and then snip the point to release the icing. Or, place the icing in a plastic bag and snip one corner.

Even the prettiest cakes require only a few pastry tips. If you plan to take up cake decorating in a serious way, such as making wedding or birthday cakes, you will want to invest in special tips for roses, drop flowers, and the like. For the cakes in this book, you will only need a few basic tips. The sizes here are for Ateco tips. Star tips in the larger sizes, already suggested for other desserts, such as #4, #5, #7, and #8, are perfect. For names or other writing, a large, plain tip #1 or #2 will serve nicely. You will need to have the larger #5, #7, and #8 plain tips for other preparations. Add to the list as you develop skill, or as other needs arise, rather than buy a set.

Using a Pastry Bag. To prevent the filling from oozing out of the tip while filling the bag, twist the bag just above the tip and press the bag into the tip. Place the bag in a tall container; I use a plastic juice pitcher. Fold the upper edge over the top of the container to keep the bag open. Scrape the icing into the bag, filling it no more than three-quarters full. Lift the bag over the top of the icing and twist to close. Place the twisted top of the bag between your thumb and first finger and let the other fingers gently wrap around the bag. Use only that hand to press the bag. Use the fingertips of the other hand to guide the bag, but do not apply any pressure or you will force the filling back out of the bag. Keep the outside of the bag clean so your hand can grip it firmly. Press the bag firmly at the start of the stroke, release the pressure, and finish the stroke. To practice, prepare instant mashed potatoes and pipe the mixture onto a counter or sheets of waxed paper. Scrape it up and repeat until you get the "feel" for stars, swirls, claws, etc.

Cheesecakes

Cheesecakes are amongst the simplest of desserts. Sprinkle a crumb base in the bottom of a springform or cake pan. In a mixer or a processor, puree cream cheese with sugar, possibly add sour or heavy cream, and beat in some eggs with flavoring. Turn into the pan and bake, sometimes in a water bath (see page 17), until set. Turn off the heat and cool in the oven. Refrigerate and garnish if directed.

To Unmold a Cheesecake. Run a knife around the edge of the pan. Release the sides and remove. Serve on the base of the pan, or, if desired, remove the base.

To remove the base, cover a plate with plastic wrap. Place on top of the cheesecake and turn the cake over onto the plate. Using a flexible metal spatula to help, remove the bottom of the pan. Place a platter on the bottom of the cheesecake and turn upright. Remove the plate and plastic wrap. If you are planning to remove the bottom of the pan, it is wise to line the pan with parchment before filling.

CRUMB BASE   Prepare the base from graham crackers, zwieback, crushed cookies such as gingersnaps, vanilla or chocolate wafers, or ground nuts. Add enough melted butter to moisten and sweeten with sugar, if needed. Press into the bottom of the pan and about ½ inch up the sides.

LINDY'S CHEESECAKE

For many years Lindy's restaurant in New York prepared the *sine qua non* of cheesecakes. This is an adaptation of their specialty.

¾ cup graham cracker crumbs	2 tablespoons cornstarch
2 pounds cream cheese, softened	1¼ teaspoons vanilla
2 cups sour cream	2 teaspoons grated lemon rind
½ cup butter, softened	2 teaspoons grated orange rind
1¼ cups sugar	1 teaspoon lemon juice
5 eggs, lightly beaten	

1.   Preheat the oven to 375°F. Butter the bottom and sides of a 9-inch springform pan and sprinkle with graham cracker crumbs. Wrap the outside of the pan in foil and prepare a water bath.

2.   In an electric mixer, beat the cream cheese until smooth. Beat in the sour cream and the butter until fully incorporated. Add the sugar, eggs, cornstarch, vanilla, lemon and orange rinds, and lemon juice. Beat on high speed for about 5 minutes, or until smooth.

3.   Pour into the prepared pan. Bake on the middle rack of the oven for 1 hour, or until the mixture sets and is golden on top. Turn off the oven and let the cake cool inside, with the door held ajar with a pot holder, for 1 hour. Cool in the water bath for 2 hours longer. Remove from the water bath and refrigerate overnight. Unmold.

Yields 10 to 12 servings

Can be prepared 2 days ahead or frozen.

GINGER CHEESECAKE

¾ pound pecans, ground	4 eggs, lightly beaten
2 tablespoons brown sugar	½ cup heavy cream
1 egg white, beaten until frothy	1 teaspoon vanilla
3 teaspoons ground ginger	1 cup minced ginger marmalade
1 teaspoon grated lemon rind	1 tablespoon grated gingerroot
2 pounds cream cheese, softened	1 ounce crystallized ginger, minced, optional
¾ cup sugar	

1. Preheat the oven to 300°F. Butter a 9-inch springform pan. In a bowl mix the pecans, brown sugar, egg white, 1 teaspoon of ground ginger, and lemon rind, and press across the bottom and ½ inch up the sides of the pan.

2. In an electric mixer, beat the cream cheese, sugar, eggs, cream, and vanilla until smooth. Beat in the ginger marmalade, remaining ground ginger, and grated gingerroot.

3. Pour into the pan and bake for 1 hour and 40 minutes. Cool in the turned-off oven for 1 hour with the door closed. Refrigerate until cold. Unmold. Before serving, sprinkle with candied ginger.

Yields 10 to 12 servings

Can be prepared 2 days ahead or frozen.

Variations

• Substitute ½ cup of crushed gingersnaps, ½ cup of crushed chocolate wafers, and ⅓ cup of melted butter for the pecans, brown sugar, egg white, ginger, and lemon rind.
• Garnish with 1 pint of blueberries, brushed with warm Currant Glaze (see page 36).

STRAWBERRY CHEESECAKE

This is one of the simplest and best cheesecakes.

½ cup graham cracker crumbs
2 pounds cream cheese, softened
4 eggs
1¾ cups sugar
Grated rind and juice of 1

lemon
1 teaspoon vanilla
1½ cups strawberries, hulled
Apricot Glaze, page 36, for garnish

1.   Preheat the oven to 325°F. Butter the inside of an 8-inch round cake pan with 3-inch sides and prepare a water bath. Sprinkle the inside of the pan with the crumbs and dump out the excess.

2.   In an electric mixer, beat the cream cheese, eggs, sugar, lemon rind, lemon juice, and vanilla until blended and smooth. Pour into the pan.

3.   Bake for 1½ hours. Cool in the turned-off oven for 30 minutes. Remove from the water bath and cool to room temperature. Unmold. Decorate with the strawberries and brush with the glaze. Refrigerate until ready to serve.

Yields 8 to 10 servings

Can be prepared 2 days ahead, or frozen.

Variation

· Substitute blueberries, raspberries, bananas, or other fruit for the strawberries.

Meringues

The basic recipe and preparation for meringues is in Chapter 1. Review that section before preparing these desserts. Besides large cakes, meringues are prepared in individual servings. Pipe shells or discs, and sandwich them with just enough filling to hold them together. Because these are so sweet, it is wise to make smaller individual servings, rather than larger. If the filling is moist, such as whipped cream, fill shortly before serving so the meringue does not become too soft. On the other hand, for large cakes, sometimes the goal is to soften the meringue. Fill it in advance so it will slice cleanly rather than be so crisp that it crumbles.

VACHERIN (Spanish Wind Torte)

This is a most impressive-looking dessert. Preparing the shell takes time, most of which is letting it dry in a slow oven.

2 recipes plain Meringue, page 23	2 cups fruit of choice (strawberries, peaches, raspberries, etc.), sliced or diced
1½ cups heavy cream	
2 tablespoons kirsch	
Sugar, to taste	

1.   Preheat the oven to 225°F. Fit a pastry bag with a #6 plain tip. On large baking sheets lined with parchment paper, draw five 8-inch circles. On a smaller baking sheet draw a 7-inch circle.

2.   Prepare one recipe of meringue. Fill a pastry bag fitted with a #5 plain tip with the meringue.

3.   Pipe the meringue in a spiral on one of the 8-inch circles, filling it in completely. On the remaining 8-inch circles, pipe 1-inch-thick rings around the outside edge of the drawn circles. On the 7-inch circle, spread a ½-inch layer of meringue smoothly. Put the remaining meringue into a pastry bag fitted with a #5 star tip. Pipe swirls of meringue on top of the 7-inch circle to make an attractive rococo design.

4.   Bake the meringues for about 45 minutes to an hour, or until set, white, and crisp. Prop the oven door open with a pot holder to prevent moisture from developing.

5. Dry in the turned-off oven. This can take about 4 hours longer, depending on the oven and the humidity. Set the 7-inch circle aside. (This is the top of the shell.) Place a fresh sheet of parchment on a baking sheet and place the 8-inch spiral circle on it. (This will be the base of the shell.)

6. Preheat the oven to 200°F. Prepare the second batch of meringue.

7. Frost the edge of the base with the meringue. Place one of the 8-inch meringue rings on top. Continue to stack the meringue rings to make a box, cementing them with the fresh meringue. Frost the outside of the box with a thin layer of meringue.

8. Fill another pastry bag, fitted with a #5 star tip, with the remaining fresh meringue and pipe swirls around the sides of the box. Pipe shell shapes around the base and pipe stars around the upper edge. Bake the shell for 1 hour, or until dry. Cool in the turned-off oven for 4 hours, or overnight, until dry and crisp.

9. Shortly before serving, whip the cream until it forms soft peaks. Add the kirsch and sugar, and beat until stiff.

10. Gently fold the fruit into the whipped cream and pile lightly into the vacherin shell. Place the 7-inch lid slightly askew on top.

Yields 8 to 10 servings

Serve within an hour of filling.

NOTE: Prepare the shell up to a week ahead and keep in an airy, dry place, or an airtight container to keep it crisp. Avoid preparing in humid weather unless fully air conditioned.

PAVLOVA

The national dessert of New Zealand and equally popular in Australia, this is a soft meringue version of the previous recipe.

4 **egg whites**	1 **cup heavy cream**
1 **cup sugar**	**Sugar, to taste**
4 **teaspoons cornstarch**	2 **cups cut-up fruit in season,**
2 **teaspoons vinegar**	**for garnish**
1 **teaspoon vanilla**	

1. Preheat the oven to 275°F. Butter a shallow 9 × 11-inch ovenproof serving dish.

2.   In an electric mixer, whip the egg whites until they hold soft peaks. Beat in the sugar, 1 tablespoon at a time, and beat until the mixture is stiff and glossy. Fold in the cornstarch, vinegar, and vanilla.

3.   With a rubber spatula, scrape into the prepared dish, pushing it up against sides and leaving the center hollow. Bake for 1¼ to 1½ hours, or until lightly browned. Cool.

4.   Just before serving, whip the cream to soft peaks and add sugar to taste. Pile into the meringue shell and garnish with the fruit. Serve from the pan.

Yield 6 to 8 servings

Can be prepared the day before filling.

MERINGUE CAKE WITH PEACHES

The meringue layers make this peach "shortcake" special indeed.

½ cup butter, softened	**¼ cup chopped walnuts or**
1½ cups sugar	**pecans**
4 eggs, separated	**1 cup heavy cream**
¼ cup milk	**2 tablespoons confectioners'**
½ teaspoon vanilla	**sugar**
1 cup flour	**2 fresh peaches, peeled, pitted**
1½ teaspoons baking powder	**and diced**
Pinch of salt	

1.   Preheat the oven to 350°F. Butter two 8-inch cake pans and line with waxed paper.

2.   In a processor, cream the butter and ½ cup of sugar until light and fluffy. Beat in the egg yolks, one at a time, and add the milk and the vanilla.

3.   Sift the flour and the baking powder together and add to the egg mixture, beating until just mixed. Divide between the pans and smooth the top.

4.   In an electric mixer, beat the egg whites and the salt until they form soft peaks and add the remaining sugar, 1 tablespoon at a time, beating until the mixture is stiff and glossy. Spread the meringue over the cake batter and sprinkle the nuts over 1 layer of meringue.

5.   Bake for 30 minutes, or until a knife inserted in the middle comes out clean. Cool on a rack for 10 minutes. Unmold carefully and cool with the meringue right side up.

6.   In a bowl, whip the cream and sweeten with the confectioners' sugar. Fold in the peaches.

7.   Place the plain meringue layer, meringue side down, on a cake plate. Spread with the whipped cream and peaches. Add the second layer, nutted side up. Refrigerate for 2 hours.

Yields 6 to 8 servings

Prepare the cakes the day before, but assemble shortly before serving.

CONCORDE

This adaptation of Gaston Le Notre's spectacular dessert, named for the Concorde jet, is no more than meringue layers with chocolate mousse.

1 recipe Cocoa Meringue,	**for Filling, page 249**
page 24	**Confectioners' sugar**
1 recipe Chocolate Mousse	

1.   Preheat the oven to 300°F. Butter and flour 2 baking sheets or cover with parchment.

2.   Draw three $10 \times 5\frac{1}{2}$-inch ovals on one of the baking sheets. Using a pastry bag fitted with a #5 plain tip, pipe out the meringue to fill the ovals on the baking sheet.

3.   Using a pastry bag fitted with a #4 plain tip, pipe meringue strips the length of the second baking sheet.

4.   Bake the strips about 50 minutes and check the color; they should be barely brown on the bottom and almost dry. Bake the disks about 1 hour and 20 minutes, or until dry and crisp. Cool.

5.   No more than 30 minutes before assembling, prepare the chocolate mousse.

6.   Place a meringue layer on a plate and spread with a layer of mousse. Cover with another meringue layer, spread with more mousse, and top with the final layer. Frost the top and sides of the cake with the remaining mousse.

7. With a sharp knife cut the chocolate meringue strips into 1-inch sections and press onto the sides and top of the cake.

8. Place a 2-inch strip of paper diagonally across the cake and sprinkle the top of the cake generously with confectioners' sugar. Remove the paper strip and refrigerate until ready to serve.

Yields 8 to 10 servings

Prepare up to 1 day before serving. Prepare the meringue layers weeks before, if desired. Store in an airtight container at room temperature.

NOTE: Spread the mousse lightly to form a thick coating. For the nicest effect, press the meringue strips haphazardly into the mousse.

Variation

• Pipe 3½-inch sticks of meringue. Arrange the sticks upright, like fence posts, around the assembled cake. Swirl the mousse on top attractively.

RASPBERRY–CHOCOLATE MERINGUE CAKE

1 recipe Cocoa Meringue, page 24	**chocolate**
8 ounces semisweet	**1 recipe Raspberry Mousse, see page 263**

1.   Preheat the oven to 300°F. Butter and flour a baking sheet or cover with parchment.

2.   Draw three $10 \times 5\frac{1}{2}$-inch ovals on one of the baking sheets. Using a pastry bag fitted with a #5 plain tip, pipe out the meringue to fill the ovals on the baking sheet. (See illustration.) Use all of the meringue making the ovals.

3.   Bake about 1 hour and 20 minutes, or until dry and crisp. Cool.

4.   Melt 4 ounces of the chocolate. Line a baking sheet with waxed paper and spread the chocolate on the paper and refrigerate until firm. Break the chocolate into small flakes.

5.   Reserve 1½ cups of the mousse. Fold the chocolate flakes into the remaining mousse. Spread half of the mousse with the chocolate flakes on a meringue layer, cover with a second meringue layer. Spread the remaining mousse on top.

6.   Melt the remaining chocolate. Spread a thin layer on the smooth side of the third meringue layer. Refrigerate until the chocolate is firm. Place on the cake, chocolate side up, and press down gently. Spread the mousse that oozes out between the layers around the cake, thinly.

7.   Make a chocolate band with the remaining melted chocolate. (See page 42.) Wrap the strips around the cake. Refrigerate any unused chocolate until firm and break into flakes.

8.   Pipe the reserved mousse through a pastry bag fitted with a #5 star tip around the top edge of the cake. Sprinkle the center of the top of the cake with the chocolate flakes. Refrigerate until ready to serve.

Yields 8 servings

Best served the same day.

GÂTEAU D'AUTOMNE (Autumn Meringue Cake)

This is another adaptation of a LeNôtre dessert.

3 (7-in) plain Meringue	**for Filling, page 249**
layers, page 23	**6 ounces semisweet chocolate**
½ recipe Chocolate Mousse	

1.   Spread each meringue layer with some of the chocolate mousse.

Assemble and frost the entire cake with the remaining chocolate mousse. Refrigerate for 1 hour.

2.   Melt the chocolate. Make Chocolate Ruffles and Chocolate Bands (see pages 41–42).

3.   Arrange the ruffles on the cake, starting at the outside edge and working in concentric circles toward the center. Wrap the bands of chocolate around the sides of the cake, placing them under any overhanging frill. Refrigerate until ready to serve.

Yields 8 servings

Can be prepared the day before serving.

Variations

• *Lemon Curd Cake.*   Substitute Lemon Curd (see page 28), for the chocolate mousse.
• For a lighter dessert, use Lemon Soufflé (see page 254), but first stabilize the mousse with gelatin or it will ooze out as the cake sets.

MERINGUE CUPS WITH VARIOUS FILLINGS

12 plain Meringue cups,
  page 24
  3 cups filling, see Variations

1.   About 1 hour before serving, fill the cups and garnish.

2.   Refrigerate until ready to serve.

Yields 12 servings

The meringue cups can be prepared weeks ahead and stored in an airtight container.

Variations

• *Cream.* Whip 1 cup of heavy cream and flavor with vanilla. Fold in 1½ cups of the fruit of your choice.
• *Fruit.* Fill the cups with berries or diced fruit, mixed with kirsch, orange, or other liqueur. Top with a dollop of whipped cream.
• *Ganache.* Fill with Ganache (see page 34), and garnish with shaved chocolate. White chocolate shavings give a nice contrast.

- *Lemon.* Fill with Lemon Curd (see page 28), and garnish with fresh berries.
- *Orange.* Fill with Orange Curd filling (see page 28), and garnish with grated chocolate, Candied Orange pieces (see page 38), or minced Chocolate Coated Orange Rind (see page 527).
- *Alternate Method Mousse.* Fill meringue cups with a mousse from Chapter 7.

Meringue Shells. Pipe the meringue in large shells using a #8 open star tip. Once baked, press the flat side slightly to make an indentation and fill with whipped cream, buttercream, or lemon or orange curd. Sandwich two halves and, to further enhance them, spread the outside of the shells thinly with the filling and roll in grated chocolate, ground nuts, or coconut.

CHOCOLATE AND COFFEE DACQUOISE

This version has a lot of filling in relation to the amount of succès. It is equally delicious made in 10- or even 12-inch layers using the same quantities.

10 ounces semisweet	**25**
chocolate, chopped	**4 cups Coffee Buttercream,**
5½ cups heavy cream	**page 31**
¼ cup confectioners' sugar	**¾ cup toasted sliced almonds**
4 (8-in) Succès circles, page	

1. Melt the chocolate in 3½ cups of the heavy cream. Stir until smooth. Refrigerate the ganache about 1 hour, or until cold, stirring occasionally.

2. Whip the chocolate ganache to soft peaks and refrigerate for half an hour.

3. Whip the remaining cream and the confectioners' sugar until firm peaks form.

4. Place one of the succès layers on a serving platter and spread with the ganache. Top with another succès layer and spread with half of the buttercream. Add a third succès layer and spread with the whipped cream. Top with the last succès layer, flat side up. Spread the top and sides of the cake with the remaining buttercream. Press the almonds against the side. Refrigerate until ready to serve. Serve cold or at room temperature.

Yields 8 to 10 servings

Can be prepared 2 days before serving or frozen.

NOTE: This particular version has an undecorated top. Spread with the remaining ganache or dust with confectioners' sugar if you want a more finished look.

Variations

- *Chocolate Mousse*. Fill the layers with Chocolate Mousse for filling (see page •••). Sprinkle the top layer with confectioners' sugar.
- *Ganache*. Fill layers with Ganache (see page 34).
- *Hazelnut*. Prepare succès with hazelnuts and substitute 4 cups of Praline Buttercream (see page 31) for the Coffee Buttercream.
- *Dacquoise with Raspberry Pastry Cream Filling*. Bake the succès in an 11 × 17 inch rectangle and cool. Cut into 3 long strips. Spread one layer with 1 cup Vanilla Pastry Cream (see page 26). Add another succès layer spread with 1 cup of pastry cream and arrange 1 cup raspberries on the cream. Cover with the final succès layer and sprinkle generously with confectioners' sugar. Refrigerate until set. Trim the sides and serve garnished with ½ cup of raspberries and pass the raspberry sauce (see page 552).

SMALL DACQUOISE CAKES

These small cakes are oval or circular sandwiches of succès.

20 (2½-in) Succès circles, page 25	**filling, page 349 or Classic Buttercream, page 31**
2 cups Chocolate Mousse for	**Chocolate Glaze, page 35**

1.   Sandwich the succès layers with half the mousse.

2.   Frost the tops and sides with the remaining mousse. Refrigerate about 2 hours, or until set.

3.   Coat with chocolate glaze and let stand until set.

Yields 10 cakes

Can be prepared the day before serving. For the fullest flavor, let come almost to room temperature before serving.

NOTE: Professional bakers assemble each cake in metal rings to make perfect circles or ovals. Once chilled, they wipe the sides with a warm sponge to release the cakes. You can use thin sheets of foil-wrapped cardboard shaped into rings, and cut them off once the filling sets. Smooth the sides with a spatula dipped in hot water if needed. Or, leave them more free-form.

Variations

- *Almond-Raisin Buttercream.* Soak ½ cup of raisins in 1½ tablespoons of rum for 30 minutes. Spread half the succès layers with rum-flavored buttercream, and sprinkle with the raisins. Top with remaining layers of succès and coat with the remaining buttercream. Refrigerate until set. Coat with the Chocolate Glaze (see page 35).
- *Chocolate Buttercream.* Substitute 2 cups of Chocolate Buttercream (see page 31) for the mousse.
- *Cocoa-Dusted.* Fill and frost the succès layers with chocolate mousse. Refrigerate until set and sprinkle with ⅓ cup of sugar sifted with 2 tablespoons of cocoa powder in place of the chocolate glaze.
- *Hazelnut.* Substitute Almond Buttercream (see page 31) for the mousse. Frost half the succès layers and sprinkle each cake with hazelnuts. Top with the remaining succès layers and spread with 1 tablespoon of the remaining buttercream. Refrigerate until set. Serve sprinkled with confectioners' sugar or coat with Chocolate Glaze.

Nutted Cakes

Nuts are the base of many cakes. Sometimes nuts replace all the flour or starch and in other cakes they are mixed with the starch to create an interesting texture.

MOCHA WALNUT ROLL

1 cup heavy cream	2 tablespoons dark rum
⅓ cup strong coffee	11 × 17-in Basic Nut Cake
12 ounces semisweet	prepared with walnuts and
chocolate, chopped	rolled, page 22
4 tablespoons butter,	12–14 walnut halves, for garnish
softened	

1. In a saucepan or a microwave, bring the cream and the coffee to a boil. Remove from the heat and stir in the chocolate. Cool for 5 minutes. Add the butter and rum and whisk until smooth. Refrigerate until cold and whip until fluffy.

2. Unroll the cake and place on a sheet of waxed or parchment paper. Spread half of the ganache over the cake. Starting from one of the long sides, roll the cake. Wrap in the waxed paper and seal. Refrigerate for 30 minutes.

3.   Unwrap and place on a platter. Spread the remaining ganache over the roll and draw a fork through the ganache to make a design. Trim the ends and arrange the walnuts on the top.

4.   Refrigerate until ready to serve.

Yields 12 to 14 servings

Can be prepared the day before or frozen.

ILONA TORTE

Mocha buttercream fills and covers walnut-chocolate cake layers.

1 cup sugar	1¾ plus ⅔ cups chopped
¼ cup water	walnuts
5 ounces semisweet	2 tablespoons dried bread
chocolate, chopped	crumbs
6 tablespoons butter,	3 cups Mocha Buttercream,
softened	page 31
8 eggs, separated	Walnut halves, for garnish

1.   Preheat the oven to 375°F.

2.   Butter a 10-inch springform pan and line with waxed paper. Butter and flour the paper and sides of the pan.

3.   In a saucepan, dissolve the sugar and the water over medium heat. Add the chocolate, remove from the heat, and stir until the chocolate melts. Cool for 15 minutes.

4.   In an electric mixer, cream the butter until light. Beat in the egg yolks, one at a time. Add the chocolate mixture, 1¾ cups of walnuts, and the bread crumbs, mixing after each addition.

5.   In another bowl, using clean beaters, beat the egg whites to form stiff peaks. In two batches, fold the egg whites into the chocolate mixture and pour into the pan.

6.   Bake for 35 to 40 minutes, or until the center feels firm when pressed. Cool in the pan for 15 minutes. Unmold onto a rack covered with a paper towel. Remove the pan bottom and the waxed paper. Cool.

7. Split the torte into two layers. Set aside 1 cup of buttercream. Fill and frost the cake with the remaining buttercream, spreading it smoothly. Press the remaining chopped walnuts onto the sides of the cake.

8. Fit a pastry bag with a #4 open star tip and pipe rosettes of the remaining buttercream around the rim of the cake. Place a walnut on each rosette.

Yields 10 to 12 servings

Can be made the day before or frozen.

BLACK BREAD TORTE

Pumpernickel bread crumbs give an extraordinary flavor to this walnut-chocolate cake. Serve with whipped cream or ice cream.

¼ **cup rum**	⅓ **cup ground walnuts**
2 **cups pumpernickel bread crumbs**	¾ **cup grated semisweet chocolate**
6 **eggs, separated**	1½ **cups heavy cream, whipped, sweetened, and flavored with rum**
Pinch of salt	
1 **cup sugar**	
1 **teaspoon vanilla**	

1. Preheat the oven to 350°F. Butter the bottom but not the sides of a 9-inch tube pan.

2. In a bowl, pour the rum over the bread crumbs, mix, and set aside.

3. Beat the egg whites with the salt until they hold soft peaks. Add the sugar, 1 tablespoon at a time, and beat until the mixture holds stiff peaks.

4. In another bowl, stir the egg yolks and the vanilla together. Fold one-fourth of the egg whites into the yolk mixture. Fold in the bread crumb mixture, nuts, and chocolate. Fold in the remaining egg whites. Pour into the prepared pan.

5. Bake 50 to 60 minutes, or until the cake is brown and springy to the touch. Cool in the pan before removing. Serve with the whipped cream.

Yields 10 to 12 servings

Prepare the day before.

HAZELNUT TORTE

Versions of this classic cake appear on many fine dessert tables.

11 × 17-inch Basic Nut Cake, prepared with hazelnuts, page 22	**11 Chocolate Circles, page 44**
4 cups Classic Buttercream, page 31	**4 ounces semisweet chocolate, melted**
	11 Chocolate-dipped Hazelnuts, page 527

1. Cut the cake into four 4 × 11-inch layers. Set aside 1 cup of buttercream.

2. Place one layer on the back of a baking sheet and spread with buttercream. Repeat with the other layers and buttercream. Spread the sides and the top with more buttercream. Refrigerate for 1 hour.

3. Cut the chocolate circles in half and press them against the base of the cake round side up.

4. Using a paper cone, pipe the melted chocolate in diagonal lines in two directions over the top of the cake to create a crosshatch design. Score the cake into 1-inch slices.

5. Using a pastry bag fitted with a #4 open star tip, pipe a rosette of the reserved buttercream in the center of each slice and top with a hazelnut. Refrigerate until set and transfer to a serving platter.

Yields 11 servings

Can be prepared 2 days ahead or frozen.

Variations

• Bake as 2 (9-inch) round cakes.
• Substitute Hazelnut-flavored Buttercream (see page 31) for the vanilla.
• Fill with a layer of Chocolate Ganache or Chocolate Buttercream (see page 31) and 2 layers of hazelnut buttercream.

PECAN ROLL WITH
CHOCOLATE WHIPPED CREAM

4 eggs, separated	1 cup heavy cream
1 cup sifted confectioners' sugar, plus additional, for garnish	3 tablespoons sugar
	2 teaspoons cocoa
	½ teaspoon vanilla
2 cups ground pecans	

1. Preheat the oven to 375°F. Butter an 11 × 17-inch jelly roll pan, line with parchment or waxed paper and butter the paper.

2. In a bowl, beat the egg yolks with 1 cup of confectioners' sugar until thickened and pale.

3. Using clean beaters, beat the egg whites until stiff, but not dry, peaks form. Fold the pecans into the egg yolk mixture, then fold in the whites.

4. Spread evenly in the pan and bake for 15 to 20 minutes, or until lightly browned. It will spring back when touched on the surface. Remove from the pan. Starting from one of the long sides, roll the cake lengthwise, still covered with the paper, and cool.

5. In a bowl, beat the cream, sugar, cocoa, and vanilla until the mixture forms soft peaks. Unroll the cooled cake and peel off the paper. Spread with the cream and reroll. Place on a serving plate. Dust the top with confectioners' sugar.

Yields 12 servings

Prepare the cake the day before and fill up to 6 hours before serving.

Variations

- Substitute almonds, hazelnuts or walnuts for the pecans.
- Omit the cocoa and flavor the cream with 1 teaspoon of vanilla and 1 tablespoon of kirsch, orange-, or nut-flavored liqueur.
- Fold 1 cup of fruit or berries into the cream.
- Use 2 cups of Lemon or Orange Curd (see page 28) for the filling.
- Fill the cake with 2 cups of a favorite buttercream (see pages 31–33).
- Omit the cocoa and flavor the cream with 1 teaspoon of ground ginger and ½ cup of minced crystallized ginger.

PARROZZO (Almond and Chocolate Cake)

5 tablespoons plus 4 teaspoons butter	5 eggs, separated
1 cup almonds	½ teaspoon vanilla
¾ cup sugar	5 ounces semisweet chocolate
½ cup flour	1 tablespoon water
6 tablespoons potato flour or potato starch	Chocolate Strands or Vermicelli, page 45, for garnish
Pinch of cinnamon	

1.   Preheat the oven to 350°F. Butter and flour a 9-inch cake pan. Melt the 5 tablespoons of butter and allow it to cool.

2.   In a processor, grind the almonds with 3 tablespoons of sugar. In a bowl, sift the flour, potato flour, and cinnamon.

3.   In a large bowl, beat the egg yolks, vanilla and the remaining sugar until thickened and pale. Beat in the ground almond mixture. Add the flour mixture, a little at a time, beating between each addition. Beat in the cooled melted butter.

4.   In a mixer, beat the egg whites until stiff, but not dry, peaks form and fold into the batter. Pour into the prepared pan and bake for 40 minutes, or until it tests done. Cool in the pan and unmold.

5.   Melt the chocolate with the remaining butter and the water. Stir until smooth. Pour over the cake and spread evenly. Let the chocolate glaze set for 30 minutes. Decorate with the chocolate strands.

Yields 8 to 10 servings

Can be prepared the day before serving or frozen.

PINE NUT ALMOND AND BERRY TORTE

6 eggs, separated
1¼ cups ground blanched
   almonds
1 cup sugar
⅓ cup flour
½ teaspoon baking powder
Pinch of salt
Pinch of cream of tartar
½ cup lightly toasted pine
   nuts

1 cup heavy cream
1 tablespoon confectioners'
   sugar
1 teaspoon vanilla
1 pint strawberries, hulled
½ pint blackberries
½ cup currant jelly, melted
Slivered blanched almonds

1. Preheat the oven to 350°F. Butter a 10-inch springform pan.

2. In a bowl, beat the egg yolks until thickened and pale. Beat in the almonds and ½ cup of sugar.

3. In another bowl, mix the flour and baking powder. Stir into the almond mixture.

4. In a mixer, beat the egg whites with the salt and cream of tartar until they hold soft peaks. Gradually add the remaining sugar and beat until the mixture holds firm peaks. Fold into the almond mixture, with the pine nuts, one-third at a time.

5. Pour into the prepared pan. Bake for 40 minutes, or until it tests done. Cool on a rack. Remove the cake from the pan.

6. In a bowl, whip the cream, confectioners' sugar, and vanilla until stiff. Spread one-fourth of the whipped cream on top of the cake. Put the remaining cream into a pastry bag fitted with a #5 open star tip. Pipe a border on top of the cake.

7. Arrange the berries in the center. Brush the fruit with the currant jelly and sprinkle the slivered almonds around the edge of the fruit.

Yields 8 to 10 servings

Prepare the cake up to 4 days before serving or freeze. Garnish no more than 6 hours before serving.

TARTE AU CITRON (Lemon Tart)

"Tart" as in shape, "tart" as in flavor, this is a nutted cake layer topped with lemon slices and "frosted" with nutted meringue.

3 eggs, separated	**1 tablespoon flour**
1 cup sugar	**2 lemons, peeled and thinly**
Grated rind of 1 lemon	**sliced**
1¾ cups finely ground almonds	**2 egg whites**

1.   Preheat the oven to 350°F. Butter an 8-inch springform pan.

2.   Beat the egg yolks and ¾ cup of sugar until thickened and pale. Beat in the lemon rind and mix well. Blend in 1 cup of almonds and the flour.

3.   In a bowl, using clean beaters, beat 3 egg whites until stiff peaks form. Fold into the almond mixture. Pour into the pan. Bake for 20 minutes, or until the cake is lightly browned.

4.   Remove from the oven and cover the top with overlapping lemon slices. Beat the remaining whites until they form soft peaks. Gradually beat in the remaining sugar and fold in the remaining almonds.

5.   With a spatula dipped in cold water, carefully spread the egg white mixture evenly over the lemon slices, covering them completely. Bake for 15 minutes, or until the meringue is golden. Remove the sides of pan and serve.

Yields 6 to 8 servings

Although it can be prepared the day before serving, it is best served on the same day.

MACEDONIAN ORANGE CAKE

This is a particularly delicious cake, presented simply.

4 ounces unsweetened	**Grated rind and juice of 1**
chocolate	**orange**
9 eggs, separated	**Pinch of salt**
2 cups confectioners' sugar	**⅔ cup butter**
1 cup ground almonds	**2 whole eggs**

1.   Preheat the oven to 350°F. Line the bottom of a 10-inch springform pan with parchment paper or waxed paper. Melt the chocolate and bring to room temperature.

2. In a bowl, beat the 9 egg yolks with 1 cup of the confectioners' sugar until thickened and pale. Beat in the almonds, orange rind, and orange juice.

3. Using clean beaters, beat 9 egg whites and the salt until they form soft peaks. Fold into the almond mixture and pour into the prepared pan. Bake 1 hour, or until it tests done. Cool in the pan.

4. In a processor, cream the butter and the remaining confectioners' sugar. Blend in the chocolate and the whole eggs.

5. Remove the cake from the pan, and place on a serving plate. Frost the cake with the icing.

Yields 8 to 10 servings

Can be prepared the day before serving or can be frozen.

STRAWBERRY-WALNUT CREAM CAKE

4 eggs	**¾ cup flour**
½ cup sugar	**½ cup chopped walnuts**
1 tablespoon instant coffee granules	**1 pint strawberries, hulled**
	1 cup heavy cream, whipped

1. Preheat the oven to 350°F. Butter an 8-inch cake pan and sprinkle with sugar and flour.

2. In a mixer, beat the eggs, sugar, and coffee until the mixture thickens to the consistency of mayonnaise. Gently fold in the flour and the walnuts.

3. Pour into the pan. Bake for 30 to 35 minutes, or until the cake springs back when touched. Unmold onto a wire rack and cool.

4. Set aside 6 to 8 whole strawberries and slice the remainder. Whip the cream until it forms soft peaks. Fold the sliced berries into two-thirds of the whipped cream.

5. Cut the cake in half horizontally and fill with the plain whipped cream. Top with the other layer and spread with the strawberry-flavored whipped cream. Garnish with the whole strawberries.

Yields 6 to 8 servings

Fill no more than 6 hours before serving.

FONDANT DE NOIX AU CHOCOLAT
(Walnut Fondant)

4 egg yolks	1 cup plus 2 tablespoons
1½ cups confectioners' sugar	butter, softened
2½ teaspoons cornstarch	3 cups finely chopped walnuts
2½ teaspoons flour	Walnut halves, for garnish
5 tablespoons kirsch	Chocolate Sauce, page 540
1½ cups heavy cream	

1.   Line the bottom of a 1-quart charlotte mold with parchment. In a bowl, beat the egg yolks and ¼ cup of sugar until thickened and pale. Beat in the cornstarch and the flour. Blend in the kirsch.

2.   In a saucepan, bring the cream to a boil and stir into the yolk mixture. Return to the saucepan and cook, stirring constantly, until the mixture just comes to a boil and thickens. Refrigerate, covered, until cold.

3.   In a mixer, cream the butter and the remaining 1¼ cups of sugar until smooth. Whisk in the cooled cream mixture and fold in the walnuts. Pour into the mold and refrigerate about 4 hours, or until firm.

4.   Unmold and garnish with walnut halves. Serve with the sauce.

Yields 8 servings

Can be prepared up to 2 days before serving.

KARIDOPETA (Nut Cake)

Like so many Middle Eastern desserts, this Greek nut cake is moistened with a sugar syrup.

6 eggs, separated	8 zwieback, crushed
1¾ cups sugar	Grated rind of 1 orange
1 teaspoon vanilla	2¼ cups water
1½ cups ground walnuts	Cinnamon stick
1½ cups ground blanched	1 lemon slice
almonds	¼ cup light rum

1.   Preheat oven to 350°F. Butter a 13 × 9-inch baking pan.

2.   In a bowl, beat the egg yolks with ¾ cup of sugar until thickened and pale. Beat in the vanilla. Stir in the nuts, zwieback, and orange rind.

3.   Using clean beaters, beat the egg whites until stiff peaks form. Fold into the nut mixture. Pour into the prepared pan and bake for 1 hour, or until it tests done.

4.   Meanwhile, in a saucepan, simmer the remaining sugar, water, cinnamon, and lemon, until the sugar dissolves. Remove from the heat and stir in the rum.

5.   As soon as the cake is removed from the oven, pour the hot syrup over the cake. Cool before serving. Cut into diamond shapes.

Yields 24 servings

Can be prepared several days before serving.

ALMOND PASSOVER CAKE

4 eggs, separated	**½ teaspoon almond extract**
½ cup plus 2 tablespoons sugar	**1 pint large strawberries, hulled and sliced, for garnish**
¾ cup ground blanched almonds	**Sugar, for garnish**

1.   Preheat the oven to 350°F. Oil an 8-inch springform pan and dust with matzoh meal.

2.   In a mixer, beat the egg yolks until foamy. Add the measured sugar. Beat until thickened and pale. Mix in the almonds and the almond extract.

3.   Using clean beaters, beat the egg whites until stiff peaks form. Fold into the almond mixture.

4.   Pour into the prepared pan. Bake for 30 to 35 minutes, or until golden and it tests done. Cool. Serve topped with the strawberries, and sprinkled with the sugar.

Yields 6 to 8 servings

Can be prepared the day before or can be frozen.

Fruitcakes and Cakes with Fruit

Fruitcake, the Christmas specialty, is among the finest of desserts. It is, perhaps, even more wonderful for tea in July than after a heavy Christmas dinner. It is also much maligned. It seems every year writers attempt to outdo themselves with comic comments about the eternity of these cakes. They claim there are only ten that pass from house to house, etc. The commercial offerings may be less than pleasing, with too much dry cake and too few, yet still too many, gummy fruits.

I offer only one recipe for this type of cake. It has a small amount of cake holding together a plethora of fruit. Wrap it in brandy- or rum-soaked cloths for at least a month to mature the flavor. The longer it sits the more the flavor improves, within reason. Many of the versions of fruitcake concentrate on the quantity and proof of the alcohol. A student of mine from Jamaica insisted her rum cake was only suitable when prepared with 150 proof rum. She was right as long as the only interest was the rum. A true fruitcake should have a balance of fruit and liquor flavors.

Also included in this chapter are cakes with fruit which are cake batters with fruit added to them. Usually there is more batter by far than there is fruit, such as in Blueberry Pound Cake (see page 458). Serve these for tea or when you want a simpler sweet.

DARK FRUITCAKE

Leo White, my mentor, prepared great quantities of these every year to sell through his catering business. Customers shipped them around the world, wrapped in white cloths soaked in brandy, greaseproof paper, and plain brown paper. (This was before plastic wrap.)

2½ **cups butter, softened**	2½ **teaspoons cinnamon**
3¾ **cups brown sugar**	2½ **teaspoons mace**
10 **eggs**	2½ **teaspoons allspice**
3¾ **cups raisins**	2½ **teaspoons ground cloves**
3¾ **cups currants**	2½ **teaspoons lemon extract**
2½ **cups citron**	**Brandy or rum, as needed**
10 **cups flour**	**Confectioners' Sugar Glaze**
2½ **cups molasses**	**page 36**
2½ **cups milk**	

1.   Preheat the oven to 300°F. Butter five 9 × 5-inch loaf pans, line with parchment paper, and butter the paper.

2. In an electric mixer, cream the butter and add the brown sugar. Beat until light and fluffy. Add the eggs gradually, beating well after each addition.

3. In a very large bowl or pot, combine the raisins, currants, and citron, and mix well. Add 1 cup of flour and toss to coat the fruit. By hand, fold in the butter mixture with the molasses, milk, spices, lemon extract, and the remaining flour. Mix all the ingredients until evenly combined.

4. Spoon into prepared pans, smoothing the tops. Bake for 1½ hours, or until it tests done.

5. Unmold, peel off the parchment, and place the cakes on a rack. Spoon 2 tablespoons of the brandy over each cake and let cool.

6. Cut squares of cotton sheeting or cheesecloth large enough to wrap each cake. In a bowl, soak the cloths in 1 cup of brandy. Wrap each cake with one of the brandy-soaked cloths and then wrap in plastic wrap. Store in an airtight container for at least 1 month before serving.

7. After a month check the cakes. If keeping longer, you may need to soak the cloths in more brandy. Check the cakes monthly.

8. Before serving, drizzle the glaze over the cakes, letting it run down the sides.

Yields 5 loaves

The cakes will keep up to a year wrapped in liqueur-soaked cloths in an airtight container.

NOTE: The quantities may seem large, but if you are doing this much work, making some to give away or to keep for use over the year makes sense.

Variation

• Substitute Candied Orange or Lemon Rind (see page 39), candied pineapple, or glacéed cherries for some of the raisins, currants, and citron.

PANFORTE (Sienese Christmas Cake)

This is very different from the traditional British/American fruitcake. It is more like a candy and equally delicious.

½ **cup finely ground almonds**
4 **cups blanched almonds**
2 **cups chopped Candied Lemon Rind, page 39**
2 **cups chopped candied orange rind, page 39**
1 **cup blanched hazelnuts**
Grated rind of 1 orange
Grated rind of 1 lemon
¼ **teaspoon ground cloves**
¼ **teaspoon cinnamon**

¼ **teaspoon ground coriander**
¼ **teaspoon nutmeg**
1 **cup ground almonds or hazelnuts**
¼ **cup flour**
2 **cups sugar**
1 **cup honey**
¼ **cup butter**
1 **teaspoon salt**
Confectioners' sugar

1.   Preheat the oven to 300°F. Butter two 9-inch springform pans. Line the bottom and sides with parchment paper and butter the paper. (If using a tart pan with fluted sides, line the bottom and butter the sides well without lining.) Dust the pans with the ½ cup of finely ground almonds.

2.   In a large bowl, combine the blanched almonds, candied lemon and orange rinds, blanched hazelnuts, grated orange and lemon rinds, cloves, cinnamon, coriander, nutmeg, remaining ground almonds, and flour.

3.   In a large saucepan, heat the sugar, honey, butter, and salt over low heat until the sugar melts. Increase the heat and cook, stirring, until mixture registers 260°F. Pour over the nut mixture and mix well.

4.   Divide between the pans. Bake about 35 minutes, or until bubbles appear on the surface. Cool in the pans.

5.   Sift a thick layer of confectioners' sugar onto a sheet of waxed paper and invert the cakes onto the sugar. Remove the pans and the parchment paper. Sprinkle generously with confectioners' sugar. Turn the cakes right side up. Store in an airtight container for at least a week before serving.

Yields 16 to 24 servings

Can be prepared up to 6 months before serving.

HOT APPLE CAKE WITH CARAMEL SAUCE

1 cup butter	½ teaspoon salt
1 cup sugar	3 apples, peeled, cored, and
2 eggs	chopped
1½ cups flour	¾ cup chopped walnuts
1 teaspoon nutmeg	1 teaspoon vanilla
1 teaspoon cinnamon	Caramel Sauce II, page 539
1 teaspoon baking soda	

1.   Preheat the oven to 350°F. Butter a 10-inch pie pan and set aside.

2.   In a bowl, cream the butter and sugar until light and fluffy. Beat in the eggs one at a time.

3.   Sift together the flour, nutmeg, cinnamon, baking soda, and salt. Stir into the butter mixture with the apples, nuts, and vanilla. Pour into the pie pan. Bake about 45 minutes, or until lightly browned. Serve warm or at room temperature with the caramel sauce.

Yields 6 to 8 servings

Can be prepared the day before.

GÂTEAU AUX POMMES LYONNAISE (Apple Cake from Lyon)

1½ cups sugar	1 pound apples, peeled, cored,
5 eggs	and sliced
Pinch of salt	⅓ cup sliced almonds
Grated rind of 1 lemon	½ cup Praline Powder, page 30
½ teaspoon almond extract	½ cup butter, melted
2½ tablespoons oil	Heavy cream or Crème
⅔ cup milk	Fraîche, page 39
2½ cups cake flour	
2 teaspoons baking powder	

1.   Preheat the oven to 375°F. Butter and flour a 9-inch springform pan.

2.   In a bowl, beat ¾ cup of sugar and 3 eggs until thickened and pale. Add the salt, lemon rind, and almond extract. Mix well. Beat in the oil and the milk.

3.   Sift the flour and the baking powder together. Add to the batter and blend well. Pour into the prepared pan.

4.   Arrange half the apple slices neatly over the batter, leaving a ½-inch border. Sprinkle the almonds over the apples and sprinkle with 2 table-spoons of praline powder. Cover with the remaining apples and sprinkle with 2 more tablespoons of praline powder.

5.   Bake for 30 minutes, or until it tests done.

6.   Meanwhile, beat the remaining eggs and sugar into the melted butter. Set aside.

7.   Remove the cake from the oven and prick the top in several places with a small knife. Pour the egg mixture over the cake and let soak in. Sprinkle with the remaining praline powder and bake for 15 minutes, or until it tests done. Remove from the oven and cool. Let stand for one day before serving.

8.   Unmold the cake and serve with the heavy cream or crème fraîche.

Yields 8 to 10 servings

Can be frozen.

BLUEBERRY POUND CAKE

2 **cups blueberries**	1 **cup butter, softened**
2 **tablespoons grated lemon**	1 **cup sugar**
rind	4 **eggs**
2 **cups flour**	

1.   Preheat the oven to 300°F. Lightly butter a 6-cup loaf or tube pan.

2.   In a bowl, mix the blueberries, lemon rind, and 3 tablespoons of flour.

3.   In a large bowl, cream the butter and sugar until light and fluffy. Beat in the eggs, one at a time. Gently fold in the remaining flour. Fold the blueberry mixture into the batter.

4.   Scrape into the pan and bake for 1 hour, or until it tests done. Cool. Remove the cake from the pan. Store overnight before serving.

Yields 18 ½-inch-thick slices

Should be prepared the day before or frozen.

BLUEBERRY STREUSEL KUCHEN

1½ cups plus ⅓ cup sifted flour	1 cup sugar
2½ teaspoons baking powder	2½ cups blueberries
½ teaspoon salt	¼ cup butter, softened
¼ cup milk	½ teaspoon cinnamon
1 egg, beaten	Heavy cream or whipped
½ cup butter, melted	cream

1. Preheat the oven to 375°F. Butter and flour a 9-inch layer cake pan.

2. Sift 1½ cups of flour, baking powder, and salt together.

3. In a bowl, beat the milk, egg, melted butter, and ½ cup of sugar. Stir in the flour mixture and pour into the pan. Cover with the blueberries.

4. In another bowl, mix the remaining flour, remaining sugar and the softened butter with the cinnamon to the consistency of a coarse meal. Sprinkle over the berries.

5. Bake for 40 to 50 minutes, or until it tests done. Unmold and serve warm with heavy cream or whipped cream.

Yields 6 to 8 servings

Can be prepared the day before, although best served warm.

GÂTEAU BIGARREAU (Cherry Cake)

½ cup plus 2 teaspoons sugar	¾ cup plus 2 tablespoons
¾ cup plus 2 teaspoons flour,	Praline Powder, page 30
sifted	3 tablespoons apricot jam
3 eggs	3 tablespoons currant jelly
1 teaspoon baking powder	1–2 tablespoons water
Pinch of salt	1½ pounds cherries, pitted
½ cup heavy cream	

1. Preheat the oven to 350°F. Butter an 8-inch cake pan, line with parchment paper, and butter the paper. Sprinkle with 2 teaspoons of flour and 2 teaspoons of sugar.

2. In a bowl, beat the eggs and the remaining sugar until thick and pale.

3.   In another bowl, mix the remaining flour, baking powder, and salt. Fold into the egg mixture.

4.   Pour into the prepared pan and bake for 25 minutes, or until it tests done.

5.   In a bowl, whip the cream until stiff peaks form. Fold in 2 tablespoons of praline powder.

6.   In a saucepan, simmer the jam, jelly, and water until melted. Strain and cool.

7.   Cut the cake in half horizontally. Place one cake layer on a serving plate and spread with the whipped cream. Place the second layer on top. Spread some of the melted jam glaze over the top of the cake. Arrange the cherries on top and brush the fruit and sides of the cake with the remaining glaze. Press the remaining praline powder around the side of the cake.

Yields 6 to 8 servings

Can be prepared the day before serving.

DATE-NUT CAKE

1 pound pitted dates, chopped	1 cup walnuts, chopped
1 cup boiling water	2 eggs, beaten
1 teaspoon baking soda	½ teaspoon salt
¾ cup butter	4½ tablespoons dark rum, optional
1½ cups dark brown sugar	1½ cups confectioners' sugar
1 cup flour	¾ cup butter, softened

1.   Preheat the oven to 350°F. Line the bottom of a 10-inch tube pan with parchment paper and butter the paper.

2.   In a bowl, soak the dates in the water and the baking soda for 5 minutes.

3.   In a mixer, cream the butter and the brown sugar until light and fluffy. Blend in the date mixture, flour, walnuts, eggs, and salt.

4.   Pour into the prepared pan. Bake for 1 hour, or until it tests done. If desired, pour 2 tablespoons of rum over the top of the warm cake and let stand until the outside of the pan is cool. Unmold the cake and finish cooling.

5.   In a bowl, beat the confectioners' sugar, butter, and remaining rum or 2½ tablespoons of water until smooth. Spread over the cake.

Yields 8 to 10 servings

Can be prepared up to 2 days before serving or frozen.

STICKY GINGER CAKE

An old-fashioned favorite that is delicious served warm.

½ **cup butter, softened, plus additional, optional**	1 **teaspoon ginger**
½ **cup brown sugar**	¾ **cup golden raisins**
2 **eggs**	½ **teaspoon baking soda**
1 **cup molasses**	2 **tablespoons warm milk**
2 **cups flour**	**Gouda or Swiss cheese, optional**
Pinch of salt	**Apple slices, optional**

1.   Preheat the oven to 325°F. Butter and flour an 8-inch springform pan.

2.   In a bowl, cream the butter and the sugar until light and fluffy. Beat in the eggs, one at a time. Stir in the molasses.

3.   Sift the flour, salt, and ginger together. Fold into the egg mixture with the raisins.

4.   Dissolve the baking soda in the milk and stir into the batter. Pour into the pan and bake 1 hour, or until it tests done. Cool in the pan.

5.   Unmold and cut into wedges. Spread with additional butter and serve with a slice of cheese and crisp apple slices, if desired.

Yields 6 to 8 servings

Can be prepared the day before.

Variation

• Omit the cheese and apples and serve with warm applesauce, cold heavy cream, cold Custard Sauce (see page 545), whipped cream, or ice cream.

GÂTEAU AU CITRON (French Lemon Cake)

Grated rind and juice of 1	**2 eggs**
lemon	**1 cup less 2 tablespoons flour**
½ cup sugar	**1 teaspoon baking powder**
½ cup butter, softened	**½ cup confectioners' sugar**

1.   Preheat the oven to 350°F. Butter and flour an 8-inch round or square cake pan.

2.   In a bowl, cream the grated lemon rind, sugar, and butter and until light and fluffy. Beat in the eggs, one at a time. Beat in the flour and baking powder until combined. Pour into the prepared pan.

3.   Bake for 25 minutes, or until it tests done. Cool in the pan 10 minutes. Unmold the cake and place on a serving platter.

4.   In a bowl, mix the lemon juice and the confectioners' sugar and spoon over the cake. Repeat until the cake absorbs all of the glaze.

Yields 6 to 8 servings

Can be prepared the day before serving.

LEMON CAKE WITH YOGURT

1 cup butter, softened	**1 teaspoon baking powder**
1½ cups sugar	**1 teaspoon baking soda**
4 eggs	**½ teaspoon salt**
1 tablespoon grated lemon	**1 cup plain yogurt**
rind	**¾ cup ground blanched**
1 teaspoon vanilla	**almonds**
2½ cups flour	**½ cup lemon juice**

1.   Preheat the oven to 350°F. Butter a 9-inch tube pan.

2.   In a processor, cream the butter and 1 cup of sugar. With the machine running, add the eggs one at a time. Add the lemon rind and vanilla and process with on/off turns.

3.   Add the flour, baking powder, baking soda, and salt. With the machine running, add the yogurt and almonds and process until mixed.

4.   Turn into the prepared pan and bake 1 hour, or until it tests done. Let cool in the pan for 5 minutes.

5. Meanwhile, in a small saucepan, simmer the lemon juice and the remaining sugar for 5 minutes. Brush over the warm cake, letting it soak in. Cool the cake in the pan. Unmold and place on a serving platter.

Yields 12 to 16 servings

Can be prepared the day before or frozen.

VICTORIAN ORANGE CAKE

Rind of 3 large oranges	2 cups flour
1 cup raisins	1 teaspoon baking soda
1½ cups sugar	½ teaspoon salt
½ cup butter, softened	½ cup chopped walnuts
2 eggs	1 cup orange juice
¾ cup buttermilk	2 tablespoons dark rum

1. Preheat the oven to 325°F. Butter a 9-inch springform or tube pan.

2. In a processor, finely grind the orange rind and the raisins. Place in a large bowl and set aside.

3. In the processor, cream 1 cup of sugar and the butter until light and fluffy. Add the eggs and buttermilk and process until completely mixed. Incorporate the flour, baking soda, and salt with on/off turns.

4. Scrape into the bowl with the orange-raisin mixture and fold in the walnuts.

5. Scrape into the prepared pan and bake for 45 to 50 minutes, or until a cake tester inserted in the center comes out clean. Cool 10 minutes. Invert onto a wire rack.

6. In a saucepan, heat the orange juice, remaining sugar, and rum until the sugar dissolves. Pour the orange juice, 1 tablespoon at a time, over the cake. Cover and let flavors meld overnight or for several days.

Yields 8 to 10 servings

Can be kept for several days at room temperature or frozen.

ORANGE POPPYSEED CAKE

½ cup butter	rind
¾ cup sugar	1 teaspoon vanilla
2 eggs	1¼ cups flour
½ cup sour cream	½ teaspoon baking soda
⅓ cup poppyseeds, plus extra	Pinch of salt
for garnish	Sifted confectioners' sugar,
¼ cup orange juice	for garnish
1 tablespoon grated orange	

1. Preheat the oven to 350°F. Butter and flour a 4-cup ring mold.

2. In a processor, cream the butter and the sugar until light and fluffy. Mix in the eggs, one at a time. Mix in the sour cream, poppyseeds, orange juice, orange rind, and vanilla.

3. In a bowl, mix the flour, baking soda, and salt and add to the processor. Incorporate with on/off turns. Pour into the mold and bake for 40 minutes, or until it tests done. Invert onto a rack and cool. Dust with confectioners' sugar and remaining poppy seeds.

Yields 8 to 10 servings

Can be made a day before serving or frozen.

TORTA DI PERE ALLA PAESANA
(Country Cake with Fresh Pears)

½ cup dry bread crumbs	1½ cups flour
2 eggs	2 pounds pears, peeled, cored
¼ cup milk	and sliced
1 cup sugar	2 tablespoons butter
Pinch of salt	

1. Preheat the oven to 350°F. Butter a 9-inch cake pan and sprinkle with the bread crumbs. Turn over and tap out the excess crumbs.

2. In a bowl, mix the eggs and the milk. Stir in the sugar and salt. Add the flour and mix well. Stir in the pears. Pour into the prepared pan, smoothing with a spatula. Dot with the butter and bake for 45 minutes, or until the top colors lightly. Cool in the pan for 20 minutes, and unmold. Serve warm or cold.

Yields 8 to 10 servings

Best served the same day.

PLUM TORTE

1 cup plus 1 tablespoon sugar	2 eggs
½ cup butter, softened	12 plums, halved and pitted
1 cup flour	2 teaspoons lemon juice
1 teaspoon baking powder	1 tablespoon cinnamon
Salt, to taste	Heavy cream, whipped and sweetened, optional

1. Preheat the oven to 350°F. Butter a 9-inch springform pan.

2. In a processor, cream 1 cup of sugar and the butter until light and fluffy. Add the flour, baking powder, and salt with on/off turns.

3. Add the eggs and incorporate with on/off turns. Pour into the prepared pan.

4. Arrange the plums, cut side down, on top of the cake. Sprinkle with the remaining sugar, the lemon juice, and cinnamon. Bake 1 hour. Cool to lukewarm. Unmold and serve. Serve with whipped cream, if desired.

Yields 6 to 8 servings

Can be made the day before serving.

Variation

• Substitute 1 pound of pitted cherries for the plums.

Sponge and Génoise Cakes

Sponge cake, and its partner génoise, are the most common European cakes. Leavened with beaten egg and, for génoise, enriched with melted butter, the cakes serve as the base for dozens if not hundreds of different torten and gâteaux.

Bake the cakes as rounds, squares, rectangles, or sheets. Stack the layers, use them as the containers of Bavarian cream for charlottes, or roll to make cake rolls.

Fill the cakes with buttercream, whipped cream, pastry cream, jam, ganache, or mousse. Use any of those as icings, dust with a snow of confectioners' sugar, or sprinkle with granulated sugar. Coat with a chocolate glaze or a generous sprinkling of cocoa mixed with sugar. The only limit to the creations is your imagination. Please use some of the suggestions here as starting points to your signature desserts.

BEAU TENEBREAUX (Sponge Cake Filled with Whipped Cream Flavored with Calvados)

⅔ plus ¼ cup sugar	1 cup heavy cream
4 eggs, separated	1 teaspoon Calvados
4 tablespoons cornstarch	Confectioners' sugar, for
2 tablespoons flour	garnish

1. Preheat the oven to 325°F. Lightly butter and flour an 8-inch cake pan.

2. In a bowl, beat ⅔ cup of sugar with the yolks until they are thickened and pale. Fold in the cornstarch and the flour.

3. Using clean beaters, beat the egg whites until stiff peaks form and fold into the egg yolk mixture.

4. Pour into the prepared pan and bake for 25 minutes, or until it springs back when tapped. Cool in the pan on a rack for 5 minutes. Turn out onto a rack and cool completely.

5. Cut a thin slice off the top of the cake and set aside. Make a cake shell by cutting a 7-inch circle (¾-inch-deep) from the center of the cake. Cut the circle of cake into small cubes.

6. In a bowl, whip the cream, the remaining sugar, and Calvados until the mixture forms soft peaks. Fold in the diced cake. Spoon the mixture into the cake shell. Return the top to the cake. Sprinkle with confectioners' sugar.

Yields 6 to 8 servings

Can be prepared 6 hours before serving or frozen.

Variation

• Substitute raspberries or blueberries for all or part of the diced cake.

ZUCCOTTO ALLA MICHELANGELO
(Michelangelo's Pumpkin)

A favorite of Northern Italy, once unmolded this should resemble a pumpkin.

2 (10-in) round Sponge Cake layers, page 19	**¾ cup chopped candied fruit**
1¼ cups sugar	**⅔ cup chopped pecans**
⅔ cup water	**1½ cups grated semisweet chocolate**
1 cup orange liqueur	**Spun sugar, page 37,**
7 cups heavy cream	**optional for garnish**
⅔ cup cocoa	

1.   Cut each cake layer in half horizontally. Cut 2 of those layers into 8 wedges each.

2.   Line a 5-quart round-bottomed mixing bowl with plastic wrap. Arrange the cake wedges, slightly overlapping, around the bowl.

3.   In another bowl, dissolve ½ cup of sugar in the water and add the orange liqueur. Brush generously over the cake wedges.

4.   In a mixer, whip the cream until almost stiff and add the remaining sugar and beat until stiff. Place two-thirds of the whipped cream into another bowl and fold in the cocoa. Set aside.

5.   Fold the candied fruit, pecans, and 1 cup of grated chocolate into the remaining plain whipped cream. Spoon into the bowl and arrange a layer of cake on top. Brush with the syrup.

6.   Spoon the cocoa-flavored whipped cream into the bowl, saving any extra. Top with the final sponge cake layer and brush with the remaining syrup. Refrigerate at least 6 hours, until set.

7.   When ready to serve, unmold onto a platter and spread the remaining cocoa cream over the cake or, using a pastry bag fitted with a #5 open star tip, pipe a decoration over the top. Sprinkle with the remaining ½ cup grated chocolate. Surround with spun sugar, if desired.

Yields 8 to 12 servings

Can be prepared 2 days ahead or frozen.

GÂTEAU DE FRUITS (Fruit Shortcake)

10-in round Nutted Sponge Cake layer, prepared with almonds, page 20	Orange liqueur, to taste
	2 cups fruit, such as bananas,
1½ cups heavy cream	cherries, oranges, pineapple,
Sugar, to taste	etc.
	½ cup Apricot Glaze, page 36

1. Cut the cake into two layers and place one layer on a serving platter.

2. Beat the cream, sugar, and orange liqueur until stiff peaks form.

3. Spread a layer of whipped cream on the bottom layer. Top with the second layer of cake. Spread the remaining cream over the top of the cake.

4. Arrange the fruits in an attractive design on top. Brush the apricot glaze over the fruits. Refrigerate until ready to serve.

Yields 8 to 10 servings

Can be prepared up to 4 hours before serving.

LEMON CREAM ROLL

2 tablespoons confectioners' sugar, or as needed	1½ cups heavy cream
	⅔ cup sugar
11 × 17-in Sponge Cake, freshly baked, page 19	Grated rind of 2 lemons

1. Cut two 20-inch sheets of waxed paper and place on a counter, overlapping, so they are wider than the sponge sheet. Sprinkle the paper with the confectioners' sugar and unmold the warm cake on top. Tightly roll the warm cake in the waxed paper. Wrap in a damp towel for at least 20 minutes.

2. Up to 6 hours before serving, unroll the cake and peel off the waxed paper. In a bowl, whip the cream with the sugar and lemon rind until firm peaks form. Spread over the cake.

3. Reroll the cake and cut off the ragged ends. Sprinkle generously with confectioners' sugar and place on a serving platter.

Yields 8 to 12 servings

Can be prepared the day before. Fill about 6 hours before serving.

MANDARIN SLICES

Use this recipe as a base to make other slices using the fruit, jam, and buttercream of your choice.

11 × 17-in Sponge Cake, page 19	2 tablespoons orange liqueur
4 cups mandarin orange segments	3 cups Orange Buttercream, page 31
12-ounce jar orange marmalade, sieved	2 ounces Chocolate Vermicelli or Strands, page 45

1. Cut the sponge cake lengthwise into 3 strips. On the back of a baking sheet, place a cake layer and carefully arrange 2 cups of the orange segments on top.

2. In a small saucepan, boil the strained marmalade and orange liqueur for 3 minutes. Brush over the orange segments. Cool.

3. Spread half of the buttercream on a second layer of cake and place on top of the orange segments. Cover with the third layer of cake and frost the sides of the cake with the remaining buttercream. Press the chocolate vermicelli onto the sides of the cake.

4. Arrange the remaining orange segments on top and brush with the remaining glaze. Refrigerate until set. Cut into 1-inch-thick slices.

Yields 14 to 15 servings

Can be prepared the day before serving.

GÂTEAU POIRE WILLIAM
(Pear and Chocolate Cake)

5½ ounces semisweet chocolate	1 tablespoon gelatin
9-in round Chocolate Sponge Cake layer, page 20	7 tablespoons water
	2 cups heavy cream
3½ tablespoons Poire William, or other pear liqueur	Chocolate Vermicelli or Strands, page 45, for garnish
4 Vanilla Poached Pears, halved, page 40	Cocoa, for garnish
	½ cup heavy cream, whipped and sweetened, for garnish

1. Melt the chocolate. Lightly oil a 9-inch springform pan. Place the cake in the pan and brush with the liqueur. Arrange the pears, rounded sides down, with the stem ends toward the center of the cake.

2. In a saucepan, soften the gelatin in the water and dissolve over low heat. Stir into the melted chocolate and blend well. Cool to room temperature.

3. In a mixer, whip the cream until stiff. Fold into the melted chocolate mixture and spread over the pears. Smooth the top. Refrigerate about 3 hours, or until set.

4. Remove the sides of the pan and pat the chocolate vermicelli against the moist sides of the cake.

5. Cut a 3-inch circle of cardboard and place on the center of the top of cake. Sift a thick layer of cocoa over the cake around the cardboard. Remove the cardboard.

6. Using a pastry bag fitted with a #5 open star tip, pipe rosettes of whipped cream around the edge of the cake.

Yields 8 to 10 servings

Can be prepared the day before serving.

RASPBERRY BUTTERCREAM CAKE

9-in round Sponge Cake layer, page 19	**page 31**
¼ cup Dessert Syrup, flavored with framboise, page 30	**2 cups fresh raspberries**
	1½ cups heavy cream
1¼ cups Classic Buttercream, flavored with framboise,	**2 tablespoons confectioners' sugar**
	1 tablespoon framboise

1. Cut the cake in half horizontally. Brush each layer with the dessert syrup. Place one layer on a serving plate and spread with the buttercream. Scatter with half of the raspberries and press them gently into the buttercream. Top with the second layer of cake.

2. In a bowl, whip the cream with the confectioners' sugar and framboise until firm peaks form. Spread three-fourths over the top and sides of the cake.

3. Using a pastry bag fitted with a #5 open star tip, pipe rosettes of the remaining whipped cream around the edges. Garnish with the remaining raspberries.

Yields 8 to 10 servings

Can be prepared the day before serving.

GALETTE AUX FRAISES
(Strawberry Cake)

¼ cup sugar	7-in round Sponge Cake
5 tablespoons water	layer, page 19
2 tablespoons maraschino or	1½ cups sifted confectioners'
orange liqueur	sugar
½ pint strawberries, thinly	Juice of ½ orange
sliced	

1. In a saucepan, dissolve the sugar in the water and boil until it reaches 230°F. Cool. Stir in the liqueur and pour over the strawberries. Let stand for 10 minutes. Drain the strawberries, reserving the syrup.

2. Cut the cake horizontally into two layers and place one layer on a serving plate. Arrange the strawberries on the bottom layer. Spoon half the syrup over the strawberries. Cover with the second layer and spoon the remaining syrup over the top.

3. About 30 minutes before serving, in a saucepan, heat the confectioners' sugar and orange juice over low heat, stirring until the mixture is of a spreading consistency. Add a little water if it is too thick. Spread over the top of the cake.

Yields 6 to 8 servings

Prepare no more than 4 hours before serving.

STRAWBERRY GRAND MARNIER CAKE WITH MARZIPAN ICING

9-in Sponge Cake layer, baked in a springform pan, page 19	**3 cups Classic Buttercream, flavored with orange liqueur, page 31**
¾ cup Dessert Syrup, flavored with orange liqueur, page 30	**10½ ounces marzipan**
	Red or green food coloring, see Note
3 pints strawberries, hulled and sliced	**Strawberries, for garnish**

1.   Cut the cake horizontally into 3 layers. Set one layer on a serving plate, sprinkle with ¼ cup of dessert syrup, and cover with a layer of strawberries. Place the middle layer on top and brush with ¼ cup of syrup. Spread with 1 cup of buttercream. Cover with a layer of strawberries.

2.   Sprinkle the remaining syrup on the cut side of the top layer and place on the cake, cut side down. Spread the top and sides of the cake with the remaining buttercream.

3.   In a bowl, mixer, or processor, mix the marzipan with 1 drop of food coloring. Add a second drop to get a delicate pink or green shade. Between sheets of waxed paper, roll the marzipan into a 16-inch circle.

4.   Place the marzipan on the cake, easing out any creases, and trim evenly with the bottom of the cake. Arrange a decoration of sliced strawberries on top of the cake. Garnish the base with additional strawberries.

Yields 8 to 10 servings

Can be prepared the day before serving.

NOTE: Food coloring often darkens when exposed to the air, so tint the marzipan very lightly to keep the shade delicate.

Variations

• Omit the marzipan.
• Roll the marzipan into a circle just large enough to cover the top of the cake.
• Roll a strip of marzipan as tall as the cake and long enough to wrap the sides. Cut a circle to place on top. Use buttercream to garnish the top edge.

Strawberry Cream Cakes

Strawberries and cream are as traditional as peaches and cream—a marriage truly made in heaven. Here are several presentations of this marvelous combination. Substitute any berry or any other soft fruit for the strawberries.

STRAWBERRY ROLL

1 quart strawberries, hulled	2 cups heavy cream
11 × 17-in Sponge Cake, rolled, page 19	Sugar, to taste

1. Slice half of the strawberries.

2. As soon as the cake is baked, turn out onto sheets of waxed paper dusted with confectioners' sugar. Roll and cool for at least 20 minutes.

3. Whip cream to soft peaks and sweeten to taste.

4. Unroll the cake and spread a thick layer of the whipped cream over the cake. Sprinkle the sliced strawberries over the whipped cream. Roll and spread the roll with the remaining whipped cream.

5. Arrange the whole strawberries over the top and along the sides of the cake roll.

Yields 12 to 15 servings

Can be prepared 6 to 8 hours before serving.

Variation

• Flavor the cream with orange liqueur, kirsch, or rum.

STRAWBERRY SPONGE LAYERS

11 × 17-in Sponge Cake sheet, page 19	Sugar and kirsch, to taste
1 quart strawberries	3 cups heavy cream
	Currant Glaze, page 36

1. Cut the sponge sheet lengthwise into three strips.

2. Hull the berries. Cut 3 cups of berries in half and place in a bowl. Set the whole berries aside. Add the sugar and kirsch, to taste, to the halved berries. Place 1 cake layer on a serving platter.

3.   Whip the cream until stiff peaks form. Reserve 1 cup for garnishing the cake. Spread a thin layer of the remaining whipped cream on the cake layer. Arrange half of the cut berries on top and cover with another cake layer. Spread with more whipped cream and the remaining halved berries. Add the final cake layer and spread with the remaining whipped cream.

4.   Using a pastry bag fitted with a #5 open star tip, pipe rosettes of the reserved whipped cream on each serving. Garnish each rosette with a whole strawberry. Brush the berries with currant glaze.

Yields 12 to 15 servings

Best if served on the same day.

TORTA ALLA CREMA DI FRAGOLE
(Strawberry Cream Cake)

This is an Italian version of strawberries, cream, and cake.

1½ **pints strawberries, hulled**	9-**in round Sponge Cake**
6 **ounces strawberry**	**layer, page 19**
preserves, pureed	2 **cups heavy cream**
½ **cup sweet sherry**	⅓ **cup sugar**

1.   In a bowl, mash 1 pint of berries and combine with half of the preserves and the sherry. Macerate for 30 minutes. Puree in a processor.

2.   Cut the cake horizontally into three layers and place one layer on a platter. Spread with one-third of the puree.

3.   In a bowl, whip the cream with the sugar. Fold in the remaining preserves. Spread one-third of the whipped cream over the layer. Top with another cake layer and spread with another third of the puree, and another third of the whipped cream. Top with the final cake layer and spread with the remaining puree.

4.   Using a pastry bag fitted with a #4 plain tip, pipe the remaining cream in a lattice on the top of the cake. Place the whole strawberries in the spaces of the lattice. Refrigerate for at least 2 hours.

Yields 8 to 10 servings

Can be prepared up to 8 hours before serving.

MAESTRO GÂTEAU

This European specialty is a rum-flavored hazelnut génoise cake, topped with apricot-flavored jelly roll, and garnished with toasted hazelnuts.

11 × 17-in Sponge Cake, cut
in half, page 19
1½ cups apricot jam
9-in round Nutted Génoise
layer, prepared with
hazelnuts, page 21

3 tablespoons rum
2 cups Classic Buttercream,
flavored with rum, page 31
1½ cups hazelnuts, chopped,
and toasted

1. Spread the sponge cake layer with ½ cup of jam. Roll tightly into a jelly roll.

2. Sprinkle the génoise cake layer with the rum and spread the top with ¾ cup of buttercream.

3. Cut the jelly roll into ½-inch-thick slices and arrange them, cut side down, on the génoise cake layer.

4. Heat the remaining jam until melted. Glaze the top of the cake. When the glaze has set, spread the sides of the cake with the remaining 1¼ cups buttercream. Press the nuts into the sides of the cake.

Yields 8 servings

Can be prepared the day before.

GÂTEAU MADAME

8-in round Chocolate
Génoise layer, page 21
⅔ cup Dessert Syrup, flavored
with kirsch, page 30
3 cups Chocolate Mousse for
Filling, page 549

2 cups heavy cream, whipped
and sweeteened
⅓ cup cocoa, sifted
2 ounces semisweet chocolate,
shaved, for garnish

1. Cut the cake horizontally into 3 layers

2. Brush the cake layers with the syrup. Place one layer on a platter and spread with half of the mousse. Top with the second layer and spread with the remaining mousse. Top with the third layer and refrigerate for 30 minutes to set the mousse.

3.   Frost the top and sides of the cake with the whipped cream. Dust the sides with sieved cocoa by putting into a squeeze bottle and pumping the bottle. Garnish the top with the chocolate shavings.

Yields 8 to 10 servings

Can be prepared the day before serving or frozen.

CHOCOLATE CARAMEL TORTE

I created this cake with layers of chocolate Génoise, caramel buttercream, and a wrapping of chocolate.

11 × 17-in Chocolate Génoise, page 21	**1 recipe Caramel Buttercream, page 33**
½ cup Dessert Syrup, flavored with Cognac, page 30	**8 ounces semisweet chocolate, melted**

1.   Cut the génoise lengthwise into 3 equal strips. Brush each strip with the dessert syrup.

2.   Place one strip on a baking sheet and spread with a ¼-inch-thick layer of buttercream. Top with a second cake strip and spread with another ¼-inch-thick layer of buttercream. Place the third cake layer on top. Even the sides of the cake and trim. Spread the sides with a thin layer of buttercream. Using a pastry bag fitted with a #6, #7, or #8 pastry tip, pipe 16 rows of buttercream decorations, such as rosettes or shells.

3.   Use the melted chocolate to make a decorative chocolate band to surround the cake. (See page 42.) Refrigerate until ready to serve.

Yields 12 to 16 servings

Can be prepared the day before or frozen.

SCHWARZWALDER KIRSCH TORTE
(Black Forest Cherry Cake)

A classic of European pastry shops, this cake is simple to prepare and deserves its reputation.

3 (7-in) round Chocolate Génoise layers, page 21	**½ cup confectioners' sugar**
1⅓ cups Dessert Syrup, flavored with kirsch, page 30	**¼ cup kirsch**
	1 cup pitted cherries
	Maraschino or fresh cherries, for garnish
3 cups heavy cream	**Grated chocolate, for garnish**

1. Prick the cake layers with a fork and spoon the dessert syrup over each layer.

2. In a mixer, beat the cream until it forms soft peaks. Add the confectioners' sugar and the kirsch and beat until stiff.

3. Place a cake layer on a serving platter and spread with a ½-inch-thick layer of whipped cream. Strew with the pitted cherries and set a second layer on top. Spread with a ½-inch-thick layer of whipped cream and place the third layer on top. Spread the top and sides of the cake with the remaining cream.

4. If desired, garnish the top of the cake with the maraschino cherries. Press the grated chocolate into the sides of the cake. Refrigerate for at least 3 hours.

Yields 8 servings

Can be prepared the day before serving.

LE SEVILLAN
(Chocolate and Orange Gâteau)

Chocolate ganache, orange flavoring, and hazelnuts combine to make a superior gâteau.

1¾ cups heavy cream
1 pound semisweet chocolate, chopped
8-in square Génoise layer, page 20
⅔ cup Dessert Syrup, flavored with orange liqueur, page
30
⅔ cup chopped toasted hazelnuts
Chocolate Curls, page 42, for garnish
Confectioners' sugar, for garnish

1. In a saucepan, bring the cream to a boil. Add the chocolate, remove from the heat, and cover for 5 minutes. Stir until melted and smooth. Refrigerate until cold, about 3 hours.

2. In a mixer, beat the chocolate ganache until fluffy and soft enough to spread.

3. Cut the génoise horizontally into three layers. Place one layer, cut side up, on a serving platter.

4. Sprinkle one-third of the syrup over the cut layer and spread with ¾ cup of ganache. Repeat with the second layer. Top with the third layer and sprinkle the remaining syrup. Refrigerate 1 hour.

5. Frost the cake with the remaining ganache and press the hazelnuts into the sides of the cake. Arrange the chocolate curls on top and dust with confectioners' sugar.

Yields 8 servings

Can be prepared the day before.

CHOCOLATE-ORANGE CAKE

20 ounces semisweet chocolate, chopped
2 cups heavy cream
9-in round Chocolate Génoise layer, page 21
⅓ cup Dessert Syrup, flavored
with orange liqueur, page 30
⅓ cup orange marmalade
2 tablespoons orange liqueur
Candied Orange Rind, page 38, for garnish

1.   Melt 12 ounces of chocolate in 1 cup of cream, stirring until smooth. Refrigerate 1 hour, or until thick and set. Beat the ganache until light and fluffy.

2.   Cut the cake horizontally into 3 layers. Brush each layer with one-third of the dessert syrup. Place the bottom layer on a serving plate.

3.   In a bowl, mix the marmalade and the orange liqueur. Spread the bottom layer with half of the marmalade mixture and one-fourth of the ganache. Put a second layer on top and spread with the remaining marmalade and one-fourth of the ganache. Top with remaining layer and spread the top and sides with one-fourth of the ganache. Reserve the remaining ganache at room temperature for garnishing. Refrigerate the cake until set.

4.   In a saucepan or microwave, melt the remaining chocolate in the remaining cream. Whisk until smooth and cool to lukewarm. Pour the glaze over the cake and smooth over the sides. Refrigerate until set.

5.   Fill a pastry bag fitted with a #4 open star tip with remaining ganache and pipe 12 rosettes on the top of the cake. Decorate each rosette with candied peel.

Yields 12 servings

Can be prepared the day before or frozen.

ORANGE TORTE

This cake is for those who like chocolate in smaller doses. It has chocolate génoise layers filled with orange marmalade and whipped cream and it is garnished with orange segments.

1 tablespoon gelatin	sugar
2 tablespoons water	10-in round Chocolate
6 tablespoons orange juice	Génoise layer, page 21
Grated rind of 1 orange	2 tablespoons orange
2 cups heavy cream	marmalade
4 tablespoons confectioners'	12–16 orange segments, for garnish

1.   In a small saucepan, soften the gelatin in the water. Over low heat, stir until the gelatin dissolves. Stir in the orange juice and grated rind and cool to room temperature.

2.   In a mixer, beat the cream until almost stiff. Beat in the gelatin and the confectioners' sugar. Beat until stiff peaks form.

3.   Cut the cake horizontally into 3 layers. Spread the bottom layer with the orange marmalade and one-third of the cream. Add the middle layer and spread with one-third of the remaining whipped cream. Add the top layer. Frost the top and sides with the remaining whipped cream. Mark the cake into 12 to 16 servings.

4.   Using a pastry bag fitted with a #3 open star tip, pipe a rosette of whipped cream on each slice. Garnish with the orange segments.

Yields 12 to 16 servings

Can be prepared the day before serving.

ROSACE À L'ORANGE
(Orange Custard Cake)

This adaptation of a dessert by Gaston LeNôtre is one of my all-time favorites. Cake, custard, and glacéed orange slices combine to make a divine dessert.

4 cups water	page 20
2¾ cups sugar	1 cup whipped heavy cream
4 oranges, thinly sliced	⅔ cup Dessert Syrup, flavored
1¼ cups Pastry Cream, page 26	with orange liqueur, page 30
9-in round Génoise layer,	

1.   Bring the water and the sugar to a boil, add the oranges and gently simmer for 2 hours. Pour oranges and syrup into a bowl and cool. Drain well. Set aside half of the prettiest orange slices and dice the remaining.

2.   Fold the orange pieces into the pastry cream. Fold in the whipped cream.

3.   Butter a 9-inch cake pan and dust with sugar. Line the bottom and sides of the pan with the orange slices and scrape half of the pastry cream over the oranges. Cut the cake horizontally into 2 layers. Brush with the dessert syrup. Place a layer on top of the pastry cream, trimming to fit if necessary. Cover with the remaining pastry cream and another cake layer.

4.   Weight with a small plate for 2 hours in the refrigerator. To unmold, dip the pan into hot water and turn it over onto a platter.

Yields 8 to 10 servings

Serve within 48 hours.

BAGATELLE AUX FRAISES
(Strawberry Cream Torte)

8-in square Genoise layer, page 20	**4 cups strawberries, hulled, or other fruit**
⅔ cup Dessert Syrup, flavored with kirsch, page 30	**½ cup Apricot Glaze, page 36**
2 cups heavy cream, whipped and sweetened	

1. Cut the cake horizontally into 2 layers. Brush each layer with the syrup and place the bottom layer on a serving plate.

2. Spread a layer of whipped cream over the cake layer. "Plant" 2 cups of the strawberries, hulled end down, into the whipped cream. Spread with the remaining whipped cream and place the second layer on top. Refrigerate until set.

3. Cut about ¼ inch off each side of the cake. Brush half the apricot glaze on the top layer and arrange the remaining 2 cups strawberries on top. Brush the strawberries with the remaining glaze. Refrigerate for at least 3 hours.

Yields 8 to 10 servings

Can be prepared the day before serving.

NOTE: The purpose of trimming the sides in step 3 is to expose the cut sides of the strawberries.

Chocolate Desserts

These are the richest of chocolate desserts. One might question whether these are gâteaux or confections. The *Il Pellegrino* (see page 498) is more a confection than a cake. Others use chocolate mousse partially or fully cooked, or sometimes both.

Please read the section on chocolate (see page 8) to learn how to use a microwave for melting chocolate. Also read the notes on a processor. Both machines make much of baking a piece of cake.

APRICOT-CHOCOLATE SOUFFLÉ CAKE

A dense and delicious chocolate cake with apricots and walnuts.

½ cup dried apricots

1 tablespoon instant coffee
granules

1½ teaspoons water

¾ cup butter, softened

¾ cup plus 1 tablespoon
sugar

10 eggs, separated

6 ounces semisweet
chocolate

¼ cup chopped walnuts

1 cup heavy cream

½ teaspoon vanilla

8 dried apricots, see
Chocolate-dipped Fruit and
Nuts, page 527, for garnish

8 walnut halves, for garnish
Chocolate Mocha Sauce,
page 542

1. Melt the chocolate and bring to room temperature. Soak the apricots in hot water to cover for 30 minutes. Drain and chop.

2. Preheat the oven to 350°F. Butter an 8-inch round cake pan and line with parchment paper. Dissolve the coffee in the water.

3. In a mixer, cream the butter and 6 tablespoons of sugar until fluffy. Add the egg yolks, 1 at a time, blending well after each addition. Blend in the melted chocolate and the coffee. Stir in the chopped apricots and the walnuts.

4. Using clean beaters, beat the egg whites until soft peaks begin to form. Gradually beat in 6 tablespoons of sugar and beat to form soft peaks. Fold into the chocolate mixture. Pour into the pan.

5. Bake about 1 hour, or until it tests done. Cool in the pan. It will fall as it cools. Unmold onto a serving platter.

6. In a bowl, whip the cream and the remaining sugar until almost stiff. Spread half of the whipped cream on the cake. Using a pastry bag fitted with a star tip, pipe a whipped cream border around the top of the cake. Garnish with the chocolate-dipped apricots and the walnut halves. Serve with chocolate mocha sauce.

Yields 8 to 10 servings

Can be prepared the day before serving or frozen.

CHOCOLATE ROLL LEONTINE

This is an adaptation of Dione Lucas' chocolate soufflé roll.

8 ounces semisweet chocolate	½ cup cocoa
⅓ cup water	1¾ cups heavy cream
8 eggs, separated	2 tablespoons confectioners' sugar
1 cup superfine sugar	1 teaspoon vanilla
⅛ teaspoon salt	

1. Preheat the oven to 350°F. Brush an 11 × 17-inch jelly roll pan with oil and line with waxed paper or foil, letting the ends hang over the ends.

2. Melt the chocolate with the water. Stir until smooth.

3. In a bowl, whisk the egg yolks, sugar, and salt until light and fluffy. In a mixer, beat the egg whites to firm peaks. Fold the chocolate into the egg yolk mixture and fold in the egg whites.

4. Spread evenly in the prepared pan. Bake for 17 minutes, or until the top is puffed and the surface has just lost its shine. Do not overbake. Wring a towel out in cold water, place over the cake, and let cool.

5. Remove the towel and sift the cocoa over the top of the cake. Carefully loosen all 4 sides of the cake and cover with 2 overlapping sheets of waxed paper. Turn the cake over, remove the pan, and carefully peel off the waxed paper.

6. In a mixer, beat the cream, confectioners' sugar, and vanilla until stiff. Spread evenly over the cake.

7. Using the edges of the waxed paper, roll the long side gently, into a log. Lift onto a serving platter. Refrigerate at least 30 minutes. Cut off the ends. Sift more cocoa over the top.

Yields 10 to 16 servings

Can be prepared the day before serving or frozen.

NOTE: It is important not to overcook the cake or it will crack when rolled. If it does crack, sprinkle more generously with cocoa or give it an additional frosting of whipped cream.

Variations

• Substitute Mocha- or Chocolate-flavored Whipped Cream. (See page 11.)

• Add diced fruit or berries to taste to the cream.
• Substitute 2 cups of Classic Buttercream (see page 31) for the whipped cream.

CHOCOLATE ROLL WITH MOCHA CREAM

Another version of a chocolate roll with a less sweet, more intense, chocolate flavor.

**8 ounces semisweet
  chocolate, chopped**
2 tablespoons butter
6 eggs, separated
¾ cup sugar
¼ cup plus 3 tablespoons

cocoa
**1 recipe Mocha Cream, page
  11**
**⅓ cup confectioners' sugar,
  plus additional, for garnish**

1.   Preheat the oven to 350°F. Lightly butter a 10 × 15-inch jelly roll pan. Line the pan with waxed paper and butter the paper.

2.   In a small saucepan, melt the chocolate and the butter over low heat, stirring, until smooth. Cool for 3 minutes.

3.   In a large bowl, beat the egg yolks with ½ cup of sugar until thickened and pale. Beat in ¼ cup of cocoa. Fold in the cooled chocolate.

4.   Using clean beaters, beat the egg whites until soft peaks form. Add the remaining sugar gradually and beat until stiff. Stir one-fourth of the egg whites into the chocolate batter. Fold in the remaining egg whites.

5.   Pour into the pan and spread evenly. Bake for 15 to 17 minutes, or until the top feels dry. Do not overbake. Cover the cake with a towel wrung out in cold water and cool completely.

6.   Uncover the cake. Lay 2 overlapping sheets of waxed paper on the counter, sprinkle with the remaining cocoa, and unmold the cake onto the cocoa. Peel off the waxed paper. Spread with the mocha cream, leaving a ½-inch border.

7.   Using the waxed paper, roll the cake lengthwise. Transfer to a platter and refrigerate for at least 30 minutes, or until cold. Trim the ends and sprinkle with the confectioners' sugar.

Yields 10 to 16 servings

Can be prepared the day before or frozen.

CHOCOLATE MOUSSE CAKE

A variation of the Hungarian specialty *Rigo Jancsi* with thin layers of chocolate cake and a thick filling of chocolate mousse.

9 eggs, separated	2 ounces unsweetened
1¼ cups sugar	chocolate, grated
6 tablespoons instant	8 tablespoons butter, cut into
espresso powder	pieces, softened
¼ cup flour	Heavy cream, whipped and
¼ cup cocoa	sweetened, for garnish
3 cups heavy cream	
10 ounces semisweet	
chocolate, grated	

1. Preheat the oven to 350°F. Line an 11 × 17-inch jelly roll pan with waxed paper.

2. In a bowl, beat 6 egg yolks and ½ cup of sugar until thickened and pale. Beat in 3 tablespoons of espresso powder. On low speed, mix in the flour and cocoa.

3. Using clean beaters, beat 6 egg whites to form soft peaks. Add ½ cup of sugar and beat until stiff. Fold into the chocolate mixture. Spread in the prepared pan.

4. Bake 12 to 15 minutes, or until the top feels dry. Remove from the oven, place a sheet of waxed paper over the cake, cover it with a baking sheet, flip, and remove the waxed paper from the bottom of the cake.

5. Lightly oil two 9 × 5-inch loaf pans and line with plastic wrap, letting the ends extend outside the pan. Cut a rectangle of cake to fit into the bottom of each pan. Cut another cake rectangle to fit the top of each pan. Place the bottom rectangles in the pans.

6. In a large saucepan, simmer the cream until reduced to 2 cups. Stir in the remaining 3 tablespoons of the espresso powder. Add the semisweet and unsweetened chocolates to the cream and stir until blended.

7. Pour into a processor, with machine running, and gradually add the butter. Add the remaining egg yolks, one at a time, and process until smooth. Pour into a bowl.

8. In a mixer, beat the remaining egg whites with the remaining sugar until stiff and fold into the chocolate mixture. Pour half of the mousse into each pan and cover with the cake rectangles cut to fit the top of the pan. Refrigerate until set.

9.   Unmold the cakes onto serving platters. Garnish with whipped cream.

Yields 16 to 18 servings

Can be prepared two days before or frozen.

CHOCOLATE MOUSSE TORTE

There are several versions of this type of cake as well. Bake some of the chocolate mousse to make a cake and use the remaining mousse to frost the cake. Heaven.

10 tablespoons butter	**6 eggs**
10 ounces semisweet	**1 cup sugar**
chocolate, finely chopped	

1.   Preheat the oven to 350°F. Butter and lightly flour a 9-inch round cake pan.

2.   Melt the butter and the chocolate. Stir until smooth. Cool to lukewarm.

3.   In a large bowl, beat the eggs and the sugar until thickened and pale and are tripled in volume. Fold in the chocolate mixture. Place one-third of the batter in a bowl, cover, and refrigerate.

4.   Pour the remaining batter into the prepared cake pan. Bake about 25 minutes, or until it tests done. The cake will rise and fall a little. Cover a cake rack with waxed paper and invert the cake onto the rack. Turn right side up and cool.

5.   Place the cake on a serving platter. Top with the reserved mousse.

Yields 8 to 10 servings

Can be prepared the day before serving.

CHOCOLATE DECADENCE

1 pound semisweet chocolate	1 tablespoon confectioners'
5 ounces butter	sugar
4 eggs	1 teaspoon vanilla
1 tablespoon sugar	Chocolate Curls, page 41, for
1 tablespoon flour	garnish
1 cup heavy cream	Raspberry Sauce, page 552

1. Preheat the oven to 425°F. Line an 8-inch round cake pan with waxed paper.

2. Melt the chocolate and the butter. Stir until smooth. Remove from the heat.

3. In a bowl, over hot, not boiling water, heat the eggs and the sugar, stirring, until warm to the touch. In a mixer, beat the warm egg mixture until tripled in volume and the consistency of mayonnaise. Fold in the flour. Stir one-third of the egg mixture into the chocolate mixture. Fold the chocolate mixture into the remaining egg mixture. Pour into the prepared pan.

4. Bake about 15 minutes, or until the top is crusty and the center is still soft. Cool in the pan and refrigerate overnight or freeze for about 4 hours.

5. Invert the cake onto a serving plate and remove the waxed paper. If it does not come out easily, place the bottom of the cake pan on a hot stove burner for a few seconds to release the cake from the bottom of the pan.

6. In a bowl, whip the cream with the confectioners' sugar and the vanilla. Spread over the top of the cake. Or, for a more formal look, using a pastry bag fitted with a #5 open star tip, pipe the cream in rosettes on the top of the cake. Garnish with chocolate curls. Serve the sauce on the side.

Yields 8 to 10 servings

Can be prepared several days ahead or frozen.

NEMESIS AU CHOCOLAT

A rich, dense chocolate layer, baked in a water bath, and served with custard sauce.

1½ cups sugar
½ cup water
2 tablespoons vanilla
8 ounces unsweetened chocolate, chopped
4 ounces semisweet chocolate, chopped

1 cup butter, cut into pieces, softened
5 eggs
Confectioners' sugar, for garnish
Custard Sauce, page 545

1. Preheat the oven to 350°F. Butter a 9-inch round cake pan and line with waxed paper.

2. In a saucepan, bring 1 cup of sugar, the water, and vanilla to a boil. Remove from the heat. Add the unsweetened and semisweet chocolates and stir until smooth. Whisk in the butter until smooth.

3. In a mixer, beat the eggs with the remaining sugar until tripled in bulk and the consistency of mayonnaise. Fold in the melted chocolate.

4. Pour into the pan. Bake in a water bath about 30 minutes, or until the cake is firm in the center. Remove from the water bath and cool 10 minutes. Unmold onto a serving plate. Sprinkle with confectioners' sugar and serve warm or cold with custard sauce.

Yields 10 to 12 servings

Can be prepared several days before or frozen.

CHOCOLATE TRUFFLE CAKE I

A dense, rich chocolate cake, usually served with whipped cream, but it is as wonderful, if not better, with raspberry or custard sauce, or both.

1 pound semisweet chocolate, chopped
10 tablespoons butter
5 eggs, separated

1½ cups heavy cream
2 tablespoons sugar
½ teaspoon vanilla
Grated chocolate, for garnish

1. Preheat the oven to 375°F. Butter a 9-inch springform pan and line with parchment or waxed paper.

2. Melt the chocolate and the butter. Stir until smooth. Remove from the heat and cool slightly.

3. In a small bowl, mix the egg yolks, and stir into the chocolate mixture.

4. In a mixer, beat the egg whites to form stiff peaks and fold into the chocolate mixture.

5. Pour into the prepared pan and bake for 12 minutes. Do not overbake. Cool and unmold. Just before serving, whip the cream, sugar, and vanilla to stiff peaks. Spread evenly over the top of the cake. Garnish with grated chocolate.

Yields 10 to 12 servings

Can be prepared several days ahead or frozen.

CHOCOLATE TRUFFLE CAKE II

1 pound semisweet chocolate	1 teaspoon hot water
½ cup butter	4 eggs, separated
1½ teaspoons flour	1 cup heavy cream
1½ teaspoons sugar	

1. Preheat the oven to 425°F. Butter the bottom of an 8-inch springform pan and line with parchment or waxed paper.

2. Melt the chocolate and the butter. Stir until smooth. Remove from the heat and cool slightly.

3. Add the flour, sugar, and water and mix well. Add the egg yolks, one at a time, beating well after each addition.

4. In a mixer, beat the egg whites until stiff, but not dry, peaks form. Fold into the chocolate mixture.

5. Pour into the pan. Bake for 15 minutes. Do not overbake. Refrigerate for at least 3 hours. Before unmolding, remove the side of the pan. Cut the cake while still cold and then let stand at room temperature.

6. In a bowl, whip the cream to soft peaks and spoon over each serving.

Yields 8 to 10 servings

Can be prepared several days ahead or frozen.

WARM CHOCOLATE TRUFFLE CAKES

Hot chocolate cakes filled with a melted chocolate truffle.

9 ounces semisweet chocolate	**3 eggs**
11 tablespoons butter	**3 egg yolks**
3 tablespoons heavy cream	**½ cup sugar**
2 tablespoons bourbon	**⅓ cup flour**

1. In the top of a double boiler, over hot, not boiling, water, or in a microwave, heat 4 ounces of chocolate, 1 tablespoon of butter, the cream, and bourbon. Stir until smooth.

2. Refrigerate until firm enough to hold a shape. With a melon baller, shape into eight small balls. Refrigerate the truffles.

3. Preheat the oven to 350°F. Butter 8 muffin or custard cups. In the top of a double boiler, over hot, not boiling, water, or in a microwave, melt the remaining chocolate and butter. Remove from the heat.

4. In a mixer, beat the eggs, egg yolks, and sugar to the consistency of mayonnaise and are tripled in volume. Fold in the melted chocolate and flour. Spoon into the prepared cups and insert a chilled truffle into the center of each cup.

5. Bake 12 minutes, or until the top springs back when touched. Run a knife around the edges and unmold onto a baking sheet. Use a metal spatula to transfer to individual plates.

Yields 8 servings

Prepare and serve.

Truffles may be prepared a day or more ahead.

Variations

- Substitute orange liqueur, kirsch, or framboise for the bourbon.
- Serve with Grand Marnier Sauce (see page 545), or Sabayon Sauce flavored with bourbon, kirsch, or framboise (see page 544).

FLOURLESS CHOCOLATE CAKE WITH HAZELNUT-VANILLA SAUCE

14 ounces semisweet chocolate, chopped	1 teaspoon vanilla
14 tablespoons butter, cut into pieces	Pinch of salt
1½ cups sugar	Confectioners' sugar, for garnish
10 eggs, separated	Hazelnut-Vanilla Sauce, page 546
1 tablespoon orange liqueur	

1. Preheat the oven to 250°F. Butter and flour a 9-inch springform pan.

2. Melt the chocolate and the butter with ¾ cup of sugar. Stir until smooth.

3. Remove from the heat and whisk in the egg yolks. Place back over simmering water, and cook, whisking constantly, about 8 minutes, or until the mixture is shiny and thick. Remove from water and stir in the Grand Marnier and vanilla. Pour into a bowl. Cool to lukewarm.

4. In a mixer beat egg whites and the salt to form soft peaks. Beat in the remaining sugar until stiff, but not dry, peaks form. Gently fold one-third of the whites into the chocolate mixture. Fold in remaining whites.

5. Pour into prepared pan. Bake 2½ to 3 hours, or until it tests done. Cool in pan. The cake will fall.

6. Unmold and turn upright onto a serving platter. Cover and refrigerate at least 6 hours, or overnight. Dust with confectioners' sugar. Serve with sauce.

Yields 10 to 12 servings

Can be prepared the day before or frozen.

FLOURLESS CHOCOLATE FUDGE CAKE

There are many versions of flourless chocolate cake. This one is drier in texture and has a smooth chocolate glaze.

21 ounces semisweet chocolate, chopped	1⅓ cups sugar
1 cup butter, cut into pieces	5 eggs, beaten
	¾ cup cream

1.   Preheat the oven to 325°F. Butter a 9-inch springform pan.

2.   Melt 9 ounces of chocolate and the butter. Stir until smooth. Whisk in the sugar until it dissolves. Remove from the heat. Whisk in the eggs and pour into the prepared pan.

3.   Bake about 1¼ hours, or until a tester comes out almost dry. Refrigerate for at least 3 hours.

4.   In a saucepan or microwave, melt the remaining chocolate with the cream, stirring until smooth. Let the ganache cool until thick enough to spread.

5.   Unmold the cold cake onto a serving plate and frost with some of the ganache. Beat the remaining ganache until thick, put into a pastry bag fitted with a #4 open star tip, and pipe rosettes on the cake.

Yields 10 to 12 servings

Can be prepared several days before or frozen.

FUDGY FLOURLESS CHOCOLATE CAKE

This coffee-accented version is moister than the previous recipe.

7 ounces semisweet	**1 cup sugar**
chocolate, chopped	**4 eggs, lightly beaten**
½ cup strong coffee	**Whipped cream, or Custard**
1 cup butter	**Sauce, page 545**

1.   Preheat the oven to 350°F. Generously butter and flour an 8-inch spring-form pan.

2.   In a saucepan, melt the chocolate with the coffee, over medium heat, stirring. Add the butter and the sugar, a little at a time, stirring constantly. Heat until hot but not boiling. Remove from the heat. Add the eggs, one at a time, stirring constantly.

3.   Pour the batter through a fine sieve into the prepared pan. Bake 30 to 40 minutes, or until a crust forms and the mixture pulls away from the sides of the pan. Refrigerate for at least 3 hours, and unmold.

4.   Invert onto a serving platter and serve cold with whipped cream or custard sauce.

Yields 8 to 10 servings

Can be prepared several days ahead or frozen.

FLOURLESS CHOCOLATE CAKE

This cake is silkier and less fudge-like than the other flourless chocolate cakes.

4¾ ounces semisweet	**4 eggs**
chocolate, chopped	**3½ tablespoons sugar**
3 tablespoons butter	**1½ tablespoons Cognac**

1.   Preheat the oven to 275°F. Line a 9-inch round cake pan with parchment or waxed paper and butter the paper.

2.   Melt the chocolate and the butter. Stir until smooth. Remove from the heat.

3.   In a mixer, beat the eggs and the sugar until tripled in volume and the consistency of mayonnaise. Fold in the Cognac and the chocolate mixture. Pour into the prepared pan.

4.   Bake about 35 minutes, or until springy. Cool in the pan and unmold.

Yields 8 to 10 servings

Can be prepared ahead and frozen.

GÂTEAU AU CHOCOLAT DE METZ
(Metz Chocolate Cake)

This is not as dense as the previous cakes, but delicious all the same. Use it when you want a "lighter" chocolate cake.

8 ounces semisweet chocolate, chopped	½ cup blanched almonds, ground
⅓ cup milk	6 eggs, separated
½ teaspoon vanilla	Heavy cream, whipped, sweetened, and flavored
⅔ cup sugar	
¾ cup potato flour or starch	

1.   Preheat the oven to 350°F. Butter a 10-inch round cake pan.

2.   In a saucepan, melt the chocolate in the milk, stirring constantly, until smooth. Remove from the heat. Beat in the vanilla, ⅓ cup of sugar, and the potato flour.

3.   In a small bowl, mix the almonds and the egg yolks. Stir into the chocolate mixture.

4.   In a mixer, beat the egg whites until they form soft peaks. Add the remaining sugar and beat until stiff and glossy peaks form. Fold into the chocolate mixture and pour into the pan.

5.   Bake for 45 minutes. The center of the cake will be soft. Refrigerate for several hours before unmolding. Serve with whipped cream.

Yields 10 to 12 servings

Can be prepared the day before or frozen.

VELOURS AU CHOCOLAT
(Chocolate Fondant Cake)

The ingredients are very similar to the Nemesis (see page 488), but the result is quite different.

8 ounces semisweet chocolate, finely chopped	softened
2 cups superfine sugar	4 eggs, lightly beaten
½ cup strong coffee	1 tablespoon flour
1 cup butter, cut into pieces,	Confectioners' sugar, for garnish

1.   Preheat the oven to 350°F. Butter a 9-inch round cake pan and line with foil, letting the foil hang over the sides. Smooth the foil and butter it.

2.   Melt the chocolate with the sugar and the coffee, stirring until smooth. Remove from the heat and stir in the butter, a little at a time. Gradually add the eggs to the flour, beating until smooth. Add the egg mixture to the chocolate and blend well. Pour the chocolate into the prepared pan.

3.   Set in a water bath and bake for 45 minutes, without letting the water boil. Remove from the water and bake 20 minutes. Refrigerate for at least 6 hours before serving.

4.   Rub the bottom of the pan with a towel wrung out in hot water and lift the cake from the pan, using the foil overhang as handles. Peel off the foil and invert the cake onto a serving platter. Decorate with confectioners' sugar.

Yields 10 to 12 servings

Can be prepared several days before or frozen.

DARK CHOCOLATE CAKE QUAI D'ORSAY

The chocolate glaze on this cake is firmer than the usual chocolate glaze.

18 ounces semisweet chocolate, chopped	**⅓ cup sugar**
2 tablespoons milk	**7 eggs, separated**
10 tablespoons butter	**½ cup flour**
	1 egg white

1.   Preheat the oven to 400°F. Butter and flour a 9-inch round cake pan.

2.   Melt 12 ounces of chocolate in the milk. Stir until smooth.

3.   In another saucepan, melt the butter and the sugar over low heat until the sugar dissolves. Blend into the chocolate mixture.

4.   Beat in the egg yolks, 1 at a time, beating well after each addition. Gradually fold in the flour.

5.   Beat the egg whites until firm, but not dry. Fold one-fourth of the egg whites into chocolate mixture and stir to lighten the mixture. Fold in the remaining egg whites and pour into the pan.

6.   Bake for 25 to 30 minutes, or until the cake has shrunk from the sides of the pan and it tests done. Cool in the pan for 5 minutes and unmold onto a rack.

7.   Melt the remaining chocolate and stir until smooth. Pour the glaze over the cake, coating the top and sides. Refrigerate until the glaze sets. Transfer the cake to a serving platter.

Yield 10 to 12 servings

Can be prepared the day before or frozen.

DOLCE TORINESE (Chilled Chocolate Loaf)

This is not a cake in the traditional sense, but as a chocolate dessert it is unbeatable.

8 ounces semisweet chocolate	Pinch of salt
¼ cup rum	12 Petit Beurre biscuits, cut into ½ × 1-in pieces, see Note
1 cup unsalted butter	Confectioners' sugar, for garnish
2 tablespoons sugar	
2 eggs, separated	½ cup heavy cream, whipped and sweetened
1½ cups ground blanched almonds	

1.   Lightly oil a 1½ quart loaf pan with vegetable oil and line the pan with plastic wrap.

2.   Melt the chocolate. Stir in the rum and cool.

3.   Cream the butter until light and fluffy. Beat in the sugar and the egg yolks, 1 at a time. Stir in the almonds and the cooled chocolate.

4.   Using clean beaters, beat the egg whites with the salt until stiff, but not dry, peaks form. Fold into the chocolate mixture. Fold in the biscuits.

5.   Spoon into the prepared pan and smooth the top. Refrigerate for at least 4 hours or until firm. Unmold and dust with confectioners' sugar. Serve the slices with whipped cream, if desired.

Yields 12 to 18 servings

Can be prepared several days before or frozen.

NOTE: Although Petit Beurre biscuits are the best choice, other plain cookies will also work. Use a serrated knife to cut the biscuits, discarding the smaller crumbs. Slice the dessert with a serrated knife dipped in hot water.

SFORMATA AL CAFFÉ (Coffee Mold)

This is a coffee-flavored version of the previous dessert.

½ **cup butter**	1 **cup heavy cream**
⅓ **cup sugar**	1 **tablespoon confectioners'**
1 **egg yolk**	**sugar**
11 **ounces Petit Beurre Biscuit,**	**Rum, to taste**
pulverized	**Chocolate-covered coffee**
¼ **cup strong black coffee**	**beans, for garnish**

1.   Line a 9 × 5-inch loaf pan with foil or plastic wrap. Oil the foil or plastic.

2.   In a processor or an electric mixer, cream the butter and the sugar until fluffy. Add the egg yolk and mix well. Add half of the ground biscuits and mix until absorbed. Mix in the coffee and the remaining biscuits. The mixture will be a thick paste. Fill the pan with the mixture, pressing firmly. Chill at least 2 hours.

3.   Unmold onto a serving platter. Beat the cream, confectioners' sugar, and the rum, to taste, until stiff peaks form.

4.   Using a pastry bag fitted with a #4 open star tip, pipe a row of whipped cream rosettes down the center of the *sformata.* Place a coffee bean on each rosette.

Yields 12 to 18 servings

Can be prepared several days before serving.

CHOCOLAT SAINT-ÉMILION
(Chocolate Macaroon Cake)

A favorite from Normandy, this is a rich chocolate cream encasing liqueur-soaked macaroons.

1 cup butter	**chocolate, chopped**
¾ cup sugar	**½ pound small, dry Almond**
2 egg yolks	**Macaroons, page 26**
1¼ cups milk, scalded	**Dark rum**
1 pound bittersweet	

1. Oil an 8-inch springform pan.

2. In a bowl, cream the butter and sugar until light and fluffy.

3. In another bowl, gradually add the milk to the egg yolks.

4. Melt the chocolate. Stir in the milk mixture. Beat in the butter and sugar until completely smooth.

5. Brush the macaroons with the rum. Pour a thin layer of the chocolate into the prepared pan and arrange a layer of macaroons over the chocolate. Add more chocolate, another layer of macaroons, and continue to layer, finishing with the macaroons. Refrigerate overnight, or freeze. Serve cold.

Yields 6 servings

Can be prepared several days ahead, or frozen.

IL PELLEGRINO
(Chocolate Praline Ganache)

I created this dessert for a chocolate-loving client. A layer of coarsely chopped praline crumbs makes a base for a lightly whipped ganache topped with fully whipped ganache (see Notes). Serve it with caramel sauce to bring out the flavor of the base.

¾ cup coarsely chopped	**3 cups heavy cream**
Praline, page 30, see Note	**1 cup sugar**
1¼ pounds semisweet	**¼ cup water**
chocolate, chopped	**Hot water**

1. Line a 9-inch springform pan with parchment paper. Sprinkle the praline in the bottom and press into an even layer.

2. Melt 1 pound of chocolate in 1 cup of heavy cream. Stir in 1 cup of the remaining cream. Refrigerate the ganache until cold.

3. In a mixer, whip the ganache until very lightly thickened. Scrape into the prepared pan, smooth the top, and refrigerate.

4. Melt the remaining chocolate and heavy cream. Stir until smooth. Refrigerate until cold.

5. Meanwhile, in a saucepan, bring the sugar and ¼ cup of water to a full, rolling boil, swirling the pan as needed to dissolve the sugar. Boil, without stirring, until a deep golden brown. Place the pan in a sink. Add hot water, ½ cup at a time, being careful of splattering, until the caramel is the consistency of maple syrup. Refrigerate.

6. To serve, run a knife around the sides of the pan, remove the sides, and slide the cake onto a serving platter.

7. In a mixer, beat the second batch of ganache until it holds a shape and is light in color. Using a pastry bag fitted with a #5 open star tip, pipe rosettes of ganache around the edge of the cake. Pass the caramel sauce.

Yields 10 to 12 servings

Can be prepared two days before serving.

NOTES:
- The chopped praline should be the consistency of oatmeal.
- Beat the first batch of ganache until it just starts to hold a shape; the color should remain dark. If it has been whipped too much, it will lighten in color and the texture will be different.
- Beat the second batch of ganache until it holds stiff peaks, and pipe onto the cake immediately, or it will become too stiff. If the ganache does become too stiff, melt, chill, and beat it again.

Chapter *14*

COOKIES, PLAIN CAKES, AND CONFECTIONS

Many desserts need a *lagniappe,* a little something extra, to complete them. A gin and tonic is fine, but the lime finishes it. A grilled steak is delicious, but a Roquefort butter makes it special. Gravlax is grand, but the dill sauce makes it complete. For desserts, that little something extra is a cookie, a slice of plain cake, or a confection. A butter cookie makes the fruit cup dessert instead of just a bowl of fruit; a slice of Madeira Cake turns poached pears into company food. Confections such as Candied Orange Rind or truffles finish the meal. These may not be necessary, but they turn the ordinary into the extraordinary.

Many are the occasions when an assortment of cookies is dessert and more elaborate cookies are in order. Plain cake makes a fine dessert. After a lavish dinner, confections alone are the choice for many diners; for others, they are the cherry on the sundae, the last little morsel that satisfies.

Cookies, unless you are making them for the football team, should be bite-size. No more than two polite bites without puffing out the cheeks. Make plenty so guests may have as many as they want, but keep the size to about 2 inches. All too many recipes (not here, of course) suggest 3 inches or larger, which is fine for the children but not for "polite society." This often means that you will get more cookies than the recipe states. But then, who ever has too many cookies?

Americans have a passion for cookies. One cookie, the chocolate chip, created an entire industry. Ruth Wakefield created this delight at her restaurant, The Toll House in Whitman, Massachusetts, in the 1930s. Her recipe, found on the package of Nestlé's chocolate morsels, is still the standard by which all others are measured. Many cooks have tried to improve on her recipe, but with little success. They may increase the chocolate or turn it into butterscotch, but nothing matches the original.

For the cookies in this book, I use the food processor whenever possible. Follow the recipes for perfect results. If a processor is not available, you can prepare the recipes by hand or with an electric mixer. The only tedious part is creaming the butter and sugar. But as every good baker knows, ingredients should be at room temperature before you start to prepare the recipes. If the butter is refrigerator-hard, creaming will be more difficult.

A good, plain cake stands on its own without further embellishment. Sponge cake, freshly made, with no more than a dusting of confectioners' sugar, is unbeatable, as is pound cake and other cakes made with fresh unsalted butter and eggs. Sometimes, as with sponge cakes, gilding them with icings makes them even more appealing. Or, use pound cake as a base to create a special dessert. But there are many cakes that never get embellished because they are so good on their own. A midnight raid of the icebox for a glass of milk and Chocolate Mousse Cake is fine, but it is homier still, and all the more comforting, with the plain Chocolate Cake.

Confections are the little afterthoughts that make life worth living. They are as simple as candied rind or as elaborate as the magnificent Sarah Bernhardts. Chocolate Truffles get rave reviews. They can be meltingly soft in the center or somewhat firm. Enrobe them in cocoa, confectioners' sugar, or minced nuts, or encase them in melted chocolate. Or, for a quick, easy confection, prepare chocolate bark. Just be sure to follow directions carefully and never overheat the chocolate (see page 6 for handling chocolate).

STORING COOKIES, PLAIN CAKES, AND CONFECTIONS.   One of the more appealing features of most cookies, plain cakes, and confections is that you can prepare them ahead. They keep at least a day and most for several days. And generally, they freeze beautifully. Smart cooks have a supply of cookies and plain cakes in the freezer for ready use. The rest of us usually have to be ready to prepare them as we need them. Happily, most cookies take only minutes to prepare and even the plain cakes assemble and bake within an hour or so.

A chef's secret is to prepare refrigerator cookie doughs ahead and store them in the freezer. Slice off as many cookies as you need and bake during dinner. Serving warm cookies will win anyone's heart. Al Forno, a restaurant in Providence, Rhode Island, offers a platter of warm, just-baked cookies on their dessert menu. I suspect it is among its most popular desserts.

Many of the confections freeze well but, the chocolate ones are best when freshly prepared. Make them just a day or two before serving. Candied fruit rinds keep several weeks in airtight containers at room temperature.

Cookies

PALMIERS

These are the ultimate butter cookie—buttery, sweet, but not too sweet, and crisp. Perfect alone or with any dessert.

¼ recipe Classic Puff Pastry,
   page 388, see Notes
   Sugar

1.   Preheat the oven to 400°F. Run a baking sheet under cold water to dampen.

2.   Roll the pastry, in sugar instead of flour, into a rectangle about 12 × 18 inches, about ⅛ inch thick. Use more sugar than you would use flour, to prevent sticking.

3.   Fold each long side toward the center twice, so the folds almost meet. Fold the sides together to make one long strip. Cut the strip crosswise into ½-inch-thick slices. Place the slices, cut side down, on the damp baking sheet about 2 inches apart. If desired, pinch the bottom of each palmier to give it a heart shape.

4.   Bake about 20 minutes, or until the bottoms just start to turn golden. With a metal spatula, turn the palmiers over and bake until golden, about 10 minutes longer. Cool on baking racks.

Yields about 36 cookies

Can be frozen.

NOTES:

· The sugar caramelizes and is extremely hot and sticky, fresh from the oven. Should you get any on you, plunge that portion of you under cold running water immediately to stop any burning (see Chapter 1, page 5).
· Preparing puff pastry takes both skill and work, but the effort is worth it. You may prefer to purchase frozen pastry from a local market.
· Use the scraps from making other puff pastry desserts to make Palmiers. If it is a little tough, no one will notice because Palmiers are so crispy.

SHORTCAKE COOKIES

These are delicious, light, buttery cookies.

1 cup flour	**½ cup confectioners' sugar**
¾ cup butter, softened	
½ cup cornstarch	

1. Preheat the oven to 300°F.

2. In a processor, combine the flour, butter, cornstarch, and sugar. Process for 30 seconds, or until well blended. Refrigerate for an hour or until firm enough to handle.

3. Shape as desired (see Variations). Bake on ungreased baking sheets for 20 minutes, or until pale gold on the bottom. Cool on racks.

Yields about 3 dozen cookies

Store in an airtight container or freeze.

Variations

- With a rolling pin, roll the dough ¼ inch thick on a lightly floured board and use a pastry cutter to cut into shapes.
- With your hands, roll the dough into 1-inch balls, place on an ungreased cookie sheet, and flatten with a cookie stamp or the tines of a fork, to make a design.
- With your hands, roll the dough into one or two logs, 1½ inches in diameter. Wrap in waxed paper or plastic. Refrigerate for at least 1 hour, or freeze until needed. Slice ¼ inch thick and bake.
- Brush the logs with beaten egg yolk and roll in coarsely crushed sugar cubes. Slice ¼ inch thick and bake.

STRASBOURG COOKIES

Professional chefs use a pastry bag fitted with a #5 open star tip to pipe this mixture onto cookie sheets. It takes a strong arm but is the fastest way to shape the cookies.

14 tablespoons butter,	**1 teaspoon vanilla**
softened	**2 teaspoons lemon juice**
½ cup confectioners' sugar	**2½ cups flour**

1.   Preheat the oven to 450°F. Butter baking sheets.

2.   In a processor, cream the butter until light. Add the sugar and process until light and fluffy. Add the vanilla, lemon juice, and flour, and process to make a smooth, stiff dough. Add more flour, if needed.

3.   Press the dough through a cookie press onto baking sheets. Or, roll the dough into 1-inch balls, place on a baking sheet, and flatten with a cookie stamp. Bake for 8 minutes, or until lightly browned. Cool on a rack.

Yields about 3 dozen cookies

Store in an airtight container or freeze.

Variations

• Garnish each cookie with half a glacéed cherry, whole almond, or dust with colored sprinkles.

JUMBALS

Mace gives this Early American cookie a subtle flavor.

⅓ cup butter, softened	**¾ cup sifted flour**
⅓ cup sugar	**¼ teaspoon salt**
1 egg	**1 teaspoon mace**

1.   Preheat the oven to 350°F. Butter a baking sheet.

2.   In a processor, cream the butter and the sugar until light and fluffy. Add the egg and incorporate. Add the flour, salt, and mace, and process until combined.

3.   Drop the dough by teaspoonful onto the baking sheet about 4 inches apart. With a metal spatula dipped in cold water, spread the cookies about ⅛ inch thick.

4.   Bake 10 minutes, or until the edges are a light brown. Cool on a rack.

Yields about 24 cookies

Store in an airtight container or freeze.

JELLY-FILLED COOKIES

These are sometimes called Thumbprint Cookies.

1 cup butter, softened	2 cups flour
⅔ cup sugar	1 cup jam, jelly, preserves, or
2 large egg yolks	marmalade, approximately,
2 teaspoons vanilla	see Note

1.   Preheat the oven to 375°F. Butter baking sheets.

2.   In a processor or mixer, cream the butter and the sugar until light and fluffy. Add the egg yolks and the vanilla and process with on/off turns. Add the flour and process until the mixture begins to form a dough.

3.   Roll the dough into 1-inch balls and place 2 inches apart on the baking sheets.With the tip of your finger, make an indentation in the center of each cookie. Fill with ½ teaspoon of jam.

4.   Bake about 8 minutes, or until the edges turn pale gold. Cool on a rack.

Yields about 50 cookies

Store in an airtight container or freeze.

NOTE: Do not add too much jam; it will bubble over the sides of the cookies.

CROUSTILLONS (Crispy Norman Cookies)

⅓ cup sugar	¾ cup flour
3 tablespoons butter,	½ teaspoon baking powder
softened	2 egg whites
1 tablespoon milk	

1.   Preheat the oven to 375°F. Lightly butter baking sheets.

2.   In a bowl, mix the sugar, butter, and milk until creamy. Add the flour, baking powder, and egg whites, and mix until smooth. Drop tablespoonsful of the mixture onto the baking sheets about 2 inches apart. Bake for 12 minutes, or until lightly browned. Cool.

Yields about 36 cookies

Best served the same day, or store in an airtight container or freeze.

GINGERSNAPS

These are particularly good with poached fruits.

1 cup sugar	1 teaspoon cinnamon
1 cup vegetable shortening	1 teaspoon ground cloves
1 egg	½ teaspoon ginger
¼ cup dark molasses	¼ teaspoon salt
2 cups flour	Sugar
1 tablespoon baking soda	

1. Preheat the oven to 350°F.

2. In a processor, cream the sugar and the shortening. Add the egg and the molasses and process until blended.

3. In a bowl, mix the flour, baking soda, cinnamon, cloves, ginger, and salt. Add to the processor and process with on/off turns until it forms a dough. With your hands, roll into ½-inch balls. Roll the balls in sugar.

4. Place 1 inch apart on ungreased baking sheets and bake 12 minutes, or until lightly browned on the bottom. Cool on the baking sheets.

Yields about 36 cookies

Store in an airtight container or freeze.

CHOCOLATE BUTTER COOKIES

½ cup sugar	1 teaspoon almond extract
¾ cup butter, softened	1½ cups flour
1 egg yolk	¼ cup cocoa

1. Preheat the oven to 375°F.

2. In a processor or mixer, cream the sugar, butter, egg yolk, and almond extract. Gradually add the flour and the cocoa with on/off turns.

3. Shape as desired (see Variations). Bake on ungreased baking sheets for 7 to 9 minutes, or until set. Cool on racks.

Yields about 36 cookies

Store in an airtight container or freeze.

Variations

- With your hands, roll the dough into 1-inch balls, and flatten the 1-inch balls with a fork or cookie press.
- Roll into logs about ½ inch in diameter and 2 inches long, slice ¼-inch thick.
- Garnish by dipping in melted chocolate (see page 36).
- Roll the chocolate-dipped cookies in chopped nuts, candied fruits, or chocolate or colored sprinkles.
- Drizzle with Confectioners' Sugar Glaze (see page 36), or just dip the ends.

CARDAMOM BUTTER COOKIES WITH COCONUT

These are particularly good served with desserts featuring ginger.

2¼ cup sifted flour	½ teaspoon salt
1½ teaspoons baking powder	2 eggs
1¼ cups sugar	Sugar
1 cup butter, softened	Coconut
½ teaspoon cardamom	

1.   Preheat the oven to 375°F.

2.   In a bowl, mix the flour and the baking powder.

3.   In a processor or mixer, cream the butter, sugar, cardamom, and salt. Add the eggs and the flour mixture and process with on/off turns until a dough forms.

3.   Drop by ½ teaspoonsful onto ungreased baking sheets. Flatten with the bottom of a glass covered with a damp cloth. Sprinkle the tops with sugar and coconut.

4.   Bake 8 to 10 minutes, or until edges are light golden. Cool on a rack.

Yields about 8 dozen cookies

Store in an airtight container or freeze.

SABLÉES (Butter Cookies)

You must use the egg yolks for the desired sandy texture.

2 cups flour	**Pinch of salt**
½ cup butter, softened	**1 teaspoon vanilla**
½ cup sugar	**2 tablespoons milk**
5 egg yolks	

1. Preheat the oven to 350°F. Lightly butter baking sheets.

2. In a processor or mixer, mix the flour, butter, and sugar until sandy. Add 4 egg yolks, salt, and vanilla, and mix until a dough forms. Refrigerate until firm enough to roll.

3. On a lightly floured surface, or between sheets of waxed paper, roll ¼-inch thick. With a cookie cutter, cut into 1½- to 2-inch circles and place on baking sheets.

4. In a small bowl, mix the remaining egg yolk with the milk. Glaze each cookie. With the tip of a small knife or a fork, score the surface of each cookie. Bake for 15 minutes, or until golden.

Yields about 3 dozen cookies

Store in an airtight container or freeze.

NOTE: Cut the cookies as closely together as possible. The cookies made from the rerolled scraps will be tougher.

LEMON-ALMOND SABLÉES

⅔ cup ground almonds	**Pinch of salt**
⅔ cup confectioners' sugar	**1½ cups flour**
11 tablespoons butter, softened	**2 tablespoons sifted confectioners' sugar**
1 egg	**1 egg yolk**
2 teaspoons grated lemon rind	**1 tablespoon lemon juice**

1. Butter baking sheets.

2. In a processor, pulverize the ground almonds and ⅔ cup of confectioners' sugar. Transfer to a mixer, add the butter, and beat until light. Blend in the egg, lemon rind, salt, and flour and process it to a dough.

3. Shape into a flat cake and wrap in plastic. Refrigerate for 1 hour.

4. Preheat the oven to 350°F. On a lightly floured surface, or between sheets of waxed paper, roll half the dough at a time about ¼ inch thick. With a cookie cutter, cut 1½- to 2-inch rounds and place on baking sheets.

5. In a bowl, beat the sifted confectioners' sugar, egg yolk, and lemon juice. Brush the cookies with the glaze and score the tops with a fork or the point of a knife. Bake about 15 minutes, or until golden. Cool on a rack.

Yields about 50 cookies

Store in an airtight container or freeze.

NOTE: Cut the cookies as closely together as possible. The cookies made from rerolled scraps will be tougher.

PAINS AUX AMANDES (Almond Cookies)

1¼ cups flour	½ cup butter, softened
½ teaspoon ginger	½ cup brown sugar
Pinch of cinnamon	½ teaspoon baking powder
½ teaspoon allspice	3 tablespoons sliced almonds

1. Line baking sheets with foil.

2. In a processor, mix the flour, ginger, cinnamon, and allspice. Add the butter, sugar, and baking powder and process with on/off turns until the mixture starts to form a dough.

3. Turn onto a lightly floured board and knead into a dough. Shape into a 6 × 3 × 1-inch block. Wrap in waxed paper and refrigerate for 30 minutes, or until firm enough to slice.

4. Preheat the oven to 400°F. Slice ⅛ inch thick and arrange on baking sheets. Sprinkle 2 to 3 sliced almonds on each cookie and press lightly. Bake for 5 to 7 minutes, or until golden.

Yields about 50 cookies

Store in an airtight container or freeze.

NOTE: Prepare the dough in batches and freeze, to slice and bake as needed.

VIENNESE ALMOND CRESCENTS

These Old World favorites are similar to cookies found in Greece, Spain, Portugal, and Mexico.

1 cup butter, softened	**⅛ teaspoon salt**
⅓ cup sugar	**1 cup confectioners' sugar, for**
⅔ cup ground almonds	**garnish**
1⅔ cups flour	

1. Preheat the oven to 350°F. Line baking sheets with parchment paper.

2. In a processor or mixer, cream the butter and the sugar. Add the almonds, flour, and salt. Mix to form a dough. With your hands, roll table-spoonsful of the dough into logs and place on the baking sheets. Curve the ends to form crescents.

3. Bake about 12 minutes, or until the edges are barely golden. Cool on a rack. Just before serving, sprinkle heavily with confectioners' sugar.

Yields about 40 cookies

Store in an airtight container or freeze.

Variations

- For a heavier sugar coating, roll in confectioners' sugar while still warm, and again before serving.
- *Chocolate-dipped.* Dip one or both ends of the crescent in Chocolate Dip (see page 36).

PECAN SHORTBREAD COOKIES

The pecans accent the butter flavor.

1 cup pecans	**1 cup butter, softened**
2 cups flour	**Pinch of salt**
1 cup confectioners' sugar	**1 teaspoon vanilla**

1. In a processor, grind the pecans, being careful not to turn them into a paste. Add the flour and the sugar and process until combined. Add the butter, salt, and vanilla and process with on/off turns to form a dough.

2. Remove the dough from the processor and shape into a log. Refrigerate 30 minutes or until firm enough to slice.

3. Preheat the oven to 350°F. Slice the log ¼ inch thick and arrange on ungreased baking sheets. Bake 15 to 20 minutes, or until very pale brown. Cool on a rack.

Yields about 40 cookies

Store in an airtight container or freeze before or after baking.

NOTE: Place the dough on a sheet of waxed paper and use it to help roll into a round log. Or, shape into a square, rectangular, or triangular log.

PETITS BISCUITS AUX NOIX
(Crumbly Walnut Cookies)

These are short (crumbly) cookies so handle them with care.

½ **cup butter, softened**	1 **cup finely chopped walnuts**
¼ **cup plus 2 tablespoons**	1 **cup flour**
sugar	2 **tablespoons confectioners'**
2 **teaspoons vanilla**	**sugar, for garnish**

1. Preheat the oven to 300°F. Butter baking sheets.

2. In a mixer or by hand, cream the butter and, the ¼ cup of sugar until fluffy. Mix in the vanilla, nuts, and flour. Drop tablespoonfuls of dough on the baking sheets about 2 inches apart.

3. Bake about 20 minutes, or until pale golden. Carefully transfer the cookies to a rack, sprinkle with the remaining sugar, and cool. Sprinkle with confectioners' sugar.

Yields about 36 cookies

Store in an airtight container or freeze.

PALLOTTOLE AL BURRO (Butter Balls)

½ **cup butter, softened**	2 **tablespoons dark rum**
¼ **cup sugar**	1¼ **cups ground walnuts or**
2 **tablespoons honey**	**Brazil nuts**
1 **cup plus 2 tablespoons**	**Confectioners' sugar, for**
flour	**garnish**
¼ **teaspoon baking soda**	

1. Lightly butter and flour baking sheets.

2. In a mixer, cream the butter, sugar, and honey. Beat in the flour, baking soda, rum, and nuts. Refrigerate the dough about 30 minutes, or until firm.

3. Preheat the oven to 325°F. Roll the dough into 1-inch balls and arrange on sheets about 1½ inches apart. Bake about 15 to 20 minutes, or until firm and just beginning to color. Cool slightly. Roll in confectioners' sugar while still warm. Cool on racks.

Yields about 36 cookies

Store in an airtight container or freeze.

CHOCOLATE MACAROONS

See page 26 for plain Almond Macaroons.

5 ounces blanched or
  unblanched almonds,
  ground
2 ounces unsweetened
  chocolate, grated
¾ cup sugar

5 ounces egg whites (3–5 egg
  whites)
½ teaspoon almond extract
  Glacéed cherries or
  almonds, optional

1. Preheat the oven to 400°F. Line baking sheets with parchment paper or foil.

2. In a large, heavy frying pan, mix the almonds, chocolate, sugar, and egg whites. Place over medium heat and cook, stirring constantly, scraping the sides and bottom of the pan, about 5 minutes, or until the mixture is the consistency of soft mashed potatoes. Pour into a bowl and stir in the almond extract. Cool 10 minutes.

3. Using a large pastry bag fitted with a #8 star tip, pipe rosettes of the batter onto the baking sheets. Place a cherry or almond on top of each macaroon, if desired. Bake for 12 to 13 minutes, or until just beginning to color. Do not overbake. Cool on the parchment paper.

Yields about 24 macaroons

Store in an airtight container or freeze.

QUARESIMALI BISCOTTI (Italian Nut Biscuits)

When first baked, these are chewy. They soon harden to crisp cookies to dunk in coffee or red wine.

1¾ cups flour
¾ teaspoon baking powder
1 cup sugar
2 eggs
½ teaspoon cinnamon
¼ teaspoon allspice

Dash orange extract
Dash lemon extract
Dash vanilla
1½ cups whole toasted almonds
1 egg, beaten

1. Preheat the oven to 375°F. Lightly butter a large baking sheet.

2. In a bowl, mix the flour and baking powder. In a separate bowl, mix the sugar, eggs, cinnamon, allspice, orange extract, lemon extract, and vanilla. Stir in the flour mixture and the nuts.

3. Place on a lightly floured board and knead about 2 minutes, or until it forms a dough.

4. Divide the dough in half. Shape each piece of dough on a baking sheet into an 18 × 2½-inch strip. Leave at least 3 inches between the strips. Brush the top of the strips with beaten egg.

5. Bake about 20 minutes, or until the tops are slightly firm and golden. Lower the oven temperature to 300°F. Cut the logs, on the baking sheet, into 1-inch-wide slices. Turn the slices cut side down. Bake about 5 minutes, or until golden. Turn the slices to the other cut side and bake about 5 minutes longer. Cool on the baking sheet or a rack.

Yields about 36 cookies

Store in an airtight container or freeze.

Variation

• Substitute toasted hazelnuts or combine hazelnuts with the almonds.

PECAN BARS

These are pecan pie in a bar cookie shape.

1⅓ cups plus 3 tablespoons sifted flour	2 eggs
½ teaspoon baking powder	1 teaspoon vanilla
¾ cup dark brown sugar	¾ cup dark corn syrup
½ cup butter	3 cups pecan halves

1. Preheat the oven to 350°F. Butter a 10 × 15-inch jelly roll pan.

2. In a processor, mix 1⅓ cups of flour, baking powder, and ½ cup of sugar. Cut in the butter, with on/off turns, until the mixture resembles fine meal. Press into the prepared pan to make a smooth, firm layer.

3. In a bowl, beat the eggs, vanilla, remaining sugar, corn syrup, and remaining flour until smooth. Pour over the crust and spread evenly. Scatter the pecans over the top.

4. Bake for 35 to 40 minutes, or until the crust is golden. Cool in the pan for 15 to 20 minutes. Cut around the sides of the pan and invert the cake onto a baking sheet. Place a rack over it, turn over onto the rack, and cool. To make cutting easier, freeze the cookies for 30 minutes. Cut into 1 × 2-inch cookies.

Yields about 75 cookies

Store in an airtight container or freeze.

Variations

- You can arrange the pecans, rounded side up, in neat rows.
- Place the Chocolate Dip (see page 36) in a pastry bag fitted with a #1 plain tip. Drizzle it diagonally over the cookies before cutting. Or, drizzle it from a fork.

BUTTER PECAN SQUARES

1 cup butter	4 eggs
3 cups flour	2 tablespoons white vinegar
¼ cup confectioners' sugar	2 teaspoons vanilla
3 cups dark brown sugar	2 cups pecan halves
½ cup butter, melted	

1. Preheat the oven to 350°F. Butter a 10 × 15-inch jelly roll pan.

2. In a processor or mixer, cream the butter, flour, and confectioners' sugar. Press and spread in the bottom of the pan. Bake 15 minutes, or until it just starts to color.

3. In the processor or mixer, combine the brown sugar, butter, eggs, vinegar, and vanilla.

4. Scatter the pecans over the crust. Pour the filling over the pecans. Bake on the top rack of the oven for 30 minutes, or until set and browned. Cool. Refrigerate for 30 minutes to make cutting easier. Cut into 1½-inch squares.

Yields 75 squares

Store in an airtight container or freeze.

Variation

Pecan Tassies.   Press tablespoons of dough into miniature muffin pans and fill with pecans and the filling.

WALNUT BARS

2 cups flour	½ cup light corn syrup
½ cup sugar	1¼ cups brown sugar
¼ teaspoon salt	½ cup heavy cream
½ teaspoon baking powder	2 teaspoons vanilla
12 tablespoons cold butter, cut into small pieces	1 tablespoons dark rum
	3 cups walnuts, chopped
2 eggs, lightly beaten	

1. Preheat the oven to 350°F. Butter a 10 × 15-inch jelly roll pan.

2. In a processor, with on/off turns, mix the flour, sugar, salt, and baking powder. Add 8 tablespoons of the butter and process, with on/off turns, until the mixture resembles coarse meal. Pour in the eggs and process until the dough just holds together. Shape into a flat disk, wrap in plastic or waxed paper, and refrigerate about 30 minutes, or until firm enough to roll.

3. On a lightly floured board, or between sheets of waxed paper, roll the dough into a 12 × 17-inch rectangle and press into the prepared pan. Prick the surface with a fork and bake about 15 minutes, or until the crust starts to turn golden.

4. In a large saucepan, bring the corn syrup and the brown sugar to a boil, stirring often to dissolve the sugar. Add the remaining butter and the cream and simmer 3 minutes. Remove from the heat. Stir in the vanilla, rum, and walnuts. Pour over the crust and bake until the filling bubbles and the crust is lightly browned, about 15 minutes longer. Cool in the pan.

5. Refrigerate the cookies in the pan for 30 minutes to make cutting easier. Cut into 1 × 2-inch bars or cut into squares, diamonds, or triangles.

Yields 75 bars

Store in an airtight container or freeze.

NOTE: For a professional look, use a serrated knife to trim all sides before cutting into cookies.

TART LEMON BARS

There are many versions of this cookie. These are deliciously tart.

1 cup butter, softened	4 eggs
¼ cup confectioners' sugar, plus additional, for garnish	1½ cups sugar
2¼ cups flour	¼ cup lemon juice
½ teaspoon salt	1 teaspoon baking powder
¾ teaspoon grated lemon rind	½ teaspoon salt

1. Preheat the oven to 350°F. Butter a 10 × 15-inch jelly roll pan.

2. In a processor, cream the butter and ¼ cup of confectioners' sugar until light and fluffy. Add 2 cups of flour, salt, and ¼ teaspoon of lemon rind, and process until smooth. Press and spread the dough evenly in the prepared pan. Bake 15 minutes, or until it just starts to turn golden.

3. Meanwhile, in the processor, mix the eggs, sugar, remaining flour, lemon juice, baking powder, and remaining lemon rind, and salt.

4. Pour over the crust and bake about 30 to 35 minutes, or until the edges are golden. Cool in pan and sprinkle the top generously with confectioners' sugar. Use a knife dipped in hot water to cut the filling, neatly, cut into 1 × 2-inch bars.

Yields 75 bars

Store in an airtight container or freeze.

NOTES:
- If the filling absorbs the confectioners' sugar, dust again before serving.
- To make cutting easier, refrigerate for at least 30 minutes.

APRICOT HEARTS

These jam-filled pastries are delicate, light, and flavorful.

1 cup sifted flour	**softened**
½ cup butter, softened	**Apricot jam**
Pinch of salt	**1 egg, lightly beaten**
4 ounces cream cheese,	**Sugar**

1. In a processor or electric mixer, mix the flour, butter, salt, and cream cheese to form a dough. Wrap in waxed paper and refrigerate 30 minutes.

2. Preheat the oven to 400°F.

3. On a lightly floured board, roll the pastry ⅛ inch thick. Cut into small (about 2½-inch) hearts or circles.

4. Place 1 teaspoon of apricot jam on half the pastry cut-outs. Brush the edges with the egg and cover with remaining pastry cut-outs, pressing the edges to seal. Brush the tops with beaten egg and sprinkle with sugar. Bake about 12 minutes, or until golden brown. Cool on a rack.

Yields about 24 cookies

Store in an airtight container or freeze.

RASPBERRY-CHOCOLATE BARS

2 cups flour	**1 cup sugar**
¼ teaspoon baking powder	**¾ teaspoon vanilla**
Pinch of salt	**¾ cup raspberry jam**
1 cup cold butter, cut into	**12 ounces chocolate chips**
pieces	**1 cup chopped pecans**

1. Preheat the oven to 350°F. Butter a 10 × 15-inch jelly roll pan. Soften ½ cup of butter.

2. In a bowl, mix 1 cup of flour, the baking powder, and salt.

3. In a processor or a mixer, cream the softened butter, ½ cup of sugar, and ½ teaspoon of vanilla. Add the flour mixture and process to a dough. Spread and press into the prepared pan. Bake 15 minutes, or until it just starts to turn golden.

4. Spread with the jam and sprinkle with the chocolate chips.

5. Meanwhile, crumble the remaining flour, remaining butter, remaining sugar, pecans, and remaining vanilla in a bowl, with your fingertips, until it resembles coarse meal. Sprinkle the pecan mixture evenly over the chocolate chips.

6. Bake about 18 minutes longer, or until the top is bubbly and the edges start to brown. Cool in the pan. Cut into 1 × 2-inch cookies

Yields 75 cookies

Store in an airtight container or freeze.

CRISP CHOCOLATE COOKIES

3 ounces unsweetened chocolate	3 eggs
1 cup butter, softened	1½ cups flour
2 cups sugar	1 teaspoon vanilla
	1 cup chopped walnuts

1. Preheat the oven to 350°F. Butter baking sheets. Melt the chocolate.

2. In a processor, cream the butter and the sugar. Add the eggs and chocolate and mix well. Add the flour and vanilla and mix again. Transfer to a bowl and stir in the walnuts.

3. Drop teaspoonsful of dough onto the baking sheets. Flatten for thinner and crisper cookies. Bake about 8 to 10 minutes, or until just set.

Yields about 36 cookies

Store in an airtight container or freeze.

CHEWY CHOCOLATE COOKIES

Do not overbake these cookies, to keep them chewy.

2 ounces unsweetened
  chocolate
5 tablespoons butter,
  softened
2 eggs
1 cup sugar

1 teaspoon vanilla
1 cup flour
1 teaspoon baking powder
Pinch of salt
Confectioners' sugar

1.   Melt the chocolate. Line baking sheets with parchment paper.

2.   In a bowl, mix the chocolate, butter, eggs, sugar, and vanilla.

3.   In another bowl, mix the flour, baking powder, and salt. Stir into the chocolate mixture, cover with plastic wrap, and refrigerate about 1 hour, or until firm.

4.   Preheat the oven to 350°F. Roll into 1-inch balls and roll the balls in confectioners' sugar. Bake for 10 minutes, or until the cookies flatten and firm slightly. They will look underbaked. Cool about 1 minute and transfer to racks to finish cooling.

Yields about 36 cookies

Store in an airtight container or freeze.

SPICED MOLASSES-GINGER COOKIES

2 cups flour
2 teaspoons baking soda
2 teaspoons cinnamon
2 teaspoons ginger
1 teaspoon ground cloves
1 teaspoon salt
½ cup vegetable shortening

¼ cup butter
1 cup brown sugar
1 egg
¼ cup dark molasses
Ice water
Sugar

1.   Butter two baking sheets.

2.   In a bowl, mix the flour, baking soda, cinnamon, ginger, cloves, and salt.

3. In a processor or mixer, cream the shortening, butter, and sugar. Mix in the egg and molasses. Add the flour mixture and mix well. Refrigerate about 1 hour, or until firm enough to roll into balls.

4. Preheat the oven to 350°F. Roll into 1-inch balls, dip into ice water, and roll in sugar. Arrange on baking sheets, 2 inches apart. Bake about 10 minutes, or until golden and cracked on top, but still soft to the touch. Cool 1 minute, transfer to a rack and cool completely.

Yields about 45 cookies

Store in an airtight container or freeze.

BRANDY SNAPS

These delicious, crisp cookie rolls are tedious to prepare but well worth the effort.

½ **cup butter**	2 **cups heavy cream**
½ **cup dark corn syrup**	½ **cup sugar**
¼ **cup brown sugar**	2 **tablespoons brandy**
¾ **cup flour**	

1. Preheat the oven to 375°F. Butter a baking sheet and the handle of a wooden spoon.

2. In a small saucepan, over medium heat, melt the butter, corn syrup, and brown sugar. Mix in the flour and bring to a boil, stirring constantly. Remove from the heat and cool until slightly thickened but still warm. Keep in a pan of warm water to maintain consistency.

3. Drop the batter by scant teaspoonsful onto the baking sheet, making no more than five at a time. Bake about 4 to 5 minutes, or until bubbly and golden. Cool slightly and quickly roll each hot cookie on the handle of the wooden spoon, forming ¾-inch cylinders. Transfer to a rack to cool. If the cookies become too firm to wrap around the spoon handle, return to the oven to soften.

4. Just before serving, whip the cream with the sugar and brandy until stiff. Using a pastry bag fitted with a #5 star tip, pipe the whipped cream into the cookie cylinders.

Yields about 24 cookies

Store in an airtight container or freeze.

NOTES:

- Do not attempt these in a humid kitchen; they will not get crisp.
- To freeze, put them into a metal or plastic box with crumpled waxed paper to protect them from breakage.

Variation

- Drape the hot cookies over a buttered rolling pin to make tile shapes. Serve without the whipped cream.

CORNETS DE MURAT
(Rolled Cream-filled Wafers)

These are as wonderful as the previous cookies and only slightly less tedious to prepare.

5 tablespoons butter, softened	2 cups plus 1 teaspoon heavy cream
1 cup confectioners' sugar	1 tablespoon rum
3 egg whites, stirred	2 tablespoons sugar
½ cup flour	1 teaspoon vanilla

1.   Preheat the oven to 400°F. Butter baking sheets.

2.   In a processor, cream the butter and the confectioners' sugar. Add half of the egg whites and mix. Mix in 1 heaping tablespoon of flour and the remaining egg whites. Add the remaining flour, 1 teaspoon of cream, and rum and mix well.

3.   Drop teaspoonsful of the batter, spaced well apart, on the baking sheets and tap the sheet sharply on the counter to flatten the mounds. Refrigerate the remaining mixture.

4.   Bake the cookies for 4 to 5 minutes, or until brown around the edges. Loosen the cookies on the baking sheet. Roll each cookie into a horn shape, set inside a pastry tip, and cool about 2 minutes, or until set. Remove from the tip and place on a rack. If the cookies become too crisp before rolling, reheat in the oven for a minute to soften. Continue with the remaining mixture, working with one baking sheet at a time.

5.   Just before serving, whip the remaining cream until it starts to thicken. Add the sugar and vanilla and beat until stiff. Using a pastry bag fitted with a #5 star tip, pipe the whipped cream into the cookies

Yields about 30 cookies

Store unfilled cookies in an airtight container or freeze. They are best made and served on the same day.

Variations

- Stud the whipped cream with a small strawberry or raspberry.
- Fill with Chocolate Whipped Cream (see page 11).
- Serve unfilled.

MADELEINES

There are two versions of madeleines—these and a harder, more substantial version. Both versions require special molds shaped like small shells. These madeleines, based on génoise, are delicate, and best eaten within hours of baking. If you cannot serve them immediately, freeze them as soon as they are cool.

10 tablespoons butter	Grated rind of 1 lemon
⅔ cup plus 1 tablespoon flour	⅓ cup cake flour
4 eggs	Confectioners' sugar, for
⅔ cup sugar	garnish
2 teaspoons vanilla	

1.   Preheat the oven to 375°F.

2.   In a saucepan, melt the butter over medium heat until it is lightly browned and smells nut-like. Cool to room temperature. In a small bowl, mix 2 tablespoons of butter with 1 tablespoon of flour. With a pastry brush, brush the flour and butter mixture in 48 madeleine molds.

3.   In the bowl, over hot, not boiling, water, whisk the eggs until warm to the touch. Remove the bowl. Beating on slow speed, add the sugar, 1 tablespoon at a time. Add the vanilla and the lemon rind and beat constantly until the batter triples in volume, is pale, and is the consistency of mayonnaise.

4.   In a bowl, mix the remaining flour and the cake flour and fold into the egg mixture. When half of the flour is incorporated, gently fold in the remaining liquid, browned butter. Do not add the browned milk solids at bottom of pan.

5.   Spoon 1 tablespoon of batter into each mold. Bake for 12 minutes, or until golden and the cakes start to shrink from the sides of the molds. Unmold immediately. Sprinkle with confectioners' sugar before serving.

Yields 48 madeleines

Serve within 2 or 3 hours or freeze.

NOTE: As with génoise, you heat the eggs for greater volume. The melted, cooled butter must be fluid enough to pour, but if it is too hot it will sink to the bottom of the bowl. If too cold, it will not incorporate evenly.

Plain Cakes

MADEIRA CAKE

This old-fashioned cake was originally served with a glass of Madeira.

1 **cup butter, softened**	3¼ **cups flour**
Grated rind of ½ lemon	**Pinch of salt**
1¼ **cups sugar**	2 **teaspoons baking powder**
4 **eggs**	1 **cup milk**

1.   Preheat the oven to 350°F. Butter and flour a 9-inch Bundt or tube cake pan.

2.   In a processor, cream the butter, lemon rind, and sugar until light and fluffy. Add the eggs and blend. Add the flour, salt, and baking powder and process with on/off turns to incorporate partially. Add the milk and mix to blend.

3.   Pour into the pan. Bake about 45 minutes, or until it tests done. Cool in the pan 5 minutes and unmold onto a rack to finish cooling.

Yields 1 cake

Serve within 2 days or freeze.

Variation

• Glaze with Confectioners' Sugar Glaze (see page 36), using Madeira instead of water. Or, dust with confectioners' sugar.

MACE OR CARDAMOM CAKE

Prepare the cake with either spice for a subtly flavored treat.

1½ cups butter, softened	**2¾ cups sifted cake flour**
1 pound confectioners' sugar, plus additional, for garnish	**1 teaspoon mace or cardamom**
6 eggs	**1½ teaspoons vanilla**

1. Preheat the oven to 300°F. Butter and flour a 10- to 12-cup tube pan.

2. In a mixer, cream the butter and the sugar until fluffy. Beat in the eggs, one at a time. Beat in the flour, mace or cardamom, and vanilla. Pour into the prepared pan.

3. Bake about 1 hour, or until it tests done. Cool in the pan for 10 minutes, unmold onto a rack and cool. Dust with confectioners' sugar.

Yields 1 cake

Store in an airtight container or freeze.

CHOCOLATE CAKE

This is *the best* chocolate cake.

4 tablespoons butter	**¾ teaspoon baking soda**
2 ounces unsweetened chocolate	**1 egg**
1 cup flour	**1 cup sugar**
Pinch of salt	**¾ cup plus 2 tablespoons milk**
	1 teaspoon vanilla

1. Preheat the oven to 350°F. Butter and flour an 8-inch round cake pan.

2. Melt the butter and the chocolate. Stir until smooth.

3. In a bowl, mix the flour, salt, and baking soda.

4. In a mixer, beat the egg and sugar until thickened and pale. Stir in the melted chocolate. Fold in the flour alternately with the milk. Stir in the vanilla.

5. Pour into the prepared pan. Bake about 35 minutes, or until the surface is slightly springy to the touch. Serve warm or cooled.

Yields 6 to 8 servings

Store in an airtight container or freeze.

Variations

- Dust with confectioners' sugar before serving.
- Split horizontally and fill and frost with ½ recipe of Chocolate Ganache (see page 34).
- Brush split layers with raspberry-flavored Dessert Syrup (see page 30). Fill with 1 cup whipped cream and sprinkle 1 cup raspberries on top. Cover with the top layer and frost with 1 cup more whipped cream. Tumble raspberries over the top.

Confections

PAMELAS
(Candied Grapefruit Rind)

Use the same method to glaze thick orange rinds, or follow one of the recipes on pages 38–39.

4 to 6 grapefruits   **¼ pound coarse sugar**
   Cold water
3¼ cups sugar

1.   Cut the ends from the grapefruits and discard. Cut the fruit in quarters and pry the rind from the fruit. Set the fruit aside for another use. Cut the rind into ½-inch-wide strips.

2.   In a large saucepan, bring the grapefruit rind, with enough cold water to cover, to a boil and simmer 5 minutes. Drain and repeat 3 times. Always start with cold water.

3.   Return the drained rind to the pan and add the sugar. Simmer gently, uncovered, turning the rind often, for 1½ hours, or until glazed. Drain. Arrange the rind on a cooling rack set over a baking sheet. Drain until cool enough to handle. Roll the rind in the crystallized sugar.

Yields 100 to 150 pieces

Store in an airtight container for 5 to 6 weeks.

EUGENIE (Chocolate-coated Orange Rind)

These are extraordinary—well worth the small effort required.

2 large oranges	**2¾ cups sugar**
Boiling water	**5 ounces semisweet chocolate**
2 cups water	**¼ cup cocoa**

1. With a sharp knife or vegetable peeler, peel 1-inch strips of the colored rind. Cut the strips into 1-inch squares.

2. Blanch the rind in boiling water for 3 minutes, drain, and repeat. Drain.

3. In the saucepan, bring 2 cups of water and the sugar to a boil. Add the rind and simmer for 2 hours over very low heat. Drain and arrange the rind on racks and cool for 3 hours.

4. Melt the chocolate. Dip each piece of rind into the melted chocolate to coat completely. Cool on the rack until the chocolate starts to look dull. Place the cocoa in a bowl and toss the chocolate-coated rinds in the cocoa.

Yields 60 to 100 pieces

Store in an airtight container for 2 to 3 weeks.

CHOCOLATE-DIPPED FRUIT OR NUTS

8 ounces semisweet chocolate, tempered, page 9	**strawberries, dried apricots, fresh blueberries, raspberries, sliced ginger)**
Fruit of choice (whole	**Almonds or hazelnuts**

1. Melt the chocolate, heating to no more than 100°F. Cool to 85°F. and then reheat to 90°F. Keep at 90°F.

2. Dip fruit or nuts in the tempered chocolate (see Variations).

3. Place the chocolate-dipped fruit or nuts on waxed paper-lined baking sheets. Refrigerate for 5 minutes, or until the chocolate sets. Store at room temperature.

Yields approximately 1 quart of fruit or 1 pound of nuts

For best taste, serve fresh fruits within 2 to 3 hours. Dried fruits and nuts keep up to one week at room temperature.

Variations

- *Apricots or other dried fruits.*   Dip dried apricots halfway into chocolate and let excess chocolate drain. Will keep several days.
- *Blueberries or Raspberries.*   To coat blueberries or raspberries, place in tiny paper chocolate cups and spoon ½ teaspoon of melted chocolate on each. Refrigerate for 10 minutes, and keep at room temperature for up to 4 hours before serving.
- *Strawberries.*   Dry the fruit completely. Holding the stem of a strawberry, dip halfway into the chocolate, lift, and let excess chocolate drain off. Serve within 2 to 3 hours.
- *Nuts.*   Dip the nuts individually and place on baking sheets to set. Or, arrange two or three nuts in small paper cups and pour ½ teaspoon of chocolate over them to glue them together and partially coat them. You can dip nuts in caramel first, using a fork to lift them in and out. Let the caramel set and then dip them in the chocolate.

CARAMEL-COATED FRUIT

   2 cups sugar
   ½ cup water
   Strawberries, bunches of
   2–3 grapes, see Notes

1.   In a medium saucepan, bring the sugar and water to a boil, stirring gently. Stop stirring and use a brush dipped in cold water to wash down the sides. Boil, without stirring, until the syrup turns golden. Remove the saucepan from the heat and set in a larger pan of hot water.

2.   Dry the fruit thoroughly. Dip the fruit, holding the stem, into the caramel. Shake off the excess caramel and place on a buttered baking sheet or waxed paper to cool and set.

Yields enough for 1 quart of fruit

Serve within an hour or two.

NOTES:

- Select strawberries with long stems for safety and ease of dipping.
- Do not pierce the fruit, except for dried apricots, or the juices will soften the caramel, preventing it from forming a crisp casing.
- Be extremely careful whenever using caramel (see page 5 for directions).

Variation

• Dip dried apricots into the caramel on a skewer.

CHOCOLATE-ALMOND-RAISIN-GINGER BARK

8 ounces semisweet	**coarsely chopped**
chocolate, chopped	**½ cup minced crystallized**
2 ounces unsweetened	**ginger**
chocolate, chopped	**½ cup golden raisins**
1 cup toasted almonds,	

1. Line a baking sheet with foil.

2. Melt the semisweet and unsweetened chocolates. Remove from the heat.

3. Stir the almonds, ginger, and raisins into the chocolate, pour onto the baking sheet, and spread ¼ inch thick. Refrigerate about 20 minutes, or until firm. Break into pieces.

Yields about 1¼ pounds

Store at room temperature for a week or longer.

Variations

• Substitute hazelnuts or any other favorite nut for the almonds.
• Substitute 10 ounces of milk or white chocolate for the semisweet and unsweetened chocolates.
• Melt 5 ounces of milk chocolate and spread it over the bark after it is firm. Refrigerate until set.
• Substitute well-drained Candied Orange Rind (see page 39) for the ginger and raisins.

BUTTERCRUNCH TOFFEE

2 cups toasted and finely	**½ cup butter**
chopped, not pulverized	**1 teaspoon vanilla**
almonds	**¼ teaspoon baking soda**
1¼ cups light brown sugar	**6 ounces semisweet chocolate,**
2 tablespoons water	**grated**

1. Butter a 7 × 10-inch rectangle on a baking sheet. Sprinkle 1 cup of the almonds over the buttered area.

2. In a saucepan, boil the brown sugar, water, and butter until the mixture reaches 285°F. Immediately stir in the vanilla and the baking soda. Pour over the nuts in the rectangle.

3. Sprinkle the chocolate over the top and allow it to melt for 5 minutes. Spread evenly and sprinkle with the remaining almonds. Cool at room temperature until hard. Break into chunks.

Yields about 1½ pounds

Store in an airtight container for up to 2 weeks.

Variations

• Substitute pecans, macadamias, or Brazil nuts for the almonds.
• Substitute milk chocolate for the semisweet chocolate.
• Once set, remove from the pan, melt 6 ounces of semisweet chocolate over hot, not boiling, water, or in a microwave, and spread over the uncoated toffee. Sprinkle with another cup of nuts.

CHARDONS (Thistles)

12 ounces semisweet chocolate, chopped	14 ounces almond paste
	3 tablespoons sugar
2 ounces heavy cream	2 tablespoons water

1. Melt 8 ounces of chocolate in the cream. Stir until smooth. Refrigerate for at least 30 minutes, or until firm enough to pipe.

2. Meanwhile, roll the almond paste into two strips, 18 inches long and 2½ inches wide. Trim the sides neatly.

3. In a small bowl, mix the sugar and water and brush over the almond paste.

4. Using a pastry bag fitted with a #8 plain tip, pipe a strip of chocolate ganache down each strip of almond paste. Carefully wrap the almond paste around the ganache, enclosing it completely. The sides should just meet. Refrigerate while preparing the chocolate coating.

5. Melt 3 ounces of chocolate. Stir in the remaining ounce of chocolate and stir until smooth. Cool to 85°F.

6. With a pastry brush, brush the chocolate over the almond logs, leaving a rough, bark-like surface. Refrigerate about 10 minutes, or until the chocolate sets. Cut into 1-inch slices.

Yields about 36 pieces

Store in an airtight container for up to 1 week.

COCONUT THISTLES

½ cup heavy cream	44 salted toasted almonds
¼ cup light corn syrup	¾ ounce crystallized ginger,
⅔ cup sugar	shredded
1½ cups shredded unsweetened	4 ounces semisweet chocolate,
coconut	chopped

1. Lightly butter a bowl and set aside.

2. In a small saucepan, bring the cream, corn syrup, and sugar to a boil, stirring occasionally. Wash down the sides of the pan with a brush dipped in cold water as the mixture just reaches a boil. Boil until it reaches 232°F. Remove from the heat and stir in the coconut. Pour into the buttered bowl and cover loosely with plastic wrap. Cool completely.

3. Roll the cooled coconut into two 10-inch logs on sheets of waxed paper. Pat each log until it is 2½ inches wide. Arrange the almonds and ginger down the center of each log. Using the waxed paper, lift the coconut over the almonds and ginger and shape into a tight roll. Refrigerate for at least 30 minutes, or until cold.

4. Melt 3 ounces of chocolate. Stir in the remaining ounce of chocolate and cool to 85°F.

5. With a pastry brush, brush the chocolate over the logs. It should have a rough, bark-like texture.

6. Refrigerate for 10 minutes, or until the chocolate sets. Cut into 1-inch slices with a knife dipped into hot water.

Yields about 36 pieces

Store in an airtight container at room temperature for up to 1 week.

Truffles

Chocolate truffles are the *ne plus ultra* of chocolate confections. Intense little balls of chocolate, often flavored with liqueur, that should explode in the mouth with flavor. There are many versions, some based mostly on confectioners' sugar, others (my preference) based on chocolate ganache. Here are a few variations.

CHOCOLATE TRUFFLES

½ **pound semisweet chocolate, chopped**
2 **tablespoons water**
2 **tablespoons superfine sugar**
¾ **cup butter**
2 **egg yolks, lightly beaten**
Cocoa for garnish

Melt the chocolate with the water, sugar, and butter. Stir until smooth. Remove from the heat and stir in the egg yolks. Do not refrigerate. Cool at room temperature until firm enough to roll into ½-inch balls. Roll in cocoa powder.

Yields about 36 truffles

Store at room temperature for up to 3 days.

RAISIN-BOURBON TRUFFLES

½ **cup raisins**
⅓ **cup bourbon**
1 **cup heavy cream**
10 **ounces semisweet**
chocolate, finely chopped
3 **tablespoons butter**
1–1½ **pounds semisweet chocolate**

1.   In a small bowl, soak the raisins in bourbon overnight.

2.   In a saucepan or a microwave, bring the cream to a boil, add the 10 ounces of chocolate and butter, cover, and let stand 5 minutes. Stir until smooth. Set aside until cool.

3.   Stir in the raisins and bourbon and refrigerate until firm, about 4 hours, or overnight.

4. With a spoon, make 1-inch balls of the mixture (it will be soft) and arrange on a baking sheet. Freeze until hard, about 1 hour. Temper 1 pound of chocolate (see page 9).

5. When the truffles are frozen, dip into the tempered chocolate and put on a baking sheet. Chill until set.

Yields about 50 truffles

Store in the refrigerator for up to 1 week.

NOTE: These truffles are particularly delicate; keep refrigerated until shortly before serving. Because the outer casing of chocolate is harder, it will form a solid casing around the center which will almost flow when bitten.

HARLEQUIN DUJA

This is an adaptation of Gaston LeNôtre's recipe.

7 ounces milk chocolate
4 cups Duja, page 30
7 ounces semisweet
chocolate

1. Line an 8-inch square baking pan with parchment paper.

2. Melt the milk chocolate and stir in 1½ cups of Duja. Immediately pour into the pan and smooth the top. Refrigerate for 30 minutes or until firm.

3. In the same double boiler, melt the semisweet chocolate and stir in 1½ cups of Duja. Pour over the first layer in the pan. Sprinkle the remaining Duja over the soft layer and press gently. Refrigerate until firm.

4. Unmold and cut into ¾-inch squares.

Yields about 75 candies

Store at room temperature for up to 3 days, or refrigerate for a week.

FICHI ALLA CIOCCOLATA (Figs with Chocolate)

¾ cup diced Candied Orange
Rind, page 39
Ground cloves, to taste
1 pound large dried figs,
stems removed

1 cup toasted almonds
¾ cup cocoa, for garnish
¾ cup confectioners' sugar, for
garnish

1. Preheat the oven to 350°F. In a bowl, toss the orange rind and the cloves.

2. Cut a slit in the side of each fig and stuff with an almond and a few pieces of the candied rind. Press the opening closed. Arrange the figs on a baking sheet. Bake for 15 minutes, or until they turn slightly dark.

3. In a shallow bowl, mix the cocoa and the confectioners' sugar. Roll the hot figs in the mixture. Cool on a plate.

Yields about 20 pieces

Can be prepared up to a week ahead. Store in an airtight container.

MERINGUE MUSHROOMS

1 recipe Plain Meringue, page 23

3 tablespoons cocoa

4 ounces semisweet chocolate

1. Preheat the oven to 225°F. Line a baking sheet with foil or parchment paper.

2. Using a pastry bag fitted with a #5 or #6 plain tip, pipe round mounds of the meringue for the caps. Holding the bag straight up, pipe an equal number of columns, 1 to 1½ inches tall, for the stems.

3. Put the cocoa into a sieve and tap lightly over the top of the meringues to give a very light dusting. Bake about 1 hour, or until the meringues are light and crisp. To test, remove a cap or stem and let stand outside the oven for a few minutes. It should become dry and crisp. Cool and remove the meringues from the pan.

4. Melt the chocolate. With the point of a sharp knife, scrape a small hole in the bottom of each cap. Spread the chocolate on the bottom of each cap, filling the hole with the chocolate, and push a stem into the hole. Cool upside down until the chocolate sets.

Yields 50 to 75 mushrooms

Store at room temperature; if humid, put into an airtight container. They will keep for up to 2 weeks.

NOTE: Because I prefer a natural-looking mushroom, I vary the size as I pipe and allow them to just barely color. Other bakers prefer to have them all exactly the same size. Carefully smooth the top of each cap before baking and bake them so that they do not color at all.

Variation

• Substitute Chocolate Ganache for the melted chocolate (see page 34), piped through a star tip to give the look of gills to the underside of the caps.

SARAH BERNHARDTS

Macaroons topped with chocolate whipped cream and glazed in chocolate. What could be better? Fortunately, they are easy to prepare and are worth the effort.

⅔ cup blanched almonds	12 tablespoons butter
¾ cup sugar	1 tablespoon light corn syrup
3 tablespoons egg whites (1½)	5 teaspoons water
½ teaspoon almond extract	2 tablespoons minced pistachios, for garnish
2 cups heavy cream	
1 pound semisweet chocolate, chopped	

1. Preheat the oven to 300°F. Line a baking sheet with parchment paper.

2. In a processor, finely grind the almonds and sugar. Add the egg whites and almond extract and process to a paste. Using a pastry bag fitted with a #5 plain tip, pipe the macaroon batter in 1-inch rounds, 2 inches apart. Let stand for 30 minutes.

3. Bake about 20 minutes, or until they begin to color. Remove from paper and cool on a rack.

4. In a saucepan, bring the cream to a simmer. Add ½ pound of chocolate and cover. Remove from the heat and let stand for 5 minutes. Stir until smooth. Cover the ganache with waxed paper and refrigerate at least 4 hours.

5. In a mixer, beat the ganache until light and fluffy. Using a pastry bag fitted with a #5 open star tip, pipe a ¾-inch mound of ganache on top of each macaroon. Refrigerate for at least 30 minutes.

6. Melt the remaining chocolate, butter, and corn syrup until almost melted. Stir until smooth and mix in the water. Strain into a narrow, deep bowl and cool to lukewarm.

7. Holding each confection by the macaroon, dip the ganache mound into the glaze, shake to let excess fall back into the glaze, and set upright on a baking sheet. Sprinkle with pistachios.

Yields about 50 confections

Store in the refrigerator for up to 2 days before serving.

Variation

• I make these quite small to offer as a confection. You may make them larger to serve as individual pastries. Pipe 2-inch macaroons. Double the cream to 4 cups and the chocolate to 1 pound for the ganache topping. There should be enough glaze. Pipe the ganache 2½ to 3 inches above the macaroon.

Chapter *15*

SAUCES

Macédoines and fruit cups often create their own sauce from the natural juices, but other desserts are enhanced by the addition of a separate sauce. A sauce can alter the effect of a dessert. Raspberry sauce intensifies a chocolate torte, while custard sauce offers a calming effect and a subtle counterpoint. Chocolate sauce makes it more chocolate, while mocha or caramel sauce gives the torte another dimension. Serve more than one sauce to play up these aspects both in flavor and design.

Select sauces to suit your mood, pocketbook, and what is available. Raspberry sauce, even from frozen raspberries in January, is expensive, so a caramel or custard might suit better. Raspberry and chocolate are a cliché — a delicious cliché, but still a cliché. Try Caramel Sauce or a Sauce Parisienne for a change. Oranges are inexpensive year round and ordinary until you sauce them with caramel or chocolate and raspberry sauces. (Some clichés are worth living with.)

Some sauces are traditional and are, or were, considered most complementary to a particular dessert. A few years ago, intense chocolate desserts had to have whipped cream or custard sauce to cut the richness. Today, cooks are working diligently to make them more and more intense. To avoid the same old rut, try unfamiliar pairings and sample some of the less well-known sauces. Sauce Riche, a sloe gin-flavored custard sauce, seemed questionable until I prepared it and found it mouth-watering. Serve Grand Marnier Sauce with sloe gin on poached pears or chocolate tortes, or use a honeydew melon-flavored liqueur to serve with melons and other fruits.

Sauces not only flavor desserts, but also act as a design element. Serve them from a separate container, or use them to create elaborate plate decorations. Select them for their flavor and their color to add excitement to the plate. Poached pears with custard sauce is flavorful but boring to look at. Add drizzles of raspberry, chocolate, or blueberry and they look great. Fill a plate with custard sauce and draw raspberry sauce through it to make flowers or other designs (see page 46).

YOGURT SAUCE WITH ORANGE AND POPPYSEEDS

Serve with cut-up fresh fruits.

1 cup plain yogurt	vinegar
⅓ cup sugar	1 tablespoon orange juice
Grated rind of 1 orange	1 tablespoon Grand Marnier
2 tablespoons raspberry	1 tablespoon poppyseeds

In a bowl, mix the yogurt, sugar, orange rind, vinegar, orange juice, Grand Marnier, and poppyseeds.

Yields about 1½ cups

Can be prepared the day before serving.

Variation

• Substitute sour cream for the yogurt.

BROWN SUGAR-RUM SAUCE

Serve with cut-up fresh fruits.

1½ cups sour cream	1 tablespoon light rum
¼ cup brown sugar	1 tablespoon Irish whiskey or
¼ cup raisins	scotch

In a bowl, mix the sour cream, sugar, raisins, rum, and whiskey. Refrigerate, covered for 2 hours.

Yields about 2 cups

Prepare up to 3 days before serving.

CARAMEL SAUCE I

Serve with fruit, cakes, or puddings.

1½ cups heavy cream
¼ cup water
½ cup sugar

1. In a saucepan, bring the cream almost to a simmer.

2. In another saucepan, cook the water and the sugar over moderate heat until the sugar dissolves. Raise the heat and boil, without stirring, until the mixture is a deep golden brown. Remove from the heat and carefully add the hot cream, whisking constantly. Cool. Serve warm or cold.

Yields about 2 cups

Can be prepared the day before.

NOTE: Add the cream carefully to avoid splatters from the caramel.

CARAMEL SAUCE II

A richer version of the previous sauce, served with warm puddings, cakes, or over ice cream.

½ cup sugar   **½ cup butter**
½ cup brown sugar   **¼ cup rum**
½ cup heavy cream

In a saucepan, cook the sugar, brown sugar, and cream until the sugars dissolve. Stir in the butter and rum. Serve warm.

Yields about 1½ cups

Can be prepared several days ahead and reheated.

DARK CARAMEL SAUCE

The previous sauces have a butterscotch quality; this clear caramel syrup has a stronger flavor.

1 cup sugar   **lemon juice**
¾ cup cold water
¼ teaspoon cream of tartar or

1. In a saucepan, cook the sugar, ½ cup of water, and cream of tartar over low heat until the sugar dissolves. Raise the heat and boil the sauce, without stirring, until it turns a dark brown. Place the pan in cold water to stop the cooking.

2. Stir in the remaining water. Cool. Serve warm or cold.

Yields about 1 cup

NOTE: Do not let the caramel get too dark or it will taste burnt. Let it stop bubbling before adding the final water. If the sauce should "seize," add another ¼ cup of water, put over low heat, and melt the hardened sauce.

HOT FUDGE SAUCE

Serve with ice cream, poached fruit, puddings, or cakes.

½ **cup cocoa**	½ **teaspoon salt**
½ **cup brown sugar**	3 **tablespoons butter**
½ **cup sugar**	2 **tablespoons rum**
1 **cup light corn syrup**	1 **teaspoon vanilla**
½ **cup light cream**	

1. In a saucepan, simmer the cocoa, brown sugar, sugar, corn syrup, cream, salt, and butter, stirring, about 3 minutes, or until the sugars dissolve.

2. Remove from the heat and stir in the rum and vanilla. Serve warm.

Yields about 2½ cups

Can be prepared a week before serving. Keep refrigerated.

CHOCOLATE SAUCE

Serve with Fondant aux Noix (see page 155), or, wherever you need a chocolate sauce.

8½ **ounces semisweet chocolate**	**softened**
¾ **cup coffee**	2 **tablespoons sugar**
6 **tablespoons butter,**	2 **tablespoons heavy cream**

1. In a double boiler, over hot, not boiling water, or in a microwave, melt the chocolate. Stir until smooth.

2. Stir in the coffee, butter, sugar, and cream. Serve warm.

Yields about 2 cups

Can be prepared several days ahead and reheated.

BITTERSWEET CHOCOLATE SAUCE

Serve with chocolate tortes, puddings, or poached fruit.

2 ounces unsweetened chocolate	**½ cup sugar**
¼ cup water	**3 tablespoons butter, thinly sliced**
2 tablespoons Cognac	

1. In a small saucepan, melt the chocolate in the water, stirring until smooth. Add the Cognac and sugar and stir until the sugar dissolves. Stir in the butter, bit by bit, until smooth.

2. Cool, loosely covered. Serve warm or cold.

Yields about 1¼ cups

Can be prepared several days ahead.

SALSA AL CIOCCOLATO (Chocolate Sauce)

A rich, full-flavored chocolate sauce with coffee and rum accents.

3 ounces semisweet chocolate	**1 tablespoon espresso coffee**
4 tablespoons butter	**1 cup confectioners' sugar**
1 tablespoon dark rum	**1 cup evaporated milk**
	½ teaspoon vanilla

1. In a saucepan, melt the chocolate with the butter, rum, and coffee. Remove from the heat and stir in the confectioners' sugar and the milk, alternately.

2. Return to the heat and cook, stirring constantly, about 5 minutes, or until the sugar dissolves and the sauce is thick, smooth, and creamy. Stir in the vanilla. Serve warm.

Yields about 2 cups

Can be prepared several days ahead and reheated.

CHOCOLATE MOCHA SAUCE

Particularly good with desserts featuring nuts.

1 tablespoon instant coffee granules	**6 ounces semisweet chocolate, chopped**
¼ cup hot water	**¼ cup heavy cream**

1. In a bowl, dissolve the coffee in the water and add the chocolate.

2. Bring the cream to a boil and stir into the chocolate mixture until melted and smooth. Serve warm.

Yields about 1 cup

Can be prepared a day before and reheated.

WHITE CHOCOLATE SAUCE

1 cup heavy cream
6 ounces white chocolate, finely chopped

1. In a saucepan bring ⅔ cup of cream to a simmer and add the chocolate. Cover and let stand, off the heat, for 3 minutes.

2. Stir until melted and smooth. Pour into a bowl and stir in the remaining cream. Cover and chill until ready to serve.

Yields about 1½ cups

Can be prepared several days ahead.

FOAMY SAUCE

Serve with puddings.

½ cup butter, softened
1 cup confectioners' sugar
1 egg

1 teaspoon vanilla

1. In a processor, cream the butter and the sugar. Scrape into the top of a double boiler, over hot, but not boiling, water.

2. Cook, beating in the egg and vanilla with a whisk or mixer, until the sauce is foamy.

Yields about 2 cups

Best served within an hour of making.

HARD SAUCE

Serve with plum puddings or any other warm pudding.

½ cup butter, softened
1½ cups confectioners' sugar
2 tablespoons liqueur, see
   Note

In a processor, cream the butter and sugar until light and fluffy. Beat in the liqueur of choice.

Yields about 1½ cups

store in the refrigerator for a week or longer.

Variations

• Flavor with rum, Cognac, orange liqueur, kirsch, framboise, or any other desired flavor, such as vanilla extract.
• To use as an icing, add a little cream or milk to thin and spread on cakes.
• *Orange-Rum Hard Sauce.*   Substitute ¼ cup of dark rum, 2 tablespoons of grated orange rind, and ½ teaspoon of grated nutmeg for the liqueur.

SABAYON SAUCE (Zabaglione)

The French serve it cold as a sauce for fruit, bombes, mousses, or puddings. The Italians serve this warm as a dessert.

6 egg yolks	**¼ cup Marsala, sherry, or other**
1 cup sugar	**wine or liqueur**
¼ teaspoon vanilla	**2 tablespoons cold water**

1.   In a heavy saucepan, beat the egg yolks with 2 tablespoons of sugar and the vanilla until thickened and pale. Beat in the remaining sugar.

2.   Cook over low heat, beating constantly, while adding the wine and water, 1 tablespoon at a time. Continue beating until the mixture is the consistency of mayonnaise.

3.   Serve immediately in wine glasses, or as a sauce for fruit or puddings. Or, cool, beating occasionally, and serve cold.

Yields about 3 cups

Store cold sauce for up to 3 days in the refrigerator.

NOTE: This takes considerable beating. Use a hand mixer if possible.

Variation

• *Sauce Mousseline.* Prepare the Sabayon Sauce, above, and cool. Fold in 1 cup of heavy cream, whipped until it holds soft peaks. Yields about 4½ cups. Serve cold with fruit or over Bavarian creams or ice creams.

GRAND MARNIER SAUCE

This orange-flavored sauce mousseline is heavenly over strawberries and other cold fruits. Serve with intense chocolate desserts, alone or with a tart fruit sauce.

5 egg yolks

8 tablespoons sugar

4 tablespoons Grand Marnier

1 cup heavy cream

1. In the top of a double boiler, beat the egg yolks with 2 tablespoons of sugar and 2 tablespoons of Grand Marnier, over hot, not boiling water about 20 minutes, or until very thick. The mixture will double in volume. Refrigerate until cold.

2. In a mixer, beat the cream to soft peak forms and sweeten with the remaining sugar and Grand Marnier. Fold into the sauce.

Yields about 3½ cups

Store in the refrigerator for up to 2 days.

CRÈME À L'ANGLAISE
(Vanilla Custard Sauce or English Custard Sauce)

Serve this sauce with almost everything. It is light, creamy, and easily prepared.

1 cup milk

1 cup heavy cream

1 (3-in) piece vanilla bean

5 egg yolks

½ cup sugar

1. In a heavy saucepan, scald the milk and cream with the vanilla bean.

2. In another heavy saucepan, beat the egg yolks and sugar until they are thickened and pale. Gradually whisk in the hot milk. Cook over low heat, stirring constantly, in a figure-eight pattern, with a wooden spoon, reaching into the corners of the pan, until the sauce is thick enough to coat the back of a spoon (180°F).

3. Strain through a fine sieve into a bowl and cool, covered with plastic wrap or waxed paper pressed directly onto the surface. Refrigerate.

Yields about 2½ cups

546   *The Book of Great Desserts*

Can be prepared several days before serving.

Here are some suggestions to help you make it perfectly.
- I prefer to prepare this over direct heat; many people prefer to use a double boiler with hot, not boiling, water.
- All heavy cream makes a sauce that is too thick. All milk makes a sauce that is acceptable, but not as good.
- If vanilla bean is not available, substitute vanilla extract. Make the sauce as indicated, and stir the extract into the sauce after straining.
- You do not have to heat the milk and cream, but it makes cooking the sauce faster. You can heat them in a microwave on high heat for 2 to 3 minutes. Do not boil.
- Stirring in a figure-eight pattern is not a whim; it keeps the sauce moving uniformly and allows the heat to cook the egg evenly. The sauce must not boil.
- To tell if it coats the back of a wooden spoon, dip the spoon into the custard, lift with the back uppermost, and run your finger down the center of the spoon. The line should remain. A more scientific method is to check the temperature with an instant-read thermometer; it should read 180°F.
- Strain the sauce to remove any hardened bits of cooked chalaza (egg threads).
- To prevent a skin forming on the surface, stir the sauce often as it cools and cool quickly by placing in a sink of cold water. Change the water as needed. Or, cover tightly with plastic wrap and refrigerate until cold.

Variations

- *Coffee.* Add ¼ cup instant coffee powder.
- *Orange.* For the vanilla, substitute ⅓ cup of Grand Marnier or other orange liqueur.
- *Tangerine.* Omit the vanilla and add mirabelle liqueur to taste and the grated rind of 1 tangerine or ⅓ cup of tangerine liqueur.
- *Liqueur-flavored.* Omit the vanilla and add 1 tablespoon of a favorite liqueur, or to taste.
- *Hazelnut-Vanilla Sauce.* Prepare Vanilla Custard Sauce (see page 544) and stir in ½ cup of finely chopped toasted hazelnuts and 1 tablespoon of hazelnut-flavored liqueur.
- *Sauce à la Ritz (Ritz Sauce).* In a bowl, mix ½ cup of Vanilla Custard Sauce (see page 544) with ¼ cup of Grand Marnier. Fold in ½ cup of heavy cream, whipped and tinted with a drop or two of orange food coloring, if desired. Yields about 1¾ cups. Serve with fresh fruits or bombes.

• *Sauce Parisienne (Parisian Sauce).* In a bowl, fold ½ cup of Vanilla Custard Sauce, ½ cup of pureed strawberries (see page 545), ¼ cup of maraschino liqueur, and ¾ cup of heavy cream, whipped to soft peak form, together. Yields about 2¾ cups. Serve with fresh fruits, creams or bombes.
• *Sauce Riche (Rich Sauce).* In a bowl, fold ½ cup of Vanilla Custard Sauce (see page 545), ¼ cup of prunelle or sloe gin and ½ cup of heavy cream, whipped to soft peak , together. Yields about 1¾ cups. Serve with fruit, bombes, creams.

APRICOT SAUCE

Serve with fruits or as glaze for plain cakes.

1½ cups apricot preserves, see Note	**2 tablespoons kirsch or Cognac**
½ cup water	
2 tablespoons sugar	

1. In a saucepan, simmer the preserves, water, and sugar for 5 minutes, stirring frequently. Force through a sieve and stir in the liqueur.

2. Serve warm or cold.

Yields about 2 cups

Prepare up to 2 weeks before using. Keep refrigerated.

NOTE: Some brands of preserves are very fluid while others have large chunks of fruit. Pureeing in a processor before straining may help.

APRICOT-LEMON SAUCE

Serve with fresh fruits or over ice cream.

1 cup apricot preserves	**1 teaspoon grated lemon rind**
2 tablespoons lemon juice	**⅓ cup apricot brandy, see Note**
2 tablespoons sugar	

1. In a saucepan, simmer the preserves, lemon juice, sugar, and lemon rind until the sugar dissolves. Add the brandy and press through a sieve.

2. Serve cold.

Yields 1½ cups

Prepare up to a week before serving.

NOTE: Substitute rum or Cognac for the apricot brandy, if desired.

ORANGE-APRICOT SAUCE

Serve with fruit, as glaze for plain cakes, with ice cream, meringues, or puddings.

1½ cups orange juice	3 tablespoons grated orange
¾ cup sieved apricot	rind
preserves	3 tablespoons orange liqueur

1.   In a bowl, mix the orange juice, preserves, orange rind, and liqueur together.

2.   Serve cold.

Yields about 2½ cups

Prepare up to a week before serving.

APRICOT-WALNUT SAUCE

Serve warm or cold over puddings, ice cream, or fruit.

1½ cups apricot preserves	rind
½ cup water	2 tablespoons rum
1 tablespoon sugar	½ cup chopped walnuts
1 teaspoon grated orange	

1.   In a saucepan, simmer the apricot preserves, water, sugar, and orange rind until the sugar dissolves, stirring frequently. Remove from the heat and stir in the rum and walnuts.

2.   Serve warm or cold.

Yields about 2½ cups

Prepare up to a week before serving.

NOTE: For a smoother sauce, force through a sieve before adding the walnuts.

BLUEBERRY SAUCE

Serve with Lemon Soufflé (see page 254), over ice cream, with cakes, or on chocolate tortes.

1 pint fresh or frozen blueberries
½ cup sugar

Grated rind of 1 lemon

In a saucepan, simmer the blueberries, sugar, and lemon rind for 5 minutes. Cool.

Yields about 2½ cups

Prepare up to a week before serving.

BLUEBERRY-CASSIS SAUCE

Serve with mousses, creams, cakes, or puddings.

1 tablespoon butter
1 tablespoon cornstarch
¼ cup crème de cassis
¾ cup dry white wine

1 tablespoon lemon juice
1 pint fresh or frozen blueberries

1. In a saucepan, melt the butter. In a small bowl, stir the cornstarch and crème de cassis together and gradually stir into the butter.

2. Stir in the wine and lemon juice and cook, stirring, until the mixture thickens and clears. Stir in the blueberries and cook until they begin to burst. Cool.

Yields about 2½ cups

Prepare up to a week before serving.

CHERRY SAUCE

Serve with ice cream, puddings, or mousses.

1 pound tart cherries, pitted
2–3 tablespoons sugar
Pinch of cinnamon
½ cup water

Lemon juice
1 tablespoon cornstarch
1 tablespoon cold water

1. In a saucepan, simmer the cherries, sugar, and cinnamon over low heat until the juices run freely. Remove the cherries with a slotted spoon. Add the water to the juices and simmer 5 minutes. Adjust the sweetness with more sugar or with lemon juice.

2. In a small bowl, mix the cornstarch and cold water. Stir into the simmering liquid and cook until the mixture thickens and clears.

3. Return the cherries to the sauce and cool.

Yields about 3 cups

Prepare up to a week before serving.

CINNAMON-BOURBON SAUCE

Serve with warm puddings.

½ **cup butter**	1 **tablespoon hot water**
⅔ **cup sugar**	½ **cup heavy cream**
2 **eggs**	½ **cup bourbon**
½ **teaspoon cinnamon**	

1. Melt the butter.

2. In a bowl, beat the sugar, eggs, and cinnamon together. Stir into the melted butter with the hot water and cook, stirring, about 7 minutes, or until the mixture coats the back of a spoon.

3. Cool and stir in the cream and bourbon.

Yields about 2½ cups

Prepare up to a week before serving.

LEMON SAUCE

Serve with puddings or mousses.

½ **cup sugar**	2 **tablespoons butter**
1 **tablespoon cornstarch**	1½ **tablespoons lemon juice**
1 **cup boiling water**	½ **teaspoon grated lemon rind**

1. In a saucepan, mix the sugar and the cornstarch together. With a whisk, beat in the boiling water and cook over medium heat until the sauce thickens and clears.

2. Remove from the heat and whisk in the butter, lemon juice, and rind. Serve warm.

Yields about 1½ cups

Prepare up to 3 days ahead and reheat.

LEMON CURD SAUCE

A full-flavored lemon sauce.

1½ cups lemon juice	**2 cups sugar**
Pared rind of 4 lemons,	**2 eggs**
minced	**4 egg yolks**
1 cup butter	

1. In a bowl, macerate the lemon juice and the rind for 4 hours. Strain the juice into a clean bowl and discard the rind.

2. In a saucepan, over low heat, melt the butter, and stir in the sugar and lemon juice.

3. In a bowl, mix the eggs and egg yolks and stir in a spoonful of the warm lemon mixture. Return to the saucepan and cook, stirring, until thick enough to coat the back of a spoon. Pour the sauce through a sieve into a bowl and cover with plastic wrap.

Yields 3½ cups

Refrigerate, stored in covered containers, for up to 2 weeks.

LEMON CREAM SAUCE

Serve with warm puddings.

2 eggs	**Grated rind of ½ lemon**
1 cup sugar	**½ cup cream**
Juice of 1 lemon	

1. In a saucepan, beat the eggs and the sugar until thickened and pale. Add the lemon juice and the grated rind.

2. Heat, stirring, until the sugar dissolves and the sauce is lukewarm.

3. In another saucepan, heat the cream. Beat into the sauce. Cook 1 minute. Serve warm.

Yields about 1½ cups

Prepare shortly before serving.

EUNICE'S ORANGE-WALNUT SAUCE

Eunice Ehrlich, a superb cook and good friend, gave me the recipe for this creation. Serve with ice cream, crêpes, or soufflés.

3 oranges	**1 tablespoon lemon juice**
¾ cup sugar	**Pinch of salt**
½ cup light corn syrup	**¼ cup chopped walnuts**

1. With a vegetable peeler or sharp paring knife, remove the orange rind without the pith and cut the rind into fine julienne. Squeeze 1 cup of juice from the oranges.

2. In a saucepan, simmer the juice and rind for 5 minutes. Stir in the sugar, corn syrup, lemon juice, and salt, and cook, stirring until the sugar dissolves. Simmer about 20 minutes longer, or until the sauce is syrupy. Cool and stir in the nuts. Serve warm or cold.

Yields about 1½ cups

Prepare up to a week before.

RASPBERRY SAUCE

12-ounce package unsweetened frozen raspberries, thawed	**Sugar, to taste**
	1 tablespoon framboise, or to taste

1. Drain off the juices and reserve. In a processor, puree the raspberries. Sieve the pulp and discard the seeds.

2. Add sugar and framboise, to taste, and thin to the desired consistency with reserved juice. Serve warm or cold.

Yields about 1 cup

Prepare a week before use or freeze.

Variation

• *Raspberry-Almond Sauce.*   Substitute almond liqueur for the framboise.

MELBA SAUCE

A fresh version of the sauce above, to use when fresh raspberries are available.

2 cups raspberries
¼ cup sugar

In a processor, puree the raspberries. Force through a sieve and discard the seeds. In a saucepan, simmer the raspberry puree and sugar for 3 minutes. Cool.

Yields 1 cup

Prepare up to 3 days before serving or freeze.

RASPBERRY CREAM

1¼ cups heavy cream
¼ teaspoon vanilla
12 ounces frozen raspberries,
pureed and strained

2 tablespoons confectioners'
sugar
1 tablespoon framboise

In a bowl, beat the cream and vanilla until stiff. Fold in the raspberry puree, sugar, and framboise.

Yields 2½ cups

Refrigerate up to 6 hours.

SAUCE CARDINALE (Cardinal Sauce)

Serve in place of either raspberry or strawberry sauce. Particularly suited to poached pears.

1 cup crushed strawberries	**1 teaspoon cornstarch**
1 cup crushed raspberries	
1 cup sugar	

1.   In a saucepan, simmer the strawberries, raspberries, sugar, and cornstarch until slightly thickened, stirring frequently.

2.   Puree in a processor or blender and press the pulp through a sieve. Serve warm or cold.

Yields about 2½ cups

Prepare up to 3 days before serving or freeze.

STRAWBERRY SAUCE

Serve with cakes, mousses, or crêpes.

1 pint strawberries, hulled	**2 to 3 tablespoons kirsch or**
and sliced	**orange liqueur**
¼ cup sugar	

In a bowl, mix the strawberries, sugar, and liqueur. Cover and macerate at room temperature for 1 hour, stirring occasionally.

Yields about 2 cups

Prepare up to 6 hours before serving.

HOT STRAWBERRY SAUCE

Serve this with puddings, crêpes, or soufflés.

6 tablespoons butter	**1 quart strawberries, hulled,**
½ cup sugar	**see Note**
¼ cup kirsch or framboise	

1. In a skillet, melt the butter; stir in the sugar, liqueur, and strawberries. Cook, over high heat, shaking the pan, just until the berries are heated and have released some of their juices.

2. Serve immediately.

Yields about 3 cups

Prepare an hour or two ahead and reheat, if desired.

NOTE: If the berries are small, use whole; otherwise, cut in halves or quarters. The object is to serve the berries hot without cooking them.

WINE SAUCE

Serve with plain cake, over puddings, or with fresh, chilled apricots.

1 cup sugar	**1 cup water**
1 tablespoon flour	**2 tablespoons sherry**
¼ teaspoon salt	**¼ teaspoon nutmeg**

1. In a bowl, mix the sugar, flour, and salt.

2. In a small saucepan, bring the water to a boil, stir in the sugar mixture, and cook over medium heat, stirring, until thickened.

3. Add the sherry and nutmeg and simmer 10 minutes longer. Serve warm.

Yields about 1½ cups

Prepare a day ahead and reheat.

Index

· · · · · · · · · · ·